DOCUMENTS OF
WESTERN CIVILIZATION

VOLUME I: TO 1715

Candace Gregory
California State University, Sacramento

THOMSON
WADSWORTH

Australia • Canada • Mexico • Singapore • Spain • United Kingdom • United States

THOMSON

™

WADSWORTH

Documents of Western Civilization Volume I: To 1715
Candace Gregory, California State University, Sacramento

Publisher: Clark Baxter
Assistant Editor: Paul Massicotte
Editorial Assistant: Lucinda Bingham
Technology Project Manager: David Lionetti
Marketing Manager: Lori Grebe Cook
Marketing Assistant: Theresa Jessen
Project Manager, Editorial Production: Katy German

Art Director: Maria Epes
Print Buyer: Judy Inouye
Permissions Editor: Joohee Lee
Compositor: Candace Gregory
Cover Designer: tani hasegawa
Cover Image: Erich Lessing / Art Resource, NY
Printer: Webcom

Library of Congress Control Number: 2005924648

ISBN-13: 978-0-495-03010-2
ISBN-10: 0-495-03010-4

Thomson Higher Education
10 Davis Drive
Belmont, CA 94002-3098
USA

CONTENTS

VOLUME I: TO 1715

PART 5: THE ROMAN REPUBLIC

PART 6: THE ROMAN EMPIRE

PART 7: CHRISTIANITY: THE NEW FAITH

PART 8: THE EMERGING MEDIEVAL STATES

PART 9: THE EARLY MIDDLE AGES

PREFACE

History is a lived experience. Reading the primary sources — the original thoughts, spoken words, opinions, and experiences of the people of the past — is one way for the student in the present to hope to understand history and, in a sense, relive it. Textbooks and other secondary studies are an indispensable tool of historical understanding, yet they can only convey the basic facts as we now understand them. It is from the original documents that the past gains color and dimension, and becomes the lives of real people rather than just a list of dates, events, and figures.

Documents of Western Civilization brings together a wide array of primary sources from across the spectrum of Western (i.e., European) history, illustrating the formation and development of Western cultures and states. The guiding principles of selection were twofold: to include documents that represented the most fundamental aspects of Western history, and to include documents that also represented the wide variety of cultures and peoples that have made up the West. Defining what was important and fundamental for each period of Western history was itself a challenge. The kinds of texts included in this source reader, and thus defined as important, are diverse. They include texts of law, politics, religion, science, philosophy and myth; testimonials; biographies; poetry and literature; speeches; and proclamations. Selections include lesser known works as well as "classic" texts. Women, marginal groups, outsiders, and other groups normally silent in the historical record are revealed through these documents to have been crucial to the development of the West. These groups, who are less often reflected in primary source readers, are clearly represented here, but are not segregated on their own. They are incorporated into the larger scope of their own particular part of Western civilization. For instance, there is no section on "Women in the Reformation," but the section on the Reformation includes Teresa of Avila's counter-reformation mysticism. Documents were also chosen for their user-friendliness. None of them are so esoteric or removed from our own culture so as to be impossible for students to understand. If anything, most students will probably find — in how people lived and felt — that the past is remarkably like the present.

The sources in this reader have been arranged in both a chronological and thematic manner. Although each source can be used individually to illustrate characteristics of a particular culture and period in Western civilization, they are arranged to reflect general trends in the development of the West. Each document is followed by a few discussion questions, while each section of documents concludes with questions that compare and contrast the individual documents in relation to the overall theme of the section.

A brief introduction precedes each document; these introductions place the documents in the larger context of Western history, and provide a background against which the aforementioned questions of interpretation and discovery can be addressed. However, these introductions are deliberately brief, so as not to distract from the reader's discovery of the past. While this sourcebook can be read on its own, it is perhaps best approached with a textbook in hand for further information on chronology and the broader historical picture. *Documents of Western Civilization* is intended to be a supplement to *Western Civilization* by Jackson J. Spielvogel. However, it is designed to be of use to any general survey of Western European history.

ACKNOWLEDGEMENTS

Thanks are due to the editors at Wadsworth Group/Thomson Learning, particularly Paul Massicotte; to my colleagues of the History Department of California State University, Sacramento, who provided advice and support in assembly of this reader, especially Barbara Keys, Mona Siegel, Afshin Marashi, and Katerina Lagos; the professors of history from whom I took classes over the years; and to my mother for her support as well. Thanks are also due to Larry Brooks. More importantly, thanks are due to all the students I have taught over the years for their responses, reactions, and reflections on the use of primary source material in history classes.

HOW TO READ
A PRIMARY SOURCE DOCUMENT

Every primary source should be approached like a puzzle, the solution of which builds a small picture of a Western culture piece-by-piece, word-by-word. All primary sources are both puzzles in themselves and clues to larger puzzles. Knowing how to read a document, how to decode it for clues and decipher its meaning, is a learnable skill. Most importantly, it is an entertaining exercise in puzzle solving.

Every primary source is shaped by a particular context and contains specific content. Each is equally important, yet in different ways and in different situations. Answering the questions that establish the context is your first priority as a reader, though you will find that you must decipher the content to do so. Furthermore, answering one question may help answer another question, but will more than likely lead to more questions. Here is a list of five general questions that should be asked about the context of any primary source:

1. *What is the content of the document? (What does it say?)*
2. *Who created/wrote it?*
3. *Where did it originate?*
4. *When was the source created/written?*
5. *Why was the source created/written down?*

The first question is that of content, which must be deciphered and interpreted. It is important to recognize and to remember that every act of reading a primary source document, whether from a recent period or the ancient past, is an act of interpretation. It is essential that you, as the reader, recognize your own context and biases, but not allow them to overpower your understanding of the document at hand. In other words, we use primary sources to understand the past, not to judge it. Furthermore, it is important to read a document for all levels of content: explicit and implicit. It is also important to use, whenever possible, other sources than the document itself in interpreting it. Comparison with other primary source documents and research into secondary sources is useful, and often necessary.

Secondly, perhaps the simplest question to ask of a primary source: who wrote it? Sometimes the author of the primary source is known explicitly, but as one goes further back into the historical record such information becomes scarce. Details (such as gender, occupation, social class, education level, biases, intentions, etc.) about the author or authors can often be discerned from the primary source itself, if one reads it carefully enough. Similar details about the culture (political system, religious beliefs, etc.) that produced the primary source can often also be detected in the documents.

The third question any reader should ask: where did the primary source originate? The "West" is a bit of a misnomer; the term has always referred to a wide geographic region of diverse peoples and cultures, although the primary focus of this sourcebook is the development of Western Europe. This diversity is reflected in the array of primary sources produced since the beginning of Western civilization. The context of each primary source reveals unique details about the specific region and culture that created it.

The fourth question relates to situating the document in time: when was it created? In what ways was this document shaped by the concerns of a particular era? There is second part to this question, in that one must also consider when the source was written down. The distinction between acts of creation and acts of writing — distinct from one another — is particularly important to consider for the earliest periods of Western history, when oral transmission of sources occurred before then act of writing down those sources. The reader must always consider hat there may be a gap in time between creation and writing.

The fifth question concerns purpose. Content alone usually provides answers to the riddle of why, although the why is not always clear or simple to explain. Nor is there necessarily only one answer to the question of purpose.

Consider the following example of how to read a primary source document, *The Sixty-Seven Articles of Zwingli*:

The articles and opinions below, I, Ulrich Zwingli, confess to have preached in the worthy city of Zurich as based upon the Scriptures which are called inspired by God, and I offer to protect and conquer with the said articles, and where I have not now correctly understood said Scriptures I shall allow myself to be taught better, but only from said Scriptures.

I. *All who say that the Gospel is invalid without the confirmation of the Church err and slander God.*

II. *The sum and substance of the Gospel is that our Lord Jesus Christ, the true Son of God, has made known to us the will of his heavenly Father, and has with his innocence released us from death and reconciled God.*

III. *Hence Christ is the only way to salvation for all who ever were, are, and shall be.*

IV. *Who seeks or points out another door errs, yea, he is a murderer of souls and a thief.*

V. *Hence all who consider other teachings equal to or higher than the Gospel err, and do not know what the Gospel is.*

VI. *For Jesus Christ is the guide and leader, promised by God to all human beings, which promise was fulfilled.*

VII. *That he is an eternal salvation and head of all believers, who are his body, but which is dead and can do nothing without him.*

VIII. *From this follows first that all who dwell in the head are members and children of God, and that is the church or communion of saints, the bride of Christ, Ecclesia catholica.*

IX. *Furthermore, that as the members of the head, so no one in the body of Christ can do the least without his head, Christ.*

X. *As that man is mad whose limbs (try to) do something without his head, tearing, wounding, injuring himself; thus when the members of the Church undertake something without their head, Christ, they are mad, and injure and burden themselves with unwise ordinances.*

XI. Hence we see in the clerical (so-called) ordinances, concerning their splendor, riches, classes, titles, laws, a cause of all foolishness, for they do not also agree with the head.

What can be known about and from this document? How does research into sources help us read this document?

1. *What is the content of the document? What does it say?* Here you would summarize what the text states. It begins by identifying who the author is, Ulrich Zwingli, who proclaims that this is a confession of preaching he has done in the city of Zurich. This particular excerpt includes eleven articles of faith and the administration of that faith, covering such topics as what a Christian should believe and who should determine what doctrines should be, and simultaneously dismisses "clerical" ordinance, which implies that this is a rejection of some existing church.

2. *Who created/wrote it?* The authorship is clearly stated in the first line; it was written by Ulrich Zwingli. Even if you did not know before reading the document that Zwingli was a Protestant reformer, his religious beliefs are evident from the text. Thus, authorship is more than just determining the name of the person who wrote it, it is also about the character of the person that wrote it, the author's educational background (what he or she learned, how they learned, for example), what his or her profession was, his or her social class, and his or her motivation. In the preceding example, the frequency with which the author (Zwingli) invokes God and Jesus Christ clearly identifies him as a Christian. That he specifically refers to Jesus Christ as the Son of God marks him as a Trinitarian Christian, one who believes in the trinity of Father, Son, and Holy Spirit. His Protestant sympathies are indicated by the frequent reference to the Gospels; Protestantism was based on the reliance on scripture as the primary authority for faith, whereas the Catholic Church recognized the importance of scripture but restricted to itself the right to interpret scripture. However, it is also clear that Zwingli had some training in Catholic doctrine. In Article II above he refers to Jesus Christ as the "true Son of God" which echoes the doctrinal claim of the Nicene Creed, the basic statement of faith for the Catholic Church.

3. *Where did it originate?* Again, this document tells us explicitly that it was written in Zurich. However, many of the clues mentioned above about authorship would also indicate that someone of Western culture wrote it.

4. *When was the source created/written?* There is no date in the document itself to answer this question. You could look up the life dates of Zwingli and estimate a range of dates in which he could have written it. Internal evidence indicates that it was written during or shortly after the Reformation began in the early sixteenth century. The author (Zwingli) is careful to distinguish himself as a Christian whose faith is based entirely on Scripture, a commonly held belief among Protestants. Furthermore he criticizes those who follow "clerical (so-called) ordinances," clearly distinguishing himself from the Catholic clergy and its hierarchy. This kind of direct confrontation between scriptural based Christianity and a hierarchical faith of law, clerics, and titles (i.e., Roman Catholicism) was typical of the early Reformation. Furthermore, Zwingli uses the phrase "to have preached." According to canon law and the medieval Catholic Church, only ordained priests (those who followed the "clerical ordinances") were legally allowed to preach. Zwingli's articles are so critical of the Catholic Church that he is either an ordained cleric preaching against his own superiors or a layperson who is preaching without church authority. Neither one would have been tolerated by the medieval church for very long. If this text were typical of Zwingli's writing, without

any clear retribution from the Catholic Church, it indicates that the Protestant schism has already begun, and that there is now the potential for preaching without the papal approval. It is also more than likely that Zwingli was speaking in a place that was at least sympathetic to his beliefs.

There is one very interesting phrase in the above that illustrates why *close* and careful reading of every primary source document is necessary. In Article VIII above, the author uses the phrase *Ecclesia catholica* to refer to the Church; it is a Latin phrase and is a sign of a faith in transition. The medieval Catholic Church which Zwingli grew up in, but which he is trying to reform, was a Latin-based church; although he wants to introduce a vernacular church, he still slips and reveals his own religious background. Couple this clue with the reference earlier to Zwingli's use of "true Son of God" and it becomes clear that this source dates from a period in Western history that was still influenced by Catholic belief, even as it is clear that Zwingli was moving away from it.

5. *Why was the source created/written down?* Actually, the answers to who, where, and when, above, are probably also the answers to the why. Zwingli used his list of *Sixty-Seven Articles* as a way to establish the authority of his own belief over that of the Roman Catholic Church he opposed. The *Articles* are a way for Zwingli to establish several of the tenets of his own particular sect of Christianity. He is a Trinitarian Christian and thus believes in a tri-partite God that is Father, Son, and Holy Spirit. He believes in the basic story of Christianity; that Jesus Christ was the Son of God, and that he was born and died in order to ensure the salvation of his believers. Zwingli has a thorough understanding of Catholic doctrines and the hierarchical nature of the Catholic Church, yet rejects both in favor of scripture and faith without mediation. He also believes in the necessity (he sees it as a requirement from God) that the state and church be one and the same identity; for him, the city of Zurich is to be run as not as a secular society but as a Christian city, a community of the faithful. In rejecting the hierarchy of the Church, Zwingli in effect authorizes himself to preach; thus in the *Articles* he empowers himself to issue said *Articles* in the first place.

PART 1

ORIGINS OF THE WEST

Western civilization begins not in the West proper but in the ancient Near East of Mesopotamia and Egypt. Long before there were states, or even cities, in Western Europe, the Near East invented everything that the West would come to identify as civilization: agriculture, cities, metallurgy, writing, laws, religion, and myth. Due to subsequent historical events, such as the conquest of the region by first the Greeks and then the Romans, these Near Eastern civilizations and their cultures came to have tremendous influence over the developing Western world. Trade in goods and ideas, as well as conquest and integration into those later Western empires, brought the West and the Near East together.

The two earliest Near Eastern civilizations, Sumer and Egypt, are explored here; subsequent chapters will explore two later and even more influential (to the West) cultures from that region: the Hebrews and the first Christians.

1.1

MESOPOTAMIAN EPIC OF CREATION

In an area once known as the cradle of civilization, the Fertile Crescent between the Tigris and Euphrates rivers, is found the earliest known civilization of Sumer. Between 3500-2340 BC, the Sumerians developed all the characteristics of what are considered to be the essential elements of civilization: agriculture, the building of cities, writing, government and law, a sophisticated religious system, metallurgy, extensive public works, etc. It is also from the Sumerians that the first written texts are known, inscribed in cuneiform marks on clay tablets that have proved to be wondrously durable, as were their ideas, which were shared with subsequent Mesopotamian states as well as all later Western cultures.

The following is from one version of the Sumerian creation myth.

---------- ✦ ----------

QUESTIONS

1. Why does Tiamat become so enraged with Apsu?
2. Mesopotamian city-states, such as Sumer, were prone to violence and warfare with one another. How is this reflected in their mythology?
3. Mesopotamian kings (such as Hammurabi in the next selection) had a personal relationship with their gods. What does the story of Marduk say about the relationship kings might have had with him? In other words, what lessons of leadership does Marduk teach?

THE EPIC OF CREATION

TABLET I

When skies above were not yet named
　　Nor earth below pronounced by name,
Apsu, the first one, their begetter
And maker Tiamat, who bore them all,
Had mixed their waters together,
But had not formed pastures, nor discovered reed-beds;
When yet no gods were manifest,
Nor names pronounced, nor destinies decreed,
Then gods were born within them.
Lahmu (and) Lahamu emerged, their names pronounced.
As soon as they matured, were fully formed,
Anshar (and) Kishar were born, surpassing them.
They passed the days at length, they added to the years.
Anu their first-born son rivalled his forefathers:
Anshar made his son Anu like himself,
And Anu begot Nudimmud in his likeness.
He, Nudimmud, was superior to his forefathers:
Profound of understanding, he was wise, was very strong at arms.
Mightier by far than Anshar his father's begetter,
He had no rival among the gods his peers.
The gods of that generation would meet together
And disturb Tiamat, and their clamour reverberated.
They stirred up Tiamat's belly,
They were annoying her by playing inside Anduruna.
Apsu could not quell their noise
And Tiamat became mute before them;
However grievous their behaviour to her,
However bad their ways, she would indulge them.
Finally Apsu, begetter of the great gods,

Called out and addressed his vizier Mummu,
    'O Mummu, vizier who pleases me!
    Come, let us go to Tiamat!'
And discussed affairs concerning the gods their sons.
Apsu made his voice heard
And spoke to Tiamat in a loud voice,
    'Their ways have become very grievous to me,
    By day I cannot rest, by night I cannot sleep.
    I shall abolish their ways and disperse them!
    Let peace prevail, so that we can sleep.'
When Tiamat heard this,
She was furious and shouted at her lover;
She shouted dreadfully and was beside herself with rage,
But then suppressed the evil in her belly.
    'How could we allow what we ourselves created to perish?
    Even though their ways are so grievous, we should bear it patiently.'
(Vizier) Mummu replied and counseled Apsu;
The vizier did not agree with the counsel of his earth mother.
    'O father, put an end to (their) troublesome ways,
    So that she may be allowed to rest by day and sleep at night.'
Apsu was pleased with him, his face lit up
At the evil he was planning for the gods his sons.
(Vizier) Mummu hugged him,
Sat on his lap and kissed him rapturously,
But everything they plotted between them
Was relayed to the gods their sons.
The gods listened and wandered about restlessly;
They fell silent, they sat mute.
Superior in understanding, wise and capable,
Ea who know everything found out their plot,
Made for himself a design of everything, and laid it out correctly,
Made it cleverly, his pure spell was superb.
He recited it and it stilled the waters.
He poured sleep upon him so that he was sleeping soundly,
Put Apsu to sleep, drenched with sleep.
Vizier Mummu the counsellor (was in) a sleepless daze.
He (Ea) unfastened his belt, took off his crown,
Took away his mantle of radiance and put it on himself.
He held Apsu down and slew him;...
And inside Apsu, Marduk was created;
Inside pure Apsu, Marduk was born.
Ea his father created him,
Damkina his mother bore him.
He suckled the teats of goddesses;
The nurse who reared him filled him with awesomeness.

Proud was his form, piercing his stare,
Mature his emergence, he was powerful from the start.
Anu his father's begetter beheld him,
And rejoiced, beamed; his heart was filled with joy.
He made him so perfect that his godhead was doubled.
Elevated far above them, he was superior in every way.
His limbs were ingenuously made beyond comprehension,
Impossible to understand, too difficult to perceive.
Four were his eyes, four were his ears;
When his lips moved, fire blazed forth.
The four ears were enormous
And likewise the eyes; they perceived everything.
Highest among the gods, his form was outstanding.
His limbs were very long, his height (?)
      (Anu cried out)
   'Mariutu, Mariutu,
   Son, majesty, majesty of the gods!'
Clothed in the radiant mantle of ten gods, worn high above his head
Five fearsome rays were clustered above him.
Anu created the four winds and gave them birth,
Put them in his (Marduk's) hand,
    'My son, let them play!'
He fashioned dust and made the whirlwind carry it;
He made the flood-wave and stirred up Tiamat.
Tiamat was stirred up, and heaved restlessly day and night.
The gods, unable to rest, had to suffer…
They plotted evil in their hearts, and
They addressed Tiamat their mother, saying,
    'Because they slew Apsu your lover and
    You did not go to his side but sat mute,
    He has created the four, fearful winds
    To stir up your belly on purpose, and we simply cannot sleep!
    Was your lover Apsu not in your heart?
    And (vizier) Mummu who was captured? No wonder you sit alone!
    Are you not a mother? You heave restlessly
    But what about us, who cannot rest? Don't you love us?
    Our grip(?) [is slack], (and) our eyes are sunken.
    Remove the yoke of us restless ones, and let us sleep!
    Set up a [battle cry] and avenge them!
    Con[quer the enemy] and reduce them to nought!'
Tiamat listened, and the speech pleased her.
    'Let us act now, (?) as you were advising!
    The gods inside him (Apsu) will be disturbed,
    Because they adopted evil for the gods who begot them.'
They crowded round and rallied beside Tiamat.

They were fierce, scheming restlessly night and day.
They were working up to war, growling and raging.
They convened a council and created conflict.
Mother Hubur, who fashions all things,
Contributed an unfaceable weapon: she bore giant snakes,
Sharp of tooth and unsparing of fang (?).
She filled their bodies with venom instead of blood.
She cloaked ferocious dragons with fearsome rays
And made them bear mantles of radiance, made them godlike,...

    'O Marduk, are you our champion!
    We hereby give you sovereignty over all of the whole universe.
    Sit in the assembly and your word shall be pre-eminent!
    May your weapons never miss (the mark), may they smash your enemies!
    O lord, spare the life of him who trusts in you,
    But drain the life of the god who has espoused evil!'

They set up in their midst one constellation,
And then they addressed Marduk their son,

    'May your decree, O lord, impress the gods!
    Command to destroy and to recreate, and let it be so!
    Speak and let the constellation vanish!
    Speak to it again and let the constellation reappear.'

He spoke, and at his word the constellation vanished.
He spoke to it again and the constellation was recreated.
When the gods his fathers saw how effective his utterance was,
They rejoiced, they proclaimed: 'Marduk is King!'
They invested him with sceptre, throne, and staff-of-office.
They gave him an unfaceable weapon to crush the foe.

    'Go, and cut off the life of Tiamat!
    Let the winds bear her blood to us as good news!'

The gods his fathers thus decreed the destiny of the lord
And set him on the path of peace and obedience.
He fashioned a bow, designated it as his weapon,
Feathered the arrow, set it in the string.
He lifted up a mace and carried it in his right hand,
Slung the bow and quiver at his side,
Put lightning in front of him,
His body was filled with an ever-blazing flame.
He made a net to encircle Tiamat within it,
Marshalled the four winds so that no part of her could escape:
South Wind, North Wind, East Wind, West Wind,
The gift of his father Anu, he kept them close to the net at his side.
He created the *imhullu*-wind (evil wind), the unfaceable facing wind.
He released the winds which he had created, seven of them.
They advanced behind him to make turmoil inside Tiamat.
The lord raised the flood-weapon, his great weapon,

And mounted the frightful, unfaceable storm-chariot.
He had yoked to it a team of four and had harnessed to it side
'Slayer', 'Pitiless', 'Racer', and 'Flyer';
Their lips were drawn back, their teeth carried poison.
They know not exhaustion, they can only devastate.
He stationed on his right Fiercesome Fight and Conflict,
On the left Battle to knock down every contender (?).
Clothed in a cloak of awesome armour,
His head was crowned with a terrible radiance.
The Lord set out and took the road,
And set his face towards Tiamat who raged out of control.
In his lips he gripped a spell,
In his hand he grasped a herb to counter poison.
Then they thronged about him, the god thronged about him;
The Lord drew near and looked into the middle of Tiamat:
He was trying to find out the strategy of Qingu her lover.
As he looked, his mind became confused,
His will crumbled and his actions were muddled.
As for the gods his helpers, who march(ed) at his side,
When they saw the warrior, the leader, their looks were strained.
Tiamat cast her spell. She did not even turn her neck.
In her lips she was holding falsehood, lies, (wheedling),
        '[How powerful is] your attacking force, O lord of the gods!
        The whole assembly of them has gathered to your place!'
              (But he ignored her blandishments)
The Lord lifted up the flood-weapon, his great weapon
And sent a message to Tiamat who feigned goodwill, saying:
        'Why are you so friendly on the surface
        When your depths conspire to muster a battle force?
        Just because the sons were noisy (and) disrespectful to their fathers,
        Should you, who gave them birth, reject compassion?
        You named Qingu as your lover,
        You appointed him to rites of Anu-power, wrongfully his.
        You sought out evil for Anshar, king of the gods,
        So you have compounded your wickedness against the gods my fathers!
        Let your host prepare! Let them gird themselves with your weapons!
        Stand forth, and you and I shall do single combat!'
When Tiamat heard this,
She went wild, she lost her temper.
Tiamat screamed aloud in a passion,
Her lower parts shook together from the depths.
She recited the incantation and kept casting her spell.
Meanwhile the gods of battle were sharpening their weapons.
Face to face they came, Tiamat and Marduk, sage of the gods.
They engaged in combat, they closed for battle.

The Lord spread his net and made it encircle her,
To her face he dispatched the *imhullu*-wind, which had been behind:
Tiamat opened her mouth to swallow it,
And he forced in the *imhullu*-wind so that she could not close her lips.
Fierce winds distended her belly,
Split her down the middle and slit her heart,
Vanquished her and extinguished her life.
He threw down her corpse and stood on top of her.
When he had slain Tiamat, the leader,
He broke up her regiments; her assembly was scattered.
Then the gods her helpers, who had marched at her side,
Began to tremble, panicked, and turned tail.

From *Myths from Mesopotamia: Creation, the Flood, Gilgamesh, and Others*, trans. by Stephanie Dalley. Copyright © 1989 by Oxford University Press. Reprinted by permission of Oxford University Press.

1.2

❖

LAW CODE OF HAMMURABI

Hammurabi was a king of Amorite kingdom of Old Babylon from 1792-1750 BC. He is best remembered for compiling one of the most extensive law codes of the ancient Near East. It is a comprehensive code that covers all concerns of a civilized society, including agriculture, business, labor regulations, crime and punishment, marriage and divorce, inheritance, and the activities of public officials, to name just a few. Hammurabi said that the god of justice, Shamash, gave him this code, although it in fact draws on existing Mesopotamian laws. One of the most important legacies of this law code for future Western cultures was its principle of equity. The following excerpts deal with slavery and marriage issues.

❖

QUESTIONS

1. Why does Hammurabi claim to have received these laws from Shamash? How do you think that affected how people living under the laws viewed them?
2. How are slaves protected by Hammurabi's law code? Are they strictly property in this society?
3. What power do wives have over husbands and children in the law code? What is her function within the marriage unit?

15. If any one take a male or female slave of the court, or a male or female slave of a freed man, outside the city gates, he shall be put to death.
16. If any one receive into his house a runaway male or female slave of the court, or of a freedman, and does not bring it out at the public proclamation of the major domus, the master of the house shall be put to death.

17.   If any one find runaway male or female slaves in the open country and bring them to their masters, the master of the slaves shall pay him two shekels of silver.

18.   If the slave will not give the name of the master, the finder shall bring him to the palace; a further investigation must follow, and the slave shall be returned to his master.

19.   If he hold the slaves in his house, and they are caught there, he shall be put to death.

20.   If the slave that he caught run away from him, then shall he swear to the owners of the slave, and he is free of all blame....

128.   If a man take a woman to wife, but have no intercourse with her, this woman is no wife to him.

129.   If a man's wife be surprised with another man, both shall be tied and thrown into the water, but the husband may pardon his wife and the king his slaves.

130.   If a man violate the wife (betrothed or child-wife) of another man, who has never known a man, and still lives in her father's house, and sleep with her and be surprised, this man shall be put to death, but the wife is blameless.

131.   If a man bring a charge against one's wife, but she is not surprised with another man, she must take an oath and then may return to her house.

132.   If the "finger is pointed" at a man's wife about another man, but she is not caught sleeping with the other man, she shall jump into the river for her husband.

133.   If a man is taken prisoner in war, and there is a sustenance in his house, but his wife leave house and court, and go to another house: because this wife did not keep her court, and went to another house, she shall be judicially condemned and thrown into the water.

134.   If any one be captured in war and there is no sustenance in his house, if then his wife go to another house this woman shall be held blameless.

135.   If a man be taken prisoner in war and there be no sustenance in his house and his wife go to another house and bear children; and if later her husband return and come to his home: then this wife shall return to her husband, but the children follow their father.

136.   If any one leave his house, run away, and then his wife go to another house, if then he return, and wishes to take his wife back: because he fled from his home and ran away, the wife of this runaway shall not return to her husband.

137.   If a man wish to separate from a woman who has borne him children, or from his wife who has borne him children: then he shall give that wife her dowry, and a part of the usufruct of field, garden, and property, so that she can rear her children. When she has brought up her children, a portion of all that is given to the children, equal as that of one son, shall be given to her. She many then marry the man of her heart.

138.   If a man wishes to separate from his wife who has borne him no children, he shall give her the amount of her purchase money and the dowry which she brought from her father's house, and let her go.

139.   If there was no purchase price he shall give her one mina of gold as a gift of release.

140.   If he be a freed man he shall give her one-third of a mina of gold.

141.   If a man's wife, who lives in his house, wishes to leave it, plunges into debt, tries to ruin her house, neglects her husband, and is judicially convicted: if her husband offer her release, she may go on her way, and he gives her nothing as a gift of release. If her husband does not wish to release her, and if he take another wife, she shall remain as servant in her husband's house.

142.   If a woman quarrel with her husband, and say: "You are not congenial to me," the reasons for her prejudice must be presented. If she is guiltless, and there is no fault on her part, but he leaves and neglects her, then no guilt attaches to this woman, she shall take her dowry and go back to her father's house.

143.   If she is not innocent, but leaves her husband, and ruins her house, neglecting her husband, this woman shall be cast into the water.

144.   If a man take a wife and this woman give her husband a maid-servant, and she bear him children, but this man wishes to take another wife, this shall not be permitted to him; he shall not take a second wife.

145.   If a man take a wife, and she bear him no children, and he intend to take another wife: if he take this second wife, and bring her into the house, this second wife shall not be allowed equality with his wife.

146.   If a man take a wife and she give this man a maid-servant as wife and she bear him children, and then this maid assume equality with the wife: because she has borne him children her master shall not sell her for money, but he may keep her as a slave, reckoning her among the maid-servants.

147.   If she have not borne him children, then her mistress may sell her for money.

148.   If a man take a wife, and she be seized by disease, if he then desire to take a second wife he shall not put away his wife, who has been attacked by disease, but he shall keep her in the house which he has built and support her so long as she lives.

149.   If this woman does not wish to remain in her husband's house, then he shall compensate her for the dowry that she brought with her from her father's house, and she may go.

150.   If a man give his wife a field, garden, and house and a deed therefor, if then after the death of her husband the sons raise no claim, then the mother may bequeath all to one of her sons whom she prefers, and need leave nothing to his brothers.

151.   If a woman who lived in a man's house made an agreement with her husband, that no creditor can arrest her, and has given a document therefor: if that man, before he married that woman, had a debt, the creditor can not hold the woman for it. But if the woman, before she entered the man's house, had contracted a debt, her creditor can not arrest her husband therefor.

152.   If after the woman had entered the man's house, both contracted a debt, both must pay the merchant.

153.   If the wife of one man on account of another man has their mates (her husband and the other man's wife) murdered, both of them shall be impaled.

154.   If a man be guilty of incest with his daughter, he shall be driven from the place (exiled).

155.   If a man betroth a girl to his son, and his son have intercourse with her, but he (the father) afterward defile her, and be surprised, then he shall be bound and cast into the water (drowned).

156.   If a man betroth a girl to his son, but his son has not known her, and if then he defile her, he shall pay her half a gold mina, and compensate her for all that she brought out of her father's house. She may marry the man of her heart.

Source: Charles F. Horne, ed., *The Sacred Books of Early Literature and of the East: Volume I, Babylonia and Assyria* (New York: Parke, Austin, and Libscomb, Inc., 1917), pp. 118, 127-130.

1.3

❖

EGYPTIAN CREATION MYTH

Every culture has its own unique creation mythology. A Mesopotamian creation myth has already been explored; here is an Egyptian version of how the world began. Its original form dates from the first dynasty of c. 3100 BC, with the story of Atum who arose out of the primeval waters to produce the world alone of his own power. In subsequent renderings of the myth, Atum was conflated with the sun god Ra to become Atum-Ra (also known as Amon-Ra), a more all-encompassing deity. The name of Atum/Amon-Ra was also known as Khephera. Each name of the creator deity actually reflects a particular stage in the theological development of Atum and Ra. This is a later version of the myth in which Atum, as Khephera, exists alone in the waters and sets about to create a host of other deities as well as things of the earth.

❖

QUESTIONS

1. What is the role of the waters in Khephera's act of creation? What does this say about ancient Egyptians' attitudes toward the water?
2. What is the significance of sex in this act of creation?
3. Why does Khephera create more gods in the first place?

Shāt — The Book
enti — of
rekh — knowing
kheperu — the evolutions
nu — of
Rā, — Rā,

sekher — [and] of overthrowing
Āpep — Āpep.
tcheṭṭu — The words of
Neb-er-tcher — Neb-er-tcher
tcheṭ - f — [which] he spake

em-khet — after
kheper - f — he had come into being.
nuk — I am
pu — he who
kheper — came into being

em — in the form of
Kheperȧ — Khepera
kheper-nȧ — I was (or, became)
kheper — the creator
kheperu — of what came into being

kheper — the creator
kheperu — of what came into being
neb *em-khet* — all; after
kheper-ȧ — my coming into being
āsht — many

kheperu — [were] the things which came into being
em *per* — coming forth
em — from
re-ȧ — my mouth.
ȧn — Not

kheper *pet* — existed heaven,
ȧn — not
kheper *ta* — existed earth,
ȧn — not
qemam — had been created

satat	*tchetfet*	*em*	*bet*	*pui*
the things of the earth, (i.e., plants)	and creeping things	in place		that;

thes - ná	*ám - sen*	*em*	*Nu*
I raised up them	from out of		Nu (i.e., the primeval abyss of water

em	*enen*	*án*	*qem-ná*	*bet*	*áḥá-ná*
from a state of inactivity.		Not	found I	a place	I could stand

ámi	*khut-ná*	*em*	*ábt-á*
wherein.	I worked a charm	upon (or, with)	my heart.

senti-ná	*em*	*Maā*	*ári-ná*	*áru*	*nebt*
I laid a foundation	in	Maā	[and] I made	attribute	every.

uā-k[uá]	*án*	*áshesh-ná*	*em*	*Shu*	*án*
I was alone,	[for] not	had I spit	in the form of Shu,		not

tef-ná	*em*	*Tefnut*	*án*	*kheper*	*ki*
had I emitted		Tefnut.	not	existed	another

ȧri-nef   *ḥenȧ-ȧ.*   *senti-nȧ*   *em*   *ȧbt-ȧ*   *tches-ȧ*

who worked with me.   I made a foundation   in my heart my own, (or, by means of my own will)

kheper   *ȧsht*   *kheperu*   *nu*   *kheperu*

[and] there came into being   the multitudes of things   which came into being   of the things which came into being

em   *kheperu*   *nu*   *mesu*   *em*

from out of   the things which came into being   of   births,   from out of

kheperu   *nu*   *mesu-sen*   *ȧnuk*   *pu*   *hat-ȧ*

the things which came into being   of   their births,   I, even I,   had union

em   *khefȧ-ȧ*   *tataȧt-nȧ*   *em*

with   my clenched hand,   I joined myself in an embrace   with

khaibit-ȧ   *kher-nȧ*   *em*   *re-ȧ*   *tches-ȧ*

my shadow,   I poured seed   into my mouth   my own,

ȧshesh-nȧ   *em*   *Shu*   *tefnet-nȧ*

I sent forth issue   in the form of Shu   I sent forth moisture

em	Ṭafnut	ȧn	ȧtef-ȧ	Nu	satet-sen
in the form of Tefnut.		Saith	my father	Nu,	"They make to be weak

maat-ȧ	em-sa-sen	tcher	ḥenḥenti	uau-sen
my eye	behind them,	because	for double *henti* periods	they proceeded

er-ȧ	em-khet	kheper-ȧ	em	neter	uā	neter	khemt
from me	after	I became	from	god	one	gods	three,

pu	er-ȧ	kheper-nȧ	em	ta	pen	ḥāā
that is	from out of myself,	[and after] I came into being	in	earth	this.	Were raised up

ȧref	Shu	Ṭȧfnut	em	enenu
therefore	Shu	[and] Tefnut	in	the inert watery mass

un-sen	ȧmi · f	ȧn-sen	nȧ	maat-ȧ
wherein they were,		brought they	to me	my eye

em	khet-sen	em-khet	ȧref	sam-nȧ	āt-ȧ
in	their train.	After	therefore	I had united	my members

rem-nȧ   *ḥer-sen*   *kheper*   *reth*   *pu em*

I wept   over them,   [and] came into   men and   from
being   women

remu   *per*   *em*   *maat-ȧ*   *khȧru-s*

the tears   [which] came forth   from my eye,   [and] it raged

er-ȧ   *em khet*   *i-s*   *qemi-s*   *ȧri-nȧ*   *ket*

against me   after   it came   [and] found   [that] I had made another

em   *ȧst-s*   *ṭebi-s*   *em*   *khut*   *ȧru-nȧ*

in   its place.   [I] endowed it   with   the power   I had made.
(or, splendour) which

sekhenti   *ȧref*   *ȧst-s*   *em*   *ḥrȧ-ȧ*   *em-khet*

Having made to approach therefore its place in my face, afterwards

ȧref   *ḥeq-s*   *ta*   *pen*   *er*   *tcher - f*   *kher*

therefore   it ruleth   earth   this   to   its whole extent.   Fall

en at-sen   *ȧu uabu-sen*   *ṭebui-nȧ*

their moments (or, seasons)   upon their plants,   I endowed it

thet-s   *ȧmi-s*   *per-nȧ*   *em*   *uabu*

with what it hath   in it.   I came forth   from (or in   the plants,
taken possession of   the form of)

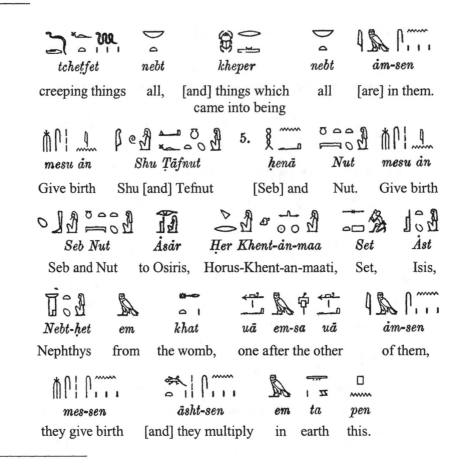

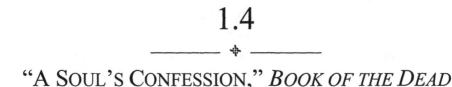

Source: E. A. Wallis Budge, *The Gods of the Egyptians*, Vol. 1, p. 308-313. © 1969 Dover. Originally published in 1904.

1.4

"A SOUL'S CONFESSION," *BOOK OF THE DEAD*

The Book of the Dead *was compiled during the New Kingdom period of Egyptian history, between 1500-1350 BC. It is a wide-ranging collection of documents that includes prayers, hymns, spells and charms, histories, mythology, even medical treatises are found in it. One of the most famous and most frequently quoted sections is the so-called "negative confession" of the soul facing final judgment by Osiris. The following are two versions of the "negative confession."*

--- ✦ ---

QUESTIONS

1. Notice that the list of "not" confessions claims that the deceased vows that *he or she has neither committed murder nor*, in a separate confession, *has not given orders for murder*. Is there is any sense that one of these is viewed as more sinful than the other?
2. Many of the confessions concern agricultural sins; why is this so important?
3. What does the speaker mean when he/she says "I am not a transgressor against a god?"

CHAPTER CXXV.

PART I.

Said on arriving at the Hall of Righteousness, that *N* may be loosed from all the sins which he hath committed and that he may look upon the divine countenances.

He saith: Hail to thee mighty god, lord of Righteousness! I am come to thee, oh my Lord: I have brought myself that I may look upon thy glory. I know thee, and I know the name of the Forty-two gods who make their appearance with thee in the Hall of Righteousness; devouring those who harbour mischief, and swallowing their blood, upon the Day of the searching examination in presence of Un-neferu.

Verily, 'Thou of the Pair of Eyes, Lord of Righteousness' is thy name.

Here am I; I am come to thee; I bring thee Right and have put a stop to Wrong.

I am not a doer of wrong to men.

I am not one who slayeth his kindred.

I am not one who telleth lies instead of truth.

I am not conscious of treason.

I am not a doer of mischief.

I do not exact as the first fruits of each day more work than should be done for me.

My name cometh not to the Bark of the God who is at the Helm.

I am not a transgressor against a god.

I am not a tale-bearer.

I am not a detractor.

I am not a doer of that which the gods abhor.

I hurt no servant with his master.

I cause no famine.

I cause not weeping.

I am not a murderer.

I give not orders for murder.

I cause not suffering to men.

I reduce not the offerings in the temples.

I lessen not the cakes of the gods.

I rob not the dead of their funeral food.

I am not an adulterer.

I am undefiled in the Sanctuary of the god of my domain.

I nether increase nor diminish the measures of grain.

I am not one who shorteneth the palm's length.

I am not one who cutteth short the field's measure.

I do not press upon the beam of the balance.

I snatch not the milk from the mouth of infants.

I drive not the cattle from their pastures.

I net not the birds of the manors of the gods.

I catch not the fish of their ponds.

O stop not the water at its appointed time.

I divide not an arm of the water in its course.

I extinguish not the lamp during its appointed time.

I do not defraud the Divine Circle of their sacrificial joints.

I drive not away the cattle of the sacred estate.

I stop not a god when he cometh forth.

I am pure, I am pure, I am pure.

My purity is that of the Great Bennu in Sutenhunen, for I am the Nose of the Lord of the Air, who giveth life to all mortals: on the day when the Eye is full in Annu, on the last day of Mechir; in the presence of the Lord of this land.

And I am one who see the fulness of the Eye in Annu, let no harm come to me in this land, in the Hall of Righteousness; because I know the names of the gods who make their appearance in it.

PART II.

1. Oh thou of long strides, who makest thine appearance in Annu; I am not a doer of wrong.
2. Oh thou who holdest the fire, and makest thine appearance in Cheraba, I am not a man of violence.
3. Oh thou of the Nose, who makest thine appearance at Chemunnu; I am not evil-minded.
4. Oh Eater of the Shadow, who makest thine appearance at Elephantine; I am not rapacious.
5. Oh thou of the Serpent face, who makest thine appearance at Re-Stau; I am not a slayer of men.
6. Oh thou of Lion form, who makest thine appearance in Heaven; I am not fraudulent in measures of grain.
7. Oh thou whose eyes (pierce) like swords, who makest thine appearance in Sechem; I commit no fraud.
8. Oh thou of fiery face, whose motion is backwards; I am not a robber of sacred property.
9. Oh Breaker of bones, who makest thine appearance in Sutenhunen; I am not a teller of lies.
10. Oh thou who orderest the flame, who makest thine appearance in Memphis; I am not a robber of food.
11. Oh thou of the Two Caverns, who makest thine appearance in Amenta; I am not sluggish.
12. Oh thou of the Bright Teeth, who makest thine appearance in the Unseen Land; I am not a transgressor.
13. Oh Eater of Blood, who makest thine appearance at the Block; I have not slaughtered the sacred animals.
14. Oh Eater of Livers, who makest thine appearance at Mabit, I deal not fraudulently.
15. Oh Lord of Righteousness, who makest thine appearance in the place of Righteousness; I am not a land-grabber.

16. Oh thou who turnest backwards, who makest thine appearance in Bubastis; I am not an eaves-dropper.
17. Oh Aati, who makest thine appearance at Annu; I am not one of prating tongue.
18. Oh Tutuf, who makest thine appearance in Ati; I trouble myself only with my own affairs.
19. Oh Uammetu, who makest thine appearance at the Block; I commit not adultery with another's wife.
20. Oh maa-antu-f, who makest thine appearance in Pa-Amsu, I am not unchaste with anyone.
21. Oh thou who are above Princes, who makest thine appearance in Amu; I do not cause terrors.
22. Oh Chemiu, who makest thine appearance in Kauu; I am not a transgressor.
23. Oh thou who raisest thy voice, and makest thine appearance in Urit; I am not hot of speech.
24. Oh divine Babe, who makest thine appearance in Annu; I lend not a deaf ear to the words of Righteousness.
25. Oh high-voiced one, who makest thine appearance in Unsit; I am not boisterous in behavior.
26. Oh Basit, who makest thine appearance at the Shetait; I am not a cause of weeping to any.
27. Oh thou whose face is behind thee, and who makest thine appearance at thy cavern; I am not given to unnatural lust.
28. Oh thou, hot of foot, who makest thine appearance at even; I indulge not in anger.
29. Oh Kenemtu, who makest thine appearance in Kenemit; I am not given to cursing.
30. Oh thou who carriest thine own offering, and makest thine appearance in Syut; I am not of aggressive hand.
31. Oh thou who hast different faces, and makest thine appearance in Netefit; I am not of inconstant mind.
32. Oh Busy one, who makest thine appearance at Utenit; I do not steal the skins of sacred animals.
33. Oh thou Horned one, who makest thine appearance at Sais; I am not noisy in my speech.
34. Oh Nefertmy, who makest thing appearance in Memphis; I am neither a liar nor a doer of mischief.
35. Oh Tem-sepu, who makest thine appearance in Tattu; I am not one who curseth the king.
36. Oh thou who doest according to thine own will, and makest thine appearance in Tebuu, I put no check upon the water in it flow.
37. Oh Striker, who makest thine appearance in Heaven; I am not of loud voice.
38. Oh thou who makest mortals to fourish, and who makest thine appearance at Sais; I curse not a god.
39. Oh thou of the beautiful shoulder, who makest thine appearance at ———; I am not swollen with pride.
40. Oh Neheb-kau, who makest thine appearance at the cavern; I have no unjust preferences.
41. Oh thou of the raised head, who makest thine appearance at thy cavern; I have no strong desire except for my own property.
42. Oh thou who liftest thy arm, who makest thine appearance in the Netherworld, I do not that which offendeth the god of my domain.

Source: Oliver J. Thatcher, ed., *The Ideas that have Influenced Civilization in the Original Documents, Vol. II: The Ancient World* (Boston: Roberts-Manchester Publishing Co., 1901), pp. 72-75.

———— ✦ ————

QUESTIONS FOR PART 1

1. Compare and contrast the Mesopotamian and Egyptian creation myths. What do the differences between the myths tell us about the differences between the two civilizations?
2. What is the relationship between religion and government in these earliest Western civilizations?
3. Much of Western culture has been concerned with answering the "big" questions of human existence. In what ways do these two earliest civilizations ask and answer those questions?

PART 2

❧

THE FIRST WESTERN EMPIRES

Just as Western civilization began in the Near East, so too did the concept of empire, which would be the defining concept of Western state building for centuries. Although there were many individual city-states and kingdoms scattered throughout the Fertile Crescent, none were truly independent of one another. As early 2340 BC, Sargon of Akkad, a city-state north of Sumer, the first civilization, created the first Mesopotamian Empire. Egypt too was prone to imperial impulses; conquests to the south and east brought new territories under the control of pharaohs. Even relatively small states, such as that of the Hebrews, built empires. The earliest history of Western civilization is the story of the rise and fall of empires, as one conquered another only to be conquered in turn. The following four selections highlight four of the most significant early empires: Egypt, the Hebrews, Neo-Babylonian, and Persia.

The Near East and the West collide when the Persian Empire attempted to conquer Greece, which was a response in itself to Greeks of the fourth century BC colonizing into the Near East. Although there had been much trade and cultural exchanges between the two regions before this, and earlier Near Eastern civilizations had colonized farther west along the southern coast of the Mediterranean (the Phoenician colonies of the eighth and ninth centuries BC), nothing that had come before had the impact of the wars between Persia and Greece. The result, ultimately, would be the first super-empire of the ancient world: the empire of Alexander the Great.

2.1

✤

A VICTORY OF RAMSES II

Ramses II (c. 1279-1213 BC) extended the borders of Egypt into Palestine. He won a significant victory over the Hittites, which was commemorated in a poem which he had inscribed on the walls of the temple of Karnak. The poem is written as if from Ptah-Tutem to Ramses II. In the theological school associated with Memphis, Ptah was the creator god, while Atum (whose creation myth was recounted in Source 1.3) was demoted to his son. The following is a prose translation of the poem.

QUESTIONS

1. Why is the inscription written as if from Ptah to Ramses, if it is the exploits of Ramses that are being applauded?
2. How does the document let us know that it was written shortly after an Egyptian victory over the Hittites?
3. How does this text explain the need of the ancient Egyptians to build large statues and monuments to themselves?

(This extract from a much longer inscription found at Abu-Simbel, Egypt, gives, perhaps better than any other passage, an idea of the divine perfection, majesty, and almighty power o the Egyptian king as the son and incarnation of the chief deity. Interesting is the incidental reference to the successful close of the war with the Hittites and to the king's marriage with the Hittite princess. Records of the Past, xii. 85-89.)

V. RAMESES II, SON AND SECOND SELF OF THE GOD PTAH-TOTUNEN

Thus speaks Ptah-Totunen with the high plumes, armed with horns, the father of the gods, to his son who loves him....

Num and Ptah have nourished thy childhood, they leap with joy when they see thee made after my likeness, noble, great, exalted. The great princesses of the house of Ptah and the Hathors of the temple of Tem are in festival, their hearts are full of gladness, their hands take the drum with joy, when they see thy person beautiful and lovely like my Majesty.... King Rameses, I grant thee to cut the mountains into statues immense, gigantic, everlasting; I grant that foreign lands find for thee precious stone to inscribe the monuments with thy name.

I give thee to succeed in all the works which thou hast done. I give thee all kinds of workmen, all that goes on two or four feet, all that flies and all that has wings. I have put in the heart of all nations to offer thee what they have done; themselves, princes great and small, with one heart seek to please thee, King Rameses. Thou hast built a great residence to fortify the boundary of the land, the city of Rameses; it is established on the earth like the four pillars of the sky; hast constructed within a royal palace, where festivals are celebrated to thee as is done for me within. I have set the crown on thy head with my own hands, when thou appearest in the great hall of the double throne; and men and gods have praised thy name like mine when my festival is celebrated.

Thou hast carved my statues and built my shrines as I have done in times of old. I have given thee years by periods of thirty; thou reignest in my place on my throne; I fill thy limbs with life and happiness, I am behind thee to protect thee; I give thee health and strength; I cause Egypt to be submitted to thee, and I supply the two countries with pure life. King Rameses, I grant that the strength, the vigor, and the might of thy sword be felt among all countries; thou castest down the hearts of all nations; I have put them under thy feet; thou comest forth every day in order that be brought to thee the foreign prisoners; the chiefs and the great of all nations offer thee their children. I give them to thy gallant sword that thou mayest do with them what thou likest. King Rameses, I grant that the fear of thee be in the minds of all and thy command in their hearts. I grant that thy valor reach all countries, and that the dread of thee be spread over all lands; the princes tremble at thy remembrance, and thy majesty is fixed on their heads; they come to thee as supplicants to implore thy mercy. Thou givest life to whom thou wishest, and thou puttest to death whom thou pleasest; the throne of all nations is in thy possession....

King Rameses, I have exalted thee through such marvelous endowments that heaven and earth leap for joy and those who are within praise thy existence; the mountains, the water, and the stone walls which are on the earth are shaken when they hear thy excellent name, since they have seen what I have accomplished for thee; which is that the land of the Hittites should be subjected to thy palace; I have put in the heart of the inhabitants to anticipate thee themselves by their obeisance in bringing thee their presents. Their chiefs are prisoners, all their property is the tribute in the dependency of the living king. Their royal daughter is at the head of them; she comes to soften the heart of King Rameses; her merits are marvelous, but she does not know the goodness which is in they heart.

Source: George Willis Botsford and Lillie Shaw Botsford, eds., *A Sourcebook of Ancient History* (New York: The Macmillan Company, 1927), pp. 10-12.

2.2

CONQUEST OF CANAAN BY THE HEBREWS

The principal source for Jewish history is the Hebrew scripture, the Old Testament. Much of the early books recount the creation of an empire promised to descendents of Abraham by his God. The following excerpt depicts the conquest of Canaan by Joshua, c. 1200. It takes place after Moses has led the Israelites out of slavery in Egypt. City by city, kingdom by kingdom, Joshua and the Israelites systematically conquered the region of Canaan.

QUESTIONS

1. Why does the author of this account describe the war between the Israelites and the Amorite kings as "vengeance?"
2. What are some of the roles that the Israelites' God plays in the battle?
3. Why do the people of Gibeon, having been enslaved by Joshua and the Israelites, then turn to them for help against the Amorite kings?

THE BOOK OF JOSHUA

Prelude to the conquest of Canaan

1 After the death of Moses the LORD's servant, the LORD said to Joshua son of Nun, Moses' assistant, 'Now that my servant Moses is dead, get ready to cross the Jordan, you and all this

people, to the land which I am giving to the Israelites. Every place where you set foot is yours: I have given it to you, as I promised Moses. From the desert and this Lebanon to the great river, the Euphrates, and across all the Hittite country westwards to the Great Sea, all of it is to be your territory. As long as you live no one will be able to stand against you: as I was with Moses, so shall I be with you; I shall not fail you or forsake you. Be strong, be resolute; it is you who are to put this people in possession of the land which I swore to their forefathers I would give them. Only be very strong and resolute. Observe diligently all the law which my servant Moses has given you; if you would succeed wherever you go, you must no swerve from it either to right or to left. This book of the law must never be off your lips; you must keep it in mind day and night so that you may diligently observe everything that is written in it. Then you will prosper and be successful in everything you do. This is my command: be strong, be resolute; do not be fearful or discouraged, for wherever you go the LORD your God is with you.'

Then Joshua instructed the officers to pass through the camp and give this order to the people: 'Get food ready to take with you for within three days you will be crossing this Jordan to occupy the country which the LORD your God is giving you to possess.

The conquest of the south

10 When King Adoni-zedek of Jerusalem heard that Joshua had captured and destroyed Ai, dealing with Ai and its king as he had dealt with Jericho and its king, and also that the inhabitants of Gibeon had come to terms with Israel and were living among them, he was greatly alarmed; for Gibeon was a large place, like a royal city: it was larger than Ai, and its men were all good fighters. So King Adoni-zedek of Jerusalem sent this message to King Hoham of Hebron, King Piram of Jarmuth, King Japhia of Lachish, and King Debir of Eglon: 'Come up and assist me to attack Gibeon, because it has come to terms with Joshua and the Israelites.'

The five Amorite kings, the kings of Jerusalem, Hebron, Jarmuth, Lachish, and Eglon, advanced with their united forces to take up position for the attack on Gibeon. The Gibeonites sent word to Joshua in the camp at Gilgal: 'Do not abandon your slaves; come quickly to our relief. Come and help us, for all the Amorite kings in the hill-country have joined forces against us.' When Joshua went up from Gilgal followed by his whole force, all his warriors, the LORD said to him, 'Do not be afraid; I have delivered these kings into your hands, and not one of them will be able to withstand you.' After a night march from Gilgal, Joshua launched a surprise assault on the five kings, and the LORD threw them into confusion before the Israelites. Joshua utterly defeated them at Gibeon; he pursued them down the pass of Beth-horon and kept up the attack as far as Azekah and Makkedah. As they fled from Israel down the pass, the LORD hurled great hailstones at them out of the sky all the way to Azekah, and they perished: more died from the hailstones than were slain by the swords of the Israelites.

On that day when the LORD delivered up the Amorites into the hands of Israel, Joshua spoke with the LORD, and in the presence of Israel said:

'Stand still, you sun, at Gibeon; you moon, at the vale of Aijalon.'

The sun stood still and the moon halted until the nation had taken vengeance on it enemies, as indeed is written in the Book of Jashar. The sun stayed in mid-heaven and made no haste to set for almost a whole day.

Never before or since has there been such a day as that on which the LORD listened to the voice of a mortal. Surely the LORD fought for Israel! Then Joshua returned with all the Israelites to the camp at Gilgal.

The five kings fled and his in a cave at Makkedah, and Joshua was told that they had been found hiding there. Joshua replied, 'Roll large stones against the mouth of the cave, and post men there to keep watch over the kings. But you yourselves must not stay. Keep up the pursuit, attack your enemies from the rear and do not let them reach their towns; the LORD your God has delivered them into your hands.'

When Joshua and the Israelites had completed the work of slaughter and everyone had been put to the sword — all except a few survivors who escaped into the fortified towns — the whole army returned safely to Joshua at Makkedah; not one of the Israelites suffered so much as a scratch.

From *The Oxford Study Bible*, edited by M. Jack Suggs, K. B. Sakenfeld & J. R. Mueller, copyright © 1992 by Oxford University Press, Inc. Used by permission of Oxford University Press, Inc.

2.3

❖

INSCRIPTION OF NEBUCHADNEZZAR II

Nebuchadnezzar II ruled the Chaldean Empire from 604-562 BC, at what can be arguably described as its golden age. He led the final defeat of the Assyrian Empire, expanded the economic resources of his empire, and rebuilt Babylon so extensively that it became renowned as one of the true wonders of the ancient world. This neo-Babylonian heyday was brief; in 539 the Chaldeans were defeated by the Persians, led by Cyrus the Great. Much of what is known about Nebuchadnezzar II is known from the Hebrew Old Testament, which has a definite bias in its description of the king, who captured the city of Jerusalem in 586 BC and enslaved its citizens. Here is an excerpt from an inscription on a temple wall; it is very revealing of how the Chaldeans saw their own king.

❖

QUESTIONS

1. Compare how Marduk is referred to here to how he is referred to in the Mesopotamian Creation Myth of Source 1.1
2. Although Nebuchadnezzar II is generally known as a military hero, what accomplishments is he most proud of here?
3. In his descriptions of buildings, why is cedar mentioned so many times? What is the significance of cedar in Mesopotamian culture?

Column I

Nebuchadrezzar...
King of Babylon, am I.

After that the lord my god had created me,
that Marduk had framed

the creature in the mother;
when I was born,
when I was created, even I,
the holy places of the god I regarded,
the way of the god I walked in.
Of Marduk, the great lord, the god my creator,
his cunning works
highly do I extol.
Of Nabu, his true son,
the beloved of my Majesty,
the way of this supreme godhead
steadfastly do I exalt;
with all my true heart
I love the fear of their godhead,
I worship their lordship.
When Marduk, the great lord,
lifted up the head of my Majesty and
with lordship over the multitude of peoples
    invested me; and
Nabu, the overseer of the multitude of heaven
    and earth,
for the governing of the peoples
a righteous scepter
placed in my hands:
for me, of them I am heedful,
I have regard unto their godhead;
for the mention of their glorious name,
I worship the god and Ishtar.
To Marduk my lord I made supplication,
prayers to him I undertook, and
the word which my heart looked for,
to him I spake:
"of old, O prince, lord of all that is!
for the king whom thou lovest, and
whose name thou callest,
that to thee is pleasing;
thou leadest him aright,
a straight path thou appointest him.
I am a prince obedient unto thee,
a creature of thy hands;
thou it was that madest me, and
with sovereignty over the multitude of the
    peoples

didst invest me;
according to thy goodness, O lord,
wherewith thou crownest
all of them.
Thy lordship supreme do thou make loving, and
the fear of thy godhead
cause thou to be in my heart!
Yes, grant that to thee is pleasing,

Column II

for my life truly thou makest."
Himself, the leader glorious,
the open-eyed of the gods, the prince Marduk,
my supplications heard and
received my prayers.
Yea, he made gracious his supreme lordship,
the fear of his godhead
he implanted in my heart;
to draw his car
he made me submit the heart;
I worshiped his lordship.
In his high trust,
to far-off lands,
distant hills,
from the Upper Sea
to the Lower Sea,
immense journeys,
blocked ways,
a place where the path is broken,
feet are not;
a road of hardships,
a journey of straits,
I pursued, and the unyielding I reduced,
I fettered the rebels.
The land I ordered aright, and
the people I made to thrive;
bad and good
among the people I removed.
Silver, gold, glitter of precious stones,
copper, *mismakanna*-wood, cedar
what thing soever is precious,
a large abundance;

the produce of mountains,
the fulness of seas,
a rich present,
a splendid gift,
to my city of Babylon
into his presence I brought....
The bright seat, the place of them that
        determine destinies,
which is the Quarter of Assembly, the chapel of
        the Fates,
wherein, at Zagmuku, the opening of the year,
on the 8th day and the 11th day,
the divine king, the god of heaven and earth,
        the lord of heaven,
taketh up his abode;
the gods of heaven and earth
with awe submit unto him;
they bow, they take their stand before him;
a destiny of enduring days,
as the destiny of my life,
they predestine in the midst thereof —

Column III

that chapel, a chapel of majesty,
the chapel of the lordship
of the open-eyed of the gods, the prince
        Marduk,
whose fabric a former king
in silver had fabricated,
with shining gold, a splendid decoration,
I overlaid it.
The vessels of the house Esagilla
with large gold —
the Bark of Marduk with *Zariru*-stones —
I made bright,
as the stars of the heavens.
The temples of Babylon
I made, I filled.
Of Etimmen-ana-ki

in burnt brick and fine *uknu* stone,
I reared its summits.
To make Esagilla
my heart lifted me up;
in chief have I regarded it.
The choicest of my cedars,
which from Lebanon,
the noble forest,
I brought,
for the roofing of Ekua,
the cell of his lordship,
I looked out, and my heart vowed.
The huge cedar-beams
for the roofing of Ekua
with shining gold I overlaid.
The panels under the cedar of the roofing
with gold and precious stones
I made bright.
For the making of Esagrilla
daily I besought
the king of the gods, the lord of lords.
Borsippa the city of his abode
I beautified, and
Ezida, the Eternal House,
in the midst thereof I made.
With silver, gold, precious stones,
copper, *mismakanna*-wood, cedar-wood,
I finished the work of it.
The cedar of the roofing
of the cells of Nabu
with gold I overlaid.
The cedar of the roofing of the gate of Nana,
I overlaid with shining silver.
The bulls, the leaves of the gate of the cell,
the lintels, the bards, the bolt,
the door-sill, *Zariru*-stone.
The cedar of the roofing
of its chambers
with silver I made bright....

Source: Charles F. Horne, ed., *The Sacred Books of Early Literature and of the East: Volume I, Babylonia and Assyria* (New York: Parke, Austin, and Libscomb, Inc., 1917), pp. 118, 127-130.

2.4

--- ✦ ---

PERSIAN INVASION OF GREECE

Herodotus (c. 484-425 BC) wrote his History of the Persian Wars *as an attempt to not only record the events of the past, but to also explain why they happened. His interest in analyzing the purpose of human events as well as their chronology gives him the title of the Father of Western History. Here he describes what happened in 480 BC, when the Persian king Xerxes led an expedition to conquer Greece, one of many attempts by Persian kings to take over Greek colonies in Ionia as well as the Greek mainland. It was a quest for the Persians that began with Cyrus the Great in 547 BC, and would not end until the final defeat of Darius III in 330 BC by Alexander the Great. The ongoing wars between Persia and the Greek city states represent one of the most drawn out wars of early empire in the ancient world.*

--- ✦ ---

QUESTIONS

1. How do Herodotus' careful descriptions of landscape and geography lend a type of veracity to his history?
2. What is the Persian impression of the Spartan forces and their ability to fight?
3. Where is Xerxes while the battle is taking place?

The position, then, was that Xerxes was lying with his force at Trachis in Malian territory, while the Greeks occupied the pass known locally as Pylae — though Thermopylae is the common Greek name. Such were the respective positions of the two armies, one being in control of al the country from Trachis northward, the other of the whole mainland to the south. The Greek force which here awaited the coming of Xerxes was made up of the following contingents: 300 heavy-armed infantry from Sparta, 500 from Tegea, 500 from Mantinea, 120 from Orchomenus in Arcadia, 1000 from the rest of Arcadia; from Corinth there were 400, from Phlius 200, and from Mycenae 80. In addition to these troops from the Peloponnese, there were the Boeotian contingents of 700 from Thespiae and 400 from Thebes. The Locrians of Opus and the Phocians had also obeyed the call to arms, the former sending all the men they had, the latter one thousand. The other Greeks had induced these two towns to send troops by a message to the effect that they themselves were merely an advance force, and that the main body of the confederate army was daily expected; the sea, moreover, was strongly held by the fleet of Athens and Aegina and the other naval forces. Thus there was no cause for alarm — for, after all, it was not a god who threatened Greece, but a man, and there neither was nor ever would be a man who was not born with a good chance of misfortune — and the greater the man, the greater the misfortune. The present enemy was no exception; he too was human, and was sure to be disappointed of his great expectations.

The appeal succeeded, and Opus and Phocis sent their troops to Trachis. The contingents of the various states were under their own officers, but the most respected was Leonidas the Spartan, who was in command of the whole army. Leonidas traced his descent directly back to Heracles, through

Anaxandrides and Leon (his father and grandfather), Anaxander, Eurycrates, Polydorus, Alcamenes, Teleches, Archelaus, Agesilaus, Doryssus, Labotas, Echestratus, Agis, Eurysthenes, Aristodemus, Aristomachus, Cleodaeus — and so to Hyllus, who was Heracles' sons. He had come to be king of Sparta quite unexpectedly, for as he had two elders brothers, Cleomenes and Dorieus, he had no thought of himself succeeding to the throne. Dorieus, however, was killed in Sicily, and when Cleomenes also died without an heir, Leonidas found himself next in the succession. He was older than Cleombrotus, Anaxandrides' youngest son, and was, moreover, married to Cleomenes' daughter. The three hundred men whom he brought on this occasion to Thermopylae were chosen by himself, all fathers of living sons. He also took with him the Thebans I mentioned, under the command of Leontiades, the son of Eurymachus. The reason why he made a special point of taking troops from Thebes, and from Thebes only, was that the Thebans were strongly suspected of Persian sympathies, so he called upon them to play their part in the war in order to see if they would answer the call, or openly refuse to join the confederacy. They did send troops, but their secret sympathy was nevertheless with the enemy. Leonidas and his three hundred were sent by Sparta in advance of the main army, in order that the sight of them might encourage the other confederates to fight and prevent them from going over to the enemy, as they were quite capable of doing if they knew that Sparta was hanging back; the intention was, when the Carneia was over (for it was that festival which prevented the Spartans from taking the field in the ordinary way), to leave a garrison in the city and march with all the troops at their disposal. The other allied states proposed to act similarly; for the Olympic festival happened to fall just at this same period. None of them ever expected the battle at Thermopylae to be decided soon — which was the reason why they sent only advanced parties there.

The Persian army was now close to the pass, and the Greeks suddenly doubting their power to resist, held a conference to consider the advisability of retreat. It was proposed by the Peloponnesians generally that the army should fall back upon the Peloponnese and hold the Isthmus; but when the Phocians and Locreians expressed their indignation at this suggestion, Leonidas gave his voice for staying where they were and sending, at the same time, an appeal for reinforcements to the various states of the confederacy, as their numbers were inadequate to cope with the Persians.

During the conference Xerxes sent a man on horseback to ascertain the strength of the Greek force and to observe what the troops were doing. He had heard before he left Thessaly that the small force was concentrated here, led by the Lacedaemonians under Leonidas of the house of Heracles. The Persian rider approached the camp and took a thorough survey of all he could see — which was not, however the whole Greek army; for the men on the further side of the wall which, after its reconstruction, was now guarded, were out of sight. He did, none the less, carefully observe the troops who were stationed on the outside of the wall. At that moment these happened to be the Spartans, and some of them were stripped for exercise while others were combing their hair. The Persian spy watched them in astonishment; nevertheless he made sure of their numbers and of everything else he needed to know, as accurately as he could and then rode quietly off. No one attempted to catch him, or took the least notice of him.

Back in his own camp he told Xerxes what he had seen. Xerxes was bewildered; the truth, namely that the Spartans were preparing themselves to die and deal death with all their strength, was beyond his comprehension, and what they were doing seemed to him merely absurd. Accordingly he sent for Demaratus, the son of Ariston, who had come with the army, and questioned him about the spy's report, in the hope of finding out what the behaviour of the Spartans might mean. 'Once before,' Demaratus said, 'when we began our march against Greece, you heard me speak of these men. I told you then how I saw this enterprise would turn out, and you laughed at me. I strive for nothing, my lord, more earnestly than to observe the truth in your presence; so hear me once more. These men have come to fight us for possession of the pass, and for that struggle they are preparing. It is the common practice of the Spartans to pay careful attention to their hair when they are about to risk their lives. But I assure you that if you can defeat these men and the rest of the Spartans who are still at home, there is no other people in the world who will dare to stand firm of lift a hand against you. You have now to deal with the finest kingdom in Greece, and with the bravest men.'

Xerxes, unable to believe what Demaratus said, asked further how it was possible that so small a force could fight with his army. 'My lord,' Demaratus replied, 'treat me as a liar, if what I have foretold does not take place.' But still Xerxes was unconvinced.

For four days Xerxes waited, in constant expectation that the Greeks would make good their escape; then, on the fifth, when still they had made no move and their continued presence seemed mere impudent and reckless folly, he was seized with rage and sent forward the Medes and Cissians with orders to take them alive and bring them into this presence. The Medes charged, and in the struggle which ensued many fell; but others took their places, and in spite of terrible losses refused to be beaten off. They made it plain enough to anyone, and not least to the king himself, that he had in his army many men, indeed, but few soldiers. All day the battle continued; the Medes, after their rough handling, were at length withdrawn and their place was taken by Hydarnes and his picked Persian troops — the King's Immortals — who advanced to the attack in full confidence of bringing the business to a quick and easy end. But, once engaged, they were no more successful than the Medes had been; all went as before, the two armies fighting in a confined space, the Persians using shorter spears than the Greeks and having no advantage from their numbers.

On the Spartan side it was a memorable fight; they were men who understood war pitted against an inexperienced enemy, and amongst the feints they employed was to turn their backs on a body and pretend to be retreating in confusion, whereupon the enemy would pursue them with a great clatter and roar; but the Spartans, just as the Persians were upon them, would wheel and face them and inflict in the new struggle innumerable casualties. The Spartans had their losses too, but not many. At last the Persians, finding that their assaults upon the pass, whether by divisions or by any other way they could think of, were all useless, broke off the engagement and withdrew. Xerxes was watching the battle from where he sat; and it is said that in the course of the attacks three times, in terror for his army, he leapt to his feet.

Next day the fighting began again, but with no better success for the Persians, who renewed their onslaught in the hope that the Greeks, being so few in number, might be badly enough disabled by wounds to prevent further resistance. But the Greeks never slackened; their troops were ordered in divisions corresponding to the states from which they came, and each division took it turn in the line except the Phocian, which had been posted to guard the track over the mountains. So when the Persians found that things were no better for them than on the previous day, they once more withdrew.

How to deal with the situation Xerxes had no idea; but just then, a mam from Malis, Ephialtes, the son of Eurydemus, came, in hope of a rich reward, to tell the king about the track which led over the hills to Thermopylae — and thus he was to prove the death of the Greeks who held the pass.

Later on, Ephialtes, in fear of the Spartans, fled to Thessaly, and in his absence a price was put upon his head by the Amphictyons assembled at Pylae. Some time afterwards he returned to Anticyra, where he was killed by Athenades of Trachis. Athenades killed him not for his treachery but for another reason, which I will explain further on; but the Spartans honoured him none the less on that account. According to another story, it was Onetes, the son of Phanagoras of Carystus, and Corydallus of Anticyra who spoke to Xerxes and showed the Persians the way round by the mountain track. This is entirely unconvincing, my first criterion being the fact that the Amphictyons, presumably after careful inquiry, set a price not upon Onetes and Corydallus but upon Ephialtes of Trachis, and my second, that there is no doubt that the accusation of treachery was the reason for Ephialtes' flight. Certainly Onetes, even though he was not a native of Malis, might have known about the track, if he had spent much time in the neighbourhood—but it was Ephialtes, and no one else, who showed the Persians the way, and I leave his name on record as the guilty one.

From *Herodotus, The Histories*, trans. Aburey de Selincourt, pp. 511-516. Copyright © 1954, 1978 Penguin Books. Reproduced with permission of Penguin Books Limited.

⬥

QUESTIONS FOR PART 2

1. Why do states build empires? What does the building of empires mean for the identity of a state?
2. What did these early Near Eastern empires have in common? How did they differ from one another?
3. What was role of religion in the creation of these early empires?

PART 3

☙

GREECE: FROM THE DARK AGES
TO THE CLASSICAL PERIOD

Although the first civilizations of Mesopotamia and Egypt are certainly essential elements in the story of Western civilization in general, it was with the Greeks that the West proper was invented. No other single civilization has had such a lasting impact on Western culture: religion, law, and the very concepts of politics, art, language, and philosophy all owe a debt to the ancient Greeks, particularly to the Classical period of the fifth and fourth centuries BC. Greek speaking peoples first migrated into the islands of the Aegean and the Greek mainland around 2000 BC. The first Greek civilizations, the Minoan (c. 2000-1450 BC) and the Mycenaean (c.1600-1100 BC), were only known through myth until nineteenth century archaeologists rediscovered their ruined cities.

Better known was the *polis* period of the Archaic (eighth thru sixth centuries) and Classical periods. The *polis* (Greek for "city-state") that probably had the single largest influence on Western civilization was Athens. The following sources illustrate the importance of Athens, but also acknowledge the influence of all of Greece. The fiercely independent Greek *poleis* (pl. of *polis*) were very competitive with one another politically, a struggle which came to a climax in nearly a century of warfare between Athens and Sparta, the Peloponnesian War of the fifth century. However, they poleis had a common cultural base that is illustrated by the four documents excerpted here.

3.1

❖

THE EARLY HELLENES, THUCYDIDES

Thucydides (c. 460-400 BC) wrote as both an eyewitness, and as a critical historian, about the events he attempted to analyze, the complicated series of wars between Athens and Sparta. He fought in the war on the side of Athens, but was sent into exile, and set out to find the causes of the current war in the actions of the past. In doing so, Thucydides was writing a much larger history than just of the war; he was attempting to understand how the Greeks of his day had come to be what they were. Significantly, he describes the origins of the Greeks, or Hellenes, as a history which began in conquest.

---------------- ✤ ----------------

QUESTIONS

1. According to Thucydides, how is the success of the Greek civilization dependent upon their geography?
2. Thucydides is writing during a war, but Greece began without political strife; does he see that as the natural progression of society?
3. What is the role of the *polis*, or city, in the early history of the Hellenes?

V. RAMESES II, SON AND SECOND SELF OF THE GOD PTAH-TOTUNEN

Thus speaks Ptah-Totunen with the high plumes, armed with horns, the father of the gods, to his son who loves him....

Num and Ptah have nourished thy childhood, they leap with joy when they see thee made after my likeness, noble, great, exalted. The great princesses of the house of Ptah and the Hathors of the temple of Tem are in festival, their hearts are full of gladness, their hands take the drum with joy, when they see thy person beautiful and lovely like my Majesty.... King Rameses, I grant thee to cut the mountains into statues immense, gigantic, everlasting; I grant that foreign lands find for thee precious stone to inscribe the monuments with thy name.

I give thee to succeed in all the works which thou hast done. I give thee all kinds of workmen, all that goes on two or four feet, all that flies and all that has wings. I have put in the heart of all nations to offer thee what they have done; themselves, princes great and small, with one heart seek to please thee, King Rameses. Thou hast built a great residence to fortify the boundary of the land, the city of Rameses; it is established on the earth like the four pillars of the sky; hast constructed within a royal palace, where festivals are celebrated to thee as is done for me within. I have set the crown on thy head with my own hands, when thou appearest in the great hall of the double throne; and men and gods have praised thy name like mine when my festival is celebrated.

Thou hast carved my statues and built my shrines as I have done in times of old. I have given thee years by periods of thirty; thou reignest in my place on my throne; I fill thy limbs with life and happiness, I am behind thee to protect thee; I give thee health and strength; I cause Egypt to be submitted to thee, and I supply the two countries with pure life. King Rameses, I grant that the strength, the vigor, and the might of thy sword be felt among all countries; thou castest down the hearts of all nations; I have put them under thy feet; thou comest forth every day in order that be brought to thee the foreign prisoners; the chiefs and the great of all nations offer thee their children. I give them to thy gallant sword that thou mayest do with them what thou likest. King Rameses, I grant that the fear of thee be in the minds of all and thy command in their hearts. I grant that thy valor reach all countries, and that the dread of thee be spread over all lands; the princes tremble at thy remembrance, and thy majesty is fixed on their heads; they come to thee as suppliants to implore thy mercy. Thou givest life to whom thou wishest, and thou puttest to death whom thou pleasest; the throne of all nations is in thy possession....

King Rameses, I have exalted thee through such marvelous endowments that heaven and earth leap for joy and those who are within praise thy existence; the mountains, the water, and the stone walls which are on the earth are shaken when they hear thy excellent name, since they have seen what I have accomplished for thee; which is that the land of the Hittites should be subjected to thy palace; I have put in the heart of the inhabitants to anticipate thee themselves by their obeisance in bringing thee their presents. Their chiefs are prisoners, all their property is the tribute in the dependency of the living king. Their royal daughter is at the head of them; she comes to soften the heart of King Rameses; her merits are marvelous, but she does not know the goodness which is in they heart.

3.2

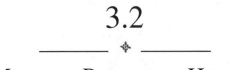

MYTH OF PANDORA, HESIOD

Hesiod was a poet in eighth century BC Boetia known for two extant works, Theogony *and* Works and Days. *He was roughly a contemporary of Homer, but vastly different in tone. Whereas Homer's epics laud the heroic action of gods and near-gods, Hesiod was much more interested in the everyday, ordinary lives of humanity. Even in his attempts to recount the divine myths, such as this story of Pandora, Hesiod revealed his "everyman" sympathies.*

QUESTIONS

1. How is Pandora destined to be an "anguishing" misery to humankind?
2. Does the use of a female figure to encapsulate all that is miserable to humanity accurately reflect how women were viewed in Archaic Greece?
3. Did the Archaic Greeks view their gods as benevolent and protective toward them?

THE PROMETHEUS-PANDORA STORY

For the gods keep hidden the livelihood of men.
  Otherwise you might easily do enough work in a day to
have enough for a full year with no further need to be working,
and might immediately hang up your rudder in the smoke of your fireplace
and release your oxen and hardworking mules from their labor.
But Zeus hid our livelihood when he was angered at heart
because Prometheus, the clever deviser, tried to deceive him.
This is why he devised anguishing miseries for men.
And he hid fire, which the goodly son of Iapetos stole back,
taking it from Zeus of the Counsels to give it to men, secretly
carrying it in a fennel stalk's hollow from Zeus of the Firebolt.

Then, stirred to anger, Zeus of the Storm Cloud addressed him as follows:
"Son of Iapetos, you who surpass all others in planning,
you rejoice in your theft of my fire and in having deceived me,
being the cause of great pain to yourself and men in the future.
I shall give them in payment of fire an evil which all shall
take to their hearts with delight, an evil to love and embrace."
Thus the Father of Gods and of Men addressed him, and laughed.
and he commanded far-famed Hephaistos immediately to make it
out of water and clay, and give it the voice of a human and
put in it strength and cause it to look like a goddess immortal,
having the lovely, desirable shape of a virgin. And then he
ordered Athena to teach her the skill of intricate weaving.
and Aphrodite the Golden he ordered to shed on her charm and
make her an object of painful love and exhausting desire.
And he ordered Hermes the Guide, the Slayer of Argos,
to put in her mind a dog's shamelessness and the deceit of a thief.
Thus spoke their king, Zeus, son of Kronos, and they obeyed him.
Immediately the famous Lame-Legged One molded of clay
and image resembling a virgin demure, as Zeus had decreed.
And the goddess gray-eyed Athena girdled and dressed her:
the Graces divine along with our Lady Persuasion hung
golden necklaces on her, and the lovely-haired Horai
crowned her head by setting upon it a garland of spring flowers,
all of which things Pallas Athena arranged in good order.
And the Guide, the Slayer of Argos, enclosed in her breast
lies and wheedling words and the treacherous ways of a thief,
following Zeus the Thunderer's degree; and he, heaven's herald,
gave her a speaking voice and announced that her name was Pandora,
"The Gift of All," because all the gods who dwell on Olympos
gave a gift to this plague for men who are eaters of bread.
But when he had completed this sheer inescapable snare,
Zeus Father had her led off as a gift to Epimetheus
by the famous Slayer of Argos, heaven's swift herald.
And Epimetheus took no heed of Prometheus's advice
not to receive any gift the Olympian Zeus might send him
but to reject it lest some evil should happen to mortals.
So he received it and learned by experience the evil he had.
For the tribes of men had previously lived on earth
free and apart from evils, free from burdensome labor
and from painful diseases, the bringers of death to men.
In the power of these evils men rapidly pass into old age.
But then woman, raising the jar's great lid in her hands and
scattering its contents, devised anguishing miseries for men.

Only Hope was left within, securely imprisoned,
caught there under the lip of the jar, unable to fly
out and away, for before this could happen she let the lid drop,
as the Lord of the Aigis, Zeus of the Storm Cloud, decreed.
But as for those others, those numberless miseries, they wander among men,
for the earth is abounding in evils and so is the sea.
And diseases come upon men by day and by night,
everywhere moving at will, bringing evil to mortals
silently, for Zeus of the Counsels has deprived them of voices.
Thus in no way can anyone escape the purpose of Zeus.

From *The Poems of Hesiod*, translated by R. M. Frazer, pp. 97-100. Copyright © 1983 University of Oklahoma Press. By permission of the publisher. All rights reserved.

3.3

APOLOGY OF PLATO

Plato (c. 429-347 BC) is best known for his political theories and his philosophy of Ideals, which he recorded in a series of dialogues featuring his teacher Socrates. However, he was also very much a pragmatic political philosopher, concerned with the potential of humanity to create and maintain a perfect state. For Plato the creation of such a state would require dedication from the lowest and youngest citizens of that idealized state. Perhaps this is why he created his Academy in Athens, to train the perfect citizens of the perfect state. Plato's dialogues are also important as one of the few sources for Socrates, the first of the trio of great Athenian philosophers (Socrates, Plato, and Aristotle). However, these are not mere transcripts of Socrates' lectures, and it is impossible to tell whether we are reading his ideas or Plato's. This source is an excerpt from the Apology, *in which Socrates attempts to answer the charges of corrupting the youth of Athens, for which he was executed in 399 BC.*

QUESTIONS

1. The word "apology" has two primary meanings in English: expressing remorse for having done something or a defense of something. Which meaning is Plato using here?
2. Socrates defends himself for having regular disciples; he says that anyone may come listen as he is "pursuing his mission." What is his mission?
3. Socrates claims that his accusers prefer deeds to words. What does he offer as his own "deeds?"

M en of Athens, do not interrupt, but hear me; there was an agreement between us that you should hear me out. And I think that what I am going to say will do you good: for I have something more to say, at which you may be inclined to cry out; but I beg that you will not do this. I would have you know that, if you kill such a one as I am, you will injure yourselves more than you will injure me. Meletus and Anytus will not injure me: they cannot; for it is not in the nature of things that a bad man should injure a better than himself. I do not deny that he may, perhaps, kill him, or drive him into exile, or deprive him of civil rights; and he may imagine, and others may imagine, that he is doing him a great injury: but in that I do not agree with him; for the evil of doing as Anytus is doing — of unjustly taking away another man's life — is greater far. And now, Athenians, I am not going to argue for my own sake, as you may think, but for yours, that you may not sin against the God, or lightly reject his boon by condemning me.

For if you kill me you will not easily find another like me, who, if I may use such a ludicrous figure of speech, am a sort of gadfly, given to the state by the God; and the state is like a great and noble steed who is tardy in his motions owing to his very size, and requires to be stirred into life. I am that gadfly which God has given the state and all day long and in all places am always fastening upon you, arousing and persuading and reproaching you. And as you will not easily find another like me, I would advise you to spare me. I dare say that you may feel irritated at being suddenly awakened when you are caught napping; and you may think that if you were to strike me dead, as Anytus advises, which you easily might, then you would sleep on for the remainder of your lives, unless God in his care of you gives you another gadfly. And that I am given to you by God is proved by this: — that if I had been like other men, I should not have neglected all my own concerns, or patiently seen the neglect of them during all these years, and have been doing yours, coming to you individually, like a father or elder brother, exhorting you to regard virtue; this I say, would not be like human nature. And had I gained anything, or if my exhortations had been paid, there would have been some sense in that: but now, as you will perceive, not even the impudence of my accusers dares to say that I have ever exacted or sought pay of anyone; they have no witness of that. And I have a witness of the truth of what I say; my poverty is a sufficient witness.

Some one may wonder why I go about in private, giving advice and busying myself with the concerns of others, but do not venture to come forward in public and advise the state. I will tell you the reason of this. You have often heard me speak of an oracle or sign which comes to me, and is the divinity which Meletus ridicules in the indictment. This sign I have had ever since I was a child. The sign is a voice which comes to me and always forbids me to do something which I am going to do, but never commands me to do anything, and this is what stands in the way of my being a politician. And rightly, as I think. For I am certain, O men of Athens, that if I had engaged in politics, I should have perished long ago and done no good either to you or to myself. And don't be offended at my telling you the truth: for the truth is that no man who goes to war with you or any other multitude, honestly struggling against the commission of unrighteousness and wrong in the state, will save his life; he who will really fight for the right, if he would live even for a little while, must have a private station and not a public one.

I can give you as proofs of this, not words only, but deeds, which you value more than words. Let me tell you a passage of my own life, which will prove to you that I should never have yielded to injustice from any fear of death, and that if I had not yielded I should have died at once. I will tell you a story — tasteless, perhaps, and commonplace, but nevertheless true. The only office of state which I ever held, O men of Athens, was that of senator; the tribe Antiochis, which is my tribe, had the presidency at the trial of the generals who had not taken up the bodies of the slain after the battle of Arginusae; and you proposed to try them all together, which was illegal, as you all thought afterwards; but at the time I was the only one of the Prytanes who was opposed to the illegality, and I gave my vote against you; and when the orators threatened to impeach and arrest me, and have me taken away, and you called and shouted, I made up my mind that I would run the risk, having law and justice with me, rather than take part in your injustice because I feared imprisonment and death. This happened in the days of the democracy. But when the oligarchy of the Thirty was in power, they sent for me and four others into the rotunda, and bade us bring Leon the Salaminian from Salamis, as they wanted to execute him. This was a specimen of the sort of commands which they were always giving with the view of implicating as many as possible in their crimes; and then I showed, not in words only, but in deed, that, if I may be allowed to use such an expression, I cared not a straw for death, and that my only fear was the fear of doing an unrighteous or unholy thing. For the strong arm of that oppressive power did not frighten me into doing wrong; and when we came out of the rotunda the other four went to Salamis and fetched Leon, but I went quietly home. For which I might have lost my life, had not the power of the Thirty shortly afterwards come to an end. And to this many will witness.

Now do you really imagine that I could have survived all these years, if I had led a public life, supposing that like a good man I had always supported the right and had made justice, as I ought, the first thing? No, indeed, men of Athens, neither I nor any other. But I have been always the same in all my actions, public as well as private, and never have I yielded any base compliance to those who are slanderously termed my disciples or to any other. For the truth is that I have no regular disciples: but if anyone likes to come and hear me while I am pursuing my mission, whether he be young or old, he may freely come. Nor do I converse with those who pay only, and not with those who do not pay; but anyone, whether he be rich or poor, may ask and answer me and listen to my words; and whether he turns out to be a bad man or a good one, that cannot be justly laid to my charge, as I never taught him anything. And if anyone says that he has ever learned or heard anything from me in private which all the world has not heard, I should like you to know that he is speaking an untruth.

But I shall be asked, Why do people delight in continually conversing with you? I have told you already, Athenians, the whole truth about this: they like to hear the cross-examination of the pretenders to wisdom; there is amusement in this. And this is a duty which the God has imposed upon me, as I am assured by oracles, visions, and in every sort of way in which the will of divine power was ever signified to anyone. This is true, O Athenians; or, if not true, would be soon refuted. For if I am really corrupting the youth, and have corrupted some of them already, those of them who have grown up and have become sensible that I gave them bad advice in the days of their youth should come forward as accusers and take their revenge; and if they do not like to come themselves, some of their relatives, fathers, brothers, or other kinsmen, should say what evil their families suffered at my hands. Now is their time. Many of them I see in the court. There is Crito, who is of the same age and of the same deme with myself; and there is Critobulus his son, whom I also see. Then again there is Lysanias of Sphettus, who is the father of Aeschines — he is present; and also there is Antiphon of Cephisus, who is the father of Epignes; and there are the brothers of several who have associated with me. There is Nicostratus the son of Theosdotides, and the brother of Theodotus (now Theodotus himself is dead, and therefore he, at any rate, will not seek to stop him); and there is Paralus the son of Demodocus, who had a brother Theages; and Adeimantus the son of Ariston, whose brother Plato is present; and Aeantodorus, who is the brother of Apollodorus, whom I also see. I might mention a great many others, any of whom Meletus should have produced as witnesses in the course of his speech; and let him still produce them, if he has forgotten — I will make way for him. And let him say, if he has any testimony of the sort which he can produce. Nay, Athenians, the very opposite is the truth. For all these are ready to witness on behalf of the corrupter, of the destroyer of their kindred, as Meletus and Anytus call me; not the corrupted youth only

— there might have been a motive for that — but their uncorrupted elder relatives. Why should they too support me with their testimony? Why, indeed, except for the sake of truth and justice, and because they know that I am speaking the truth, and that Meletus is lying.

Well, Athenians, this and the like of this is nearly all the defence which I have to offer. Yet a word more. Perhaps there may be someone who is offended at me, when he calls to mind how he himself, on a similar or even a less serious occasion, had recourse to prayers and supplications with many tears, and how he produced his children in court, which was a moving spectacle, together with a posse of his relations and friends; whereas I, who am probably in danger of my life, will do none of these things. Perhaps this may come into his mind, and he may be set against me, and vote in anger because he is displeased at this. Now if there be such a person among you, which I am far from affirming, I may fairly reply to him: My friend, I am a man, and like other men, a creature of flesh and blood, and not of wood or stone, as Homer says; and I have a family, yes, and sons. O Athenians, three in number, one of whom is growing up, and the two others are still young; and yet I will not bring any of them hither in order to petition you for an acquittal. And why not? Not from any self-will or disregard of you. Whether I am or am not afraid of death is another question, of which I will not now speak. But my reason simply is that I feel such conduct to be discreditable to myself, and you, and the whole state. One who has reached my years, and who has a name for wisdom, whether deserved or not, ought not to debase himself. At any rate, the world has decided that Socrates is in some way superior to other men. And if those among you who are said to be superior in wisdom and courage, and any other virtue, demean themselves in this way, how shameful is their conduct! I have seen men of reputation, when they have been condemned, behaving in the strangest manner: they seemed to fancy that they were going to suffer something dreadful if they died, and that they could be immortal if you only allowed them to live; and I think that they were a dishonor to the state, and that any stranger coming in would say of them that the most eminent men of Athens, to whom the Athenians themselves give honor and command, are no better than women. And I say that these things ought not to be done by those of us who are of reputation; and if they are done, you ought not to permit them; you ought rather to show that you are more inclined to condemn, not the man who is quiet, but the man who gets up a doleful scene, and makes the city ridiculous.

But, setting aside the question of dishonor, there seems to be something wrong in petitioning a judge, and thus procuring an acquittal instead of informing and convincing him. For his duty is, not to make a present of justice, but to give judgment; and he has sworn that he will judge according to the laws, and not according to his own good pleasure; and neither he nor we should get into the habit of perjuring ourselves — there can be no piety in that. Do not then require me to do what I consider dishonorable and impious and wrong, especially now, when I am being tried for impiety on the indictment of Meletus. For if, O men of Athens, by force of persuasion and entreaty, I could overpower your oaths, then I should be teaching you to believe that there are no gods, and convict myself, in my own defence, of not believing in them. But that is not the case; for I do believe that there are gods, and in a far higher sense than that in which any of my accusers believe in them. And to you and to God I commit my cause, to be determined by you as is best for you and me....

Someone will say: Yes, Socrates, but cannot you hold your tongue, and then you may go into a foreign city, and no one will interfere with you? Now I have great difficulty in making you understand my answer to this. For if I tell you that this would be a disobedience to a divine command, and therefore that I cannot hold my tongue, you will not believe that I am serious; and if I say again that the greatest good of man is daily to converse about virtue, and all that concerning which you hear me examining myself and others, and that the life which is unexamined is not worth living — that you are still less likely to believe. And yet what I say is true, although a thing of which it is hard for me to persuade you.

Moreover, I am not accustomed to think that I deserve any punishment. Had I money I might have proposed to give you what I had, and have been none the worse. But you see that I have none, and can only ask you to proportion the fine to my means. However, I think that I could afford a minae, and therefore I propose that penalty; Plato, Crito, Critobulus, and Apollodorus, my friends here, bid me say thirty minae, and they will be the sureties. Well then, say thirty minae, let that be the penalty; for that they will be ample security to you.

Not much time will be gained, O Athenians, in return for the evil name which you will get from the detractors of the city, who will say that you killed Socrates, a wise man; for they will call me wise even although I am not wise when they want to reproach you. If you had waited a little while, your desire would have been fulfilled in the course of nature. For I am far advanced in years, as you may perceive, and not far from death. I am speaking now only to those of you who have condemned me to death. And I have another thing to say to them: You think that I was convicted through deficiency of words — I mean, that if I had thought fit to leave nothing undone, nothing unsaid, I might have gained an acquittal. Not so; the deficiency which led to my conviction was not of words — certainly not. But I had not the boldness or impudence or inclination to address you as you would have liked me to address you, weeping and wailing and lamenting, and saying and doing many things which you have been accustomed to hear from others, and which, as I say, are unworthy of me. But I thought that I ought not to do anything common or mean in the hour of danger: nor do I now repent of the manner of my defence, and I would rather die having spoken after my manner, than speak in your manner and live. For neither in war nor yet at law ought any man to use every way of escaping death. For often in battle there is no doubt that if a man will throw away his arms, and fall on his knees before his pursuers, he may escape death; and in other dangers there are other ways of escaping death, if a man is willing to say and do anything. The difficulty, my friends, is not in avoiding death, but in avoiding unrighteousness; for that runs faster than death. I am old and move slowly, and the slower runner has overtaken me, and my accusers are keen and quick, and the faster runner, who is unrighteousness, has overtaken them....

Source: Plato, *The Republics and Other Works by Plato*, trans. B. Jowett, (New York: Anchor Books, 1989), pp. 452-467.

3.4

✣

A GREEK WOMAN'S VENGEANCE: *MEDEA*

Greek theatre flourished in the Classical period, beginning near the end of the Peloponnesian War. Drama developed first, then comedy. Greek theatre is particularly important as a source of information on Greek women, although one should be careful not to mistake the stage for real life. One of the three great Athenian dramatists known to us, Euripides (c. 406 BC), is best known for complex characters who face realistic problems (rather than mythological and divine predicaments). In addition to giving us one of the most powerful women in the history of Western theatre, Medea *also presents a non-traditional view of the great mythic hero Jason, and asks the question: what happens when the hero becomes just a man? Here, the betrayals by Jason of his wife and family, and his all-too human weaknesses, have tragic consequences.*

QUESTIONS

1. What is Medea's greatest fault: as a wife or as a citizen?
2. Without political or military power, what power is left to women such as Medea?
3. Is there a difference between a good female citizen and a good male citizen?

MEDEA. Women of Corinth, do not criticize me, I come forth from the palace. Well I know that snobbery is a common charge, that may be levelled against recluse and busy man alike. And the former, by their choice of a quiet life, acquire an extra stigma: they are deficient in energy and spirit. There is no justice in the eyes of men; a man who has never harmed them they may hate at sight, without ever knowing anything about his essential nature. An alien, to be sure, should adapt himself to the citizens with whom he lives. Even the citizen is to be condemned if he is too selfwilled or too uncouth to avoid offending his fellows. So…but this unexpected blow which has befallen me has broken my heart.

It's all over, my friends; I would gladly die. Life has lost it savor. The man who was everything to me, well he knows it, has turned out to be the basest of men. Of all creatures that feel and think, we women are the unhappiest species. In the first place, we must pay a great dowry to a husband who will be a tyrant of our bodies (that's a further aggravation of the evil); and there is another fearful hazard: whether we shall get a good man or a bad. For separations bring disgrace on the woman and it is not possible to renounce one's husband. Then, landed among strange habits and regulations unheard of in her own home, a woman needs second sight to know how best to handle her bedmate. And if we manage this well and have a husband who does not find the yoke of intercourse too galling, ours is a life to be envied. Otherwise, one is better dead. When the man wearies of the company of his wife, he goes outdoors and relieves the disgust of his heart [having recourse to some friend or the companions of his own age], but we women have only one person to turn to.

They say that we have a safe life at home, whereas men must go to war. Nonsense! I had rather fight three battles than bear one child. But be that as it may, you and I are not in the same case. You have your city here, your paternal homes; you know the delights of life and association with your loved ones. But I, homeless and forsaken, carried off from a foreign land, am being wronged by a husband, with neither mother nor brother nor kinsman with whom I might find refuge from the storms of misfortune. One little boon I crave of you, if I discover any ways and means of punishing my husband for these wrongs: your silence. Woman in most respects is a timid creature, wit no heart for strife and aghast at the sight of steel; but wronged in love, there is no heart more murderous that hers.

LEADER. Do as you say, Medea, for just will be your vengeance. I do not wonder that you bemoan your fate. But I see Creon coming, the ruler of this land, bringing tidings of new plans.

[Enter Creon.]

CREON. You there, Medea, looking black with rage against your husband; I have proclaimed that you are to be driven forth in exile from this land, you and your two sons. Immediately. I am the absolute judge of the case, and I shall not go back to my palace till I have cast you over the frontier of the land.

MEDEA. Ah! Destruction, double destruction is my unhappy lot. My enemies are letting out every sail and there is no harbor into which I may flee from the menace of their attack. But ill-treated and all, Creon, still I shall put the question to you. Why are you sending me out of the country?

CREON. I am afraid of you — there's no need to hide behind a cloak of words — afraid you will do my child some irreparable injury. There's plenty logic in that fear. You are a wizard possessed of evil knowledge. You are stung by the loss of your husband's love. And I have heard of you threats — they told me of them — to injure bridegroom and bride and father of the bride. Therefore before anything happens to me, I shall take precautions. Better for me now to be hateful in your eyes than to relent and rue it greatly later....

JASON. Often and often ere now I have observed that an intractable nature is a curse almost impossible to deal with. So with you. When you might have stayed on in this land and in this house by submitting quietly to the wishes of your superiors, your forward tongue has got you expelled from the country. Not that your abuse troubles *me* at all. Keep on saying that Jason is a villain of the deepest dye. But for your insolence to royalty consider yourself more than fortunate that you are only being punished by exile. I was constantly mollifying the angry monarch and expressing the wish that you be allowed to stay. But in unabated folly you keep on reviling the king. That is why you are to be expelled.

MEDEA. Rotten, heart-rotten, that is the word for you. Words, words, magnificent words. In reality a craven. You come to me, you come, my worst enemy! This isn't bravery, you know, this isn't valor, to come and face your victims. No! it's the ugliest sore on the face of humanity, Shamelessness. But I thank you for coming. It will lighten the weight on my heart to tell your wickedness, and it will hurt you to hear it. I shall begin my tale at the very beginning.

I saved your life, as all know who embarked with you on the Argo, when you were sent to master with the yoke the fire-breathing bulls and to sow with dragon's teeth that acre of death. The dragon, too, with wreathed coils, that kept safe watch over the Golden Fleece and never slept — I slew it and raised for you the light of life again. Then, forsaking my father and my own dear ones, I came to Iolcus where Pelias reigned, came with you, more than fond and less than wise. On Pelias too I brought death, the most painful death there is, at the hands of his own children. Thus I have removed every danger from your path.

And after all those benefits at my hands, you basest of men, you have betrayed me and made a new marriage, though I have borne you children. If you were still childless, I could have understood this love of your for a new wife. Gone now is all reliance on pledges. You puzzle me. Do you believe that the gods of the old days are no longer in office? Do you think that men are now living under a new dispensation? For surely you know that you have broken all your oaths to me. Ah my hand, which you so often grasped, and oh my knees, how all for nothing have we been defiled by this false man, who has disappointed all our hopes.

But come, I shall confide in you as though you were my friend, not that I expect to receive any benefit from you. But let that go. My questions will serve to underline your infamy. As things are now, where am I to turn? Home to my father? But when I came here with you, I betrayed my home and my country. To the wretched daughters of Pelias? They would surely give me a royal welcome to their home; I only murdered their father. For it is how it is. My loved ones at home have learned to hate me; the others, whom I need not have harmed, I have made my enemies to oblige you. And so in return for these services you have made me envied among the women of Hellas! A wonderful, faithful husband I have in you, if I must be expelled from the country into exile, deserted by my friends, alone with my friendless children! A fine story to tell of the new bridegroom, that his children and the woman who saved his life are wandering about in aimless beggary! O Zeus, why O why have you given to mortals sure means of knowing gold from tinsel, yet men's exteriors show now mark by which to descry the rotten heart?

LEADER. Horrible and hard to heal is the anger of friend at strife with friend.

JASON. It looks as if I need no small skill in speech if, like a skilful steersman riding the storm with close-reefed sheets, I am to escape the howling gale of your verbosity, woman. Well, since you are making a mountain out of the favors you have done me. I'll tell *you* what *I* think. It was the goddess of Love and none other, mortal or immortal, who delivered me from the dangers of my quest. You have indeed much subtlety of wit, but it would be an invidious story to go into, how the inescapable shafts of Love compelled you to save my life. Still, I shall not put too fine a point on it. If you helped me in some way or other, good and well. But as I shall demonstrate, in the matter of my rescue you got more that you gave.

In the first place, you have your home in Greece, instead of in a barbarian land. You have learned the blessing of Laws of Justice, instead of the Caprice of the Strong. And all the Greeks have realized your wisdom, and you have won great fame. If you had been living on the edges of the earth, nobody would ever have heard of you. May I have neither gold in my house nor skill to sing a sweeter song than Orpheus if my fortune is to be hid from the eyes of men. That, then is my position in the matter of the fetching of the Fleece. (It was you who proposed the debate.)

There remains my wedding with the Princess, which you have cast in my teeth. In this connection I shall demonstrate, one, my wisdom; two, my rightness; three, my great service of love to you and my children. (Be quiet, please.) When I emigrated here from the land of Iolcus, dragging behind me an unmanageable chain of troubles, what greater windfall could I have hit upon, I an exile, than a marriage with the king's daughter? Not that I was weary of your charms (that's the thought that galls you) or that I was smitten with longing for a fresh bride; still less that I wanted to outdo my neighbors in begetting numerous children. Those I have are enough, there I have no criticism to make. No! what I wanted, first and foremost, was a good home where we would lack for nothing (well I knew that the poor man is shunned and avoided by all this friends); and secondly, I wanted to bring up the children in a style worthy of my house, and, begetting other children to be brothers to the children born of you, to bring them all together and unite the families. Then my happiness would be complete. What do *you* want with more children? As for me, it will pay me to advance the children I have by means of those I intend to beget. Surely that is no bad plan? You yourself would admit it, if jealousy were not pricking you.

You women have actually come to believe that, lucky in love, you are lucky in all things, but let some mischance befall that love, and you will think the best of all possible worlds a most loathsome place. There ought to have been some other way for men to beget their children, dispensing with the assistance of women. Then there would be no trouble in the world.

LEADER. Jason, you arrange your arguments very skillfully. And yet in my opinion, like it or not, you have acted unjustly in betraying your wife.

MEDEA. Yes! I do hold many opinions that are not shared by the majority of people. In my opinion, for example, the plausible scoundrel is the worst type of scoundrel. Confident in his ability to trick out his wickedness with fair phrases he shrinks from no depth of villainy. But there is a limit to his cleverness.

As there is also to yours. You may as well drop that fine front with me, and all that rhetoric. One word will floor you. If you had been an honorable man, you would have sought my consent to the new match and not kept you plans secret from your own family.

JASON. And if I had announced to you my intention to marry, I am sure I would have found you a most enthusiastic accomplice. Why! even now you cannot bring yourself to master your heart's deep resentment.

MEDEA. That's not what griped you. No! your foreign wife was passing into an old age that did you little credit.

JASON. Accept my assurance, it was not for the sake of a woman that I made the match I have made. as I told you once already, I wanted to save you and to beget princes to be brothers to my own sons, thereby establishing our family.

MEDEA. May it never be mine…a happiness that hurts, a blessedness that frets my soul.

JASON. do you know how to change your prayer to show better sense? "May I regard nothing useful as grievous, no good fortune as ill."

MEDEA. Insult me. *You* have a refuge, but I am helpless, face with exile.

JASON. It is your own choice. Don't blame anyone else.

MEDEA. What did I do? Did I betray you and marry someone else?

JASON. You heaped foul curses on the king.

MEDEA. And to your house also I shall prove a curse.

From *Euripides, Ten Plays of Euripides*, trans. Moses Hadas and John McLean, pp. 37-39, 42-45. Copyright © 1960, 1963 Bantam Books.

QUESTIONS FOR PART 3

1. Greek civilization is often referred to as a period of revolutionary thought. Is that claim supported or refuted by these documents, in comparison with the earlier civilizations of Mesopotamia and Egypt?
2. Compare and contrast the complaints about women in the Pandora myth with the complaints by women in the *Medea* selection.
3. Both Mesopotamia and Greece were civilizations based on city-states. How did their city-states differ?

PART 4

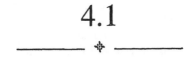

THE HELLENISTIC WORLD

In 334 BC Alexander began creating what was then the largest empire to date, when he won his first major victory against the Persians. Alexander had only been king for two years, following the death of his father Philip II of Macedon. It was Philip who had conquered Greece and incorporated the factious Greek city-states into his Macedonian kingdom. It would be up to his ambitious son Alexander to finish the Greek wars with Persia. In 330 BC Alexander and his mixed Macedonian and Greek army captured the city of Persepolis and added the title of *shahanshah*, "Great King of the Persians" to his collection of titles. He was already King of Macedon, de facto ruler of Greece, and pharaoh of Egypt (conquered in 332 BC). Before he died in 323 BC (at age thirty-two) he had pushed the boundary of his empire up to the Indus River in Asia.

The empire did not survive the death of its founder; it was quickly divided up into smaller states ruled by three of his generals. The Antigonids of Macedonia and Greece, the Ptolemies of Egypt, and the Seleucids of Persia were the political successors to Alexander. The most important legacy of Alexander was his cultural synthesis that brought together Macedonian, Greek, Persian, Egyptian, Syrian, Palestinian, Median, Parthian, and Bactrian civilizations. Most of this in turn was subsequently conquered and adopted by the Romans. The result of this cultural hodgepodge was the Hellenistic world that brought Eastern traditions to the West (for instance, see Source 4.3, on the mystery cults) and Western traditions to the East (such as Greek art and architecture, which spread throughout the East).

4.1

---✤---

HELLENISTIC WOMEN: TIMOCLEA AND ERYXO

Plutarch was a Greek writer living in the first century AD who wrote biographical sketches of people living throughout the Roman Empire. His best-known work, Parallel Lives, *compared Greeks and Romans. However, he was in fact chronicling the vast diversity of the Hellenistic world: Greeks, Romans, Egyptians, Persians, and people from many other cultures.*

In one of his shorter works, "Virtues in Women" from the Moralia, *Plutarch presented brief portraits of twenty-seven courageous and extraordinary women of the Hellenistic world. Few of the women described were well known to the Plutarch's readers; instead he chose women of unusual accomplishment and almost mythic qualities of daring and determination. Here are two of the portraits.*

The first is of Timoclea, who stood up to Alexander himself, and the second is of Eryxo, from the North African city of Cyrene, at war with the Ptolemaic kingdom of Egypt.

QUESTIONS

1. Timoclea's story gives us a glimpse of what the conquests of Alexander were like for those conquered. What reason does Plutarch give for her refusal to submit to Alexander?
2. Why does Alexander not kill Timoclea for her crime, and what does this say about Hellenistic values?
3. In the story of Eryxo, why are Egyptian soldiers in the city of Cyrene and what does this reveal about the political situation of the Eastern Mediterranean world in the early Hellenistic world?

TIMOCLEA

Theagenes of Thebes, who had the same patriotic views as Epaminondas and Pelopidas and the other notables of the city, fell at Chaeronea, in the common ruin of Greece, at the very moment of routing and pursuing his opponents. He was the man who, when asked 'How far are you going to pursue them?' replied 'All the way to Macedonia.' He was survived by a sister, who herself gave proof that his greatness and distinction came from a family tradition of valour. She, however, gained some profit from her deeds, and so endured more easily the share of the common misfortunes that fell upon her.

When Alexander had defeated the Thebans, and his soldiers were sacking various areas of the city, Timoclea's house fell into the hands of a man of violent and thoughtless temper, without any decency or good feeling. He was the commanding officer of a company of Thracians, and he bore the same name as the king, though he in no way resembled him. He had no respect for the lady's family or her way of life, and, after dinner, when he had drunk enough, he summoned her to his bed. Nor was that the end of it: he asked after any gold or solver she might have kept hidden, accompanying his demands by threats or by promises to make her his wife. She seized the opportunity he gave. 'I wish I had died,' she exclaimed, 'before this night, so as at least to keep my body safe from insult, though everything else was lost! But as things have gone, if I must regard you as guardian, master and husband to me, because Fortune has done this, I will not deprive you of what is your own. I see I am now whatever you wish me to be. I had my jewellery, I had silver drinking-cups, and I had some gold and some coin. When the city fell, I told the maids to gather it all up, and I threw it, or rather hid it for security, down a dry well. Not many people know this well; there is a cover over it, and dense bushes all around. Take it, and good luck with it. It shall be token and proof to you of the prosperity and splendour of my family.' The Macedonian did not wait till morning. He made straight for the spot, Timoclea guiding him. Ordering the garden door to be shut, so that no one should notice, he went down the well in his shirt. His guide was 'loathly Clotho,' the avenging fate sent by Timoclea, who stood waiting at the top. When she could tell by his voice that he had reached the bottom, she and her servants all brought a lot of big stones and rolled them down on to him, until they battered and smothered him to death. When the Macedonians got to know, they recovered the body. Orders had already gone out that they were not to kill any of the Thebans, and so they merely seized her, took her to the king, and reported her daring deed. Alexander saw the pride and nobility in her stead gaze and stately walk, and he began by asking who she was. Her reply was undaunted and confident, 'My brother was Theagenes, who fell at Chaeronea, commanding the troops and fighting against you for the liberty of Greece, in order that we should not suffer like this. But since we have suffered in ways our family does not deserve, we do not seek to escape death. It is surely better not to survive to endure another such night, unless you forbid it.' The more humane of those present wept for her; Alexander felt no pity for the woman — her deed was too great for forgiveness — but he admired her courage and the words with which she had cut him to the quick. He ordered his officers to take every precaution to prevent such violence being offered to a house of note again; and he released Timoclea and all of her family who could be found.

ERYXO

Arcesilaus, the son of Battus the Fortunate, was a very different person than his father. Even in his father's lifetime, he built a defensive stockade around his house, and was fined by his father a talent for doing so. After Battus' death, he proved a tyrant rather than a king, owing partly to his own cruel nature (he was called 'the Cruel'), and partly to his wicked friend Laarchus. This man, who was himself scheming for the tyranny, engaged in expelling or murdering the leading men in Cyrene, whifting the responsibility for this on to Arcesilaus, whom he finally killed by means of a drink containing sea-hare, which led to painful wasting disease. He then assumed power, claiming to hold it on behalf of Arcesilaus' son Battus. The boy was held of no account — he was only a child, and he was lame — but many people paid court to his mother, an honourable and humane woman, who had many powerful connections. Laarchus also courted and wooed her; he proposed to marry her, and adopt Battus as a son and make him his colleague on the throne. Eryxo (that was the lady's name) sought the advice of her brothers, and invited Laarchus to meet them; she herself, she said, welcomed the marriage. But when he did meet them, they deliberately misled him with the message that her brothers were at present against the marriage, but would cease their objections and give their consent once the union was consummated. So, if he pleased, he should come to her at night: the beginning once made, the rest would go well. Laarchus was delighted. Excited by her willingness, he agreed to go to her any time she chose. All this Eryxo was doing in collusion with her eldest brother, Polyarchus. A time for the meeting was fixed, and Polyarchus was secretly introduced into his sister's bedroom, together with two young men, armed with swards, who were anxious to avenge their father, whom Laarchus had recently put to death. On receiving Eryxo's summons, Laarchus went into the room without a bodyguard. The young men attacked him, and he died under the blows of their swords. They threw his body out over the wall, and brought out Battus to proclaim him king on the terms that his father had enjoyed. Polyarchus thus restored the original constitution to Cyrene.

But there was in the town a force of soldiers belonging to Amasis, the king of Egypt. Laarchus had relied upon these, and his power to terrorize the citizens had rested largely upon them. They sent a message to Amasis, denouncing Polyarchus and Eryxo. Amasis was angry, and contemplated going to war against Cyrene. But it happened that his mother had died, and the messengers arrived while he was occupied in conducting the funeral. Polyarchus accordingly decided to go and make his own defence. Eryxo would not be left behind, but insisted on accompanying him and sharing the risks. Nor would their old mother, Critola, stay behind. She was a greatly respected lady, sister of Battus the Fortunate. When they reached Egypt, their action won general admiration. After honouring both Polyarchus and the two ladies with gifts and service appropriate to royalty, he sent them home to Cyrene.

4.2

—— ✦ ——

ANCIENT MACHINERY: ARCHIMEDES' SCREW

Archimedes (287-212 BC) is one of the best known of the ancient mathematicians and inventors, yet very little is in fact known about his early machines and discoveries. Schematics and drawings do not exist, nor do we have detailed instructions on how to build these devices. What we do have, instead, are brief descriptions of Archimedes' devices in use. Mathematically he is best remembered as the discoverer of pi and the founder of geometry; as an inventor, he is best known for the lever and the screw. Here is an all-to-brief description of the latter.

—— ✦ ——

QUESTIONS

1. Archimedes was also famous for creating military machinery; what is the primary function of the screw?
2. In terms of Hellenistic culture, what is the significance of where Archimedes first conceived of the idea of the screw?
3. Why does Diodorus make such careful mention of the amount of gold and silver being mined?

Great also is the contrast these mines show when they are compared with those of Attica. The men, that is, who work the Attic mines, although they have expended large sums on the undertakings, yet "Now and then, what they hoped to get, they did not get, and what they had, they lost," so that it would appear that they met with misfortune in a kind of riddle; but the exploiters of the mines of Spain, in their hopes, amass great wealth from the undertakings. For their first labours are remunerative, thanks to the excellent quality of the earth for this sort of thing, and they are ever coming upon more splendid veins, rich in both silver and gold; for all the ground in that region is a tangled network of veins which wind in many ways. and now and then, as they go down deep, they come upon glowing subterranean rivers, but they overcome the might of these rivers by diverting the streams which flow in on them by means of channels leading off at an angle. For being urged on as they are by expectations of gain, which indeed do not deceive them, they push each separate undertaking to its conclusion, and what is the most surprising thing of all, they draw out the waters of the streams they encounter by means of what is called by men the Egyptian screw, which was invented by Archimedes of Syracuse at the time of his visit to Egypt; and by the use of such screws they carry the water in successive lifts as far as the entrance, drying up in this way the spot where they are digging and making it well suited to the furtherance of the operations. Since this machine is an exceptionally ingenious device, an enormous amount of water is thrown out, to one's astonishment, by means of a trifling amount of labour, and all the water from such rivers is brought up easily from the depths and poured out on the surface. And a man may well marvel at the inventiveness of the craftsman, in connection not only with this invention but with many other greater ones as well, the fame of which has encompassed the entire inhabited world and of which we shall give a detailed and precise account when we come to the period of Archimedes.

4.3

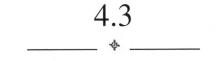

MYSTERY CULT OF OSIRIS

Hellenistic religion came in two basic forms: new philosophies (such as that of Epicurus in Source 4.4) or the mystery cults, such as the one described here by Plutarch, c. 110 AD. Mystery cults incorporated deities from across the Mediterranean world; Egyptian, Greek, and Roman gods and goddesses were worshipped side by side, and their mythologies intertwined. Mystery cults focused on the secret initiation rituals and a personal quest for union with a god. Plutarch dedicated this piece, as well as the collection on "Virtues in Women" (Source 4.1), to a priestess of the oracle of Delphi, itself a mystery cult.

QUESTIONS

1. Plutarch uses both the Greek (Dionysius) and Roman (Bacchus) names for the same deity, whom he then compares to the Egyptian deity of Osiris. What does this say in general about Hellenistic culture?
2. According to this account, what is Osiris the deity of?
3. How does a participant in this mystery cult worship Osiris?

Let this, then, be stated incidentally, as a matter of record that is common knowledge. But the wiser of the priests call not only the Nile Osiris and the Sea Typhon, but they simply give the name of Osiris to the whole source and faculty creative of moisture, believing this to be the cause of generation and the substance of life-producing seed; and the name of Typhon they give to all that is dry, fiery, and arid, in general, and antagonistic to moisture. Therefore, because they believe that he was personally of a reddish sallow color, they are not eager to meet men of such complexion, nor do they like to associate with them.

Osiris, on the other hand, according to their legendary tradition, was dark, because water darkens everything, earth and clothes and clouds, when it comes into contact with them. In young people the presence of moisture renders their hair black, while greyness, like a paleness as it were, is induced by dryness in those who are passing their prime. Also the spring-time is vigorous, prolific, and agreeable; but the autumn, since it lacks moisture, is inimical to plants and unhealthful for creatures.

The bull kept at Heliopolis which they call Mneuis and which is sacred to Osiris—some hold it to be the sire of Apis—is black and has honors second only to Apis. Egypt, moreover, which has the blackest of soils, they call by the same name as the black portion of the eye, "Chemia," and compare it to a heart; for it is warm and moist and is enclosed by the southern portions of the inhabited world and adjoins them, like the heart in a man's left side.

They say that the sun and moon do no use chariots, but boats in which to sail round in their courses; and by this they intimate that the nourishment and origin of these heavenly bodies is from moisture. They think also that Homer, like Thales, had gained his knowledge from the Egyptians, when he postulated water as the source and origin of all things; for, according to them, Ocean is Osiris, and Tethys is Isis, since she is the kindly nurse and provider for all things. In fact, the Greeks call emission *apousia* and coition *synousia*, and the son (*hyios*) from water (*hydor*) and rain (*hysai*); Dionysos also they call Hyes since he is the lord of the nature of moisture; and he is no other than Osiris. In fact, Hellanicus seem to have heard Osiris pronounced Hysiris by the priests, for he regularly spells the name in this way, deriving it, in all probability, from the nature of Osiris and the ceremony of finding him.

That Osiris is identical with Dionysos who could more fittingly know than yourself, Clea? For you are at the head of the inspired maidens of Delphi, and have been consecrated by your father and mother in the holy rites of Osiris. If, however, for the benefit of others it is needful to adduce proofs of this identity, let us leave undisturbed what may not be told, but the public ceremonies which the priests perform in the burial of the Apis, when they convey his body on an improvised bier, do not in any way come short of a Bacchic procession; for they fasten skins of fawns about themselves, and carry Bacchic wands (thyrsi) and indulge in shoutings and movements exactly as do those who are under the spell of the Dionysiac acstasies. For the same reason many of the Greeks make statues of Dionysos in the form of a bull; and the women of Elis involke him, praying that the god may come with the hoof of a bull; and the epithet applied to Dionysos among the Argives is "Son of the Bull." They call him up out of the water by the sound of trumpets, at the same time casting into the depths a lamb as an offering to the Keeper of the Gate. The trumpets they conceal in Bacchic wands, as Socrates has stated in his treatise on *The Holy Ones*. Furthermore, the tales regarding the Titans and rites celebrated by the night agree with the accounts of the dismemberment of Osiris and his revivification and regenesis. Similar agreement is found too in the tales about their sepulchers. The Egyptians, as has already been stated, point out tombs of Osiris in many places, and the people of Delphi believe that the remains of Dionysos rest with them close beside the oracle; and the Holy Ones offer a secret sacrifice in the shrine of Apollo whenever the devotees of Dionysos wake the God of the Mystic Basket (Liknites). To show that the Greeks regard Dionysos as the lord and master not only of wine, but of the nature of every sort of moisture, it is enough that Pindar be our witness, when he says,

> May gladsome Dionysos swell the fruit upon the trees,
> The hallowed splendor of harvest-time.

For this reason all who reverence Osiris are prohibited from destroying a cultivated tree or blocking up a spring of water.

Not only the Nile, but every form of moisture they call simply the effusion of Osiris; and their holy rites the water jar in honor of the god heads the procession. And by the picture of a rush they represent a king and the southern region of the world, and the rush is interpreted to mean the watering and fructifying of all things, and in its nature it seems to bear some resemblance to the generative member. Moreover, when they celebrate the festival of the Pamylia which, as had been said, is of a phallic nature, they expose and carry about a statue of which the male member is triple; for the god is the Source, and every source, by its fecundity, multiples what proceeds from it; and for "many times" we have a habit of saying "thrice," as, for example, "thrice happy," and Bonds, even thrice as many, unnumbered, unless, indeed, the word "triple" is used by the early writers in its strict meaning; for the nature of moisture, being the source and origin of all things, created out of itself three primal material substances, Earth, Air and Fire. In fact, the tale that is annexed to the legend to the effect that Typhon cast the male member of Osiris into the river, and Isis could not find it, but constructed and shaped a replica of it, and ordained that it should be honored and borne in processions, plainly comes round to this doctrine, that the creative and germinal power of the god, at the very first, acquired moisture as its substance, and through moisture combined with whatever was by nature capable of participating in generation.

But let us now take up again the proper subject of our discussion. Isis is, in fact, the female principle of Nature, and is receptive of every form of generation, in accord with which she is called by Plato the gentle nurse and the all-receptive, and by most people has been called by countless names, since, because of the force of Reason, she turns herself to this thing or that and is receptive of all manner of shapes and forms. She has an innate love for the first and most dominant of all things, which is identical with the good, and this she yearns for and pursues; but the portion which comes from evil she tries to avoid and to reject, for she serves them both as place and means of growth, but inclines always towards the better and offers to it opportunity to create from her and to impregnate her with effluxes and likenesses in which she rejoices and is glad that she is made pregnant and teeming with these creations. For creation is the image of being in matter, and the thing created is a picture of reality.

It is not, therefore, out of keeping that they have a legend that the soul of Osiris is everlasting and imperishable, but that his body Typhor oftentimes dismembers and causes to disappear, and that Isis wanders hither and yon in her search for it, and fits it together again; for that which really is and is perceptible and good is superior to destruction and change. The images from it with which the sensible and corporeal is impressed, and the relations, forms, and likenesses which this takes upon itself, like impressions of seals in wax, are not permanently lasting, but disorder and distrubance overtakes them, being driven hither from the upper reaches, and fighting against Horus, whom Isis brings forth, beholden of all, as the image of the perceptible world. Therefore it is said that he is brought to trial by Typhon on the charge of illegitimacy, as no being pure nor uncontaminated like his father, reason unalloyed and unaffected of itself, but contaminated in his substance because of the corporeal element. He prevails, however, and wins the case when Hermes that is to say Reason, testifies and points out that Nature, by undergoing changes of form with reference to the perceptible, duly bring about the creation of the world. The birth of Apollo from Isis and Osiris, while these gods were still in the womb of Rhea, has the allegorical meaning that before this world was made visible and its rough material was completely form by Reason, it was put to the test by Nature and brought forth of itself the first creation imperfect. This is the reason why they say that this god was born in the darkness of a cripple, and they call him the elder Horus; for there was then no world, but only an image and outline of a world to be.

But this Horus is himself perfected and complete; but he has not done away completely with Typhon, but has taken away his activity and strength. Hence they say that at Kopto the statue of Horus hold in one hand the privy members of Typhon, and they relate a legend that Hermes cut out the sinews of Typhon, and used them as strings for his lyre thereby instructing us that Reason adjusts the Universe and creates concord out of discordant elements, and that it does not destroy but only cripples the destructive force. Hence this is weak and inactive here, and combines with the susceptible and changeable elements and attaches itself to them, becoming the artificer of quakes and tremblings in the earth, and of droughts and tempestuous winds in the air, and of lightning-flashes and thunderbolts. Moreover, it taints waters and winds with pestilence, and it runs forth wanton even as far as the moon, often-times confounding and darkening the moon's brightness; according to the belief and account of the Egyptians, Typhon at one time smites the eye of Horus, and at another time snatches it out and swallows it, and then later gives it back again to the Sun. By the smiting, they refer allegorically to the monthly waning of the moon, and by the crippling, to it eclipse, which the Sun heals by shining straight upon it as soon as it has escaped the shadow of the earth.

them; for they do not pay a respect to them which accords with the ideas that they entertain of them. And that man is not impious who discards the god believed in by many, but he who applies to the gods the opinions entertained of them by the many. For the assertions of the many about the gods are not anticipations, but false opinions. And in consequence of these, the greatest evils which befall wicked men, and the benefits which are conferred on the good, are all attributed to the gods; for they connect all their ideas of them with a comparison of human virtues, and everything which is different from human qualities, they regard as incompatible with the divine nature.

"Accustom yourself also to think death a matter with which we are not at all concerned, since all good and evil is in sensation, and since death is only the privation of sensation. On which account, the correct knowledge of the fact that death is no concern of ours, makes the mortality of life pleasant to us, insomuch as it sets forth no illimitable time, but relieves us of the longing for immortality. for there is nothing terrible in living to a man who rightly comprehends that there is nothing terrible in ceasing to live; so that he was a silly man who said that he feared death, not because it would grieve him when it was present, but because it did grieve him while it was future. For it is very absurd that that which does not distress a man when it is present, should afflict him when only expected. Therefore, the most formidable of all evils, death, is nothing to us, since, when we exist, death is not present to us; and when death is present, then we have no existence. It is no concern then either of the living or of the dead; since to the one it has no existence, and the other class has no existence itself. But people in general, at times flee from death as the greatest of evils, and at times wish for it as a rest from the evils of life. Nor is the not living a thing feared, since living is not connected with it; nor does the wise man think not living an evil; but, just as he chooses food, not preferring that which is most abundant, but that which is nicest; so too, he enjoys time, not measuring it as to whether it is of the greatest length, but as to whether it is agreeable. And he who enjoins a young man to live well, and an old man to die well, is a simpleton, not only because of the constantly delightful nature of life, but also because the care to live well is identical with the care to die well. And he was still wrong who said:—

"'Tis well to taste of life, and then weh born
To pass with quickness to the shades below.

"For if this really was his opinion why did he not quit life? For it was easily in his power to do so, if it really was his belief. But if he was joking, then he was talking foolishly in a case where it ought not to be allowed; and, we must recollect, that the future is not our own, nor, on the other hand, is it wholly not our own, I mean so that we can never altogether await it with a feeling of certainty that it will be, nor altogether despair of it as what will never be. And we must consider that some of the passions are natural, and some empty; and of the natural ones some are necessary, and some merely natural. And of the necessary ones some are necessary to happiness, and others, with regard to the exemption of the body, from trouble; and other with respect to living itself; for a correct theory, with regard to these things, can refer all choice and avoidance to the health of the body and the freedom from disquietude of the soul. Since this is the end of living happily; for it is for the sake of this that we do everything, wishing to avoid grief and fear; and when once this is the case, with respect to us, then the storm of the soul is, as I may say, put an end to; since the animal is unable to go as if to something deficient, and to seek something different from that by which the good of the soul and body will be perfected.

"For then we have need of pleasure when we grieve, because pleasure is not present; but when we do not grieve, then we have no need of pleasure; and on this account, we affirm, that pleasure is the beginning and end of living happily; for we have recognized this as the first good, being connate with us;

and with reference to it, it is that we begin every choice and avoidance; and to this we come as if we judged of all good by passion as the standard; and, since this is the first good and connate with us, on this account we do not choose every is likely to ensue from them; and we think many pains better than pleasures, when a greater pleasure follows them, if we endure the pain.

"Every pleasure is therefore a good on account of its own nature, but it does not follow that every pleasure is worthy of being chosen; just as every pain is an evil, and yet every pain must not be avoided. But it is right to estimate all these things by the measurement and view of what is suitable and unsuitable; for at times we may feel the good as an evil, and at times, on the contrary, we may feel the evil as good. And, we think, contentment a great good, not in order that we may never have but a little, but in order that, if we have not much, we may make use of a little, being genuinely persuaded that those men enjoy luxury most completely who are the best able to do without it; and that every thing which is natural is easily provided, and what is useless is not easily procured. and simple flavours give as much pleasure as costly fare, when everything that can give you pain, and everything feeling of want, is removed; and corn and water give the most extreme pleasure when anyone in need eats them. To accustom one's self, therefore, to simple and inexpensive habits is a great ingredient in the perfecting of health, and makes a man free from hesitation with respect to the necessary uses of life. And when we, on certain occasion, fall in with more sumptuous fare, it makes us in a better disposition towards it, and renders us fearless with respect to fortune. When, therefore, we say that pleasure is a chief good, we are not speaking of the pleasures of the debauched man, or those which lie in sensual enjoyments, as some think who are ignorant, and who do not entertain our opinions, or else interpret them perversely; but we mean the freedom of the body from pain, and of the soul from confusion. For it is not continued drinkings and revels, or the enjoyment of female society, or feasts of fish and other such things, as a costly table supplies, that make life pleasant, but sober contemplation, which examines into the reasons for all choice and avoidance, and which puts to flight the vain opinions from which the greater part of the confusion arises which troubles the soul.

"Now, the beginning and the greatest good of all these things is prudence, on which account prudence is something more valuable than even philosophy, inasmuch as all the other virtues spring from it, teaching us that it is not possible to live pleasantly unless one also lives prudently, and honorably, and justly; and that one cannot live prudently, and honestly, and justly without living pleasantly; for the virtues are connate with living agreeably, and living agreeably is inseparable from the virtues. Since, who can you think better than that man who has holy opinions respecting the gods, and who is utterly fearless with respect to death, and who has properly contemplated the end of nature, and who comprehends that the chief good is easily perfected and easily provided; and the greatest evil lasts but a short period, and causes but brief pain. And who has no belief in necessity, which is set up by some as the mistress of all things, but he refers some things to fortune, some to ourselves, because necessity is an irresponsible power, and because he sees that fortune is unstable, while our own will is free; and this freedom constitutes, in our case, a responsibility which makes us encounter blame and praise. Since it would be better to follow the fables about the gods than to be a slave to the fate of the natural philosopher; for the fables which are told give us a sketch, as if we could avert the wrath of God by paying him honour; but the other presents us with necessity who is inexorable.

"And he, not thinking fortune a goddess, as the generality esteem her (for nothing is done at random by a god), nor a cause which no man can rely on, for he thinks that good or evil is not given by her to men so as to make them live happily, but that the principles of great goods or great evils are supplied by her; thinking it better to be unfortunate in accordance with reason, than to be fortunate in accordance with reason, than to be fortunate irrationally; for that those actions which are judged to be the best, are rightly done in consequence of reason.

"Do you then study these precepts, and those which are akin to them, by all means day and night, pondering on them by yourself, and discussing them with any one like yourself, and then you will never be disturbed by either sleeping or waking fancies, but you will live like a god among men; for a man living amid immortal gods, is in no respect like a mortal being."

— Diogenes Laertius

Translation of C. D. Younge.

Source: Oliver J. Thatcher, ed., *The Ideas that have Influenced Civilization is the Original Documents; Vol. II The Greek World* (Boston: Roberts-Manchester Publishing Co., 1901), pp. 426-430.

QUESTIONS FOR PART 4

1. The Hellenistic world was heavily influenced by its Greek past. What is peculiarly Greek about the preceding sources?
2. Compare the mystery cult worship of Osiris with Epicureanism. Can you identify the Eastern and Western influences on each?
3. Was there a lack of creativity or cultural progress in the Hellenistic world? Was it, as often described, a stagnant period?

PART 5

❧

THE ROMAN REPUBLIC

Long before there was a Rome, there were people living on the Italian peninsula. The Italic speaking tribes of Indo-European origin had moved into the region by 2000 BC. Within the next millennium two more peoples had moved into the area. These two late arrivals to Italy were the Greeks, another Indo-European speaking people, and the Etruscans, whose language is not Indo-European, and whose exact origins are unknown. The peninsula juts into the Mediterranean, which makes it perfectly placed for migration of people and goods; this would later help the Romans, providing access to trade and empire. The Greeks set up colonies in southern Italy, naming the region *Magna Graecia*, or Greater Greece, as well as on Sicily. The Etruscans set up a series of city-states, similar to the Greek *poleis*, scattered across northern Italy, urbanizing the peninsula. In the sixth century the Etruscans controlled much of Italy; soon however they were in retreat before expanding Romans. The Etruscan influence, particularly cultural, remained vital. By the fifth century the Romans had established not only their own city-state in central Italy but had begun to build an alliance of other cities. From the start the Roman state was committed to a republic style of government, as opposed to the monarchy favored by the Etruscans, or the democratic or tyranny styles of government favored by most Greek city-states.

The Romans were well aware of the cultural legacy they owed to both the Etruscans and the Greeks, but also felt an intense competition to outdo the Greek civilization. The following sources illustrate the mythic origins of the Roman Republic, the establishment of a peculiarly Roman law code, and the gradual disintegration of the Republic politically and culturally.

5.1

✤

TARQUIN THE PROUD AND THE RAPE OF LUCRETIA

The Roman Republic began, according to its own mythology, in the year 509 BCE, when the citizens of Rome overthrew the last of the Etruscan kings, Tarquin the Proud. According to the Roman historian Livy, the Etruscan kings were corrupt and abusive tyrants. Having deposed their king, the Romans then created a state in which power was distributed amongst several leaders. For the Romans, the following account of Tarquin's final offenses against Rome highlighted the danger in having a king with all power over a state's citizens.

✤

QUESTIONS

1. For Romans of the Republic, what virtues were expected in a good Roman woman?
2. At the time of their defeat, were the Etruscans a weak civilization?
3. What is the relationship between the Etruscans and Greek civilization?

In view of all this, Tarquin became more extravagant in his ideas — so much so that the money raised from the sale of material captured at Pometia, which was intended to carry the building up to the roof, hardly covered the cost of the foundations. This inclines me to accept the statement of Fabius — who is, moreover, the older authority — that the money was not more than forty talents, rather than the statement of Piso, who writes that 40,000 pounds' weight of silver was put aside for this work. A huge sum like that could hardly be expected from material taken from a single town in those days, and it would be more than enough for the foundations of any of the most splendid buildings even of the present time....

The attempt was made to take Ardea by assault. It failed; siege operations were begun, and the army settled down into permanent quarters. With little prospect of any decisive action, the war looked like being a long one, and in these circumstances leave was granted, quite naturally, with considerable freedom, especially to officers. Indeed, the young princes, at any rate, spent most of their leisure enjoying themselves in entertainments on the most lavish scale. They were drinking one day in the quarters of Sextus Tarquinius — Collatinus, son of Egerius, was also present — when someone chanced to mention the subject of wives. Each of them, of course, extravagantly praised his own; and the rivalry got hotter and hotter, until Collatinus suddenly cried: 'Stop! What need is there of words, when in a few hours we can prove beyond doubt the incomparable superiority of my Lucretia? We are all young and strong: why shouldn't we ride to Rome and see with our own eyes what kind of women our wives are? There is no better evidence, I assure you, than what a man finds when he enters his wife's room unexpectedly.'

They had all drunk a good deal, and the proposal appealed to them; so they mounted their horses and galloped off to Rome. They reached the city as dusk was falling; and there the wives of the royal princes were found enjoying themselves with a group of young friends at a dinner-party, in the greatest luxury. the riders then went on to Collatia, where they found Lucretia very differently employed: it was late at night, but there, in the hall of her house, surrounded by her busy maid-servants, she was still hard at work at lamplight upon her spinning. Which wife had won the contest in womanly virtue was no longer in doubt.

With all courtesy Lucretia rose to bid her husband and the princes welcome, and Collatinus, pleased with his success, invited his friends to sup with him. It was at that fatal supper that Lucretia's beauty, and proven chastity, kindled in Sextus Tarquinius the flame of lust, and determined him to debauch her.

Nothing further occurred that night. The little jaunt was over, and the young men rode back to camp.

A few days later, Sextus, without Collatinus's knowledge, returned with one companion to Collatia, where he was hospitably welcomed in Lucretia's house, and, after supper, escorted, like the honoured visitor he was thought to be, to the guest-chamber. Here he waited till the house was asleep, and then, when all was quiet, he drew his sword and made his way to Lucretia's room determined to rape her. She was asleep. Laying his left hand on her breast, 'Lucretia,' he whispered, 'not a sound! I am Sextus Tarquinius. I am armed — if you utter a word, I will kill you.' Lucretia opened her eyes in terror; death was imminent, no help at hand. Sextus urged his love, begged her to submit, pleaded, threatened, used every weapon that might conquer a woman's heart. But all in vain; not even the fear of death could bend her will. 'If death will not move you,' Sextus cried, 'dishonour shall. I will kill you first, then cut the throat of a slave and lay his naked body by your side. Will they not believe that you have been caught in adultery with a servant — and paid the price?' Even the most resolute chastity could not have stood against this dreadful threat.

Lucretia yielded, Sextus enjoyed her, and rode away, proud of his success.

The unhappy girl wrote to her father in Rome and to her husband in Ardea, urging them both to come at once with a trusted friend — and quickly, for a frightful thing had happened. Her father came with Valerius, Volesus's son, her husband with Brutus, with whom he was returning to Rome when he was met by the messenger. They found Lucretia sitting in her room, in deep distress. Tears rose to her eyes as they entered, and to her husband's question, 'Is is well with you?' she answered, "No. What can be well with a woman who has lost her honour? In your bed, Collatinus, is the impress of another man. My body only has been violated. My heart is innocent, and death will be my witness. Give me your solemn promise that the adulterer shall be punished — he is Sextus Tarquinius. He it is who last night came as my enemy disguised as a guest, and took his pleasure of me. That pleasure will be my death — and his, too, if you are men.'

The promise was given. One after another they tried to comfort her. They told her she was helpless, and therefore innocent; that he alone was guilty. It was the mind, they said, that sinned, not the boy; without intention there could never be guilt.

'What is due to *him*,' Lucretia said, 'is for you to decide. As for me I am innocent of fault, but I will take my punishment. Never shall Lucretia provide a precedent for unchaste women to escape what they deserve.' With these words she drew a knife from under her robe, drove it into hear, and fell forward, dead.

Her father and husband were overwhelmed with grief. While they stood weeping helplessly, Brutus drew the bloody knife from Lucretia's body, and holding it before him cried: 'By this girl's blood — none more chaste till a tyrant wronged her — and by the gods, I swear that with sword and fire, and whatever else can lend strength to my arm, I will pursue Lucius Tarquinius the Proud, his wicked wife, and all his children, and never again will I let them or any other man be King in Rome.'

He put the knife into Collatinus's hands then passed it to Lucretius, then to Valerius. All looked at him in astonishment: a miracle had happened — he was a changed man. Obedient to his command, they swore their oath. Grief was forgotten in the sudden surge of anger, and when Brutus called upon them to make war, from that instant, upon the tyrant's throne, they took him for their leader.

Lucretia's body was carried from the house into the public square. Crowds gathered, as crowds will, to gape and wonder — and the sight was unexpected enough, and horrible enough, to attract them. Anger at the criminal brutality of the king's son and sympathy with the father's grief stirred every heart; and when Brutus cried out that it was time for deeds not tears, and urged them, like true Romans, to take up arms against the tyrants who had dared to treat them as a vanquished enemy, not a man amongst them could resist the call. The boldest spirits offered themselves at once for service; the rest soon followed their lead. Lucretia's father was left to hold Collatia; guards were posted to prevent news of the rising from reaching the place, and with Brutus in command the armed populace began their march on Rome.

In the city the first effect of their appearance was alarm and confusion, but the sight of Brutus, and others of equal distinction, at the head of the mob, soon convinced people that this was, at least no mere popular demonstration. Moreover the horrible story of Lucretia had had hardly less effect in Rome than in Collatia. In a moment the forum was packed, and the crowds, by Brutus's order, were immediately summoned to attend the Tribune of Knights—an office held at the time by Brutus himself. There, publicly throwing off the mask under which he had hitherto concealed his real character and feelings, he made a speech painting in vivid colours the brutal and unbridled lust of Sextus Tarquinius, the hideous rape of the innocent Lucretia and her pitiful death, and the bereavement of her father, for whom the cause of her death was an even bitterer and more dreadful thing than the death itself. He went on to speak of the king's arrogant and tyrannical behaviour; of the sufferings of the commons condemned to labour underground clearing or constructing ditches and sewers; of gallant Romans—soldiers who had beaten in battle all neighbouring peoples—robbed of their swords and turned into stone-cutters and artisans. He reminded them of the foul murder of Servius Tullius, of the daughter who drove her carriage over her father's corpse, in violation of the most sacred of relationships—a crime which God alone could punish. Doubtless he told them of other, and worse things, brought to his mind in the heat of the moment and by the sense of this latest outrage, which still lived in his eye and pressed upon his heart; but a mere historian can hardly record them.

The effect of his words was immediate: the populace took fire, and were brought to demand the abrogation of the king's authority and the exile of himself and his family.

With an armed body of volunteers Brutus then marched for Ardea to rouse the army to revolt. Lucretius, who some time previously had been appointed by the king Prefect of the City, was left in command in Rome. Tullia fled from the palace during the disturbances; where-ever she went she was met with curses; everyone, men and women alike, called down upon her head the vengeance of the furies who punish sinners against the sacred ties of blood.

When the news of the rebellion reached Ardea, the king immediately started for Rome, to restore order. Brutus got wind of his approach, and changed his route to avoid meeting him, finally reaching Ardea almost at the same moment as Tarquin arrived at Rome. Tarquin found the city gates shut against him and his exile decreed. Brutus the Liberator was enthusiastically welcomed by the troops, and Tarquin's sons were expelled from the camp. Two of them followed their father into exile at Caere in Etruria. Sextus Tarquinius went to Gabu—his own territory, as he doubtless hoped; but his previous record there of robbery and violence had made him many enemies, who now took their revenge and assassinated him.

From *Livy, The Early History of Rome*, trans. Aubrey de Selincourt, pp. 97-101. Copyright © 1960, 1981 Penguin Books. Reprinted by permission of Penguin Books Limited.

5.2

TWELVE TABLES

Having overthrown their Etruscan kings in 509 BC, the Romans set up a republic in which power was shared amongst a few aristocratic, or Patrician, families. Patrician status was determined more by bloodline than by wealth. The lower classes, or Plebeians, included a few wealthy families and the bulk of the Roman population, which had neither status nor money. This oligarchy dominated the city's political community through oral laws and customs, and often ruled arbitrarily. The Struggle of the Orders began almost immediately, and in 451 BC the Plebeians won their first major victory when they forced the Patricians to write the laws down on the Twelve Tables, *which ensured the same laws would be applied to all Roman citizens equally, regardless of class.*

QUESTIONS

1. Why is slander (Tablet VIII) a capital offense?
2. How do the laws characterize a "spendthrift?" Why was this such a serious issue for the Romans?
3. Compare these laws with the account of Tarquin in the previous source. What was more important for the Romans: state or individual?

TABLE IV: *Patria Potestas: Rights of Head of Family*

Quickly kill…a dreadfully deformed child.

If a father thrice surrender a son for sale, the son shall be free from the father.

A child born ten months after the father's death will not be admitted into a legal inheritance.

TABLE V: *Guardianship; Succession*

Females shall remain in guardianship even when they have attained their majority…except Vestal Virgins.

Conveyable possessions of a woman under guardianship of agnates cannot be rightfully acquired by *usucapio*, save such possessions as have been delivered up by her with a guardian's sanction.

According as a person shall will regarding his [household], chattels, or guardianship of his estate, this shall be binding.

If a person dies intestate, and has no self-successor, the nearest agnate kinsman shall have possession of deceased's household.

If there is no agnate kinsman, deceased's clansmen shall have possession of his household.

To persons for whom a guardian has not been appointed by will, to them agnates are guardians.

If a man is raving mad, rightful authority over his person and chattels shall belong to his agnates or to his clansmen.

A spendthrift is forbidden to exercise administration over his own goods….A person who, being insane or a spendthrift, is prohibited from administering his own goods shall be under trusteeship of agnates.

The inheritance of a Roman citizen-freedman shall be made over to his patron if the freedman has died intestate and without self-successor.

Items which are in the category of debts are not included in the division when they have with automatic right been divided into portions of an inheritance.

Debt bequeathed by inheritance is divided proportionally amongst each heir with automatic liability when the details have been investigated.

TABLE VI: *Acquisition and Possession*

When a party shall make bond or conveyance, the terms of the verbal declaration are to be held binding.

Articles which have been sold and handed over are not acquired by a buyer otherwise than when he has paid the price to the seller or has satisfied him is some other way, that is, by providing a guarantor or a security.

A person who has been ordained a free man [in a will, on condition] that he bestow a sum of 10,000 pieces on the heir, though he has been sold by the heir, shall win his freedom by giving the money to the purchaser.

It is sufficient to make good such faults as have been named by word of mouth, and that for any flaws which the vendor had expressly denied, he shall undergo penalty of double damage.

Usucapio of movable things requires one year's possession for its completion; bue *usucapio* of an estate and buildings, two years.

Any woman who does not wish to be subjected in this manner to the hand of her husband should be absent three nights in succession every year, and so interrupt the *usucapio* of each year.

A person shall not dislodge from a framework a [stolen] beam which has been fixed in buildings or a vineyard....action [is granted] for double damages against a person found guilty of fixing such [stolen] beam....

TABLE VIII: *Torts or Delicts*

If any person has sung or composed against another person a song such as was causing slander or insult to another, he shall be clubbed to death.

If a person has maimed another's limb, let there be retaliation in kind unless he makes agreement for settlement with him.

If he has broken or bruised a freeman's bone with his hand or a club, he shall undergo penalty of 300 *as* pieces; if a slave's, 150.

If he has done simple harm [to another], penalties shall be 25 *as* pieces.

If a four-footed animal shall be said to have caused loss, legal action...shall be either the surrender of the thing which damaged, or else the offer of assessment for the damage.

For pasturing on, or cutting secretly by night, another's crops acquired by tillage, there shall be capital punishment in the case of an adult malefactor...he shall be hanged and put to death as a sacrifice to Ceres. In the case of a person under the age of puberty, at the discretion of the praetor [see note 23] either he shall be scourged or settlement shall be made for the harm done by paying double damages.

Any person who destroys by burning any building or heap of corn deposited alongside a house shall be bound, scourged, and put to death by burning at the stake, provided that he has committed the said misdeed with malice aforethought; but if he shall have committed it by accident, that is, by negligence, it is ordained that he repair the damage, or, if he be too poor to be competent for such punishment, he shall receive a lighter chastisement.

Any person who has cut down another person's trees with harmful intent shall pay 25 *as* pieces for every tree.

If theft has been done by night, if the owner kill the thief, the thief shall beheld lawfully killed.

It is forbidden that a thief be killed by day...unless he defend himself with a weapon; even though he has come with a weapon, unless he use his weapon and fight back, you shall not kill him. And even if he resists, first call out.

In the case of all other thieves caught in the act, if they are freemen, they should be flogged and adjudged to the person against whom the theft has been committed, provided that the malefactors have committed it by day and have not defended themselves with a weapon; slaves caught in the act of theft should be flogged and thrown from the Rock; boys under the age of puberty should, at the praetor's discretion, be flogged, and the damage done by them should be repaired.

If a person pleads on a case of theft in which the their has not been caught in the act, the their must compound for the loss by paying double damages.

A stolen thing is debarred from *usucapio*.

No person shall practice usury at a rate more than one twelfth…A usurer is condemned for quadruple amount.

Arising out of a case concerning an article deposited…action for double damages.

Guardians and trustees…the right to accuse on suspicion…action…against guardians for double damages.

If a patron shall have defrauded his client, he must be solemnly forfeited.

Whosoever shall have allowed himself to be called as witness or shall have been scales-balancer, if he do not as witness pronounce his testimony, he must be deemed dishonoured and incapable of acting as witness.

Penalty…for false witness…a person who has been found guilty of giving false witness shall be hurled down from the Tarpeian Rock….

No person shall hold meetings by night in the city.

Members [of associations]…are granted…the right to pass any binding rule they like for themselves provided that they cause no violation of public law….

TABLE X: *Sacred Law*

A dead man shall not be buried or burned within the city.

One must not do more than this [at funerals]; one must not smooth the pyre with an axe.

…three veils, one small purple tunic, and ten flute-players….

Women must not tear cheeks or hold chorus of "Alas!" on account of funeral.

When a man is dead one must not gather his bones in order to make a second funeral. An exception [in the case of] death in war or in a foreign land….

Anointing by slaves is abolished, and every kind of drinking bout.

5.3

⚜

THE GRACCHI BROTHERS AND REFORM

By the second century the Republic was clearly in trouble politically, socially, and economically. The Gracchi brothers, Tiberius (d. 133 BC) and Gaius (d. 121 BC), were each successively tribune (leader of the Plebeian Tribal Assembly). Each in turn suggested economic reforms, such as land redistribution or extending citizenship to non-Romans, which brought them and their followers into open and violent conflict with the Senate.

---- ✦ ----

QUESTIONS

1. The toga was a sign of senatorial class; why is it significant that the senators were wearing their togas when they attacked Tiberius?
2. Why is it significant that none of the followers of Tiberius were executed with a sword?
3. How did the people of Rome feel about the Gracchi brothers after they had been killed?

At the same time also many of his friends on the Capitol came running to Tiberius with urgent appeals to hasten thither, since matters there were going well. And in fact things turned out splendidly for Tiberius at first; as soon as he came into view the crowd raised a friendly shout, and as he camp up the hill they gave him a cordial welcome and ranged themselves about him, that no stranger might approach.

XVIII. But after Mucius began once more to summon the tribes to the vote, none of the customary forms could be observed because of the disturbance that arose on the outskirts of the throng, where there was crowding back and forth between the friend of Tiberius and their opponents, who were striving to force their way in and mingle with the rest. Moreover, at this juncture Fulvius Flaccus, a senator, posted himself in conspicuous place, and since it was impossible to make his voice heard so far, indicated with his hand that he wished to tell Tiberius something meant for his ear alone. Tiberius ordered the crowd to part for Flavius, who made his way up to him with difficulty, and told him that a session of the senate the party of the rich, since they could not prevail upon the consul to do so, were purposing to kill Tiberius themselves, and for his purpose had under arms a multitude of their friends and slaves.

XIX. Tiberius, accordingly, reported this to those who stood about him, and they at once girded up their togas, and breaking in pieces the spear-shafts with which the officers keep back the crowd, distributed the fragments among themselves, that they might defend themselves against their assailants. Those who were farter off, however, wondered at what was going on and asked what it meant. Where-upon Tiberius put his hand to his head, making this visible sign that his life was in danger, since the questioners could not hear his voice. But his opponents, on seeing this, ran to the senate and told that body that Tiberius was asking for a crown; and that his putting his hand to his head was a sign having that meaning. All the senators, of course, were greatly disturbed, and Nasica demanded that the consul should come to the rescue of the state and put down the tyrant. The consul replied with mildness that he would resort to no violence and would put no citizen to death without a trial; if, however, the people, under persuasion or compulsion from Tiberius, should vote anything that was unlawful, he would not regard this vote as binding. There-upon Nasica sprang to his feet and said: "Since, then, the chief magistrate betrays the state, do ye who wish to succour the laws follow me." With these words he covered his head with the skirt of this toga and set out for the Capitol. All the senators who followed him wrapped their togas about their left arms and pushed aside those who stood in their path, no man opposing them, in view of their dignity, but all taking to flight and trampling upon one another.

Now, the attendants of the senators carried clubs and staves which they had brought from home; but the senators themselves seized the fragments and legs of the benches that were shattered by the crowd in its flight, and went up against Tiberius, at the same time smiting those who ere drawn up to protect him. Of these there was a rout and a slaughter; and as Tiberius himself turned to fly, someone laid hold of his garments. So he let his toga go and fled in his tunic. But he stumbled and fell to the ground amond some bodies that lay in front of him. As he strove to rise to his feet, he received his first blow, as everybody admits, from Publius Satyreius, one of his colleagues, who smote him on the head with the leg of a bench; to the second blow claim was made by Lucius Rufus, who plumed himself upon it as upon some noble deed. And of the rest more than three hundred were slain by blows from sticks and stones, but not one by the sword....

XVII. So then, as Caius fled, his foes pressed hard upon him and were overtaking him at the wooden bridge over the Tiber, but his two friends bade him go on, while they themselves withstood his pursuers, and, fighting there at the head of the bridge, would suffer no man to pass, until they were killed. Caius had with him in his flight a single servant, by name Philocrates, and though all the spectators, as at a race, urged Caius on to greater speed, no a man came to his aid, or even consented to furnish him with a horse when he asked for one, for his pursuers were pressing close upon him. He barely succeeded in escaping into a sacred grove of the Furies, and there fell by the hand of Philocrates, who then slew himself upon his master. According to some writers, however, both were taken alive by the enemy, and because the servant had thrown his arms about his master, no one was able to strike the master until the slave had first been dispatched by the blows of many. Someone cut off the head of Caius, we are told, and was carrying it along, but was robbed of it by a certain friend of Opimius, Septimuleius; for proclamation had been made at the beginning of the battle that an equal weight of gold would be paid the men who brought the head of Caius or Fulvius. So Septimuleius stuck the head of Caius on a spear and brought it to Opimius, and when it was placed in a balance it weighed seventeen pounds and two thirds, since Septimuleius, besides showing himself to be a scoundrel, had also perpetrated a fraud; for he had taken out the brain and poured melted lead in its place. But those who brought the head of Fulvius were of the obscurer sort, and therefore got nothing. The bodies of Caius and Fulvius and of the other slain were thrown into the Tiber, and they numbered three thousand; their property was sold and the proceeds paid into the public treasury. Moreover, their wives were forbidden to go into mourning, and Licinia, the wife of Caius, was also deprived of her marriage portion. Most cruel of all, however, was the treatment of the younger son of Fulvius, who had neither lifted a hand against the nobles nor been present at the fighting, but had come to effect a truce before the battle and had been arrested; after the battle he was slain. However, what vexed the people more than this or anything else was the erection of a temple of Concord by Opimius; for it was felt that he was priding himself and exulting and in a manner celebrating a triumph in view of all this slaughter of citizens. Therefore at night, beneath the inscription on the temple, somebody carved this verse: — "A work of mad discord produces a temple of Concord."

XVIII. And yet this Opimius, who was the first consul to exercise the power of a dictator, and put to death without trial, besides three thousand other citizens, Caius Gracchus and Fulvius Flaccus, of whom one had been consul and had celebrated a triumph, while the other was the foremost man of his generation in virtue and reputation — this Opimius could not keep his hands from fraud, but when he was sent as ambassador to Jugurtha the Numidian was bribed by him, and after being convicted most shamefully of corruption, he spent his old age in infamy, hated and abused by the people, a people which was humble and cowed at the time when the Gracchi fell, but soon afterwards showed how much it missed them and longed for them. For it had statues of the brothers made and set up in a conspicuous place, consecrated the places where they were slain, and brought thither offerings of all the first-fruits of the seasons, nay, more, many sacrificed and fell down before their statues every day, as though they were visiting the shrines of gods.

5.4

REPUBLICAN THEATRE: *THE EUNUCH* BY TERENCE

The playwright Terence (d. 159 BC) was a former Carthaginian slave who wrote comedies based on Greek plays. He took simple—and often crude—Greek plots and transformed them into sophisticated Latin theatre. His plays are emblematic of the merger between Greek and Roman cultures, in particular of the Latinization of the Greek past. The Eunuch was Terence's version of the Greek play by Menander; most revealing is the playwright's introduction to the play. His biting attacks on a rival playwright's own translations of Greek plays give us a glimpse of how competitive the Roman theatre world had been.

QUESTIONS

1. Although the character of Phaedria is meant to be the nobleman, and Parmeno the servant, who is really in charge here?
2. What kinds of wares and services could a Roman of the second century find at the market? What does this reveal about the economic vitality of the city?
3. How would you describe the position of slaves in Roman society from this excerpt?

[*The young man* PHAEDRIA *comes out of his father's house talking to his slave* PARMENO, *a middle-aged attendant.*]

PHAEDRIA: Well, then, what am I to do? I can't refuse to go now she's asking me herself, can I? Or had I better think of making a stand against these insults from such women? She slammed her door on me once, and now she opens it again. Shall I go back? No, not if she goes down on bended knees.
PARMENO: Of course, sir, if you can do that, it's the best and boldest course. But if you make a start and can't stick it out, and then go running back to her when you can't stand it any longer, unasked and no terms fixed, letting her see you're in love and can't bear it — then it'll all be over and done with. It will be the end of you, sir; she'll stop play once she find you're beaten. So while there's

time, do think, and think again, sir. Reason can't solve what hasn't got rhyme nor reason, and all these upsets—insults, jealousies, quarrels, reconciliations, war, then peace again—they're all part of love, and if you insist on a method to settle all your uncertainties, why, you might as well think up a method for madness. You're angry now, muttering away to yourself: 'I'll show her! She...with him...and me...and then no...just let her try! I'd rather die! She'll learn what sort of a man I am!' But believe me, it won't take more than a single tiny false tear — which she can hardly squeeze out by force after all that rubbing of her eyes — to damp down all those hot words. Then she'll turn the attack on you, and you'll be the one to suffer.

PHAEDRIA: Monstrous! At last I can see her wickedness and my own sorry state. I'm eaten up with love and I'm sick of it, I'm dying on my feet, eyes open, awake and aware, but what on earth can I do?

PARMENO: Do? Buy your freedom as cheap as possible, and if you can't get it cheap, pay up what you can and stop worrying yourself to death.

PHAEDRIA: That's your advice?

PARMENO: Yes, if you've any sense. Love provides enough troubles anyway — just you face up to those properly and don't go adding to them. Look, she's coming out, that blight on our fortunes! Every penny we ought to have goes to *her*.

[THAIS *comes out of her house without seeing them; she is an attractive young woman.*]

THAIS: Oh dear, I'm afraid Phaedria was annoyed and misunderstood me when I wouldn't let him in yesterday.

PHAEDRIA [*clutching* PARMENO]: The mere sight of her sets me all trembling and shivering.

PARMENO: Courage sir! Go nearer the fire and you'll warm up all right.

THAIS [*coming forward*]: Who's that? Phaedria my dear, is that you? Why are you waiting here? You should have come straight in.

PARMENO: Not a word about shutting her door to him!

THAIS: Why don't you say something?

PHAEDRIA [*bitterly*]: I always find the door open, don't I — I always come first with you.

THAIS: Please, no more.

PHAEDRIA: Why 'no more'? Oh Thais, Thais, if only love meant the same thing to you as it does to me and we ere on equal terms! Then you would suffer for this as much as I do, or I would think nothing of what you have done!

THAIS: Phaedria, my own, my darling, don't torture yourself, please. I swear I didn't do this because I care for anyone or love anyone more than you. In the circumstances it had to be done.

PARMENO: Quite so. Poor soul, I suppose you shut the door for love of him!

THAIS: You think that of me, Parmeno? All right: but let me tell you why I sent for you.

PHAEDRIA [*eagerly*]: Tell me.

THAIS: First of all, can *he* keep his mouth shut?

PARMENO: Me? Of course I can. Listen, I stick to a promise — but there are conditions. When I hear the truth spoken I can hold my tongue and keep quiet as well as anyone, but it it's a lie or an invention or a trumped-up tale, it's out at once; I'm full of cracks and leak all over. So if you want a secret kept, madam, tell the truth.

THAIS: [*ignoring him*]: My mother came from Samos and lived in Rhodes.

PARMENO: I can keep *that* secret.

THAIS: While she was there, a merchant made her a present of a little girl stolen from here, from Attica.

PHAEDRIA: A citizen born?

THAIS: I think so, but we can't be sure. All she could tell us herself was her father's and mother's name, and she didn't know her country or anything else to identify her — she was too young. The merchant added that he had heard from the pirates who sold her that she had been carried off from Sunium. As soon as my mother had taken her in she took care to teach her all she could and bring her up as her own child. She was generally believed to be my sister. Then I found a protector, my first and only one, and came here to Athens with him. It was he who set me up with what I have.

PARMENO: Two lies: they'll both leak out.

THAIS: What do you mean?

PARMENO: One wasn't enough for you and he wasn't the only to give you something. My master here has also made a handsome contribution.

THAIS: Very well, but let me come to my point. It wasn't long before my soldier friend went of to Caria, and that was when I came to know you. You know yourself how dear you have been to me ever since and how I have always told you everything.

PHAEDRIA [bitterly]: There's another thing for Parmeno to let out.

PARMENO: No doubt about that, sir.

THAIS: Please listen, both of you. My mother died recently at Rhodes, leaving a brother who is always greedy for money. Seeing the girl was a beauty and knows how to play the lyre, he hoped she would fetch a good price, so he put her up for sale and sold her on the spot. Luckily my friend happened to be there and bought her as a present for me, knowing nothing of course of all I've just told you. Now he's back in Athens, but since he found out about my relations with you too he's busy finding excuses not to give me her. He says he'd be willing to do so if he could be sure he came first with me and wasn't afraid I should leave him once I had her, only that is what he *is* afraid of. Personally I have my suspicions that he's taken a fancy to the girl.

PHAEDRIA: Is it more than a fancy?

THAIS: No; I've made inquiries. Now there are many reasons, Phaedria dear, why I want to get her away from him. In the first place she's spoken of as my sister, and then there's the chance I may be able to restore her to her family. I'm alone here, Phaedria, without a single friend or relative, and I should like to make some friends by doing a kindness. Please help me with this and make things easier: let the man have first place with me for the next few days…Can't you answer me?

PHAEDRIA: You wretched woman, what answer can I give to conduct like yours?

PARMENO: Well done, sir, congratulations! It's come home to you at last; you're a man!

PHAEDRIA: Do you think I couldn't see what you were leading up to? 'A little girl was carried off from here, my mother brought her up as her own, she was taken for my sister and I want to get her away to restore her to her family.' In fact all you've just said amounts to this — I'm kept out and he's let in. and why? Obviously because you love him more than you love me; and now you're afraid that girl he brought here may snatch him from you — for what he's worth.

THAIS: *I'm* afraid of *that*?

PHAEDRIA: What else is worrying you? Tell me that. Is he the only one who gives you presents? Have you ever know me set a limit to my generosity? When you told me you wanted an Ethiopian slave-girl, didn't I leave everything to look for one? And then you said you'd like a eunuch because only queens employ them; well I've found one, and only yesterday I paid two thousand drachmas for the pair. Badly treated as I was by you, I didn't forget; and in return for what I've done you kick me out!

THAIS: There, there, Phaedria. I want to get the girl away and I still think my plan is the best way to do this, but rather than lose your affection I'll do anything you bid me.

PHAEDRIA: If only you spoke from your heart and really meant 'rather than lose your affection'! If only I could believe you are sincere in what you say, I could endure anything!

PARMENO [*aside*]: He's weakening. Beaten by a word and all too soon!

THAIS: Alas, don't I speak from the heart? Have you ever wanted anything from me, even in fun, without getting it? I can't get what *I* want — I can't persuade you to give me a mere couple of days.

PHAEDRIA: If it's only a couple...but it might turn into twenty.

THAIS: I promise you, only a couple or —

PHAEDRIA: I'm not have 'or'.

THAIS: It shan't be more. Just let me have this.

PHAEDRIA: Oh all right, have it your own way.

THAIS: [*embracing him*]: No wonder I love you, you're so kind.

PHAEDRIA: I'll leave town and endure my misery in the country — two days of it. That's settled then; Thais must have her way. Parmeno, see that those two are brought across.

PARMENO: Very good, sir.

PHAEDRIA: For two day then, Thais — good-bye.

THAIS: Good-bye, dear Phaedria. That's all, then?

PHAEDRIA: All — except this. When you are with your soldier in person, be absent in spirit. Night and day, love me, long for me, dream of me, wait for me, think of me, hope for me, find joy in me, and be all mine. You have my heart: try to give me yours.

[*He walks firmly into* DEMEA*'s house without a backward glance, followed by* PARMENO.]

THAIS: Oh dear...Perhaps he doesn't trust me and judges my character by other women. But knowing myself, I can swear I've told nothing but the truth, and no man is dearer to me than my Phaedria. All I have done in this I did for the girl's sake, for I have hopes that I've already found her brother, a young man of good family. He's arranged to visit me this very day, so I'll go in and wait for him.

[*She goes into her house. After a short pause* PHAEDRIA *comes out, ready for departure, followed by* PARMENO.]

From Terence, *The Comedies*, trans. Betty Radice, pp. 167-172. Copyright © 1965, 1976 Penguin Books, Ltd. Reproduced by permission of Penguin Books Limited.

QUESTIONS FOR PART 5

1. If the Roman Republic set out with such high ideals — to be everything they thought the Etruscans were not — why does the Republic end in such corruption?
2. Compare the play by Terence to the story of Lucretia. By what social and ethical standards were Roman women judged?
3. What was place of religion in the Roman Republic?

PART 6

THE ROMAN EMPIRE

The rise of Octavian to the role of emperor in 31 BC established peace again in the Italian world, brought new economic prosperity with the conquest of Egypt, brought more land and peoples under Roman control, and created the Roman Golden Age for the duration of Octavian's reign. The emperors that followed Octavian were not always the most capable or even, at times, sane, and the empire faced new internal and external difficulties from its very beginning (particularly from the new Christian faith and the Germanic tribes), yet the great *Pax Romana*, or Roman Peace, lasted unchecked until 180 AD. The slow breakdown of the Empire lasted another three hundred years, and even then Roman institutions of law, religion, culture, and urban cities continued in the form of the Byzantine Empire and the Roman Catholic Church.

The five source excerpts in this chapter highlight the early Empire, and show both the greatness and the weakness of that Empire.

6.1

THE DEEDS OF THE DIVINE AUGUSTUS

After defeating the forces of Mark Antony and Cleopatra at the battle of Actium in 31 BC, Octavia became the first Roman emperor. He was granted the title of Augustus by the senate, although he preferred to be called princeps *("First Citizen"). Shortly before he died in 14 AD, he presented a list of his accomplishments, the* Res Gestae *(or* Deeds*), inscribed in bronze and exhibited them in Rome. Copies of the list were displayed throughout the empire.*

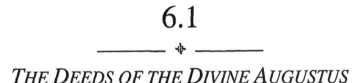

QUESTIONS

1. Although Augustus called himself a citizen of Rome, how does he establish himself through these *Deeds* as an emperor in power if not in name?
2. Why does Augustus list so many of his economic expenditures? How are these "deeds?"
3. In *Deed* 34, Octavian describes being awarded the title of "Augustus." What does it mean?

B elow is a copy of the accomplishments of the deified Augustus by which he brought the whole world under the empire of the Roman people, and of the moneys expended by him on the state and the Roman people, as inscribed on two bronze pillars set up in Rome.

1. At the age of nineteen, on my own initiative and at my own expense, I raised an army be means of which I liberated the republic, which was oppressed by the tyranny of a faction. For which reason the senate, with honorific decrees, made me a member of its order in the consulship of Gaius Pansa and Aulus Hirtius [43 B.C.], giving me at the same time consular rank in voting, and granted me the *imperium*. It ordered me as propraetor, together with the consuls, to see to it that the state suffered no harm. Moreover, in the same year, when both consuls had fallen in the war, the people elected me consul and a triumvir for the settlement of the commonwealth [cf. § 115].

2. Those who assassinated my father I drove into exile, avenging their crime by due process of law; and afterwards when they waged war against the state, I conquered them twice on the battlefield [the two battles of Phillippi (42 B.C.)].

3. I waged many wars throughout the whole world by land and by sea, both civil and foreign, and when victorious I spared all citizens who sought pardon. Foreign peoples who could safely be pardoned I preferred to spare rather than to extirpate. About 500,000 Roman citizens were under military oath to me. Of these, when their terms of service were ended, I settled in colonies or sent back to their own municipalities a little more than 300,000, and to all of these I allotted lands or granted money as rewards for military service. I captured 600 ships, exclusive of those which were of smaller class than triremes....

5. The dictatorship offered to me in the consulship of Marcus Marcellus and Lucius Arruntius [22 B.C.] by the people and by the senate, both in my absence and in my presence, I refused to accept. In the midst of a critical scarcity of grain I did not decline the supervision of the grain supply, which I so administered that within a few days I freed the whole people from imminent panic and danger by my expenditures and efforts. The consulship, too, which was offered to me at that time as an annual office for life, I refused to accept.

6. In the consulship of Marcus Vinicius and Quintus Lucretius, and again in that of Publius Lentulus and Gnaeus Lentulus, and a third time in that of Paullus Fabius Maximus and Quintus Tubero [in 19, 18, and 11 B.C.], though the Roman senate and people unitedly agreed that I should be elected sole guardian of the laws and morals with supreme authority, I refused to accept any office offered me which was contrary to the traditions of our ancestors. The measures which the senate desired at that time to be taken by me I carried out by virtue of the tribunician power. In this power I five times voluntarily requested and was given a colleague by the senate.

7. I was a member of the triumvirate for the settlement of the commonwealth for ten consecutive years. I have been ranking senator for forty years, up to the day on which I wrote this document. I have been *pontifex maximus*, augur, member of the college of fifteen for performing sacrifices, member of the Arval Brotherhood, one of the *Titii sodales*, and a fetial....

10. My name was inserted, by decree of the senate, in the hymn of the Salian priests. And it was enacted by law that I should be sacrosanct in perpetuity and that I should posses the tribunician power as long as I live. I declined to become *pontifex maximus* in place of a colleague while he was still alive, when the people offered me that priesthood, which my father had held. A few years later, in the consulship of Publius Sulpicius and Gaius Valgius, I accepted this priesthood, when death removed

the man who had taken possession of it at a time of civil disturbance; and from all Italy a multitude flocked to my election such as had never previously been recorded at Rome....

14. My sons Faius and Lucius Caesar, whom fortune took from me in their youth, were, in my honor, made consuls designate by the Roman senate and people when they were fifteen years old, with permission to enter that magistracy after a period of five years. The senate further decreed that from the day on which they were introduced into the forum they should attend its debates. Moreover, the whole body of Roman *equites* presented each of them with silver shields and spears and saluted each as *princeps iuventutis*.

15. To the Roman plebs I paid 300 sesterces apiece in accordance with the will of my father [i.e., Julius Caesar]; and in my fifth consulship [29 B.C.] I gave each 400 sesterces in my own name out of the spoils of war; and a second time in my tenth consulship [24 B.C.] I paid out of my own patrimony a largess of 400 sesterces to every individual; in my eleventh consulship [23 B.C.] I made twelve distributions of food out of grain purchased at my own expense; and in the twelfth year of my tribunician power [12 B.C.] for the third time I gave 400 sesterces to every individual. These largesses of mine reached never less than 250,000 persons. In the eighteenth year of my tribunician power and my twelfth consulship [5 B.C.] I gave sixty *denarii* to each of 320,000 persons of the urban plebs. And in my fifth consulship [29 B.C.] I gave out of the spoils of war 2,000 sesterces apiece to my soldiers settled in colonies. This largess on the occasion of my triumph was received by about 120,000 persons in the colonies. In my thirteenth consulship [2 B.C.] I gave sixty *denarii* apiece to those of the plebs who at that time were receiving public grain; the number involved was a little more than 200,000 persons.

16. I reimbursed municipalities for the lands which I assigned to my soldiers in my fourth consulship, and afterwards in the consulship of Marcus Crassus and Gnaeus Lentulus the augur [30 and 14 B.C.]. The sums involved were about 600,000,000 sesterces which I paid for Italian estates, and about 260,000,000 sesterces which I paid for provincial lands. I was the first and only one to take such action of all those who up to my time established colonies of soldiers in Italy or in the provinces. And afterwards, in the consulship of Tiberius Nero and Gnaeus Piso, and likewise of Gaius Antistius and Decimus Laelius, and of Gaius Calvisius and Lucius Passienus, and of Lucius Lentulus and Marcus Messalla, and of Lucius Caninius and Quintus Fabricius [in 7, 6, 4, 3, and 2 B.C.], I granted bonuses in cash to the soldiers whom after the completion of their terms of service I sent back to their municipalities; and for this purpose I expended about 400,000,000 sesterces.

17. Four times I came to the assistance of the treasury with my own money, transferring to those in charge of the treasury 150,000,000 sesterces. And in the consulship of Marcus Lepidus and Lucius Arruntius [A.D. 6; cf. § 199] I transferred out of my own patrimony 170,000,000 sesterces to the soldier's bonus fund, which was established on my advice for the purpose of providing bonuses for soldiers who had completed twenty or more years of service.

18. From the year in which Gnaeus Lentulus and Publius Lentulus [18 B.C.] were consuls, whenever the provincial taxes fell short, in the case sometimes of 100,000 persons and sometimes of many more, I made up their tribute in grain and in money from my own grain stores and my own patrimony....

20. I repaired the Capitol and the theater of Pompey with enormous expenditures on both works, without having my name inscribed on them. I repaired the conduits of the aqueducts which were falling into ruin in many places because of age, and I doubled the capacity of the aqueduct called Marcia by admitting a new spring into its conduit. I completed the Julian Forum and the basilica which was between the temple of Castor and the temple of Saturn, works begun and far advanced by my father, and when the same basilica was destroyed by fire, I enlarged its site and began rebuilding the

structure, which is to be inscribed with the names of my sons; and in case it should not be completed while I am still alive, I left instructions that the work be completed by my heirs. In my sixth consulship [28 B.C.] I repaired eighty-two temples of the gods in the city, in accordance with a resolution of the senate, neglecting none which at the time required repair. In my seventh consulship [27 B.C.] I reconstructed the Flaminian Way from the city as far as Ariminum, and also all the bridges except the Mulvian and the Minucian.

21. On my own private land I built the temple of Mars Ultor and the Augustan Forum from spoils of war. On ground bought for the most part from private owners I built the theater adjoining the temple of Apollo which was to be inscribed with the name of my son-in-law Marcus Marcellus. In the Capitol, in the temple of the deified Julius, in the temple of Apollo, in the temple of Vesta, and in the temple of Mars Ultor I consecrated gifts from the spoils of war which cost me about 100,000,000 sesterces. In my fifth consulship [29 B.C.] I remitted to the municipalities and colonies of Italy 35,000 pounds of crown gold which they were collecting in honor of my triumphs; and afterwards, whenever I was acclaimed *imperator*, I did not accept the crown gold, though the municipalities and colonies decreed it with the same enthusiasm as before.

22. I gave a gladiatorial show three times in my own name, and fie times in the names of my sons and grandsons; at these shows about 10,000 fought. Twice I presented to the people in my own name an exhibition of athletes invited from all parts of the world, and a third time in the name of my grandson. I presented games in my own name four times, and in addition twenty-three times in the place of other magistrates. On behalf of the college of fifteen, as master of that college, with Marcus Agrippa as my colleague, I celebrated the Secular Games in the consulship of Gaius Furnius and Gaius Silanus. In my thirteenth consulship [2 B.C.] I was the first to celebrate the Games of Mars, which subsequently the consuls, in accordance with a decree of the senate and a law, have regularly celebrated in the succeeding years. Twenty-six times I provided for the people, in my own name or in the names of my sons or grandsons, hunting spectacles of African wild beasts in the circus or in the Forum or in the amphitheaters; in these exhibitions about 3,500 animals were killed.

23. I presented to the people an exhibition of a naval battle across the Tiber where the grove of the Caesars now is, having the site excavated 1,800 feet in length and 1,200 feet in width. In this exhibition thirty beaked ships, triremes or biremes, and in addition a great number of smaller vessels engaged in combat. On board these fleets, exclusive of rowers, there were about 3,000 combatants....

25. I brought peace to the sea by suppressing the pirates. In that war I turned over to their masters for punishment nearly 30,000 slaves who had run away from their owners and taken up arms against the state. The whole of Italy voluntarily took an oath of allegiance to me and demanded me as its leader in the war in which I was victorious at Actium. The same oath was taken by the provinces of the Gauls, the Spains, Africa, Sicily, and Sardinia. More than 700 senators served at that time under my standards; of that number eighty-three attained the consulship and about 170 obtained priesthoods, either before that date or subsequently, up to the day on which this document was written.

26. I extended the frontiers of all the provinces of the Roman people on whose boundaries were peoples not subject to our empire. I restored peace to the Gallic and Spanish provinces and likewise to Germany, that is to the entire region bounded by the Ocean from Gades to the mouth of the Elbe river. I caused peace to be restored in the Alps, from the region nearest to the Adriatic Sea as far as the Tuscan Sea, without undeservedly making war against any people. My fleet sailed the Ocean from the mouth of the Rhine eastward as far as the territory of the Cimbrians, to which no Roman previously had penetrated either by land or by sea. The Cimbrians, the Charydes, the Semnones, and

other German peoples of the same region through their envoys sought my friendship and that of the Roman people. At my command and under my auspices two armies were led almost at the same time into Ethiopia and into Arabia which is called Felix; and very large forces of the enemy belonging to both peoples were killed in battle, and many towns were captured. In Ethiopia a penetration was made as far as the town of Napata, which is next to Meroe; in Arabia the army advanced into the territory of the Sabaeans to the town of Mariba.

27. I added Egypt to the empire of the Roman people. Although I might have made Greater Armenia into a province when its king Artaxes was assassinated, I preferred, following the precedent of our ancestors, to hand over this kingdom, acting through Tiberius Nero, who was then my stepson, to Tigranes, son of King Artavasdes and grandson of King Tigranes. And afterwards, when this same people revolted and rebelled, after I subdued it through my son Gaius, I handed it over to the rule of King Ariobarzanes, son of Artabazus, king of the Medes, and after his death to his son Aravasdes. When the latter was killed, I dispatched to that kingdom Tigranes, a scion of the royal family of Armenia. I recovered all the provinces extending beyond the Adriatic Sea eastward, and also Cyrenae, which were for the most part already in the possession of kings, as I had previously recovered Sicily and Sardinia, which had been seized in the slave war.

28. I established colonies of soldiers in Africa, Sicily, Macedonia, in both Spanish provinces, in Achaea, Asia, Syria, Narbonese Gaul, and Pisidia. Italy, moreover, has twenty-eight colonies established by me, which in my lifetime have grown to be famous and populous....

31. Royal embassies from India, never previously seen before any Roman general, were often sent to me. Our friendship was sought through ambassadors by the Bastarnians and the Scythians and by the kings of the Sarmatians, who live on both sides of the Don River, and by the kings of the Albanians and of the Iberians and of the Medes.

32. The following kings fled to me as suppliants: Tiridates and afterwards Phraates son of King Phraates, kings of the Parthians; Artavasdes, king of the Medes; Artaxares, king of the Adiabenians; Dumnobellaunus and Tincommius, kings of the Britons; Maelo, king of the Sugumbrians, and Segimerus, king of the Marcomannian Suebians. Phraates son of Orodes, king of the Parthians, sent to me in Italy all his sons and grandsons, not because he was conquered in war, but seeking our friendship through pledge of his children. Under my principate numerous other peoples, with whom previously there had existed no exchange of embassies and friendship, experienced the good faith of the Roman people.

33. The peoples of the Parthians and of the Medes, through ambassadors who were the leading men of these peoples, received from me the kings for whom they asked: the Parthians, Vonones son of King Phraates, grandson of King Orodes; the Medes, Ariobarzanes son of King Artavasdes, grandson of King Ariobarzanes.

34. In my sixth and seventh consulships, after I had put an end to the civil wars, having attained supreme power by universal consent, I transferred the state from my own power to the control of the Roman senate and the people. For this service of mine I received the title of Augustus by decree of the senate, and the doorposts of my house were publicly decked with laurels, the civic crown was affixed over my doorway, and a golden shield was set up in the Julian senate house, which, as the inscription on this shield testifies, the Roman senate and people game me in recognition of my valor, clemency, justice, and devotion. After that time I excelled all in authority, but I possessed no more power than the others who were my colleagues in each magistracy.

35. When I held my thirteenth consulship, the senate, the equestrian order, and the entire Roman people gave me the title of "father of the country" and decreed that this title should be inscribed in the vestibule of my house, in the Julian senate house, and in the Augustan Forum on the pedestal of the chariot which was set up in my honor by decree of the senate. At the time I wrote this document I was in my seventy-sixth year.

6.2

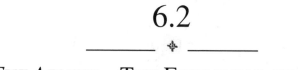

THE AENEID: THE FOUNDING OF ROME AND THE CURSE OF DIDO

It is typical of the grandeur of the Roman Empire that it created not just one, but two separate myths of its own creation. Both myths directly link the Roman state to the gods, typical of the Roman sense of their own divine destiny. The older, Republican myth linked Rome to the war between two brothers, Romulus and Remus, sons of Mars, the god of war, who were raised in the wild by a she-wolf. When Augustus came to power, he encouraged Virgil to write an epic poem to rival the epics of the Greeks. The result was The Aeneid, which traces the Roman origins back further than Romulus and Remus to Homeric time itself, and to the fall of Troy. Aeneas, a prince of Troy, flees the destruction of his homeland and sets sail for Italy, where is destined to found a state even greater than Troy. In typical Homeric tradition, he spends ten years wandering around the Mediterranean, having many adventures and facing many struggles with gods, people, and his own inclinations.

In the first of the following two excerpts, Venus-Cytherea (mother of Aeneas) asks Jupiter of her son's destiny. The second excerpt is a speech given by the Queen of Carthage, Dido, after Aeneas has abandoned her. Aeneas had stopped in Carthage to have his ships repaired and remained, distracted by his affair with Dido.

QUESTIONS

1. What did it mean for Rome to believe it was founded first by a prince of Troy? How did this allow the Romans to believe themselves superior to the Greeks?
2. What was the connection between Aeneas and Augustus?
3. How did the curse of Dido — that there be no peace between Carthage and Rome — justify the Punic Wars?

It was the day's end when from highest air
Jupiter looked down on the broad sea

Flecked with wings of sails, and the land masses,
Coasts, and nations of the earth. He stood

On heaven's height and turned his gaze toward
    Libya,
And, as he took the troubles there to heart,
Venus appealed to him, all pale and wan,
With tears in her shining eyes:
        "My lord who rule
The lives of men and gods now and forever,
And bring them all to heel with your bright
    bolt,
What in the world could my Aeneas do,
What could the Trojans do, so to offend you
That after suffering all those deaths they find
The whole world closed to them, because of
    Italy?
Surely from these the Romans are to come
In the course of years, renewing Teucer's line,
To rule the sea and all the lands about it,
According to your promise. What new thought
Has turned you from them, Father? I consoled
    myself
For Troy's fall, that grim ruin, weighing out
One fate against another in the scales,
But now, when they have borne so many blows,
The same misfortune follows them. Great king,
What finish to their troubles will you give?
After Antenor slipped through the Achaeans
He could explore Illyrian coves and reach
In safety the Liburnians' inland kingdoms
And source of the Timavus. Through nine
    openings
With a great rumble in the mountain wall
It bursts from the ground there and floods the
    fields
In a rushing sea. And yet he chose that place
For Padua and new homes for Teucrians,
Gave them a name, set up the arms of Troy,
And now rests in his peace. As for ourselves,
Your own children, whom you make heirs of
    heaven,
Our ships being lost (this is unspeakable!),
We are forsaken through one enemy's rage
And kept remote from Italy. Is this
The palm for loyalty? This our power
    restored?"
He smiled at her, the father of gods and men,

With that serenity that calms the weather,
And lightly kissed his daughter. Then he said:
"No need to be afraid, Cytherëa.
Your children's destiny has not been changed.
As promised, you shall see Lavinium's wall
And take up, then, amid the stars of heaven
Great-souled Aeneas. No new thought has turned
    me.
No, he, your son — now let me speak of him,
In view of your consuming care, at length,
Unfolding secret fated things to come —
In Italy he will fight a massive war,
Beat down fierce armies, then for the people there
Establish city walls and a way of life.
When the Rutulians are subdued he'll pass
Three summers of command in Latium,
Three years of winter quarters. But the boy,
Ascanius, to whom the name of Iulus
Now is added — Ilus while Ilium stood —
Will hold the power for all of thirty years,
Great rings of wheeling months. He will transfer
His capital from Lavinium and make
A fortress, Alba Longa. Three full centuries
That kingdom will be rule by Hector's race,
Until the queen and priestess, Ilia,
Pregant by Mars, will bear twin sons to him.
Afterward, happy in the tawny pelt
Hi nurse, the she-wolf, wears, young Romulus
Will take the leadership, build walls of Mars,
And call by his own name his people Romans.
For these I set no limits, world or time,
But make the gift of empire without end.
Juno, indeed, whose bitterness now fills
With fear and torment sea and earth and sky,
Will mend her ways, and favor them as I do,
Lords of the world, the toga-bearing Romans.
Such is our pleasure. As the years fall away,
An age comes when Assaracus' royal house
Will bring to servitude Thessalian Phthia,
Renowned Mycenae, too; and subjugate
Defeated Argos. From that comely line
The Trojan Caesar comes, to circumscribe
Empire with Ocean, fame with heaven's stars.
Julius his name, from Iulus handed down:
All tranquil shall you take him heavenward

In time, laden with plunder of the East,
And he with you shall be invoked in prayer.
Wars at an end, harsh centuries then will soften,
Ancient Fides and Vesta, Quirinus
With Brother Remus, will be lawgivers,
And grim with iron frames, the Gates of War
Will then be shut: inside, unholy Furor,
Squatting on cruel weapons, hands enchained
Behind him by a hundred links of bronze,
Will grind his teeth and howl with bloodied
    mouth."...
    Soon early Dawn, quitting the saffron bed
Of old Tithonus, cast new light on earth,
And as air grew transparent, from her tower
The queen caught sight of ships on the seaward
    reach
With sails full and the wind astern. She knew
The waterfront now empty, bare of oarsmen.
Beating her lovely breast three times, four
    times,
And tearing her golden hair,
    "O Jupiter,"
She said, "will this man go, will he have
    mocked
My kingdom, stranger that he was and is?
Will they not snatch up arms and follow him
From every quarter of the town? and dockhands
Tear our ships from moorings? On! Be quick
With torches! Give out arms! Unship the oars!
What am I saying? Where am I? What madness
Takes me out of myself? Dido, poor soul,
Your evil doing has come home to you.
Then was the right time, when you offered him
A royal scepter. See the good faith and honor
Of one they say bears with him everywhere
The hearthgods of his country! One who bore
His father, spent with age, upon his shoulders!
Could I not then have torn him limb from limb
And flung the pieces on the sea? His company,
Even Ascanius could I not have minced
And served up to his father at a feast?

The luck of battle might have been in doubt —
So let it have been! Whom had I to fear,
Being sure to die? I could have carried torches
Into his camp, filled passage ways with flame,
Annihilated father and son and followers
And given my own life on top of all!
O Sun, scanning with flame all works of earth,
And thou, O Juno, witness and go-between
Of my long miseries; and Hecatë,
Screeched for at night at crossroads in the cities;
And thou, avenging Furies, and all gods
On whom Elissa dying may call: take notice,
Overshadow this hell with your high power,
As I deserve, and hear my prayer!
If by necessity that impious wretch
Must find his haven and come safe to land,
If so Jove's destinies require, and this,
His end in view, must stand, yet all the same
When hard beset in war by a brave people,
Forced to go outside his boundaries
And torn from Iulus, let him beg assistance,
Let him see the unmerited deaths of those
Around and with him, and accepting peace
On unjust terms, let him not, even so,
Enjoy his kingdom or the life he longs for,
But fall in battle before his time and lie
Unburied on the sand! This I implore,
This is my last cry, as my last blood flows.
Then, O my Tyrians, besiege with hate
His progeny and all his race to come:
Make this your offering to my dust. No love,
No pact must be between our peoples; No,
But rise up from my bones, avenging spirit!
Harry with fire and sward the Dardan countrymen
Now, or hereafter, at whatever time
The strength will be afforded. Coast with coast
In conflict, I implore, and sea with sea,
And arms with arms: may they content in war,
Themselves and all the children of their
    children!"...

6.3

---✦---

MILITARY TRAINING, VEGETIUS

Flavius Vegetius Renatus wrote a manual on military training in the late Empire, c. 400 CE. His manual was well known throughout the Middle Ages and Renaissance, and is still read in modern times.

---✦---

QUESTIONS

1. Vegetius speaks often of the past, of "ancient custom" and of how the army once perfected the training techniques he is describing. What impression does this give of the Roman army in Vegetius' own day?
2. Does Vegetius believe that experience alone makes a soldier a good soldier?
3. Vegetius says that an army should be able to set up an armed city "wherever it pitches camp." Does he also mean that the reverse is true, that a city should be run like an army?

138. MILITARY TRAINING

Vegetius, *Military Science* I. i. ix, x, xix, xxxvi; II. xxiii, xxv

In every battle victory is granted no by mere numbers and innate courage but by skill and training. For we see that the Roman people owed the conquest of the world to no other cause than military training, discipline in their camps, and practice in warfare....

At the very beginning of their training, recruits should be taught the military step. For there is nothing to be maintained more, on the march and in the line, than the keeping of their ranks by all the soldiers. This cannot be attained in any other way than by learning through training to march quickly and together. For a separated and disorderly army exposes itself to the gravest danger at the hands of the enemy. Now, twenty miles with the military step should be done in five hours, in the summer only; with the full step, which is quicker, twenty-four miles should be completed in the same number of hours....

The soldier is to be trained in leaping also, to enable him to leap across ditches or overcome some impeding height, so that when difficulties of this nature arise he can cross without effort. Moreover, in actual combat the soldier, advancing with running and leaping, dulls the eyesight of his adversary, strikes terror into his mind, and inflicts a blow before the latter makes definite preparations to avoid it or resist....

Every recruit, without exception should in the summer months learn to swim; for it is not always possible to cross rivers on bridges, but a retreating and pursuing army is frequently compelled to swim. Sudden rains or snowfalls often cause torrents to overflow their banks, and risk is increased by ignorance not only of the enemy but of water. The ancient Romans, therefore, perfected in every branch of military science by so many wars and perpetual dangers, chose the Field of Mars next to the Tiber in which the young might wash off the sweat and dust after military exercise, and by swimming gain relaxation from their weariness in marching. It is opportune for not only the infantry but also the cavalry, the horses, and the sutlers, whom they call "helmeters," to be trained to swim, lest they be inexperienced when necessity arises and faces them....

Recruits should be obliged frequently to carry burdens weighing up to sixty pounds, and to march with the military step. For on arduous expeditions they find themselves under the necessity of carrying their provisions as well as their arms....

It was a survival of ancient custom, confirmed by enactments of the deified Augustus and Hadrian, to exercise both cavalry and infantry three times a month by marches.... The Infantry was instructed to march ten miles with the military step, wearing armor and equipped with all weapons, and return to camp; and to take part of the journey at the quicker pace. The cavalry, likewise, separated in squadrons and similarly armed, performed the same march, practicing cavalry exercises, sometimes pursuing, sometimes retreating, and then returning to the attack. They did not make these marches in plains; rather, both branches were compelled to ascend and descend sloping and steep places....

The younger soldiers and recruits used to be drilled morning and afternoon in every type of weapon; the older and experienced ones were drilled in weapons once a day.... For length of service or age alone does not bestow the science of war, but after any number of years of service an undisciplined soldier is always a recruit.... It is very desirable to drill them also at the post with wooden stakes, as they learn to attack the sides or feet or head both with the point and the edge [of the sword]. They should be accustomed also to leap and strike blows at the same time, to rise up with a bound and sink down again below the shield, now eagerly rushing forward with a leap, now leaping back to the rear. They must also practice throwing their javelins at the posts from a distance in order to increase their skill in aiming and the strength of the arm....

The legion in practice is victorious because of the number of soldiers and the type of machines. First of all, it is equipped with hurling machines which no cuirass, no shield can withstand. For the practice is to have a ballista mounted on a carriage for each century, to each of which are assigned mules and a detail of eleven men for loading and firing. The larger these are, the farther and more powerfully do they hurl missiles. Not only do they defend the camps, but they are placed in the field in the rear of the heavy-armed infantry. Before their fire power neither enemy cavalrymen with cuirasses nor infantry men with shields can hold their ground. It is customary to have fifty-five such mounted ballistas in each legion. Likewise, there are ten *onagri*, one for each cohort; they are drawn ready-armed on carriages by oxen, so that in case of an enemy attack on the rampart the camp can be defended with arrows and stones.

The legion also carries with it small boats, each hollowed out of a single piece of timer, with very long cables and sometimes iron chains. When these "single plankers," as they are called, are joined together and covered with boards, rivers which cannot be forded are crossed without bridges by the infantry and cavalry without danger. The legion is provided with grappling hooks, called "wolves," and with iron scythes fixed to the ends of long poles; likewise mattocks, hoes, spades, shovels, buckets, and baskets to carry earth in ditch-digging operations; also hatchets, axes, and saws for hewing and sawing timber. Besides these, it has workmen equipped with all tools, who make various kinds of wooden sheds, battering rams, and movable towers for besieging cities. To avoid the enumeration of more of these, I shall add that the legion ought to carry with it everywhere everything which is believed necessary to every kind of warfare, so that whenever it pitches its camp it forms an armed city.

6.4

--- ✣ ---

SATIRE ON WOMEN, JUVENAL

There is probably no portrait of a Roman woman more derisive than this satire by Juvenal (d. c. 128). No one in first-century Rome was safe from this poet's acerbic wit; in sixteen surviving satires, he lampoons men and women of all classes, the system of slavery, the power of emperors, and foreigners. He reminded his readers again and again that imperial Rome was a pale shadow of the glory that had been the Republic, or at least of the idealized Republic as he thought of it. As is typical of diatribes against women, Juvenal accuses women of the Empire of being oversexed and generally lacking in morals of any kind.

--- ✣ ---

QUESTIONS

1. Juvenal refers to the Family Encouragement Act, a law passed by Augustus in 9 AD which rewarded Romans who had families of three or more children. What does Juvenal think this law did to the Roman view of marriage?
2. When Juvenal describes what a Roman woman does in a typical day, what social class is he referring to?
3. Does Juvenal present Roman women as being incapable or unwilling to control their sexuality?

Justice withdrew to heaven, and Chastity
  went with her,
Two sisters together, beating a common retreat.
To bounce your neighbour's bed, my friend, to
  outrage
Matrimonial sanctity is now an ancient and
  long-
Established tradition. All other crimes came
  after,
With the Age of Iron; but our first adulterers
appeared in the Silver Era. And here you are in
  this
Day and age, man getting yourself engaged,
fixing up marriage-covenant, dowry, betrothal-
  party;
Any time now some high-class barber will start
Coiffeuring you for the wedding, before you
    know it the ring

Will be on her finger. Postumus, are you *really*
Taking a wife? You used to be sane enough —
    what
Fury's got into you, what snake has stung you
    up?
Why endure such bitch-tyranny when rope's
    available
By the fathom, when all those dizzying top-
    floor windows
Are open for you, when there are bridges handy
To jump from? Supposing none of these exits
    catches
Your fancy, isn't it better to sleep with a pretty
    boy?
Boys don't quarrel all night, or nag you for little
    presents
While they're on the job, or complain that you
    don't come

Up to their expectations, or demand more
  gasping passion.
But no: you staunchly uphold the Family
  Encouragement Act,
A sweet little heir's your aim, though it means
  foregoing
All those pickings — fat pigeons, bearded
  mullet, the bait
Of the legacy-hunter's market. Really, if *you*
  take a wife, I'll
Credit anything, friend. You were once the
  randiest
Hot-rod-about-town, you hid in more bedroom
  cupboards
Than a comedy juvenile lead. Can this be the
  man now
Sticking his silly neck out for the matrimonial
  halter?
And as for your insistence on a wife with old-
  fashioned
Moral virtues — man, you need your blood-
  pressure checked, you're
Crazy, you're aiming over the moon. Find a
  chaste
And modest bride, and well may you sacrifice
Your gilded heifer to Juno, well may you go
  down flat
And kiss the stones before the Tarpeian alter!
Few indeed are the girls with a ritual
  qualification
For the feast of the Corn-Goddess — nine
  whole days' abstinence! —
Or whose fathers wouldn't prefer, if they could,
  to avoid
Such tainted filial kisses. Hang wreaths on your
  doorposts,
Strew your threshold with ivy! Tell me, will
  Hiberina
Think one man enough? You'd find it much
  less trouble
To make her agree to being blinded in one eye.
But *you* maintain that a girl sho's lived a
  secluded
Life on her father's estate, way out in the
  country,

Can keep a good reputation. Just put her down
In the sleepiest outback town you can think of
  — and if she behaves
As she did back home, then I'll believe in that
  country
Estate of yours. But don't tell me nothing ever
Came off in caves, or up mountains — are Jove
  and Mars *that* senile?
Look around the arcades, try to pick out a
  woman
Who's worthy of your devotion. Check every
  tier of seats
At all the theatres in town: will they yield one
  single
Candidate you could love without qualm?
  When pansy
Bathyllus dances Leda, all *fouettés* and
  entrechats,
Just watch the women. One can't control her
  bladder,
Another suddenly moans in drawn-out ecstasy
As though she was coming. Your country girl's
  all rapt
Attention, she's learning fast.
But when the theatrical
Season is over, the stage-props all packed away,
The playhouses closed and empty, in those
  summer
Dogdays when only the lawcourts go droning
  on,
Some women relieve their boredom by taking
  in
Low-down vaudeville farces — and their
  performers.
Look at that fellow who scored such a hit in the
  late-night
Show as Actaeon's mother, camping it up like
  mad —
Poor Aelia's crazy about him. These are the
  women
Who'll pay out fancy prices for the chance to
  defibulate
A counter-tenor, to ruin a concert performer's
  voice.

One has a kink for ham actors. Are you
    surprised? What else
Do you expect them to do? Go ape on a good
    book?
Marry a wife, and she'll make some flute-player
Or guitarist a father, not you. So when you erect
Long stands in the narrow streets, and hang
    your front-door
With outsize laurel wreaths, it's all to welcome
    an infant
Whose face, in that tortoiseshell cradle, under
    its canaopy,
Recalls some armoured thug, some idol of the
    arena.
When that senator's wife, Eppia, eloped with
    her fancy swordsman
To the land of the Nile, the Alexandrian stews,
Egypt itself cried out at Rome's monstrous
    morals.
Husband, family, sister, all were jettisoned, not
One single thought for her country; shamelessly
    she forsook
Her tearful children,...
    What was the youthful
Charm that so fired our senator's wife? What
    hooked her?
What did Eppia see in him to make her put up
With being labelled 'The Gladiatress'? Her
    poppet, her Sergius
Was no chicken, forty at least, with a dud arm
    that held promise
Of early retirement. Besides, his face looked a
    proper mess —
Helmet-scarred, a great wen on his nose, an
    unpleasant
Discharge from one constantly weeping eye.
    What of it?
He was a glaidator. That name makes all the
    breed
Seem handsomer than Adonis; this was what
    she preferred
To her children and her country, her sister, her
    husband: steel
Is what they all crave for. Yet this same
    Sergius,

Once pensioned off, would soon have bored her
    as much as her husband.
Do such private scandals move you? Are you
    shocked by Eppia's deeds?
Then look at the God's rivals, hear what
    Claudius
Had to put up with. The minute she heard him
    snoring,
His wife — that whore-empress — who dared
    to prefer the mattress
Of a stews to her couch in the Palace, called for
    her hooded
Night-cloak and hastened forth, alone or with a
    single
Maid to attend her. Then, her black hair hidden
Under an ash-blonde wig, she would make
    straight for her brothel,
With its odour of stale, warm bedclothes, its
    empty reserved cell.
Here she would strip off, showing her gilded
    nipples and
The belly that once housed a prince of the
    blood. Her door-sign
Bore a false name, Lycisca, 'The Wolf girl'. A
    more than willing
Partner, she took on all comers, for cash,
    without a break.
Too soon, for her, the brothel-keeper dismissed
His girls. She stayed till the end, always the last
    to go,
Then trailed away sadly, still with a burning
    hard on,
Retiring exhausted, yet still far from satisfied,
    cheeks
Begrimed with lamp-smoke, filthy, carrying
    home
To her imperial couch the stink of the
    whorehouse.
What point in mentioning spells, or aphrodisiac
    potions,
Or that lethal brew served up to stepsons?
    Sexual compulsion
Drives women to worse crimes: lust is their
    strongest motive.

'Censennia's husband swears she's the perfect
    wife: why so?'
Because she brought him three million. In
    exchange he calls her chaste.
The shafts that waste him, the fires that burn
    him up
Have nothing to do with desire. That torch was
    lit
By cash; it was her dowry that fired those
    arrows,
And purchased her freedom. She can make
    come-hitherish signs
Or write billets-doux in front of her husband;
    your wealthy
Woman who marries a miser has widow's
    privileges....
There's nothing a woman
Baulks at, no action that gives her a twinge of
    conscience
Once she's put on her emerald choker, weighted
    down her ear-lobes
With vast pearl pendants. What's more
    insufferable
Than your well-heeled female? But earlier in
    the process
She presents a sight as funny as it's appalling,
Her features lost under a damp bread face-pack,
Or greasy with vanishing-cream that clings to
    her husband's
Lips when the poor man kisses her — though
    it's all
Wiped off for her lover. She takes no trouble
    about
The way she looks at home: those imported
    Indian
Scents and lotions she buys with a lover in
    mind.
First one layer, then the next: at last the
    contours emerge
Till she's almost recognizable. Now she
    freshens
Her complexion with asses' milk. (If her
    husband's posted
To the godforsaken North, a heard of she-asses

Will travel with them.) But all these
    medicaments
And various treatments — not least the damp
    bread-poultice —
Make you wonder what's underneath, a face or
    an ulcer.
It's revealing to study the details of such a
    woman's
Daily routine, to see how she occupies her time.
If her husband, the night before, has slept with
    his back to her, then
The wood-maid's had it, cosmeticians are
    stripped and flogged,
The litter-bearer's accused of coming late. One
    victim
Has rods broken over his back, another bears
    bloody stripes
From the whip, a third is lashed with a cat-o'-
    nine-tails:
Some women pay their floggers an annual
    salary.
While the punishment's carried out she'll be
    fixing her face,
Gossiping with her friends, giving expert
    consideration
To the width of the hem on some gold-
    embroidered robe —
Crack! Crack! — or skimming through the
    daily gazette;
Till at last, when the flogger's exhausted, she
    snaps 'Get out!'
And for one day at least the judicial hearing is
    over.
Her household's governed with all the savagery
Of a Sicilian court. If she's made some
    assignation
That *she wants* to look her best for, and is in a
    tearing hurry
Because she's late, and her lover's waiting for
    her
In the public gardens, or by the shrine (bordello
Might be a more accurate term) of Isis — why
    then, the slave-girl
Arranging her coiffure will have her own hair
    torn out.

Poor creature, and the tunic ripped from her
shoulder and breasts.
'Why isn't this curl in place?' the lady screams,
and her rawhide
Lash inflicts chastisement for the offending
ringlet.
But what was poor Psecas's crime? How could
you blame and attendant
For the shape of your own nose? Another maid
Combs out the hair on her left side, twists it
round the curlers;
The consultative committee is reinforced by
An elderly lady's-maid inherited from Mama,
And now promoted from hairpins to the wool
department.
She takes the floor first, to be followed by her
inferiors
In age and skill, as though some issue of
reputation
Or life itself were at stake, so obsessionally they
strive

In beauty's service. See the tall edifice
Rise up on her head in serried tiers and storeys!
See her heroic stature — at least, that is, from in
front:
Her back view's less impressive, you'd think it
belonged
To a different person. The effect is ultra-absurd
If she's lacking in inches, the sort who without
stilettos
Resembles some sawn-off pygmy, who's forced
to stand
On tiptoe for a kiss. Meantime she completely
Ignores her husband, gives not a moment's
thought
To all she costs him. She's less a wife than a
neighbour —
Except when it comes to loathing his friends
and slaves,
Or running up bills…

From Junvenal, "Satire VI," *The Sixteen Satires*, trans. Peter Green, pp. 127-132, 144-146. Copyright ©
1967, 1974 Penguin Books, Ltd. Reproduced by permission of Penguin Books Limited.

6.5

❖

"DINNER WITH TRIMALCHIO," PETRONIUS

*Like the preceding piece by Juvenal, Petronius' Satryricon is an uninhibited satire of the early
Roman Empire. Petronius, who died in 66 AD, was a part of Emperor Nero's inner circle, and was thus
well placed to write about the indulgences and excesses of the rich and powerful. The "Dinner with
Trimalchio" fragment is one of the most frank portraits of that overindulgence and dissipation.*

❖

QUESTIONS

1. Compare Petronius' satire with that of Juvenal. Although Petronius is more concerned with men
than women, does he have a more favorable impression than Juvenal of the women?
2. Although this satire is amusing to read, it also makes several comments about serious problems
facing the early Empire. Find at least one such reference and explain it.

3.   What is Petronius saying about Roman faith at this time?

J ust at the entrance stood the hall-porter, dressed in a green uniform with a belt of cherry red. He was shelling peas into a silver basin. Over the doorway hung — of all things — a golden cage from which a spotted magpie greeted visitors.

As I was gaping at all this, I almost fell over backwards and broke a leg. There on the left as one entered, no far from the porter's cubbyhole, was a huge dog with a chain round it neck. It was painted on the wall and over it, in big capitals, was written:

BEWARE OF THE DOG

My colleagues laughed at me, but when I got my breath back I went on to examine the whole wall. There was a mural of a slave market, price tags and all. Then Trimalchio himself, holding a wand of Mercury and being led into Rome by Minerva. After this a picture of how he learned accounting and, finally, how be became a steward. The painstaking artist had drawn it all in great detail with descriptions underneath. Just where the colonnade ended Mercury hauled him up by the chin and rushed him to a high platform. Fortune with her flowing cornucopia and the three Fates spinning their golden threads there in attendance....

Having had enough of these interesting things, we attempted to go in, but one of the slaves shouted: 'Right foot first!' Naturally we hesitated a moment in case one of us should cross the threshold the wrong way. But just as we were all stepping forward, a slave with his back bare flung himself at our feet and began pleading with us to get him off a flogging. He was in trouble for nothing very serious, he told us — the steward's clothes, hardly worth ten sesterces, had been stolen from him at the baths. Back went our feet, and we appealed to the steward, who was counting out gold pieces in the office, to let the man off.

He lifted his head haughtily: 'It is not so much the actual loss that annoys me,' he said, 'it's the wretch's carelessness. They were my dinner clothes he lost. A client had presented them to me on my birthday — genuine Tyrian purple, of course; however they had been laundered once. So what does it matter? He's all yours.'

We were very much obliged to him for this favour; and when we did enter the dining-room, that same slave whose cause we had pleased ran up to us and, to our utter confusion, covered us with kisses and thanked us for our kindness.

'And what's more,' he said, 'you'll know right away who it is you have been so kind to. "The master's wine is the waiter's gift."'

Finally we took our places. Boys from Alexandria poured iced water over our hands. Others followed them and attended to our feet, removing any hangnails with great skill. But they were not quiet even during this troublesome operation: they sang away at their work. I wanted to find out if the whole staff were singers, so I asked for a drink. In a flash a boy was there, singing in a shrill voice while he attended to me — and anyone else who was asked to bring something did the same. It was more like a musical comedy than a respectable dinner party.

Some extremely elegant hors'd'oeuvre were served at this point — by now everyone had taken his place with the exception of Trimalchio, for whom, strangely enough, the place at the top was reserved. The dishes for the first course included an ass of Corinthian bronze with two panniers, white olives on one side and black on the other. Over the ass were two pieces of plate, with Trimalchio's name and the weight of the silver inscribed on the rims. There were some small iron frames shaped like bridges supporting dormice sprinkled with honey and poppy seed. There were steaming hot sausages too, on a silver gridiron with damsons and pomegranate seeds underneath.

We were in the middle of these elegant dishes when Trimalchio himself was carried in to the sound of music and set down on a pile of tightly stuffed cushions. The sight of him drew an astonished laugh from the guests. His cropped head stuck out from a scarlet coat; his neck was well muffled up and he had put round it a napkin with a broad purple stripe and tassels dangling here and there. On the little finger of his left hand he wore a heavy guilt ring and a smaller one on the last joint of the next finger. This I thought was solid gold, but actually it was studded with little iron stars. And to show off even more of his jewellery, he had his right arm bare and set off by a gold armlet and an ivory circlet fastened with a gleaming metal plate.

After picking his teeth with a silver toothpick, he began: 'My friends, I wasn't keen to come into the dining room yet. But if I stayed away any more, I would have kept you back, so I've deprived myself of all my little pleasures for you. However, you'll allow me to finish my game.'

A boy was at his heels with a board of terebinth wood with glass squares, and I noticed the very last word in luxury — instead of white and black pieces he had gold and silver coins. While he was swearing away like a trooper over his game and we were still on the hors d'oeuvre, a tray was brought in with a basket on it. There sat a wooden hen, its wings spread round it the way hens are when they are broody. Two slaves hurried up and as the orchestra played a tune they began searching through the straw and dug out peahens' eggs, which they distributed to the guests.

Trimalchio turned to look at this little scene and said: 'My friends, I gave orders for that bird to sit on some peahens' eggs. I hope to goodness they are not starting to hatch. However, let's try them and see if they are still soft.'

We took up our spoons (weighing at least half a pound each) and cracked the eggs, which were made of rich pastry. To tell the truth, I nearly threw away my share, as the chicken seemed already formed. But I heard a guest who was an old hand say: 'There should be something good here.' So I searched the shell with my fingers and found the plumpest little figpecker, all covered with yolk and seasoned with pepper.

At this point Trimalchio became tired of his game and demanded that all the previous dishes be brought to him. He gave permission in a loud voice for any of us to have another glass of mead if we wanted it. Suddenly there was a crash from the orchestra and a troop of waiters — still singing — snatched away the hors d'oeuvre. However in the confusion one of the side-dishes happened to fall and a slave picked it up from the floor. Trimalchio noticed this, had the boy's ears boxed and told him to throw it down again. A cleaner came in with a broom and began to sweep up the silver plate along with the rest of the rubbish. Two long-haired Ethiopians followed him, carrying small skin bottles like those they use for scattering sand in the circus, and they poured wine over our hands — no one ever offered us water.

Our host was complimented on these elegant arrangements. 'You've got to fight fair,' he replied. 'That is why I gave orders for each guest to have his own table. At the same time these smelly slaves won't crowd so.'

Carefully sealed wine bottles were immediately brought, their necks labelled:

PALERNIAN
CONSUL OPIMIUS
ONE HUNDRED YEARS OLD

While we were examining the labels, Trimalchio clapped his hands and said with a sigh:

'Wine has a longer life than us poor folks. So let's wet our whistles. Wine is life. I'm giving you real Opimian. I didn't put out such good stuff yesterday, though the company was much better class.'

Naturally we drank and missed no opportunity of admiring his elegant hospitality. In the middle of this a slave brought in a silver skeleton, put together in such a way that its joints and backbone could be pulled out and twisted in all directions. After he had flung it about on the table once or twice, its flexible joints falling into various postures, Trimalchio recited:

'Man's life alas! is but a span,
So let us live it while we can,
We'll be like this when dead.

After our applause the next course was brought in. Actually it was not as grand as we expected, but it was so novel that everyone stared. It was deep circular tray with the twelve signs of the Zodiac arranged round the edge. Over each of them the chef had placed some appropriate dainty suggested by the subject. Over Aries the Ram, butter beans; over Taurus the Bull, a beef-steak; over the Heavenly Twins, testicles and kidneys; over Cancer the crab, a garland; over Leo the Lion, an African fig; over Virgo the Virgin, a young sow's udder; over Libra the Scales, a balance with a tart in one pan and a cake in the other, over Scorpio, a lobster; over Sagittarius the Archer, a bull's eye; over Capricorn, a horned fish; over Aquarius the Water-carrier, a goose; over Pisces the Fishes, two mullets. A young Egyptian slave carried bread around in a silver oven…and in a sickening voice he mangled a song from the show *The Asafoetida Man*.…

'Me now,' he said, 'I don't have a bath every day. It's like getting' rubbed with fuller's earth, havin' a bath. The water bites into you, and as the days go by, your heart turns to water. But when I've knocked back a hot glass of wine and honey, kiss-my-arse I say to the cold weather. Mind you, I couldn't have a bath — I was at a funeral today. Poor old Chrysanthus has just given up the ghost — nice man he was! It was only the other day he stopped me in the street. I still seem to hear his voice. Dear, dear! We're just so many walking bags of wind. We're worse than flies — at least flies have got some strength in them, but we're no more than empty bubbles.

'And what would he have been like if he hadn't been on a diet? For five days he didn't take a drop of water or a crumb of bread into his mouth. But he's gone to join the majority. The doctors finished him — well, hard luck, more like. After all, a doctor is just to put your mind at rest. Still, he got a good sendoff — he had a bier and all beautifully draped. His mourners — several of his slaves were left their freedom — did him proud, even though his widow was a bit mean with her tears. Suppose now he hadn't been so good to her! But women as a sex are real vultures. It's no good doing them a favour, you might as well throw it down a well. An old passion is just an ulcer.'

He was being a bore and Phileros said loudly:

'Let's think of the living. He's got what he deserved. He lived an honest life and he died an honest death. What has he got to complain about? He started out in life with just a penny and he was ready to pick up less than that from a muck-heap, if he had to use his teeth. He went up in the world. He got bigger and bigger till he got where you see, like a honeycomb. I honestly think he left a solid hundred thousand and he had the lot in hard cash. But I'll be honest about it — seeing I'm a bit of a cynic — he had a foul mouth and too much lip. He wasn't a man, he was just murder.

'Now his brother was a fine man, a real friend to his friends, always ready with a helping hand or a decent meal.

'Chrysanthus had bad luck at first, but the first vintage set him on his feet. He fixed his own price when he sold the wine. And what properly kept his head above water was a legacy he came in for, when he pocketed more than was left to him. And the blockhead, when he had a quarrel with his brother, cut him out of his will in favour of some sod we've never heard of. You're leaving a lot behind when you leave your own flesh and blood. But he took advice from his slaves and they really fixed him. It's never right to believe all you're told, especially for a business man. But it's true he enjoyed himself while he lived. You got it, you keep it. He was certainly Fortune's favourite — lead turned to gold in his hand. Mind you, it's easy when everything runs smoothly.

'And how old do you think he was? Seventy or more! But he was hard as nails and carried his age well. His hair was black as a raven's wing. I knew the man for ages and ages and he was still and old lecher. I honestly don't think he left the dog alone. What's more, he liked little boys — he could turn his hand to anything. Well, I don't blame him — after all, he couldn't take anything else with him.'…

From Petronius, *The Satryricon and the Fragments*, trans. John Sullivan, pp. 46-51, 56-57. Copyright © 1969 Penguin Books, Ltd. Reproduced by permission of Penguin Books Limited.

⊕

QUESTIONS FOR PART 6

1. Although the Golden Age of the Empire lasted until 180 AD, how did Augustus actually set up the weaknesses that would eventually help bring the Empire down?
2. Compare the *Deeds* of Augustus to the destiny of Aeneas. Was Augustus a model for Virgil's epic hero?
3. Why were so many writers of the Golden Age of the Empire looking back to the Republic as the ideal society?

PART 7

❦

CHRISTIANITY: THE NEW FAITH

Christianity arose from a combination of Greco-Roman and Jewish traditions, yet at the same time embodied a shift in ideology and customs. Although it originated as a small sect in the Jewish religion, Christianity quickly took hold of the populace of the entire Roman Empire, and as the Germanic tribes systematically destroyed the Roman state in the fifth century, it was the new faith that proved the most durable contribution to Western civilization. The transition from pagan Rome to a Christianized Europe was not a simple one, nor is the history of Christianity itself as a faith and a culture a straightforward one. There were many sects of the new faith and many interpretations of Christ's message, and even the fall of the Roman state did not necessarily represent a clear-cut triumph for the Christians. The transition actually lasted for several more centuries.

It is arguable that no one development had as much of an impact on the West as Christianity. Here are five sources that illustrate the origins of Christian beliefs, the attempt to stabilize Christian beliefs with the creation of a creed (statement of belief), and finally two sources that illustrate the complexity with which Christian and Roman cultures intersected.

7.1

✦

THE ANNUNCIATION TO MARY AND THE MAGNIFICAT, GOSPEL ACCORDING TO LUKE

Jesus Christ was born c. 6 BC, during the reign of Augustus. The religion he founded had a profound impact on Western culture, and ultimately on the entire world. In the earliest days of the faith there were many oral traditions about Jesus circulating in the eastern provinces of the Roman Empire; some of these would be gathered up in the second century to form the Christian scriptures known as the New Testament. The four main sources for the life of Christ were the gospels of Matthew, Mark, Luke, and John, written some thirty to sixty years after the death of Christ. In the following excerpt from Luke, the most detailed of the gospels about Mary and the early life of Jesus, Mary learns that she is pregnant and delivers her longest speech of any of the gospel accounts, known as the Magnificat.

QUESTIONS

1. What is the significance of Elizabeth recognizing the holiness of Mary's pregnancy before Mary has told her anything about it?
2. Where are the men of this culture while this scene is taking place? Why are they not present?
3. How does Mary understand the role of God in history?

When his period of duty was completed Zechariah returned home. His wife Elizabeth conceived, and for five months she lived in seclusion, thinking, 'This is the Lord's doing; now at last he has shown me favour and taken away from me the disgrace of childlessness.

In the sixth month the angel Gabriel was sent by God to Nazareth, a town in Galilee, with a message for a girl betrothed to a man named Joseph; a descendant of David; the girl's name was Mary. The angel went in and said to her, 'Greetings, most favoured one! The Lord is with you.' But she was deeply troubled by what he said and wondered what this greeting could mean. Then the angel said to her, 'Do not be afraid, Mary, for God has been gracious to you; you will conceive and give birth to a son, and you are to give him the name Jesus. He will be great, and will be called Son of the Most High. The Lord God will give him the throne of his ancestor David, and he will be king over Israel for ever; his reign shall never end. 'How can this be?' said Mary. 'I am still a virgin.' The angel answered, 'The Holy Spirit will come upon you, and the power of the Most High will overshadow you; for that reason the holy child to be born will be called Son of God. Moreover your kinswoman Elizabeth has herself conceived a son in her old age; and she who is reputed barren is now in her sixth month, for God's promises can never fail. 'I am the Lord's servant,' said Mary; 'may it be as you have said.' Then the angel left her.

Soon afterwards Mary set out and hurried away to a town in the uplands of Judah. She went into Zechariah's house and greeted Elizabeth. And when Elizabeth heard Mary's greeting, the baby stirred in her womb. Then Elizabeth was filled with the Holy Spirit and exclaimed in a loud voice, 'God's blessing is on you above all women, and his blessing is on the fruit of your womb. Who am I, that the mother of my Lord should visit me? I tell you, when your greeting sounded in my ears, the baby in my womb leapt for joy. Happy is she who has had faith that the Lord's promise to her would be fulfilled!'

And Mary said:

'My soul tells out the greatness of the Lord,
my spirit has rejoiced in God my Savior;
for he has looked with favour on his servant,
lowly as she is.
From this day forward
all generations will count me blessed,
for the Mighty God has done great things for me.
His name is holy,
his mercy sure from generation to generation
toward those who fear him.
He has shown the might of his arm,
he has routed the proud and all their schemes;

he has brought down monarchs from their thrones,
and raised on high the lowly.
He has filled the hungry with good things,
and sent the rich away empty.
He has come to the help of Israel his servant,
as he promised to our forefathers;
he has not forgotten to show mercy
to Abraham and his children's children forever.'

Mary stayed with Elizabeth about three months and then returned home.

From *The Oxford Study Bible*, edited by M. Jack Suggs, K. B. Sakenfeld, & J. R. Mueller. Copyright ©
1992 by Oxford University Press, Inc. Used by permission of Oxford University Press, Inc.

7.2

THE SERMON ON THE MOUNT AND THE BEATITUDES, GOSPEL ACCORDING TO MATTHEW

Matthew's gospel gives us this account of Jesus gathering followers and preaching, and serves as one of the most extensive illustrations of Jesus' message. It also contains one of the earliest Christian prayers, a series of statements beginning "Blessed are...," that make up the Beatitudes.

QUESTIONS

1. From the references Jesus makes while preaching on the mount, how would you describe the social and economic background of his audience at this sermon?
2. What did this sermon tell the early Christians about the heaven that was being promised to them?
3. How does Jesus understand the concept of "law"? Is this a new understanding of law in the West?

From that day Jesus began to proclaim the message: 'Repent, for the kingdom of Heaven is upon you.'

Jesus was walking by the sea of Galilee when he saw two brothers, Simon called Peter and his brother Andrew, casting a net into the lake; for they were fishermen. Jesus said to them, 'Come with me, and I will make you fishers of men.' At once they left their nets and followed him.

Going on farther, he saw another pair of brothers, James son of Zebedee and his brother John; they were in a boat with their father Zebedee, mending their nets. He called them, and at once they left the boat and their father, and followed him.

He travelled throughout Galilee, teaching in the synagogues, proclaiming the good news of the kingdom, and healing every kind of illness and infirmity among the people. His fame spread throughout Syria; and they brought to him sufferers from various diseases, those racked with pain or possessed by demons, those who were epileptic or paralysed, and he healed them all. Large crowds followed him, from Galilee and the Decapolis, from Jerusalem and Judaea, and from Transjordan.

5 When he saw the crowds he went up a mountain. There he sat down, and when his disciples had gathered round him he began to address them. And this is the teaching he gave:

Blessed are the poor in spirit;
the kingdom of Heaven is theirs.
Blessed are the sorrowful;
they shall find consolation.
Blessed are the gentle;
they shall have the earth for their possession.
Blessed are those who show mercy;
mercy shall be shown to them.
Blessed are those whose hearts are pure;
they shall see God.
Blessed are the peacemakers;
they shall be called God's children.
Blessed are those who are persecuted in the cause of right;
the kingdom of Heaven is theirs.

Blessed are you, when you suffer insults and persecution and calumnies of every kind for my sake. Exult and be glad, for you have a rich reward in heaven; in the same way they persecuted the prophets before you.

You are the salt to the world. And if salt becomes tasteless, how is its saltness to be restored? It is good for nothing but to be thrown away and trodden underfoot.

You are light for all the world. A town that stands on a hill cannot be hidden. When a lamp is lit, it is not put under the meal-tub, but on the lampstand, where it gives light to everyone in the house. Like the lamp, you must shed light among your fellows, so that, when they see the good you do, they may give praise to your Father in heaven.

Do not suppose that I have come to abolish the law and the prophets; I did not come to abolish, but to complete. Truly I tell you: so long as heaven and earth endure, not a letter, not a dot, will diappear from the law until all that must happen has happened. anyone therefore who set aside even the least of the law's demands, and teaches others to do the same, will have the lowest place in the kingdom of Heaven, whereas anyone who keeps the law, and teaches others to do so, will rank high in the kingdom of Heaven. I tell you, unless you show yourselves far better than the scribes and Pharisees, you can never enter the kingdom of Heaven.

You have heard that our forefathers were told, "Do not commit murder; anyone who commits murder must be brought to justice." But what I tell you is this: Anyone who nurses anger against his brother must be brought to justice. Whoever calls his brother "good for nothing" deserves the sentence of the court; whoever calls him "fool" deserves hell-fire. So if you are presenting your gift at the altar and suddenly remember that your brother has a grievance against you, leave your gift where it is before the altar. First go and make your peace with your brother; then com back and offer your gift. If someone sues you, come to terms with him promptly while you are both on your way to court; otherwise he may hand you over to the judge, and the judge to the officer, and you will be thrown into jail. Truly I tell you: once you are there you will not be let out until you have paid the last penny.

You have heard that they were told, "Do not commit adultery." But what I tell you is this: If a man looks at a woman with a lustful eye, he has already committed adultery with her in his heart. If your right eye causes your downfall, tear it out and fling it away; it is better for you to lose one part of your body than for the whole of it to be thrown into hell. If your right hand causes your downfall, cut it off and fling it away; it is better for you to lose one part of your body than for the whole of it to go to hell.

7.3

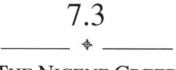

THE NICENE CREED

In the first centuries of Christianity, in what might be called its formative years, there were numerous councils of church leaders, going back to the earliest meeting between Jesus and his disciples. (The Last Supper was one such meeting.) After the conversion of Constantine the Great in 312 AD, the Roman emperors also sent representatives to these councils. One function of the councils was to determine what constituted true Christian belief, about which there was often little consensus. Divergent interpretations of Jesus' preaching was common. One result was the creations of creeds, or statements of belief; there were several popular versions of these in the early church. One creed that has remained fundamental to most Christian sects today, although it exists in different forms, was created at the council of Nicea in 325. It was subsequently revised several times; the following form dates from approximately 374.

QUESTIONS

1. What is the role of the believer in Christianity, as defined by the Creed?
2. How does the Nicene Creed present the concept of the Trinity? What are the three parts and how do they relate to one another?
3. What is the relationship of Jesus to God, as defined by this Creed?

We believe in one God the Father All-sovereign, maker of heaven and earth, and of all things visible and invisible;

And in one Lord Jesus Christ, the only-begotten Son of God, Begotten of the Father before all the ages, Light of Light, true God of True God, begotten not made, of one substance with the Father, through whom all things were made; who for us men and for our salvation came down from the heavens, and was made flesh of the Holy Spirit and the Virgin Mary, and became man, and was crucified for us under Pontius Pilate, and suffered and was buried, and rose again on the third day according to the Scriptures, and ascended into the heavens, and sitteth on the right hand of the Father, and cometh again with glory to judge living and dead, of whose kingdom there shall be no end:

And in the Holy Spirit, the Lord and the Life-giver, that proceedeth from the Father, who with Father and Son is worshipped together and glorified together, who spake through the prophets:

In one holy Catholic and Apostolic Church:

We acknowledge one baptism unto remission of sins. We look for a resurrection of the dead, and the life of the age to come.

Source: Henry Bettenson, ed., *Documents of the Christian Church*, (New York: Oxford University Press, 1963), p. 26.

7.4

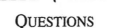

DEFENSE OF CHRISTIANITY, ST. AUGUSTINE

Augustine was Bishop of Hippo, in North Africa, from 396 to 430. He was one of the most prolific of the early Christian theologians, and although he himself claims to have destroyed some of his writings, many survive. In the City of God, *Augustine set out to write a defense of Christians from the accusation that they were responsible for the sack of Rome in 410 by the Visigoths.*

QUESTIONS

1. In writing the *City of God*, what does Augustine reveal about the relationship between Christians and Pagans at the end of the Roman Empire?
2. Why does Augustine view the destruction of Rome as an act of Divine Providence?
3. What does Augustine mean by the phrase "City of God?"

CHAPTER 1

From this earthly city issue the enemies against whom the City of God must be defended. Some of them, it is true, abjure their worldly error and become worthy members in God's City. But many others, alas, break out in blazing hatred against it and are utterly ungrateful, notwithstanding its

Redeemer's signal gifts. For, they would no longer have a voice to raise against it, had not its sanctuaries given them asylum as they fled before the invaders' swords, and made it possible for them to save that life of which they are so proud.

Have not even those very Romans whom the barbarians spared for the sake of Christ assailed His Name? To this both the shrines of the martyrs and the basilicas of the Apostles bear witness: amid the city's devastation, these buildings gave refuge not only to the faithful but even to infidels. Up to the sacred threshold raged the murderous enemy, but the slayers' fury went no further. The merciful among the enemy conducted to the churches those whom they had spared even outside the holy precincts, to save them from others who lacked such mercy. Even these ruthless men, who in other places customarily indulged their ferocity against enemies, put a rein to their murderous fury and curbed their mania for taking captives, the moment they reached the holy places. Here, the law of sanctuary forbade what the law of war elsewhere permitted. Thus were saved many of those who now cry down Christian culture and who blame Christ for the calamities that befell the city. Indeed, that very mercy to which they owe their lives and which was exercised in Christ's Name they ascribe not to our Christ but to their Fate. Yet, if they only had sense, they would see that the hardships and cruelties they suffered from the enemy came from that Divine Providence who makes use of war to reform the corrupt lives of men. They ought to see that it is the way of Providence to test by such afflictions men of virtuous and exemplary life, and to call them, once tried, to a better world, or to keep them for a while on earth for the accomplishment of other purposes. As for the fact that the fierce barbarians, contrary to the usage of war, generally spared their lives for Christ's sake and, in particular, in places dedicated to Christ's Name — which by a merciful Providence were spacious enough to afford refuge to large numbers — this they should have credited to Christian culture. They should thank God and, if they would escape the pains of eternal fire, should turn to His Name with all sincerity — as many have, without sincerity, in order to escape the results of the present ruin.

For, many of those whom you see heaping impudent abuse on the servants of Christ would not have escaped the ruin and massacre had they not falsely paraded as servants of Christ. Now, with ungrateful pride, impious madness, and perversity of heart, they work against that Name. They who turned to that Name with a lying tongue, in order to enjoy this temporal light, deserve the penalty of eternal darkness....

CHAPTER 3

Just think of the kind of gods to whose protection the Romans were content to entrust their city! No more pathetic illusion could be imagined. Yet, the pagans are angry with us because we speak so frankly of their divinities. However, they feel no anger against their own writers. They even pay them a fee to teach such nonsense, and think such teachers worthy of public salary and honors. Take Virgil. Children must read this greatest and best of all poets in order to impress their tender minds so deeply that he may never be easily forgotten, much as the well-known words of Horace suggest:

> The liquors that new vessel first contains
> Behind them leave a taste that long remains.

Now, in Virgil, Juno is pictured as the foe of the Trojans and as saying, while she goads Aeolus, King of the Winds, against them:

> The nation that I hate in peace sails by,
> With Troy and Troy's fallen gods to Italy.

Did they act wisely in placing Rome's immunity from defeat in the hands of such vanquished deities? Even assuming that Juno spoke these words in a fit of feminine anger, not knowing what she said, does not Aeneas himself, so often styled 'the pious,' relate how

> Panthus, a priest of Phoebus and the Tower,
> Rushed with his nephew and the conquered gods
> And, frantic, sought for shelter at my door.

Does he not admit that the very gods, whom he declares 'conquered' are entrusted to his protection rather than he to theirs when he is given the charge, 'To thee doth Troy commend her gods, her all'? If, then Virgil describes such gods as vanquished, and, because vanquished, needing a man's help even to escape, surely it is folly to believe that it was wise to entrust Rome to the safe-keeping of such divinities, and to believe that Rome could never be destroyed unless it lost its gods. In fact, to worship fallen gods as patrons and defenders is more like having poor odds than good gods. It is much more sensible to believe, not so much that Rome would have been saved from destruction had not the gods perished, but rather that the gods would have perished long ago had not Rome made every effort to save them.

For, who does not see, if only he stops to consider, how futile it is to presume that Rome could not be conquered when protected by conquered custodians, and that the reason it fell was that it lost its tutelary deities? Surely, the only possible reason why Rome should fall was that it wanted vincible protectors. Hence, when all these things were written and sung about the fallen gods, it was not because the poets took pleasure in lying, but because truth compelled intelligent men to avow them. However, this matter will be more fitly and more fully treated in subsequent chapters. Here I shall do my best to wind up in few words what I began to say about men's ingratitude.

These men, I say, hold Christ responsible for the evils which they deservedly suffer for their wicked lives. They have not the slightest appreciation of the fact, that, when they deserved to be punished, they were spared for Christ's sake. On the contrary, with impious perversity and bitterness, they attack His Name with those very tongues which falsely invoked that Name to save them. The very tongues which, like cowards, they held in check in the sacred places when safe, protected and unharmed by the enemy for Christ's sake, they now use to hurl malicious curses against Him....

CHAPTER 7

All the destruction, slaughter, plundering, burning, and distress visited upon Rome in its latest calamity were but the normal aftermath of war. It was something entirely new that fierce barbarians, by an unprecedented turn of events, showed such clemency that vast basilicas were designated as places where refugees might assemble with assurance of immunity. There, no one was to be slain or raped; many destined for liberation were to be led there by the compassionate enemy; from there, none was to be dragged away to captivity by a cruel foe. That this was in honor of the Name of Christ and to the credit of Christian civilization is manifest to all. To see this and not acknowledge it with praise is ingratitude. To impugn those who give us credit is utterly unreasonable. Let no man with sense ascribe this to the savage ways of the barbarians. It was God who struck awe into ruthless and blood-thirsty hearts, who curbed and wondrously tamed them. God who long ago spoke these words by the mouth of the Prophet; 'I will visit their iniquities with a rod: and their sins with stripes. But My mercy I will not take away from them.

CHAPTER 8

But, someone will say: 'How, then, is it that this divine mercy was bestowed on impious and ungrateful man?' Surely, the answer is that mercy was shown by the One who, day by day, 'maketh His sun to rise upon the good and bad, and raineth upon the just and the unjust.' For, although some who reflect on these truths repent and are converted from their wickedness, others, according to the words of the Apostle, despise 'the riches of His goodness and long-suffering, in the hardness of their heart and the impenitence' and treasure up to themselves 'wrath against the day of wrath and revelation of the just judgment of God Who will render to every man according to his works.' Nevertheless, God's patience is an invitation to the wicked to do penance, just as God's scourge is a school of patience for the good. In the like manner, God's mercy embraces the good with love, just as His severity corrects the wicked with punishment. It has pleased Divine Providence to prepare for the just joys in the world to come in which the unjust will have no part; and for the impious, pains which will not afflict the virtuous. But, as for the paltry goods and evils of this transitory world, these He allotted alike to just and unjust, in order that men might not seek too eagerly after those goods which they see even the wicked to possess, or shrink too readily from those ills which commonly afflict the just....

Source: Augustine, *City of God*, trans. Gerald G. Walsh, Demetrius B. Zema, Grace Monahan, and Daniel J. Honan (New York: Doubleday, 1958), pp. 40-44.

7.5

MARTYRDOM OF ST. PERPETUA

Perpetua, born to a pagan Roman family, was martyred in Carthage in 203, in the persecutions of Emperor Septimus Severus. The following is her own account of arrest and imprisonment, and the account by Saturus (her teacher) of her subsequent death. At the time of her arrest Perpetua was a catechumen, preparing to be baptized as a Christian.

QUESTIONS

1. Why, according to Perpetua, is she being martyred? What was her crime according to the state of Rome?
2. Why were narratives such as the account of Perpetua's martyrdom so popular with early Christians?
3. Did the violent acts in the story add to or detract from its popularity?

I f the ancient examples of faith, such as both testified to the grace of God, and wrought the edification of man, have for this cause been set out in writing that the reading of them may revive the past and so both God be glorified and man strengthened, why should not new examples be set out equally suitable to both those ends? For these in like manner will some day be old and needful for posterity, though in their own time because of the veneration secured to antiquity they are held in less esteem. But let them see to this who determine the one power of the one Spirit by times and seasons: since the more recent things should rather be deemed the greater, as being "later than the last." This follows from the pre-eminence of grace promised at the last lap of the world's race. For "In the last days, saith the Lord, I will pour forth of My Spirit upon all flesh, and their sons and their daughters shall prophesy: and on My servants and on My handmaidens will I pour forth of My Spirit: and their young men shall see visions, and their old men shall dream dreams." And so we who recognize and hold in honour not new prophecies only but new visions as alike promised, and count all the rest of the powers of the Holy Spirit as intended for the equipment of the Church, to which the same Spirit was sent bestowing all gifts upon all as the Lord dealt to each man, we cannot but set these out and make them famous by recital to the glory of God. So shall no weak or despairing faith suppose that supernatural grace, in excellency of martyrdoms or revelations, was found among the ancients only; for God ever works what He has promised, to unbelievers a witness, to believers a blessing. And so "what we have heard and handled declare we unto you also," brothers and little children, "that ye also" who were their eyewitnesses may be reminded of the glory of the Lord, and you who now learn by the ear "may have fellowship with" the holy martyrs, and through them with the Lord Jesus Christ, to whom belong splendour and honour for ever and ever. Amen.

Certain young catechumens were arrested, Revocatus and his fellow-slave Felicitas, Saturninus, and Secundulus. Among these also Vibia Perpetua, well-born, liberally educated, honourably married, having father and mother, and two brothers, one like herself a catechumen, and an infant son at the breast. She was about twenty-two years of age. The whole story of her martyrdom is from this point onwards told by herself as she left it written, hand and conception being alike her own.

"When I was still," she says, "with my companions, and my father in his affection for me was endeavouring to upset me by arguments and overthrow my resolution, 'Father,' I said, 'do you see this vessel, for instance, lying here, waterpot or whatever it may be?' 'I see it, 'he said. And I said to him 'Can it be called by any other name than what it is?' and he answered, 'No.' 'So also I cannot call myself anything else than what I am, a Christian.'

"Then my father, furious at the word 'Christian,' threw himself upon me as though to pluck out my eyes; but he was satisfied with annoying me; he was in fact vanquished, he and his Devil's arguments. Then I thanked the Lord for being parted for a few days from my father, and was refreshed by his absence. During those few days we were baptized, and the Holy Spirit bade me make no other petition after the holy water save for bodily endurance. A few days after we were lodged in prison; and I was in great fear, because I had never known such darkness. What a day of horror! Terrible heat, thanks to the crowds! Rough handling by the soldiers! To crown all I was tormented there by anxiety for my baby. Then Tertius and Pomponius, those blessed deacons who were ministering to us, paid for us to be removed for a few hours to a better part of the prison and refresh ourselves. Then all went out of the prison and were left to themselves. My baby was brought to me, and I suckled him, for he was already faint for want of food. I spoke anxiously to my mother on his behalf, and strengthened my brother, and commended my son to their charge. I was pining because I saw them pine on my account. Such anxieties I suffered for many days; and I obtained leave for my baby to remain in the prison with me; and I at once recovered my health, and was relieved of my trouble and anxiety for my baby; and my prison suddenly became a palace to me, and I would rather have been there than anywhere else....

"After a few days a rumour ran that we were to be examined. Moreover, my father arrived from the city, worn with trouble, and came up the hill to see me, that he might overthrow my resolution, saying: 'Daughter, pity my white hairs! Pity your father, if I am worthy to be called father by you; if with these hands I have brought you up to this your prime of life, if I have preferred you to all your brothers! Give me not over to the reproach of men! Look upon your brothers, look upon your mother and your mother's sister, look upon your son who cannot live after you are gone! Lay aside your pride, do not ruin all of us, for none of us will ever speak freely again, if anything happen to you!' So spoke my father in his love for me, kissing my hands, and casting himself at my feet; and with tears called me by the name not of daughter but of lade. And I grieved for my father's sake, because he alone of all my kindred would not have joy in my suffering. And I comforted him, saying: 'It shall happen on that platform as God shall choose; for know well that we lie not in our own power but in the power of God.' and, full of sorrow, he left me.

"On another day when we were having our midday meal, we were suddenly hurried off to be examined; and we came to the market-place. Forthwith a rumour ran through the neighbouring parts of the market-place, and a vast crowd gathered. We went up onto the platform. The others, on being question, confessed their faith. So it came to my turn. And there was my father with my child, and he drew me down from the step, beseeching me: 'Have pity on your baby.' And the procurator Hilarian, who had then received the power of life and death in the room of the late pro-consul Minucius Timinianus, said to me: 'Spare your father's white hairs; spare the tender years of your child. Offer a sacrifice for the safety of the Emperors.' And I answered: 'No.' 'Are you a Christian?' said Hilarian. And I answered: 'I am.' And when my father persisted in trying to overthrow my resolution, he was ordered by Hilarian to be thrown down, and the judge struck him with his rod. And I was grieved for my father's plight, as if I had been struck myself, so did I grieve for the sorrow that had come on his old age. Then he passed sentence on the whole of us, and condemned us to the beasts; and in great joy we went down into the prison. Then because my baby was accustomed to take the breast from me, and stay with me in prison, I sent at once the deacon Pomponius to my father to ask for my baby. But my father refused to give him. And as God willed, neither had he any further wish for my breasts, nor did they become inflamed; that I might not be tortured by anxiety for the baby and pain in my breasts.

"After a few days, while we were all praying, suddenly in the middle of the prayer I spoke, and uttered the name of Dinocrates; and I was astonished that he had never come into mind till then; and I grieved, thinking of what had befallen him. And I saw at once that I was entitled, and ought, to make request for him. And I began to pray much for him, and make lamentation to the Lord. At once on this very night this was shown me. I saw Dinocrates coming forth from a dark place, where there were many other dark places, very hot and thirsty, his countenance pale and squalid; and the wound which he had when he died was in his face still. This Dinocrates had been my brother according to the flesh, seven years old, who had died miserably of a gangrene in the face, so that his death moved all to loathing. For him then I had prayed; and there was a great gulf between me and him, so that neither of us could approach the other. There was besides in the very place where Dinocrates was a font full of water, the rim of which was above the head of the child; and Dinocrates stood on tiptoe to drink. I grieved that the font should have water in it and that nevertheless he could not drink because of the height of the rim. And I woke and recognized that my brother was in trouble. But I trusted that I could relieve his trouble, and I prayed for him every day until we were transferred to the garrison prison, for we were to fight with the beasts at the garrison games on the Caesar Geta's birthday. And I prayed for him day and night with lamentations and tears that he might be given me.

"During the daytime, while we stayed in the stocks, this was shown me. I saw that same place which I had seen before, and Dinocrates clean in body, well clothed and refreshed; and where there had been a wound, I saw a scar; and the font which I had seen before had its rim lowered to the child's waist; and there poured water from it unceasingly; and on the rim a golden bowl full of water. And Dinocrates came forward and began to drink from it, and the bowl failed not. And when he had drunk enough of the water, he came forward, being glad to play as children will. And I awoke. Then I knew that he had been released from punishment.

"Then after a few days Pudens the adjutant, who was in charge of the prison, who began to show us honour, perceiving that there was some great power within us, began to admit many to see us, that both we and they might be refreshed by one another's company. Now when the day of the games approached, my father came in to me, worn with trouble, and began to pluck out his beard and cast it on the ground, and to throw himself on his face, and to curse his years, and to say such words as might have turned the world upside down. I sorrowed for the unhappiness of his old age....

As for Felicitas indeed, she also was visited by the grace of God in this wise. Being eight months gone with child (for she was pregnant at the time of her arrest), as the day for the spectacle drew near she was in great sorrow for fear lest because of her pregnancy her martyrdom should be delayed, since it is against the law for women with child to be exposed for punishment, and lest she should shed her sacred and innocent blood among others afterwards who were male-factors. Her fellow-martyrs too were deeply grieved at the thought of leaving so good a comrade and fellow-traveller behind alone on the way to the same hope. So in one flood of common lamentation they poured forth a prayer to the Lord two days before the games. Immediately after the prayer her pains came upon her. And since from the natural difficulty of an eight-months' labour she suffered much in child-birth, one of the warders said to her: "You who so suffer now, what will you do when you are flung to the beasts which, when you refused to sacrifice, you despised?" And she answered: "Now I suffer what I suffer: but then Another will be in me who will suffer for me, because I too am to suffer for Him." So she gave birth to a girl, whom one of the sisters brought up as her own daughter.

But He who had said: "Ask and ye shall receive" had granted to those who asked Him that death which each had craved. For, whenever they talked amongst themselves about their hopes of martyrdom, Saturninus declared that he wished to be cast to all the beasts; so indeed would he wear a more glorious crown. Accordingly at the outset of the show he was matched with the leopard and recalled from him; he was also (later) mauled on the platform by the bear. Saturus on the other hand had a peculiar dread of the bear, but counted beforehand on being dispatched by one bite of the leopard. And so when he was offered to the wild boar, the fighter with beasts, who had bound him to the boar, was gored from beneath by the same beast, and died after the days of the games were over, whereas Saturus was only dragged. And when he was tied up on the bridge before the bear, the bear refused to come out of his den. So Saturus for the second time was recalled unhurt.

For the young women the Devil made ready a mad heifer, an unusual animal selected for this reason, that he wished to match their sex with that of the beast. And so after being stripped and enclosed in nets they were brought into the arena. The people were horrified, beholding in the one a tender girl, in the other a woman fresh from childbirth, with milk dripping from her breasts. so they were recalled and dressed in tunics without girdles. Perpetua was tossed first, and fell on her loins. Sitting down, she drew back her torn tunic from her side to cover her thighs, more mindful of her modesty than of her suffering. Then, having asked for a pin, she further fastened her disordered hair. For it was not seemly that a martyr should suffer with her hair dishevelled, lest she should seem to mourn in the hour of the glory. Then she rose, and seeing that Felicitas was bruised, approached, gave a hand to her, and lifted her up. And the two stood side by side, and the cruelty of the people being now appeased, they were recalled to the Gate of Life. There Perpetua was supported by a certain Rusticus, then a catechumen, who kept close to her; and being roused from what seemed like sleep, so completely had she been in the Spirit and in ecstasy, began to look about her, and said to the amazement of all: "When we are to be thrown to that heifer, I cannot tell." When she heard what had already taken place, she refused to believe it till she had observed certain marks of ill-usage on her body and dress. Then she summoned her brother and spoke to him and the catechumen, saying: "Stand ye all fast in the faith, and love one another; and be not offended by our sufferings."

Source: Anne Freemantle, ed., *A Treasury of Early Christianity*, (New York: Mentor Books, 1960), pp. 186-192, 195-197.

QUESTIONS FOR PART 7

1. Christianity is a religion that draws on the influences of many cultures. Using these documents, consider what connections Christianity has to Judaism, Greece, and Rome.
2. What was the role of women in early Christianity? Did that role differ in any way from how women functioned in the broader communities of the Jewish culture and Rome?
3. What was the relationship between early Christianity and the state? Christianity appears at the height of the Roman Empire, during the reign of Augustus, yet is often credited by historians with contributing to the fall of the Empire. Is early Christianity a divisive or unifying force in the late Roman world?

PART 8

❧

THE EMERGING MEDIEVAL STATES

The medieval world was a synthesis of the Greco-Roman, Christian, and Germanic worlds. It was never an easy synthesis, and well into the modern period tensions between the three legacies remain, in such debates as the relationship between church and state, law and faith.

The collapse of the Roman political system in the West left a vacuum that was quickly filled by various Germanic tribes; in the East, the Roman state continued but transmuted into the theocratic, Greek state of the Byzantine Empire. Christianity, which had been splintered into diverse sects, had synthesized into a somewhat unified religion, only to begin to break apart again into very autonomous Latin and Greek churches. In the seventh century a new religion appeared in Arabia; Islam quickly overtook the Near East, northern Africa, and reached far into western Europe through the Iberian peninsula. There were, in fact, many medieval worlds.

The sources of this chapter illustrate some of those early medieval worlds, including the introduction of Christianity into the Germanic culture (the Conversion of Clovis), the Byzantine codification of Roman law in the *Corpus Juris Civilis*, the gradual development of papal authority over the Western church, and the earliest interaction between Islam and the West.

8.1

✛

CONVERSION OF CLOVIS

Clovis became the first king of the Franks shortly before 500 AD. Until then, the Franks were ruled by a chieftain who answered to an assembly of warriors; it was a system of governance common to most Germanic tribes in the fifth and sixth centuries. At about the same time he also converted to Roman Christianity, as the following excerpt describes. It is not clear whether Clovis had pagan beliefs before this conversion, or whether he had converted to Arian Christianity, a sect viewed as heretical by the Roman church. Many of the Franks (and other Germans) had converted to Arianism by 500; gradually they would be converted to Roman Catholicism. The process of converting the Germans coincided with the conquests of several of the tribes by the Franks. Once he became king, Clovis was determined to build an empire to rule as well.

—————— ✢ ——————

QUESTIONS

1. If he had not yet converted to Catholicism, why does Clovis still punish the man who destroyed the vase from the church?
2. What role does Clotilda play in the conversion of Clovis?
3. Clovis' battlefield conversion mimics the conversion of Constantine the Great in 312, which also took place on a battlefield. Is it a coincidence that both men have the same conversion story?

27 After these events Childeric died and Clovis his son reigned in his stead. In the fifth year of his reign Siagrius, king of the Romans, son of Egidius, had his seat in the city of Soissons which Egidius, who has been mentioned before, once held. And Clovis came against him with Ragnachar, his kinsman, because he used to possess the kingdom, and demanded that they make ready a battle-field. And Siagrius did not delay nor was he afraid to resist. And so they fought against each other and Siagrius, seeing this army crushed, turned his back and fled swiftly to king Alaric at Toulouse. And Clovis sent to Alaric to send him back, otherwise he was to know that Clovis would make war on him for his refusal. And Alaric was afraid that he would incur the anger of the Franks on account of Siagrius, seeing it is the fashion of the Goths to be terrified, and he surrendered him in chains to Clovis' envoys. And Clovis took him and gave orders to put him under guard, and when he had got his kingdom he directed that he be executed secretly. At that time many churches were despoiled by Clovis' army, since he was as yet involved in heathen error. Now the army had taken from a certain church a vase of wonderful size and beauty, along with the remainder of the utensils for the service of the church. And the bishop of the church sent messengers to the king asking that the vase at least be returned, if he could not get back any more of the sacred dishes. On hearing this the king said to the messenger: "Follow us as far as Soissons, because all that has been taken is to be divided there and when the lot assigns me that dish I will do what the father asks." Then when he came to Soissons and all the booty was set in their midst, the king said: "I ask of you, brave warriors, not to refuse to grant me in addition to my share, yonder dish," that is, he was speaking of the vase just mentioned. In answer to the speech of the king those of more sense replied: "Glorious king, all that we see is yours, and we ourselves are subject to your rule. Now do what seems well-pleasing to you; for no one is able to resist your power." When they said this, a foolish, envious and excitable fellow lifted his battle-ax and struck the vase, and cried in a loud voice: "You shall get nothing here except what the lot fairly bestows on you." At this all were stupefied, but the king endured the insult with the gentleness of patience, and taking the vase he handed it over to the messenger of the church, nursing the wound deep in his heart. And at the end of the year he ordered the whole army to come with their equipment of armor, to show the brightness of their arms on the field of March. And when he was reviewing them all carefully, he came to the man who struck the vase, and said to him: "No one has brought armor so carelessly kept as you; for neither your spear nor sword nor ax is in serviceable condition." And seizing his ax he cast it to the earth, and when the other had bent over somewhat to pick it up, the king raised his hands and drove his own ax into the man's head. "This," said he, "is what you did at Soissons to the vase." Upon the death of this man, he ordered the rest to depart, raising great dread of himself by this action. He made many wars and gained many victories. In the tenth year of his reign he made war on the Thuringi and brought them under his dominion.

28. Now the king of the Burgundians was Gundevech, of the family of king Athanaric the persecutor, whom we have mentioned before. He had four sons; Gundobad, Godegisel, Chilperic and Godomar. Gundobad killed his brother Chilperic with the sword, and sank his wife in water with a stone tied to her neck. His two daughters he condemned to exile; the older of these, who became a nun, was called Chrona, and the younger Clotilda. And as Clovis often sent embassies to Burgundy, the maiden Clotilda was found by his envoys. And when they saw that she was of good bearing and wise, and learned that she was of the family of the king, they reported this to King Clovis, and he sent an embassy to Gundobad without delay asking her in marriage. And Gundobad was afraid to refuse, and surrendered her to the men, and they took the girl and brought her swiftly to the king. The king was very glad when he saw her, and married her, having already by a concubine a son named Theodoric.

29. He had a first-born son by queen Clotilda, and as his wife wished to consecrate him in baptism, she tried unceasingly to persuade her husband, saying: "The gods you worship are nothing, and they will be unable to help themselves or any one else. For they are graven out of stone or wood or some metal. And the names you have given them are names of men and not of gods, as Saturn, who is declared to have fled in fear of being banished from his kingdom by his son; as Jove himself, the foul perpetrator of all shameful crimes, committing incest with men, mocking at his kinswomen, not able to refrain from intercourse with his own sister as she herself says: *Jovisque et soror et conjunx.* What could Mars or Mercury do? They are endowed rather with the magic arts than with the power of the divine name. But he ought rather to be worshipped who created by his word heaven and earth, the sea and all that in them is out of a state of nothingness, who made the sun shine, and adorned the heavens with stars, who filled the waters with creeping things, the earth with living things and the air with creatures that fly, at whose nod the earth is decked with creatures that fly, at whose nod the earth is decked with growing crops, the trees with fruit, the vines with grapes, but whose hand mankind was created, by whose generosity all that creation serves and helps man whom he created as his own." But though the queen said this the spirit of the king was by no means moved to belief, and he said: "It was at the command of our gods that all things were created and came forth, and it is plain that your God has not power and, what is more, he is proven not to belong to the family of the gods." Meantime the faithful queen made her son ready for baptism; she gave command to adorn the church with hangings and curtains, in order that he who could not be moved by persuasion might be urged to belief by this mystery. The boy, whom they named Ingomer, died after being baptized, still wearing the white garments in which he became regenerate. At this the king was violently angry, and reproached the queen harshly, saying: "If the boy had been dedicated in the name my gods he would certainly have lived; but as it is, since he was baptized in the name of your God, he could not live at all." To this the queen said: "I give thanks to the omnipotent God, creator of all, who has judged me not wholly unworthy, that he should deign to take to his kingdom one born from my womb. My soul is not stricken with grief for his sake, because I know that, summoned from this world as he was in his baptismal garments, he will be fed by the vision of God."

After this she bore another son, whom she named Chlodomer at baptism; and when he fell sick, the king said: "It is impossible that anything else should happen to him than happened to his brother, namely, that being baptized in the name of your Christ, he should die at once." But through the prayers of his mother, and the Lord's command, he became well.

30. The queen did not cease to urge him to recognize the true God and cease worshiping idols. But he could not be influenced in any way to this belief, until at last a war arose with the Alamanni, in which he was driven by necessity to confess what before he had of this free will denied. It came about that as the two armies were fighting fiercely, there was much slaughter, and Clovis's army began to be in danger of destruction. He saw it and raised his eyes to heaven, and with remorse in his heart he burst into tears

and cried: "Jesus Christ, whom Clotilda asserts to be the son of the living God, who art said to give aid to those in distress, and to bestow victory on those who hope in thee, I beseech the glory of thy aid, with the vow that if thou wilt grant me victory over these enemies, and I shall know that power which she says that people dedicated in thy name have had from thee, I will believe in thee and be baptized in thy name. For I have invoked my own gods, but, as I find, they have withdrawn from aiding me; and therefore I believe that they possess no power, since they do not help those who obey them. I now call upon thee, I desire to believe thee, only let me be rescued from my adversaries." And when he said this, the Alamanni turned their backs, and began to disperse in flight. And when they saw that their king was killed, they submitted to the dominion of Clovis, saying: "Let not the people perish further, we pray; we are yours now." And he stopped the fighting, and after encouraging his men, retired in peace and told the queen how he had had merit to win the victory by calling on the name of Christ. This happened in the fifteenth year of this reign.

31. Then the queen asked saint Remi, bishop of Rheims, to summon Clovis secretly, urging him to introduce the king to the word of salvation. And the bishop sent for him secretly and began to urge him to believe in the true God, maker of heaven and earth, and to cease worshiping idols, which could help neither themselves nor any one else. But the king said: "I gladly hear you, most holy father; but there remains one thing: the people who follow me cannot endure to abandon their gods; but I shall go and speak to them according to your words." He met with his followers, but before he could speak the power of God anticipated him, and all the people cried out together: "O pious king, we reject our mortal gods, and we are ready to follow the immortal God whom Remi preaches." This was reported to the bishop who was greatly rejoiced, and bade them get ready the baptismal font. The squares were shaded with tapestried canapies, the churches adorned with white curtains, the baptistery set in order, the aroma of incense spread, candles of fragrant odor burned brightly, and the whole shrine of the baptistery was filled with divine fragrance: and the Lord gave such grace to those who stood by that they thought they were placed amid the odors of paradise. And the king was the first to ask to be baptized by the bishop. Another Constantine advanced to the baptismal font, to terminate the disease of ancient leprosy and wash away with fresh water the foul spots that had long been borne. And when he entered to be baptized, the saint of God began with ready speech: "Gently bend your neck, Sigamber; worship what you burned; burn what you worshipped." The holy bishop Remi was a man of excellent wisdom and especially trained in rhetorical studies, and of such surpassing holiness that he equalled the miracles of Silvester. For there is extant a book of his life which tells that he raised a dead man. And so the king confessed all-powerful God in the Trinity, and was baptized in the name of the Father, Son and holy Spirit, and was anointed with the holy ointment with the sign of the cross of Christ. And of his army more than 3000 were baptized. His sister also, Albofled, was baptized, who not long after passed to the Lord. And when the king was in mourning for her, the holy Remi sent a letter of consolation which began in this way: "The reason of your mourning pains me, and pains me greatly, that Albofled your sister, of good memory, has passed away. But I can give you this comfort, that her departure from the world was such that she ought to be envied rather than mourned." Another sister also was converted, Lanthechild by name, who had fallen into the heresy of the Arians, and she confessed that the Son and the holy Spirit were equal to the Father, and was anointed....

8.2

---- ✛ ----

CORPUS JURIS CIVILIS OF JUSTINIAN

The Corpus Juris Civilis, *or Body of Civil Law, was both a compilation and a reworking of older Roman law codes. It is the single most important law code in the history of Western civilization. It was commissioned by the Byzantine Emperor Justinian in 529 and took four years to complete. In its finished form it was divided into four parts:* Code, Digests, *and* Institutes, *which were all written in Latin and based heavily on older Roman laws, and the* Novels, *which were new laws written in Greek. The very shape of the* Corpus — *Latin and Greek, old and new laws — exemplifies the Byzantine culture, itself a synthesis of old and new, West and East. Justinian was both a Roman emperor in the style of Augustus and Constantine, and an Eastern tyrant in the Greek tradition. The laws excerpted here are from the* Institutes.

---- ✛ ----

QUESTIONS

1. Does the *Corpus* define slavery as a natural state?
2. What rationale is used to determine whether a man and woman may marry or not? What determines impediment to marriage?
3. Who has more freedom under this law code, a slave in relation to a master, or a child in relation to a father?

III. THE LAW OF PERSONS

All our law relates either to persons, or to things, or to actions. Let us first speak of persons; as it is of little purpose to know the law, if we do not know the persons for whose sake the law was made. The chief division in the rights of persons is this: men are all either free or slaves.

1. Freedom, from which men are said to be free, is the natural power of doing what we each please, unless prevented by force or by law.
2. Slavery is an institution of the law of nations, by which one man is made the property of another, contrary to natural right.
3. Slaves are denominated *servi*, because generals order their captives to be sold, and thus preserve them, and do not put them to death. Slaves are also called *mancipia*, because they are taken from the enemy by the strong hand.
4. Slaves either are born or become so. They are born so when their mother is a slave; they become so either by the law of nations, that is, by captivity, or by the civil law, as when a free person, above the age of twenty, suffers himself to be sold, that he may share the price given for him.
5. In the condition of slaves there is no distinction; but there are many distinctions among free persons; for they are either born free, or have been set free.

IV. DE INGENIUS

A person is *ingenuus* who is free from the moment of his birth, by being born in matrimony, of parents who have been either both born free, or both made free, or one of whom has been born and the other made free; and when the mother is free, and the father a slave, the child nevertheless is born free; just as he is if his mother is free, and it is uncertain who is his father; for he had then no legal father. And it is sufficient if the mother is free at the time of the birth, although a slave when she conceived; and on the other hand, if she be free when she conceives, and is a slave when she gives birth to her child. If the child is held to be born free for the misfortune of the mother ought not to prejudice her unborn infant. The question hence arose, if a female slave with child is made free, but again becomes a slave before the child is born, whether the child is born free or a slave? Marcellus thinks it is born free, for it is sufficient for the unborn child, if the mother has been free, although only in the intermediate time; and this is true.

1. When a man has been born free he does not cease to be *ingenuus*, because he has been in the position of a slave, and has subsequently been enfranchised; for it has been often settled that enfranchisement does not prejudice the rights of birth.

V. FREEDMEN...

1. Manumission is effected in various ways; either in the face of the Church, according to the imperial constitutions, or by *vindicta*, or in the presence of friends; or by letter, or by testament, or by any other expression of a man's last will. And a slave may also gain his freedom in many other ways, introduced by the constitutions of former emperors, and by our own.
2. Slaves may be manumitted by their masters at any time; even when the magistrate is only passing along, as when a praetor, or *praeses*, or proconsul is going to the baths, or the theater.

IX. THE POWER OF PARENTS

Our children, begotten in lawful marriage, are in our power.
1. Marriage, or matrimony, is a binding together of a man and woman to live in an indivisible union.
2. The power which we have over our children is peculiar to the citizens of Rome; for no other people have a power over their children, such as we have over ours.
3. The child born to you and your wife is in your power. And so is the child born to your son of his wife, that is, your grandson or granddaughter; so are your great grandchildren, and all your other descendants. But a child born of your daughter is not in your power, but in the power of its own father.

X. MARRIAGE

Roman citizens are bound together in lawful matrimony; when they are united according to law, the males having attained the age of puberty, and the females a marriageable age, whether they are fathers or sons of a family; but, of the latter, they must first obtain the consent of their parents, in whose power they are. For both natural reason and the law require this consent; so much so, indeed, that it ought to precede marriage. Hence the question has arisen, whether the daughter of a madman could be married, or his son marry? And as opinions were divided as to the son, we decided that as the daughter of a madman might, so may the son of a madman marry without the intervention of the father, according to the mode established by our constitution.

1. We may not marry every woman without distinction; for with some, marriage is forbidden. Marriage cannot be contracted between persons standing to each other in the relation of ascendant and descendant, as between a father and daughter, a grandfather and his granddaughter, a mother and her son, a grandmother and her grandson; and so on, *ad infinitum*. And, if such persons unite together, they only contract a criminal and incestuous marriage; so much so, that ascendants and descendants, who are only so by adoption, cannot intermarry; and even after the adoption is dissolved, the prohibition remains. You cannot, therefore, marry a woman who has been either your daughter or granddaughter by adoption, although you may have emancipated her.

2. There are also restrictions, though not so extensive, on marriage between collateral relations. A brother and sister are forbidden to marry, whether they are the children of the same father and mother, or of one of the two only. And, if a woman becomes your sister by adoption, you certainly cannot marry; but, if the adoption is destroyed by emancipation, you may marry her; as you may also, if you yourself are emancipated. Hence it follows, that if a man would adopt his son-in-law, he ought first to emancipate his daughter; and if he would adopt his daughter-in-law, he ought previously to emancipate his son.

3. A man may not marry the daughter of a brother, or a sister, nor the granddaughter, although she is in the fourth degree. For when we may not marry the daughter of any person, neither may we marry the granddaughter. But there does not appear to be any impediment to marrying the daughter of a woman whom your father has adopted; for she is no relation to you, either by natural or civil law.

4. The children of two brothers or two sisters, or of a brother and sister, may marry together.

5. So, too, a man may not marry his paternal aunt, even though she be so only by adoption; nor his maternal aunt; because they are regarded in the light of ascendants. For the same reason, no person may marry his great aunt, either paternal or maternal.

6. There are, too, other marriages from which we must abstain, from regard to the ties created by marriage; for example, a man may not marry his wife's daughter, or his son's wife, for they are both in the place of daughters to him; and this must be understood to mean those who have been our stepdaughters or daughters-in-law; for if a woman is still your daughter-in-law, that is, if she is still married to your son, you cannot marry her for another reason, as she cannot be the wife of two persons at once. And if your step-daughter, that is, if her mother is still married to you, you cannot marry her, because a person cannot have two wives at the same time.

7. Again, a man is forbidden to marry his wife's mother, and his father's wife, because they hold the place of mothers to him; a prohibition which can only operate when the affinity is dissolved; for if your step-mother is still your step-mother, that is, if she is still married to your father, she would be prohibited from marrying you by the common rule of law, which forbids a woman to have two husbands at the same time. So if your wife's mother is still your wife's mother, that is, if her daughter is still married to you, you cannot marry her, because you cannot have two wives at the same time.

8. The son of a husband by a former wife, and the daughter of a wife by a former husband, or the daughter of a husband by a former wife, and the son of a wife by a former husband, may lawfully contract marriage, even though they have a brother or sister born of the second marriage.

9. The daughter of a divorced wife by a second husband is not your step-daughter; and yet Julian says we ought to abstain from such a marriage. For the betrothed wife of a son is not your daughter-in-law; nor your betrothed wife your son's step-mother; and yet it is more decent and more in accordance with law to abstain from such marriage.

10. It is certain that the relationship of slaves is an impediment to marriage, even if the father and daughter or brother and sister, as the case may be, have been enfranchised.

Source: Oliver J. Thatcher, ed., *The Ideas that have Influenced Civilization in the Original Documents, Volume III* (Boston: Roberts-Manchester Publishing Co., 1901-1902), pp. 103-108

8.3

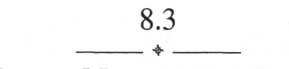

GREGORY I, LETTERS ON THE PAPACY

Gregory I, pope from 590-604, is largely responsible for establishing Rome and the Papacy as the power center of the Western Church, and is thus known as Gregory the Great. The series of letters included here illustrate the vigorous approach he took to the many impediments faced by Rome in dominating the Western Church, including plague and the war between the Ostrogoths and the Byzantines for control of Italy, complicated by the invasion of the peninsula by the Lombards in 568. Gregory was also responsible for authorizing numerous missions that sent monks into the still pagan Germanic tribes of central and eastern Europe, as well as the British Isles. He also organized the music of the liturgy into the Gregorian Chants.

QUESTIONS

1. How does Gregory interpret the calamities of the sixth century as an opportunity for Christians?
2. How does Gregory view his relationship to the temporal authorities?
3. Why does Gregory urge missionaries to incorporate local practices and the shrines of pagan idols into Christian worship?

THE PRESENT AGE

1. To the clergy of Milan

Take note that all the things of this world, which we used to hear from sacred scripture were doomed to perish, we see now in ruins. Cities are overthrown, fortresses uprooted, churches destroyed, and no tiller of the soil inhabits our land any more. The sword of man incessantly rages in our midst — we, the very few who are left. Along with this, calamities smite us from above. Thus we see before our very eyes the evils that we long ago heard would descend upon the world, and the very regions of the earth have become like pages of books to us. As all things pass away, we should reflect how all that we have loved was nothing. Look with anxious heart, therefore, upon the approaching day of the Eternal Judge and, by repenting, anticipate its terrors. Wash away all the stains of your transgressions with your tears. Use lamentations that endure only for awhile to turn aside the wrath that hangs over you eternally. When our loving Creator comes to judge us, He will comfort us in direct proportion to what He now sees as the punishment that we inflict upon ourselves for our own transgressions.

THE EMPEROR AND THE CHURCH OF CONSTANTINOPLE

2. To Emperor Maurice

Our most pious and God-appointed Lord, in addition to all the burdensome cares of empire, provides with true spiritual zeal for the preservation of Christian peace among the clergy. He righteously and correctly knows that no person can exercise proper rule on earth unless he knows how to deal with divine matters, and he also knows that the peace of the state depends on the peace of the universal Church. Indeed, Most Serene Lord, what human power, what strength of muscular arm, would dare raise a sacrilegious hand against the eminence of your most Christian empire, if all its priests strove with one mind, as they ought, to win the Redeemer's favor for you by prayer and the merit of their lives? What sword of a most savage people would advance with such cruelty to the slaughter of the faithful, were it not for the fact that the lives of us, who are called priests but who are not, are weighed down by perfidious deeds?...Our faults, which weigh down the forces of the state, sharpen the swords of the enemy. What shall we say for ourselves, who are unworthily set over God's people, when we oppress them with the burdens of our sins and destroy by example what we preach with our tongues?...Our bones are wasted by fasts, but we are bloated in our minds. Our body is covered with rags, but in the pride of our heart, we surpass the imperial purple. We lie in ashes but look down upon loftiness. Teachers of humility, we are masters of pride....God has inspired my most pious Lord to deter war against the empire by first establishing peace within the Church and by deigning to bring back the hearts of its priests to harmony. This, indeed, is what I desire, and for myself, I give glad obedience to your most serene commands.

Since, however, it is not my cause, but God's, since the holy laws, since the venerable councils, since the very commands of our Lord Jesus Christ are disturbed by the invention of a certain proud and haughty phrase, may you, My Most Pious Lord, cut out the sore and bind the resisting patient in the restraints of imperial authority. For in binding up these things tightly, you provide relief to the state, and when you cut off such things, you assure a longer reign for yourself.

To all who know the Gospel, it is clear that the Lord verbally committed to the holy apostle, Peter, the prince of all the apostles, care of the entire Church....For to Peter it was said: "You are Peter, and upon this rock I will build My Church, and the gates of hell shall not prevail against it. And I will give you the keys of the Kingdom of Heaven; whatever you bind on earth will be bound also in heaven, and whatever you loose on earth will be loosed also in heaven." Behold, Peter received the keys of the Kingdom of Heaven; the power to bind and loose is given him; the care of the entire Church is committed to him, and yet he is not called the *universal apostle*. Meanwhile, the most holy man, my fellow-priest John, attempts to be called universal bishop. I am compelled to cry out: "O tempora, O mores!"

Behold. all the regions of Europe are in the hands of barbarians, cities are overthrown, fortresses uprooted, provinces depopulated, no tiller of the soil inhabits the land, idol worshippers rage and daily dominate — all to the slaughter of the faithful — and still priests, who ought to lie weeping on the ground and in ashes, seek for themselves names of vanity, and they take pride in new and profane titles.

Do I, Most Pious Lord, defend my own cause? Am I resentful because of a wrong done me? No! It is the cause of Almighty God. It is the cause of the universal Church....In honor of Peter, prince of the apostles, [the title *universal*] was offered by the venerable synod of Chalcedon to the bishop of Rome. But not one bishop of Rome has ever consented to use this unique title, lest, by giving something special to one priest, priests in general would be deprived of the honor due them. How is it, then, that we do not seek the glory of this title, even when it is offered, but another presumes to seize it for himself, even though it has not been offered?...

Behold. We all suffer offense in this matter. Let the author of the offense be brought back to a proper way of life, and all priestly quarrels will end. For my part, I am the servant of all priests, as long as they live in a manner that befits priests. But whoever, through the swelling of vainglory, lifts up his neck against God Almighty and against the laws of the Church Fathers, I trust such a man will not bend my neck to himself, not even with a sword.

PETRINE PRIMACY

3. To Eulogius, bishop of Alexandria

Your most sweet Holiness has spoken much in you letter to me about the chair of Saint Peter, prince of the apostles, saying that he himself now sits on it in the persons of his successors,...and, indeed, I gladly accepted all that was said, inasmuch as he has spoken to me about who occupies Peter's chair. Although special honor to me in no way delights me, I greatly rejoice because you, Most Holy One, have given to yourself what you have bestowed on me. For who can be unaware that the holy church has been made firm in the strength of the prince of the apostles, who derived his name from the firmness of his spirit, so that he was called *Petrus*, which comes from *petra*. And to him it is said by the voice of Truth: "I will give you the keys of the Kingdom of Heaven." And again it is said to him: "When you are converted, strengthen your brothers." And once more: "Simon, son of Jonah, do you love Me? Then feed My sheep." It follows from this that although there are many apostles, so far as primacy is concerned, the see of the prince of the apostles alone has grown strong in authority, which in three places is one see. For Peter himself exalted the see in which he deigned to reside and end his life on earth. Peter himself honored the see to which he sent his disciple as evangelist. Peter himself strengthened the see in which, although he would leave it, he sat for seven years. Because it is the see of one, and one see over which by Divine Authority three bishops now preside, whatever good I hear of you I impute to myself. If you believe anything good of me, impute this to your merits, because we are one in Him how says: "That they all may be one, as You, Father, are in Me and I in You, and that they may be one in Us.

MISSIONARY POLICIES

4. To Augustine, bishop of the Angles

Augustine's third question.

Inasmuch as there is one faith, why do the practices of churches differ? The Roman Church has one type of mass; there is another in the churches of Gaul.

My brother, you are acquainted with the practices of the Roman Church, in which you have been nurtured. I wish, however, that if you have found any practices that might be more pleasing to God Almighty, be they the customs of the Church of Rome, or of Gaul, or of any Church whatsoever, you carefully select them out and diligently introduce to the Church of the Angles, which is still new to the faith, whatever you have been able to collect from these many Churches. We ought not love things for their location; rather, we should love locations for the good things that are attached to them. Therefore, choose from each particular Church those things that are holy, religious, and proper, and collecting them as it were into a bundle, plant them in the minds of the Angles for their use.

5. To Mellitus, abbot traveling through Gaul

Since the departure of our congregation that is with you, I have been most anxious because I have heard nothing about the success of your journey. When, however, Almighty God has brought you to our most reverend brother, Bishop Augustine, inform him that, after much deliberation, I have decided the following in regard to the issue of the Angles. The shrines of that people's idols should not be destroyed. Destroy only the idols that are in them. Take holy water and sprinkle it in these shrines. Build altars and deposit relics in them. For if the shrines are well built, it is necessary to transfer them from the worship of devils to the service of the True God. When the people see that their shrines are not destroyed, they will be able to banish error from their hearts and more comfortably come to places they are familiar with, now knowing and adoring the True God. Since they are also accustomed to kill many oxen as sacrifices to demons, they should also have some solemn festivity of this sort but in a changed form. On that day of dedication or on the feast days of the holy martyrs whose relics are deposited there, they may construct tents out of the branches of the trees that surround these shrines that have been transformed into churches, and they may celebrate that holy day with religious feasts. Do not let them sacrifice animals to the Devil any longer, but let them slay animals for their own eating in praise of God, and let them give thanks to the Giver of all for their full stomachs. In this way, while they retain some bodily pleasures they might more easily be able to incline their minds toward spiritual joys. Without a doubt, it is impossible to cut away everything all at once form hard hearts. One who strives to climb to the highest pinnacle must ascend by steps and paces, not be leaps.

Source: Alfred Andrea, ed., *The Medieval Record: Sources of Medieval History*, (Boston: Houghton Mifflin Company, 1997), pp. 116-118.

8.4

THE MUSLIM CONQUEST OF IBERIA

In invading the Iberian Peninsula in 710, Islam continued its rapid expansion, as both a religion and a state. Founded in the early seventh century by Muhammad, by the eighth century the new civilization controlled most of the Middle East, including former Persian and Byzantine territories, and most of North Africa. It was now poised to conquer parts of western Europe. In 710 a Berber (a newly converted

North African people) named Tariq was sent by his king to invade Visigothic Iberia. Tariq founded a Muslim state that would last, at least partially, until the fall of Granada in 1492. Here is a Muslim chronicle account of Tariq's invasion.

QUESTIONS

1. Why does Ilyan, a Visigoth, actually invite Tariq to invade Iberia?
2. Having accomplished the physical conquest of Iberia himself, why does Tariq hand it over to Musa Ibn Nosseyr?
3. How is this a holy war for the Muslims?

The encounter between Tariq and Ludhriq (Roderick) took place in the Wadi Lakka (Lago de la Janda) in Shudhuna (Sidonia). Allah put Roderick to flight. He was heavily encumbered with armour, and threw himself into the Wadi Lago; he was never seen again.

It is said that the Visigoth kings had a palace at Tulaitula (Toledo) in which was a sepulchre containing the Four Evangelists, on whom they swore their [coronation] oaths. The palace was greatly revered, and was never opened. When a king died, his name was inscribed there. When Roderick came to the throne, he put the crown on his head himself, which gave great offence to the Christians; then he opened the palace and the sepulchre, despite the attempts of the Christians to prevent him. Inside they found effigies of the Arabs, bows slung over their shoulders and turbans on their heads. At the bottom of the plinths it was written: "When this palace is opened and these images are brought out, a people in their likeness will come to al-Andalus and conquer it.

Tariq entered al-Andalus in Ramadan 92 (began 22 June 711). His reason for coming was as follows: One of the Spanish called Yulyan (Julian) used to come and go frequently between al-Andalus and the land of the Berbers (North Africa). Tanja (Tangiers) was [one of the places he regularly visited]. The people of Tangiers were Christian....He used to bring back from there fine horses and falcons for Roderick. The merchant's wife died, and he was left with his beautiful daughter. Roderick ordered him to proceed to al-'Udwa (North Africa), but Julian excused himself on the grounds that his wife had died and he had no-one with whom he could leave his daughter. He ordered her to be brought to the palace. When Roderick saw her, she pleased him greatly, and he took her. On his return, her father learned of this, and said to Roderick, "I have left behind horses and falcons such as you have never seen before." Roderick authorized him to go there and gave him money [to purchase them]. Julian went to Tariq b. Ziyad and excited his interest in al-Andalus, describing its fine points and the weakness of it inhabitants, and their lack of courage. Tariq b. Ziyad wrote to Musa b. Nusair with this information, and was ordered to invade al-Andalus. Tariq mustered the troops.

Once he was on board with this men, he couldn't keep his eyes open, and in his sleep he saw the Prophet (God bless him and grant him salvation), surrounded by the Muhajirun and the Ansar...girded with their swords and with their bows slung over their shoulders. The Prophet (on whom be peace) passed in front of Tariq and said to him, "Pursue your business!" Tariq saw the Prophet and his companions in his sleep until they entered al-Andalus. He took this as a good omen, and encouraged his men with the good news.

So Tariq crossed over the coast of al-Andalus and the first place he conquered was the town of Qartajanna (Carteya or Torre de Cartagena) in the district of al-Jazira (Algeciras). He ordered his men to chop up the captives whom they had killed, and boil their flesh in cauldrons. The remaining captives were set free. Those who were released told everyone they met, and God filled their hearts with fear. Then he advanced, and met Roderick, with the result already mentioned. He pushed on to Astija (Ecija) and Qurtuba (Cordova), then to Toledo and the pass known as the Pass of Tariq, through which he entered Jilliqiyya (Galicia). He overran Galicia, ending up in Usturqa (Astorga).

When Musa b. Nusair heard how successful he had been, he bacame envious of him, and set off with a large force... When he came to the coast of North Africa, he left the point from which Tariq b. Ziyad had entered and went [instead] to a place known as Marsa Musa (the anchorage of Musa; near Ceuta). He avoided the route followed by Tariq and took the Sidonia coast. He arrived one year after Tariq, and proceeded via Sidonia to Ishbiliyya (Seville), which he conquered. From there, he went to Laqant (Fuente de Cantos), to a place called Musa's Pass at the edge of Fuente de Cantos, [and from there] to Marida (Mérida). Some scholars say that the people of Mérida surrendered on terms and were not taken by storm. Musa advanced into Galicia through the pass named after him, and overran the territory he entered, and appeared before Tariq in Astorga.

When Tariq crossed over, the troops from Cordova went to meet him, and were scornful because they saw the small number of his followers. They fought a severe battle and were defeated; Tariq didn't cease slaughtering them until they reached Cordova. Roderick heard this and advanced from Toledo. They met at a place called Sidonia, on a river called today the Wadi Umm Hakim, and fought a hard battle. Almighty God killed Roderick and his men. Mughith al-Rumi, the slave of al-Walid b. 'Abd al-Malik [the Umayyad caliph, 705-15], was Tariq's cavalry commander and he marched on Cordova; Tariq went to Toledo. He entered it, and asked after the Table, which was the only thingt that concerned him. The People of the Book [the Jews or Christians] assert that it was the table of Solomon son of David [...]

[Tariq] conquered al-Andalus on behalf of Musa b. Nusair, and took from it the Table of Solomon son of David (on whom be peace!), and the crown. Tariq was told that the Table was in a fortress called Firas, two days' journey from Toledo, commanded by the son of Roderick's sister. Tariq sent him and his family a safe conduct; the prince cam down [from the castle] and Tariq carried out his promise towards him. Tariq said, "Hand over the Table to me," which he did; it had gold decoration and precious stones such as he had never seen. Tariq removed one of its legs together with its ornamentation of gold and jewels, and made a replacement leg for it. The Table was valued at 200,000 dinars because of its precious stones. Tariq took all the jewels, armour, gold, silver and plate he found there, and besides that acquired wealth such as had not been seen before. He collected it all up and went to Cordova, where he made his base. He then wrote to Musa b. Nusair informing him of the conquest of Spain and of the booty that he had acquired. [...]

It is also said that it was Musa, after his arrival in al-Andalus, who sent Tariq to Toledo, which is half way between Cordova and Arbuna (Narbonne). Narbonne marks the furthest extent of al-Andalus and the limit of where the writ of 'Umar b. 'Abd al-'Azia [Umayyad caliph, 717-720] was effective, before the polytheists overran it. It is still in their hands today. [It is also said that] it was only here that Tariq acquired the Table. Roderick was in possession of 2,000 miles of coast over and above that. [From these wide domains] the Muslims won great booty in gold and silver. "Abd al-Malik b. Maslama told me, on the authority of al-Laith b. Sa'd, "The carpets there were found [to be] woven with rods of gold, which formed a string of gold, pearls, rubies and emeralds. When the Berbers found one, and were unable to carry it away, they took an axe to it and cut it down the middle. Two of them took half each for themselves [and went off] together with a large crowd, while the troops were preoccupied with other things."

[The same authorities relate that] when al-Andalus was conquered, someone came to Musa b. Nusair and said to him, "Send someone with me and I will show you [buried] treasure." Musa sent people with him and the man said to them, "dig here." They did so, and emeralds and rubies such as they had never seen before poured out over them. When they saw it they were overawed, and said, "Musa b. Nusair will never believe us." They sent someone to get him and he saw it for himself. [The same sources] relate that when Musa b. Nusair conquered al-Andalus he wrote to [the caliph] 'Abd al-Malik: "It's not a conquest, so much as the Day of Judgment."

From *Christians and Moors in Spain, Vol. III, Arabic Sources (711-1501)*, eds., Charles Melville and Ahmed Ubaydl, pp. 3-9. Copyright © 1992 Aris & Phillips, Ltd. Reprinted with permission of Oxbow Books.

QUESTIONS FOR PART 8

1. Compare Tariq to Clovis. How are the two men similar in their approach to power? How are they different?
2. What role does the Roman Christian church play in the consolidation of Germanic and Byzantine power, respectively?
3. Which had more power in the emerging medieval world, the church or the state?

PART 9

❧

THE EARLY MIDDLE AGES

The years between the fall of Rome, c. 500, to the Carolingian empire, c. 800, used to be known as the Dark Ages. In referring to them as such, historians were dismissing that period as lacking law and order, as a gap in civilization. We now know that civilization did not retreat entirely, and that the period was not nearly as dark as was once supposed. It is however, undeniable that the emergence of a new empire in the west in 800 represented a turning point in the Early Middle Ages. Charlemagne was crowned Emperor of the Romans by Pope Leo III on Christmas Day, 800; his empire would later be termed the Holy Roman Empire. Yet it was in not a recreation of the original Roman Empire. For one thing, in 800 there was still a "Roman Emperor," as that title had remained active with the Byzantines. For another thing, Charlemagne was crowned by the head of the Roman church, which leads to future power struggles between emperors and popes. Finally, Charlemagne's real power lay in his collection of various German titles, including king of the Franks and king of the Lombards, titles that remained separate from one another.

Simultaneously the Carolingian era resulted in increased power for the papacy and the Roman church. Bolstered by the support Charlemagne gave it and the frequency with which he relied on its help, the Catholic Church continued to expand its influence and its own attempts at centralized power. The following documents illustrate how Charlemagne consolidated and expanded his power, the expansion of Catholic faith, and the Carolingian culture that resulted from both. The final document gives us a glimpse of the impeding collapse of Carolingian power, which will be weakened by internal strife (dynastic wars) and external threats (Vikings, Magyars, and Muslims) in the ninth century.

9.1

✥

CHARLEMAGNE'S WARS OF CONQUEST

Charlemagne was the first emperor in the West since 476, when the last western Roman emperor had abdicated his title in face of a Barbarian sack of Rome. He established at his court at Aachen a center for learning and manuscript production that was unrivaled in western Europe for centuries. He sought to make government more efficient, replacing independent and land-wealthy nobles known as counts with subservient administrators, many of whom were drawn from the church. Charlemagne's efforts at centralizing power in a dynastic monarchy would not long survive after his death, but it set a precedent that would be copied by later medieval states.

Much of Charlemagne's power came from his incessant wars. He continued the tradition established by Clovis in 500 of conquering and converting the still pagan Germanic tribes of the East, spreading his idea of a revived Roman state far into central Europe and enabling the Catholic Church further access to the pagans.

---- ✦ ----

QUESTIONS

1. What functions does the Catholic Church have in Charlemagne's wars of conquests?
2. How do we reconcile Charlemagne's faith with the fact that he spent most of his life at war?
3. Do the Franks recognize that they and the Saxons share a common Germanic heritage? Why or why not?

§7 Now that the war in Italy was over, the one against the Saxons, which had been interrupted for the time being, was taken up once more. No war ever undertaken by the Frankish people was more prolonged, more full of atrocities or more demanding of effort. The Saxons, like almost all the peoples living in Germany, are ferocious by nature. They are much given to devil worship and they are hostile to our religion. They think it no dishonour to violate and transgress the laws of God and man. Hardly a day passed without some incident or other which was well calculated to break the peace. Our borders and theirs were contiguous and nearly everywhere in flat, open country, except, indeed, for a few places where great forests or mountain ranges interposed to separate territories of the two peoples by a clear demarcation line. Murder, robbery and arson were of constant occurrence on both sides. In the end, the Franks were so irritated by these incidents that they decided that the time had come to abandon retaliatory measures and to undertake a full-scale war against these Saxons.

War was duly declared against them. It was waged for thirty three long years and with immense hatred on both sides, but the losses of the Saxons were greater than those of the Franks. This war could have been brought to a more rapid conclusion, had it not been for the faithlessness of the Saxons. It is hard to say just how many times they were beaten and surrendered as suppliants to Charlemagne, promising to do all that was exacted from them, giving the hostages who were demanded, and this without delay, and receiving the ambassadors who were sent to them. Sometimes they were so cowed and reduced that they even promised to abandon their devil worship and submit willingly to the Christian faith; but, however ready they might seem from time to time to do all this, they were always prepared to break the promises they had made. I cannot really judge which of these two courses can be said to have come the more easily to the Saxons, for, since the very beginning of the war against them, hardly a year passed in which they did not vacillate between surrender and defiance.

However, the King's mettlesome spirit and his imperturbability, which remained as constant in adversity as in prosperity, were not to be quelled by their ever-changing tactics, or, indeed, to be wearied by a task which he had once undertaken. Not once did he allow anyone who had offended in this way to go unpunished. He took vengeance on them for their perfidy and meted out suitable punishment, either by means of an army which he led himself or by dispatching a force against them under the command of his counts. In the end, when all those who had been offering resistance had been utterly defeated and subjected to his power, he transported some ten thousand men, taken from among those who lived both on this side of the Elbe and across the river, and dispersed them in small groups, with their wives and children, in various parts of Gaul and Germany. At long last this war, which had dragged on for so many years, came to an end on conditions imposed by the King and accepted by the Saxons. These last were to give up their devil worship and the malpractices inherited from their forefathers; and then, once they had adopted the sacraments of the Christian faith, and religion, they were to be united with the Franks and become one people with them....

§9. At a time when this war against the Saxons was being waged constantly and with hardly an intermission at all, Charlemagne left garrisons at strategic points along the frontier and went off himself with the largest force he could muster to invade Spain. He marched over a pass across the Pyrenees, received the surrender of every single town and castle which he attacked and then came back with his army safe and sound, except for the fact that for a brief moment on the return journey, while he was in the Pyrenean mountain range itself, he was given a taste of Basque treachery. Dense forests, which stretch in all directions, make this a spot most suitable for setting ambushes. At a moment when Charlemagne's army was stretched out in a long column of march, as the nature of the local defiles forced it to me, these Basques, who had set their ambush on the very top of one of the mountains, came rushing down on the last part of the baggage train and the troops who were marching in support of the rearguard and so protecting the army which had gone on ahead. The Basques forced them down into the valley beneath, joined battle with them and killed them to the last man. They then snatched up the baggage, and, protected as they were by the cover of darkness, which was just beginning to fall, scattered in all directions without losing a moment. In this feat the Basques were helped by the lightness of their arms and by the nature of the terrain in which the battle was fought. On the other hand, the heavy nature of their own equipment and the unevenness of the ground completely hampered the Franks in their resistance to the Basques. In this battle died Eggihard, who was in charge of the King's table, Anshelm, the Count of the Palace and Roland, Lord of the Breton Marches, along with a great number of others. What is more, this assault could not be avenged there and then, for, once it was over, the enemy dispersed in such a way that no one knew where or among which people they could be found....

§11. Next there suddenly broke out a war in Bavaria, but this was very soon over. It was occasioned by the pride and folly of Duke Tassilo. He was encouraged by his wife, who was the daughter of King Desiderius and thought that through her husband she could revenge her father's exile, to make an alliance with the Huns, the neighbours of the Bavarians to the East. Not only did Tassilo refuse to carry out Charlemagne's orders, but he did his utmost to provoke the king to war. Tassilo's arrogance was too much for the spirited King of the Franks to stomach. Charlemagne summoned his levies from all sides and himself marched against Bavaria with a huge army, coming to the River Lech, which divides the Bavarians from the Germans. He pitched his camp on the bank of this river. Before he invaded the province he determined to discover the intentions of the Duke by sending messengers to him. Tassilo realized that nothing could be gained for himself or his people by his remaining stubborn. He went in person to beg Charlemagne's forgiveness, handed over the hostages who had been demanded, his own son Theodo among them, and, what is more, swore an oath that he would never again listen to anyone who might try to persuade him to revolt against the King's authority. In this way a war which had all the appearance of becoming very serious was in the event brought to a swift conclusion. Tassilo was summoned to the King's presence and was not allowed to go back home afterwards. The government of the province over which he had ruled was entrusted from that moment onwards not to a single duke but to a group of counts.

§12. No sooner were these troubled over than Charlemagne declared war on the Slaves, whom we are accustomed to call Siltzes, but whose real name, in their own language, is the Welatabi. In this conflict the Saxons fought as allies alongside certain other nations who followed Charlemagne's standards, although their loyalty was feigned and far from sincere. The cause of the war was that the Welatabi refused to obey Charlemagne's orders and kept harassing with never-ending invasions the Abodrites, who earlier on had been allied to the Franks....

§13. The war Which cam next was the most important which Charlemagne ever fought, except the one against the Saxons: I mean the struggle with the Avars or Huns. He waged it with more vigour than any of the others and with much greater preparation. He himself led only one expedition into Pannonia, the province which the Huns occupied at that period. Everything else he entrusted to his son Pepin, to the governors of his provinces and to his counts and legates. The war was prosecuted with great vigour by these men and it came to an end in its eighth year.

Just how many battles were fought and how much blood was shed is shown by the fact that Pannonia is now completely uninhabited and that the site of the Khan's palace is now so deserted that no evidence remains that anyone ever lived there. All the Hun nobility died in this war, all their glory departed. All their wealth and their treasures assembled over so many years were dispersed. The memory of man cannot recall any war against the Franks by which they were so enriched and their material possessions so increased. These Franks, who until then had seemed almost paupers, now discovered so much gold and silver in the palace and captured so much precious booty in their battles, that it could rightly be maintained that they had in all justice taken from the Huns what these last had unjustly stolen from other nations....

§14. The last war which Charlemagne undertook was against those Northmen who are called Danes. They first came as pirates and then they ravaged the coasts of Gaul and Germany with a large fleet. Their King Godefrid was so puffed up with empty ambition that he planned to make himself master of the whole of Germany. He had come to look upon Frisia and Saxony as provinces belonging to him; and he had already reduced the Abodrites, who were his neighbours, to a state of subservience and made them pay him tribute. Now he boasted that he would soon come with a huge army to Aachen itself, where the King had his court. There was no lack of people to believe his boasting, however empty it really was. He was really considered to be on the point of trying some such manoeuvre, and was only prevented from doing so by the fact that he died suddenly. He was killed by one of his own followers, so that his own life and the war which he had started both came to a sudden end.

From Einhard, *Two Lives of Charlamagne*, trans. Lewis Thorpe, pp. 61-68. Copyright © 1969 Penguin Books, Ltd. Reproduced by permission of Penguin Books Limited.

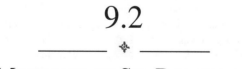

9.2

MISSIONS OF ST. BONIFACE

Boniface is the Latin name for Winfrith, who died in 754. He was born in Wessex, one of several Anglo-Saxon kingdoms in England, and was renowned for his missionary activities both in England and

*in Europe. His missions among the Hessians, Frisians, and Saxons of the continent pre-date
Charlemagne; they took place during the reign of Charlemagne's father Pepin, who was king of the
Franks from 751-768. The peoples that Boniface was trying to convert to Christianity were the same
tribes that Charlemagne spent most of his reign at war with. Later missionaries, who used the memory of
Boniface's career and martyrdom for inspiration, would follow the progress of Charlemagne's army into
Saxony and Frisia.*

QUESTIONS

1. The description of the pagan Germanic practices encountered by Boniface in 722 is nearly the
    same as descriptions from Roman writers of the first century. Why did these practices survive so
    long in the face of Christian missionary activity?
2. Boniface was not a Frank; do you think this gave him an advantage in his mission to the Frisians
    and Saxons, who were frequently at war with the Franks?
3. In the last scene, why do Boniface and his clergy refuse to fight back?

Many of the Hessians now were brought into the Catholic faith and received the sevenfold gift of the
Holy Spirit and the laying on of hands. Others, however, whose spirit was still too feeble, refused
to accept the unalloyed truths of the faith in their entirety. And there were also those who offered
clandestine sacrifice to trees and springs, and even those who did it openly. There were occult, and even
public, soothsayers who read the future in animals' entrails and in the flight of birds, and carried on all
kinds of divining and spellbinding and sacrificial rites.

But there were also pagans with more sense who abhorred all this heathen impiety and would have
nothing to do with it. With the advice of these latter he took a stand against all this by daring to cut down
an immense oak tree which the pagans, in their own ancient language, called the Oak of Thunor [Donar],
and which stood in a place called Geismar. While some of the brethren stood by, Boniface collected all
his courage — for a great mob of pagans stood there, cursing bitterly in their hearts against this enemy of
their gods — and cut into the tree. But though he had made only a small notch in the tree, suddenly its
whole mighty mass, shaken by a divine blast from on high, which splintered its topmost branches, came
crashing down and split asunder into four parts, as though by the avenging judgment of god. There for all
to see were four giant sections of the trunk, all of equal length, though none of the brethren had laid a
hand on it. At the sight of all this the pagans abruptly changed sides, left off their cursing of the moment
before, and began to believe in the Lord and to bless Him. Afterwards the holy bishop talked the matter
over with the brethren and decided to use the timber from this tree to build a wooden oratory which he
dedicated in honor of St. Peter the Apostle.

...By some mysterious presentiment he was able to foretell the approaching day of this death to
Bishop Lull and tell him even in what fashion death now at long last would come to him. He discussed
with him detailed plans for the building of churches and the teaching of the people. And he said to him:
"For I long to finish the journey which yet lies ahead of me. I am powerless to draw back from this
pilgrimage of my heart. Even now the day of my departure is at hand and the hour of my death draws
nearer. Shortly I shall escape from the prison of the body and return in freedom to claim my prize of
immortality. Yours is the destiny, my dearest son, of completing the building of these churches in
Thuringia which I have only begun. Yours is the most urgent task of leading this people out of the

wasteland of their blind wandering. And I ask you to finish that church at Fulda which I started to build, and bring my old body there, worn out with its many years." After a pause he added: "And now, my son, prepare carefully all those things which must be packed up for our use on our journey. And do not forget to put a linen cloth in my chest of books to wrap my poor old body in." […] But when the day grew light and the morning sunrise broke upon the world, it was a world turned upside down, for there advancing on them were not friends but enemies, not new Christian worshippers but new executioners. Brandishing spears and shields, a vast throng of the pagans burst into the camp. At once Boniface's escort rushed to arms on all sides and ran out against them. They stood poised to defend the saints — later martyrs — against this mindless mob of raging people, when the hero of God suddenly stepped out of his tent. At the first sound of the crowd's furious onslaught he had called the band of clergy to this side and had taken up the saints' relics which he always had with him. Now he immediately scolded his followers and forbade any fighting. "Do not fight them, lads. Lay down your weapons. What we are taught by the Gospel is true, and we must not give back evil for evil, but good for evil. This now is that very day we have long dreamed of. That moment of freedom we have yearned for is right here. So be heroic in the Lord and suffer this royal grace of his will gladly. Keep your trust in him and he will set your souls free."

Then he turned to the priests and deacons and other clerics standing beside him, God's sworn men all of them, and spoke to them like a father: "My hero brothers, be bold of heart. Have no terror of these slayers of the body, for they have no power to kill the soul, which lives forever. Take cheer in the Lord and fix the anchor of your hope in God, because in another instant he will give you your eternal reward and lead you to your rightful seat in the great hall of heaven among the fellowship of the angels noble beyond earthly measure. Do not surrender yourselves to the doomed love of this life. Snare not your heart with the base and hollow blandishments the heathen do. But submit courageously to this brief instant of death so that you may reign with Christ forever."

While he was lovingly urging his disciples on to the martyr's crown with these heartening words, suddenly the raging storm of pagans overwhelmed them with swords and every sort of weapon, and stained the bodies of the saints with the blood of a happy death.

Source: Clinton Albertson, S. J., *Anglo-Saxon Saints and Heroes* (New York: Fordham University Press, 1997), pp. 308-314.

9.3

✦

A CAROLINGIAN WOMAN: GUIBERT OF NOGENT'S *MEMOIRS*

Guibert was the abbot of Nogent from 1104-1121. His family were minor nobility (virtually a prerequisite for monastic promotion in the eleventh century) in France. His Memoirs recount not only his own story but also the story of his mother and her spiritual influence on him. The following account of his mother's conversion took place during the end of the Carolingian period.

Questions

1. Although Guibert and his mother are Christians, why do they both believe that his mother was cursed on her wedding day?
2. Does Guibert resent his mother for abandoning him in order to join a monastery?
3. Why does Guibert not give his mother's name?

CHAPTER 12

After these lengthy accounts I return to Thee, my God, to speak of the conversion of that good woman, my mother. When hardly of marriageable age, she was given to my father, a mere youth, by the provision of my grandfather, since she was of the nobility, had a very pretty face, and was naturally and most becomingly of sober mien. She had, however, conceived a fear of God's name at the very beginning of her childhood. she had learned to be terrified of sin, not from experience but from dread of some sort of blow from on high, and — as she often told me herself — this dread has so possessed her mind with the terror of sudden death that in later years she grieved because she no longer felt in maturity the same stings of righteous fear as she had in her unformed and ignorant youth.

Now, it so happened that at the very beginning of that lawful union conjugal intercourse was made ineffective through the bewitchments of certain persons. It was said that their marriage drew upon them the envy of a stepmother, who had some nieces of great beauty and nobility and who was plotting to slip one of them into my father's bed. Meeting with no success in her designs, she is said to have used magical arts to prevent entirely the consummation of the marriage. His wife's virginity thus remained intact for three years, during which he endured his great misfortune in silence; at last, driven to it by those close to him, my father was the first to reveal the facts. In all sorts of ways, his kinsmen endeavored to bring about a divorce, and by their constant pressure upon my father, who was then young and dull-witted, they tried to induce him to become a monk, although at that time there was little talk of this order. They did not do this for his soul's good, however, but with the purpose of getting possession of his property.

When their suggestion produced no effect, they began to hound the girl herself, far away as she was from her kinsfolk and harassed by the violence of strangers, into voluntary flight out of sheer exhaustion under their insults, and without waiting for divorce. She endured all this, bearing with calmness the abuse that was aimed at her, and if out of this rose any strife, she pretended ignorance of it. Besides this, certain rich men, perceiving that she was not in fact a wife, began to assail the heart of the young girl; but Thou, O Lord, the builder of inward chastity, didst inspire her with purity stronger than her nature or her youth. Thy grace it was that saved her from burning, though set in the midst of flames, Thy doing that her weak soul was not hurt by the poison of evil talk, and that when enticements from without were added to those impulses common to our human nature, like oil poured on the flames yet the young maiden's heart was always under her control and never won from her by any allurements. Are not such things solely Thy doing, O Lord? When she was in the heat of youth and continually engaged in wifely duties, yet for seven whole years Thou didst keep her is such contenence that, in the words of a certain wise man, even "rumour dare not speak lies about her."

O God, Thou knowest how hard, how almost impossible it would be for women of the present time to keep such chastity as this; whereas there was in those days such modesty that hardly ever was the good name of a married woman sullied by evil rumor. Ah! how wretchedly have modesty and honor in the state of virginity declined from that time to this our present age, and both the reality and the show of a married woman's protection fallen to ruin. Therefore coarse mirth is all that may be noted in their manners and naught but jesting heard, with sly winks and ceaseless chatter. Wantonness shows in their gait, only silliness in their behaviour. So much does the extravagance of their dress depart from the old simplicity that the enlargement of their sleeves, the tightness of their dresses, the distortion of their shoes of Cordovan leather with their curling toes, they seem to proclaim that everywhere modesty is a castaway. A lack of lovers to admire her is a woman's crown of woe, and on her crowds of thronging suitors rests her claim to nobility and courtly pride. There was a that time, I call God to witness, greater modesty in married men, who would have blushed to be seen in the company of such women, than there is now in brides. By such shameful conduct they turn men into greater braggarts and lovers of the market place and the public street.

What is the end of all this, Lord God, but that no one blushes for his own levity and licentiousness, because he knows that all are tarred with the same brush, and, seeing himself in the same case as all others, why the should he be ashamed of pursuits in which he knows all others engage? But why do I say "ashamed" when such men feel shame only if someone excels them as an example of lustfulness? A man's private boastfulness about the number of his loves or his choice of a beauty whom he has seduced is no reproach to him, nor is he scorned for vaunting his love affairs before Thee. Instead, his part in furthering the general corruption meets with the approval of all. Listen to the cheers when, with the inherent looseness of unbridled passions which deserve the doom of eternal silence, he shamelessly noises abroad what ought to have been hidden in shame, what should have burdened his soul with the guilt of ruined chastity and plunged him in the depths of despair. In this and similar ways, this modern age is corrupt and corrupting, distributing evil ideas to some, while the filth thereof, spreading to others, goes on increasing without end.

Holy God, scarcely any such thing was heard of in the time when Thy handmaid was behaving as she did; indeed, then shameful things were hidden under the cloak of sacred modesty and things of honor had their crown. In those seven years, O Lord, that virginity which Thou didst in wondrous fashion prolong in her was in agony under countless wrongs, as frequently they threatened to dissolve her marriage with my father and give her to another husband or to send her away to the remote houses of my distant relatives. Under such grievous treatment she suffered bitterly at times, but with Thy support, O God, she strove with wonderful self-control against the enticements of her own flesh and the inducements of others.

I do not say, gracious Lord, that she did this out of virtue, but that the virtue was Thine alone. For how could that be virtue that came of no conflict between body and spirit, no straining after God, but only from concern for outward honor and to avoid disgrace? No doubt a sense of shame has its use, if only to resist the approach of sin, but what is useful before a sin is committed is damnable afterward. What prostrates the self with the shame of propriety, holding it back from sinful deeds, is useful at the time, since the fear of God can bring aid, giving holy seasoning to shame's lack of savour, and can make that which was profitable at the time (that is, in the world) useful not for a moment but eternally. But after a sin is committed a sense of shame which leads to vanity is the more deadly the more it obstinately resists the healing of holy confession. The desire of my mother, Thy servant, O Lord God, was to do nothing to hurt her worldly honor, yet following Thy Gregory, whom, however, she had never read or heard read, she did not maintain that desire, for afterward she surrendered all her desires into Thy sole keeping, It was therefore good for her at that time to be attached to her worldly reputation.

Since the bewitchment by which the bond of natural and lawful intercourse was broken lasted seven years and more, it is all too easy to believe that, just as by prestidigitation the faculty of sight may be deceived so that conjurers seem to produce something out of nothing, so to speak, and to make certain things out of others, so reproductive power and effort may be inhibited by much less art; and indeed it is now a common practice, understood even by ignorant people. When that bewitchment was broken by a certain old woman, my mother submitted to the duties of a wife as faithfully as she had kept her virginity when she was assailed by so many attacks. In other ways she was truly fortunate, but she laid herself open not so much to endless misery as to mourning when she, whose goodness was ever growing, gave birth to an evil son who (in my own person) grew worse and worse. Yet Thou knowest, Almighty One, with what purity and holiness in obedience to Thee she raised me, how greatly she provided me with the care of nurses in infancy and of masters and teachers in boyhood, with no lack even of fine clothes for my little body, so that I seemed to equal the sons of kings and counts in indulgence....

While staying there, she resolved to retire to the monastery of Fly. After my master had a little house built for her there near the church, she then came forth from the place where she was staying. She knew that I should be utterly an orphan with no one at all on whom to depend, for great as was my wealth of kinsfolk and connections, yet there was no one to give me the loving care a little child needs at such an age; though I did not lack for the necessities of food and clothing. I often suffered from the loss of that careful provision for the helplessness of tender years that only a woman can provide. As I said, although she knew that I would be condemned to such neglect, yet Thy love and fear, O God, hardened her heart. Still, when on the way to that monastery she passed below the stronghold where I remained, the sight of the castle gave intolerable anguish to her lacerated heart, stung with the bitter remembrance of what she had left behind. No wonder indeed if her limbs seemed to be torn from her body, since she knew for certain that she was a cruel and unnatural mother. Indeed, she heard this said aloud, as she had in this way cut off her heart and left bereft of succor such a fine child, made worthy, it was asserted, by so much affection, since I was held in high regard not only by our own family but by outsiders. And Thou, good and gracious God, didst by Thy sweetness and love marvelously harden her heart, the tenderest in all the world, that it might not be tender to her own soul's harm. For tenderness would then have been her ruin, if she, neglecting her God, in her worldly care for me had put me before he own salvation. But "her love was strong as death," for the closer her love for Thee, the greater her composure in breaking from those she loved before.

Coming to the cloister, she found an old woman in the habit of a nun whom she compelled to live with her, declaring that she would submit to her discipline, as she gave the appearance of great piety. "Compelled," I say, because once she had tested the woman's character, she exerted all her powers of persuasion to get her companionship. And so she began gradually to copy the severity of the older woman, to imitate her meager diet, to choose the plainest food, to give up the soft mattress to which she had been accustomed, to sleep in contentment with only straw and a sheet. And since she still had much beauty and showed no sign of age, she purposely strove to assume the appearance of age with an old woman's wrinkles and bowed form. Her long flowing locks, which usually serve as a woman's crowning beauty, were frequently cut short with the scissors; her dress was black and unpleasant-looking, its unfashionable width adorned with countless patches; her cloak was undyed and her shoes were pierced with many a hole past mending, for there was within her One whom she tried to please with such mean apparel.

Since she had learned the beginning of good deeds from the confession of her old sins, she repeated her confessions almost daily. Consequently, her mind was forever occupied in searching out her past deeds, what she had thought or done or said as a maiden of tender years, or in her married life, or as a widow with a wider range of activities, continually examining the seat of reason and bringing what she found to the knowledge of a priest or rather to God through him. Then you might have seen the woman praying with such sharp sighs, pining away with such anguish of spirit that as she worshiped, there was scarcely ever a pause in the heart-rending sobs that went with her entreaties. She had learned the seven penitential psalms from the old woman I mentioned before, not by sight but by ear, and day and night she turned them over in her mind, chewing them with such savour, one might say, that the sighs and groans of those sweet angel songs never ceased to echo in Thy ears, O Lord. But whenever assemblies of people from outside disturbed her beloved solitude — for all who were acquainted with her, especially men and women of noble rank, took pleasure in conversing with her because of her wondrous wit and forbearance — on their departure, every untrue, idle, or thoughtless word she had uttered during their talk begat in her soul indescribable anguish until she reached the familiar waters of penitence or confession.

Reprinted from *Readings in Medieval History, third edition*, edited by Patrick J. Geary, Ontario: Broadview Press, 2003, pp. 369-371, 374-375. Reprinted by permission of Broadview Press.

9.4

VIKING INVASIONS

The invasions of the Vikings, or Northmen, in the ninth and tenth centuries represent the last wave of Germanic invasions, completing the process of the Germanization of Europe begun in the first century AD. These latest invaders (Danes, Swedes, and the Norse) were still pagan when they began migrating southward. Their invasions also came in many forms: violent military excursions, trade expeditions, and simple migrations of communities. By 1000 the invasions had ended, leaving Viking communities and states scattered across Europe. The most influential Viking settlements were in Greenland, Ireland, England, Francia, and Russia; an effort to establish a Viking colony in the Americas by Leif Erikson (an Icelander) in c. 1000 famously failed. Gradually, the Vikings settled into their new lands, converting to Christianity and adopting Carolingian and Anglo-Saxon titles and customs.

The following chronicle account is of the Viking invasions of Francia, the homeland of the Carolingians.

QUESTIONS

1. Compare the Viking invasions of the tenth century with the last war fought by Charlemagne against an earlier Viking invasion.
2. Why did the Vikings so frequently target Christian churches?
3. When the Vikings accept the offer of money in 885 to prevent the plunder of Paris, what does this say about the motives of these invaders?

(b) THE SIEGE OF PARIS

885. The Northmen came to Paris with 700 sailing ships, not counting those of smaller size which are commonly called barques. At one stretch the Seine was lined with the vessels for more than two leagues, so that one might ask in astonishment in what cavern the river had been swallowed up, since it was not to be seen. The second day after the fleet of the Northmen arrived under the walls of the city, Siegfred, who was then king only in name but who was in command of the expedition, came to the dwelling of the illustrious bishop. He bowed his head and said: "Gauzelin, have compassion on yourself and on your flock. We beseech you to listen to us, in order that you may escape death. Allow us only the freedom of the city. We will do no harm and we will see to it that whatever belongs either to you or to Odo shall be strictly respected." Count Odo, who later became king, was then the defender of the city. The bishop replied to Siegfred, "Paris has been entrusted to us by the Emperor Charles, who, after God, king and lord of the powerful, rules over almost all the world. He has put it on our care, not at all that the kingdom may be ruined by our misconduct, but that he may keep it and be assured of its peace. If, like us, you had been given the duty of defending these walls, and if you should have done that which you ask us to do, what treatment do you think you would deserve?" Siegfred replied: "I should deserve that my head be cut off and thrown to the dogs. Nevertheless, if you do not listen to my demand, on the morrow our war machines will destroy you with poisoned arrows. You will be the prey of famine and of pestilence and these evils will renew themselves perpetually every year." So saying, he departed and gathered his comrades.

In the morning the Northmen, boarding their ships, approached the tower and attacked it. They shook it with their engines and stormed it with arrows. The city resounded with clamor, the people were aroused, the bridges trembled. All came together to defend the tower. There Odo, his brother Robert, and the Count Ragenar distinguished themselves for bravery; likewise the courageous Abbot Ebolus, the nephew of the bishop. A keen arrow wounded the prelate, while at his side the young warrior Frederick was struck by a sword. Frederick died, but the old man, thanks to God, survived. There perished many Franks; after receiving wounds they were lavish of life. At last the enemy withdrew, carrying off their dead. The evening came. The tower had been sorely tried, but its foundations were still solid, as were also the narrow *baies* which surmounted them. The people spent the night repairing it with boards. By the next day, on the old citadel had been erected a new tower of wood, a half higher than the former one. At sunrise the Danes caught their first glimpse of it. Once more the latter engaged with the Christians in violent combat. On every side arrows sped and blood flowed. With the arrows mingled the stones hurled by slings and war-machines; the air was filled with them. The tower which had been built during the night groaned under the strokes of the darts, the city shook with the struggle, the people ran hither and thither, the bells jangled. The warriors rushed together to defend the tottering tower and to repel the fierce assault. Among these warriors two, a count and an abbot [Ebolus], surpassed all the rest in courage. The former was the redoubtable Odo who never experienced defeat and who continually revived the spirits of the worn-out defenders. He ran along the ramparts and hurled back the enemy. On those who were secreting themselves so as to undermine the tower he poured oil, was, and pitch, which, being mixed and heated, burned the Danes and tore off their scalps. Some of them died; others threw themselves into the river to escape the awful substance....

Meanwhile Paris was suffering not only from the sword outside but also from a pestilence within which brought death to many noble men. Within the walls there was not ground in which to bury the dead....Odo, the future king, was sent to Charles, emperor of the Franks, to implore help for the stricken city.

One day Odo suddenly appeared in splendor in the midst of three bands of warriors. The sun made his armor glisten and greeted him before it illuminated the country around. The Parisians saw their beloved chief at a distance, but the enemy, hoping to prevent his gaining entrance to the tower, crossed the Seine and took up their position on the bank. Nevertheless Odo, his horse at a gallop, got past the Northmen and reached the tower, whose gates Ebolus opened to him. The enemy pursued fiercely the comrades of the count who were trying to keep up with him and get refuge in the tower. [The Danes were defeated in the attack.]

Now came the Emperor Charles, surrounded by soldiers of all nations, even as the sky is adorned with resplendent stars. A great throng, speaking many languages, accompanied him. He established his camp at the foot of the heights of Montmartre, near the tower. He allowed the Northmen to have the country of Sens to plunder; and in the spring he gave them 700 pounds of silver on condition that by the month of March they leave France for their own kingdom. Then Charles returned, destined to an early death.

(c) THE BAPTISM OF ROLLO AND THE ESTABLISHMENT OF THE NORMANS IN FRANCE

The king had at first wished to give to Rollo the province of Flanders, but the Norman rejected it as being too marshy. Rollo refused to kiss the foot of Charles when he received from him the duchy of Normandy. "He who receives such a gift," said the bishops to him, "ought to kiss the foot of the king." "Never," replied he, "will I bend the knee to any one, or kiss anybody's foot." Nevertheless, impelled by the entreaties of the Franks, he ordered one of his warriors to perform the act in his stead. This man seized the foot of the king and lifted it to his lips, kissing it without bending and so causing the king to tumble over backwards. At that there was a loud burst of laughter and a great commotion in the crowd of onlookers. King Charles, Robert, Duke of the Franks, the counts and magnates, and the bishops and abbots, bound themselves by the oath of the Catholic faith to Rollo, swearing by their lives and their bodies and by the honor of all the kingdom, that he might hold the land and transmit it to his heirs from generation to generation throughout all time to come. When these things had been satisfactorily performed, the king returned in good spirits into his dominion, and Rollo with Duke Robert set out for Rouen.

In the year of our Lord 912 Rollo was baptized in holy water in the name of the sacred Trinity by Franco, archbishop of Rouen. Duke Robert, who was his godfather, gave to him his name. Rollo devotedly honored God and the Holy Church with his gifts....The pagans, seeing that their chieftain had become a Christian, abandoned their idols, received the name of Christ, and with one accord desire to be baptized. Meanwhile the Norman duke made ready for a splendid wedding and married the daughter of the king [Gisela] according to Christian rites.

Rollo gave assurance of security to all those who wished to swell in his country. The land he divided among his followers, and, as it had been a long time unused, he improved it by the construction of new buildings. It was peopled by the Norman warriors and by immigrants from outside regions. The duke established for his subjects certain inviolable rights and laws, confirmed and published by the will of the leading men, and he compelled all his people to live peaceably together. He rebuilt the churches, which had been entirely ruined; he restored the temples, which had been destroyed by the ravages of the pagans;

he repaired and added to the walls and fortifications of the cities; he subdued the Britons who rebelled against him; and with the provisions obtained from them he supplied all the country that had been granted to him.

Source: Frederic Austin Ogg, ed., *A Sourcebook of Mediaeval History* (New York: American Book Company, 1907), pp. 165-173.

QUESTIONS FOR PART 9

1. The sources in this chapter cover three and a half centuries. Why was there so much warfare during this period?
2. Compare the spiritual impulses of Boniface and Guibert's mother; why did people choose to be missionaries or nuns, when these choices bring danger or pain?
3. What role did women play in the Carolingian world?

PART 10

THE HIGH MIDDLE AGES

The High Middle Ages, c. 1000-1300 AD, was a time of renewal and development in Western civilization. After several centuries in which cities and trade remained scarce, both re-emerged in the eleventh century, as the West stabilized. With the urbanization of Europe came new theories of spirituality, education, politics, and art. Much of what had begun in the early Middle Ages came to fruition, and even more than had been imagined. Catholicism had a complete hegemony on the West, and during this period the papacy (after a shaky start) reached the zenith of its power. New kingdoms and states were created, although dynastic feuds (both at the level of the aristocracy and of the monarchies) continued. These two developments will be explored in the next chapter.

In this chapter the religious and intellectual developments of the High Middle Ages are explored. At no other point in the Middle Ages could one say that Christian faith had such universal appeal as it did during these three centuries. The results of this communal commitment to Roman Catholicism resulted in the majesty of the Gothic cathedrals, the sublime beauty of polyphonic chant and liturgical music, the reform of established monastic houses and creation of new orders (such as the Franciscans and the Dominicans of the thirteenth century), and scholasticism, which attempted to explain faith and theology using classical philosophy as well as Christian faith and mysticism. The sources of this chapter highlight some of these cultural advancements.

10.1

+

RULE OF ST. FRANCIS OF ASSISI

The first Christian monks were men and women of the third century who chose to live as solitary hermits in the deserts of Egypt and Syria. They followed the scriptural injunction of Christ, who said: "Go, sell everything you have, and give to the poor, and you will have treasure in heaven; then come and follow me" (Mark 10:21). Shortly thereafter monasteries were founded, in which men or women lived in groups, dedicating their lives to prayer. Each monastic house had its own Rule, *or regulations to follow. The earliest monastic* Rule *in western Europe was that of St. Benedict in 529. Benedictine houses, which remained popular and powerful throughout the Middle Ages, emphasized isolation from the temporal world, daily prayer, farming or manuscript work, and meditation.*

In 1210 a revolutionary approach to monasticism was created with the Rule *of St. Francis. The Franciscans, or the Order of Friars Minor, were a mendicant order. They would not remove themselves from the world but instead wandered through the cities of western Europe preaching poverty and repentance.*

——————— ✦ ———————

QUESTIONS

1. Under what circumstances could the Franciscan brothers have money?
2. What authority does the papacy have over individual Franciscans?
3. How is this a peculiarly urban *Rule*?

VIII.

THE RULE OF ST. FRANCIS OF ASSISI

("Bullarium Romanum, editio Taurinensis," vol. iii. p. 394)

1 This is the rule and way of living of the minorite brothers: namely to observe the holy Gospel of our Lord Jesus Christ, living in obedience, without personal possessions, and in chastity. Brother Francis promises obedience and reverence to our lord pope Honorius, and to his successors who canonically enter upon their office, and to the Roman Church. And the other brothers shall be bound to obey brother Francis and his successors.

2. If any persons shall wish to adopt this form of living, and shall come to our brothers, they shall send them to their provincial ministers; to whom alone, and to no others, permission is given to receive brothers. But the ministers shall diligently examine them in the matter of the catholic faith and the ecclesiastical sacraments. And if they believe all these, and are willing to faithfully confess them and observe them steadfastly to the end; and if they have no wives, or if they have them and the wives have already entered a monastery, or if they shall have given them permission to do so — they themselves having already taken a vow of continence by the authority of the bishop of the diocese, and their wives being such age that no suspicion can arise in connection with them: — the ministers shall say unto them the world of the holy Gospel, to the effect that they shall go and sell all that they have and strive to give it to the poor. But if they shall not be able to do this, their good will is enough. And the brothers and their ministers shall be on their guard and not concern themselves for their temporal goods; so that they may freely do with those goods exactly as God inspires them. But if advice is required, the ministers shall have permission to send them to some God-fearing men by whose counsel they shall dispense their goods to the poor. Afterwards there shall be granted to them the garments of probation: namely two gowns without cowls and a belt, and hose and a cape down to the belt; unless to these same ministers something else may at some time seem to be preferable in the sight of God. But, when the year of probation is over, they shall be received into obedience; promising always to observe that manner of living, and this Rule. And, according to the mandate of the lord pope, they shall never be allowed to break these bonds. For according to the holy Gospel, no one putting his hand to the plough and looking back is fit for the kingdom of God. And those who have now promised obedience shall have one gown with a cowl, and another, if they wish it, without a cowl. And those who are compelled by necessity, may wear shoes. And all the brothers shall wear humble garments, with the benediction of God. And I warn

and exhort them lest they despise or judge men whom they shall see clad in soft garments and in colours, using delicate food and drink; but each one shall the rather judge and despise himself.

3. The clerical brothers shall perform the divine service according to the order of the holy roman Church; excepting the psalter, of which they may have extracts. But the lay brothers shall say twenty four Paternosters at matins, five at the service of praise, seven each at the first, third, sixth and ninth hour, twelve at vespers, seven at the completorium; and they shall pray for the dead. And they shall fast from the feast of All Saints to the Nativity of the Lord; but as to the holy season of Lent, which begins from the Epiphany of the Lord and continues forty days, which the Lord consecrated with his holy fast — those who fast during it shall be blessed of the Lord, and those who do not wish to fast shall not be bound to do so; but otherwise they shall fast until the Resurrection of the Lord. But at other times the brothers shall not be bound to fast save on the sixth day (Friday); but in time of manifest necessity the brothers shall not be bound to fast with their bodies. But I advise, warn and exhort my brothers in the Lord Jesus Christ, that, when they go into the world, they shall not quarrel, nor contend with words, nor judge others. But they shall be gentle, peaceable and modest, merciful and humble, honestly speaking with all, as is becoming. And they ought not to ride unless they are compelled by manifest necessity or by infirmity. Into whatever house they enter they shall first say: peace be to this house. And according to the holy Gospel it is lawful for them to eat of all the dishes which are placed before them.

4. I firmly command all the brothers by no means to receive coin or money, of themselves or through an intervening person. But for the needs of the sick and for clothing the other brothers, the ministers alone and the guardians shall provide through spiritual friends, as it may seem to them that necessity demands, according to time, place and cold temperature. This one thing being always regarded, that, as has been said, they receive neither coin nor money.

5. Those brothers to whom God has given the ability to labour, shall labour faithfully and devoutly; in such way that idleness, the enemy of the soul, being excluded, they may not extinguish the spirit of holy prayer and devotion; to which other temporal things should be subservient. As a reward, moreover, for their labour, they may receive for themselves and their brothers the necessities of life, but not coin or money; and this humbly, as becomes the servants of God and the followers of most holy poverty.

6. The brothers shall appropriate nothing to themselves, neither a house, nor a place, nor anything; but as pilgrims and strangers in this world, in poverty and humility serving God, they shall confidently go seeking for alms. Nor need they be ashamed, for the Lord made Himself poor for us in this world. This is that height of most lofty poverty, which has constituted you my most beloved brothers heirs and kings of the kingdom of Heaven, has made you poor in possessions, has exalted you in virtues. This be your portion, which leads on to the land of the living. Adhering to it absolutely, most beloved brothers, you will wish to have for ever in Heaven nothing else than the name of our Lord Jesus Christ. And wherever the brothers are and shall meet, they shall show themselves as of one household; and the one shall safely manifest to the other his necessity. For if a mother loves and nourishes her son in the flesh, how much more zealously should one love and nourish one's spiritual brother? And if any of them fall into sickness, the other brothers ought to serve him, as they would wish themselves to be served.

7. But if any of the brothers at the instigation of the enemy shall mortally sin: for those sins concerning which it has been ordained among the brothers that recourse must be had to the provincial ministers, the aforesaid brothers shall be bound to have recourse to them, as quickly as they can, without delay. But those ministers, if they are priests, shall with mercy enjoin penance upon them. But if they are not priests, they shall cause it to be enjoined upon them through others, priests of the order; according as it seems to them to be most expedient in the sight of God. And they ought to be on their guard lest they

grow angry and be disturbed on account of the sin of any one; for wrath and indignation impede love in themselves and in others.

8. All the brothers shall be bound always to have one of the brothers of that order as general minister and servant of the whole fraternity, and shall be firmly bound to obey him. When he dies, the election of a successor shall be made by the provincial ministers and guardians, in the chapter held at Pentecost; in which the provincial ministers are bound always to come together in whatever place shall be designated by the general minister. And this, once in three years; or at another greater or lesser interval, according as shall be ordained by the aforesaid minister. And if, at any time, it shall be apparent to the whole body of the provincial ministers and guardians that the aforesaid minister does not suffice for the service and common utility of the brothers: the aforesaid brothers to whom the right of election has been given shall be bound, in the name of God, to elect another as their guardian. But after the chapter held at Pentecost the ministers and the guardians can, if they wish it and it seems expedient for them, in that same year call together, once, their brothers, in their districts, to a chapter.

9. The brothers may not preach in the bishopric of any bishop if they have been forbidden to by him. And no one of the brothers shall dare to preach at all to the people, unless he have been examined and approved by the general minister of this fraternity, and the office of preacher have been conceded to him. I also exhort those same brothers that, in the preaching which they do, their expressions shall be chaste and chosen, to the utility and edification of the people; announcing to them vices and virtues, punishment and glory, with briefness of discourse; for the words were brief which the Lord spoke upon earth.

10. The brothers who are the ministers and servants of the other brothers shall visit and admonish their brothers and humbly and lovingly correct them; not teaching them anything which is against their soul and against our Rule. But the brothers who are subjected to them shall remember that, before God, they have discarded their own wills. Wherefore I firmly command them that they obey their ministers in all things which they have promised God to observe, and which are not contrary to their souls and to our Rule. And wherever there are brothers who know and recognize that they can not spiritually observe the Rule, they may and should have recourse to their ministers. But the ministers shall receive them lovingly and kindly, and shall exercise such familiarity towards them, that they may speak and act towards them as masters to their servants; for so it ought to be, that the ministers should be the servants of all the brothers. I warn and exhort, moreover, in Christ Jesus the Lord, that the brothers be on their guard against all pride, vain-glory, envy, avarice, care and anxiety for this world, detraction and murmuring. And they shall not take trouble to teach those ignorant of letters, but shall pay heed to this that they desire to have the spirit of God and its holy workings; that they pray always to God with a pure heart; that they have humility, patience, in persecution and infirmity; and that they love those who persecute, revile and attack us. For the Lord saith: "Love your enemies and pray for those that persecute you and speak evil against you; blessed are they that suffer persecution for righteousness' sake, for of such is the kingdom of Heaven; He that is steadfast unto the end shall be saved."

11. I firmly command all the brothers not to have suspicious intercourse or to take counsel with women. And, with the exception of those whom special permission has been given by the Apostolic Chair, let them not enter nunneries. Neither may they become fellow god-parents with men or women, lest from this cause a scandal may arise among the brothers or concerning the brothers.

12. Whoever of the brothers by divine inspiration may with to go among the Saracens and other infidels, shall seek permission to do so from their provincial ministers. But to none shall the ministers give permission to go, save to those whom they shall see to be fit for the mission.

Furthermore, through their obedience I enjoin on the ministers that they demand from the lord pope one of the cardinals of the holy roman Church, who shall be the governor, corrector and protector of that fraternity, so that, always subjected and lying at the feet of that same holy Church, steadfast in the catholic faith, we may observe poverty and humility, and the only Gospel of our Lord Jesus Christ; as we have firmly promised.

Source: Ernest Henderson, ed. *Select Historical Documents of the Middle Ages* (New York: AMS Press, 1968), pp. 344-349.

10.2

FOUNDATION OF THE UNIVERSITY OF HEIDELBERG, 1386

The first university was created at Bologna in 1158. Emperor Frederick Barbarossa granted it a charter, primarily for the study of law. Its popularity was so immediate that other towns and other nobles wanted to charter their own universities. Most, such as the University of Paris, grew out of a pre-existing cathedral school. Each university also had its own focus: Bologna had law; Paris, Oxford and Cambridge had theology; and Salerno had medicine.

At all medieval universities, charters were signed between the students and the town or nobleman on whose land the school was to be run, such as this one between Heidelberg and a German prince, Rupert I.

QUESTIONS

1. What authority does the Bishop of Worms have over the students (or clerks)?
2. What do these regulations imply about the relationship between students and townspeople?
3. Why do you think Rupert used the University of Paris as a model?

1 We, Rupert the elder, by the grace of God count palatine of the Rhine, elector of the Holy Empire, and duke of Bavaria, — lest we seem to abuse the privilege conceded to us by the apostolic see of founding a place of study at Heidelberg similar to that at Paris, and lest, for this reason, being subjected to the divine judgement, we should deserve to be deprived of the privilege granted — do decree, with provident counsel (hich decree is to be observed unto all time), that the University of Heidelberg shall be ruled, disposed, and regulated according to the modes and manners accustomed to be observed in the University of Paris. Also that, as a handmaid of Paris — a worthy one let us hope — the latter's steps shall be imitated in every way possible; so that, namely, there shall be four faculties in it: the first, of sacred theology and divinity; the second, of canon and civil law, which, by reason of their similarity, we think best to comprise under one faculty; the third, of medicine; the fourth, of liberal arts — of the three-fold philosophy, namely, primal, natural, and moral, three mutually subservient daughters. We wish this institution to be divided and marked out into four nations, as it is at Paris; and that all these faculties shall

make one university, and that to it the individual students, in whatever of the said faculties they are, shall unitedly belong like lawful sons to one mother.

Likewise [we desire] that this university shall be governed by one rector, and that the various masters and teachers, before they are admitted to the common pursuits of our institution, shall swear to observe the statutes, laws, privileges, liberties, and franchises of the same, and not reveal its secrets, to whatever grade they may rise. Also that they will uphold the honor of the rector and the rectorship of our university, and will obey the rector in all things lawful and honest, whatever be the grade to which they may afterwards happen to be promoted. Moreover, that the various masters and bachelors shall read their lectures and exercise their scholastic functions and go about in caps and gowns of a uniform and similar nature, according as has been observed at Paris up to this time in the different faculties.

And we will that if any faculty, nation, or person shall oppose the aforesaid regulations, or stubbornly refuse to obey them, or any one of them — which God forbid — from that time forward that same faculty, nation, or person, if it do not desist upon being warned, shall be deprived of all connection with our aforesaid institution, and shall not have the benefit of our defense or protection. Moreover, we will and ordain that as the university as a whole may do for those assembled here and subject to it, so each faculty, nation, or province of it may enact lawful statutes, such as are suitable to its needs, provided that through them, or any one of them, no prejudice is done to the above regulations and to our institution, and that no kind of impediment arise from them. And we will that when the separate bodies shall have passed the statutes for their own observance, they may make them perpetually binding on those subject to them and on their successors. And as in the University of Paris the various servants of the institution have the benefit of the various privileges which its masters and scholars enjoy, so in starting our institution in Heidelberg, we grant, with even greater liberality, through these presents, that all the servants, i.e., its pedells, librarians, lower officials, preparers of parchment, scribes, illuminators, and others who serve it, may each and all, without fraud, enjoy in it the same privileges, franchises, immunities and liberties with which its masters or scholars are now or shall hereafter be endowed.

2. Lest in the new community of the city of Heidelberg, their misdeeds being unpunished, there be an incentive to the scholars of doing wrong, we ordain, with provident counsel, by these presents, that the bishop of Worms, as judge ordinary of the clerks of our institution, shall have and possess, now and hereafter while our institution shall last, prisons, and an office in our town of Heidelberg for the detention of criminal clerks. These things we have seen fit to grant to him and his successors, adding these conditions: that he shall permit no clerk to be arrested unless for a misdemeanor; that he shall restore any one detained for such fault, or for any light offense, to his master, or to the rector if the latter asks for him, a promise having been given that the culprit will appear in court and that the rector or master will answer for him if the injured parties should go to law about the matter. Furthermore, that, on being requested, he will restore a clerk arrested for a crime on slight evidence, upon receiving a sufficient pledge — sponsors if the prisoner can obtain them, otherwise an oath if he cannot obtain sponsors — to the effect that he will answer in court the charges against him; and in all these things there shall be no pecuniary exactions, except that the clerk shall give satisfaction, reasonably and according to the rule of the aforementioned town, for the expenses which he incurred while in prison. And we desire that he will detain honestly and without serious injury a criminal clerk thus arrested for a crime where the suspicion is grave and strong, until the truth can be found out concerning the deed of which he is suspected. And he shall not for any cause, moreover, take away any clerk from our aforesaid town, or permit him to be taken away, unless the proper observances have been followed, and he has been condemned by judicial sentence to perpetual imprisonment for a crime.

We command our advocate and bailiff and their servants in our aforesaid town, under pain of losing their offices and our favor, not to lay a detaining hand on any master or scholar of our said institution, nor to arrest him or allow him to be arrested, unless the deed be such that that master or scholar ought rightly to be detained. He shall be restored to his rector or master, if he is held for a slight cause, provided he will swear and promise to appear in court concerning the matter; and we decree that a slight fault is one for which a layman, if he had committed it, ought to have been condemned to a light pecuniary fine. Like-wise, if the master or scholar detained be found gravely or strongly suspected of the crime, we command that he be handed over by our officials to the bishop or to his representative in our said town, to be kept in custody.

3. By the tenor of these presents we grant to each and all the masters and scholars that, when they come to the said institution, while they remain there, and also when they return from it to their homes, they may freely carry with them, both coming and going, throughout all the lands subject to us, all things which they need while pursuing their studies, and all the goods necessary for their support, without any duty, levy, imposts, tolls, excises, or other exactions whatever. And we wish them and each one of them, to be free from the aforesaid imposts when purchasing corn, wines meat, fish, clothes and all things necessary for their living and for their rank. And we decree that the scholars from their stock in hand of provision, if there remain over on or two wagon loads of wine without their having practised deception, may after the feast of Easter of that year, sell it at wholesale without paying impost. We grant to them, moreover, that each day the scholars, of themselves or through their servants, may be allowed to buy in the town of Heidelberg, at the accustomed hour, freely and without impediment or hurtful delay, any eatables or other necessaries of life.

4. Lest the masters and scholars of our institution of Heidelberg may be oppressed by the citizens, moved by avarice, through extortionate prices of lodgings, we have seen fit to decree that henceforth each year, after Christmas, one expert from the university on the part of the scholars, and one prudent, pious, and circumspect citizen on the part of the citizens, shall be authorized to determine the price of the students' lodgings. Moreover, we will and decree that the various masters and scholars shall, through our bailiff, our judge and the officials subject to us, be defended and maintained in the quiet possession of the lodgings given to them free or of those for which they pay rent. Moreover, by the tenor of these presents, we grant to the rector and the university, or to those designated by them, entire jurisdiction concerning the payment of rents for the lodgings occupied by the students, concerning the making and buying of books, and the borrowing of money for other purposes by the scholars of our institution; also concerning the payment of assessments, together with everything that arises from, depends upon, and is connected with these.

In addition, we command our officials that, when the rector requires our and their aid and assistance for carrying out his sentences against scholars who try to rebel, they shall assist our clients and servants in this matter; first, however, obtaining lawful permission to proceed against clerks from the lord bishop of Worms, or from one deputed by him for this purpose.

Source: Frederic Austin Ogg, ed., *A Sourcebook of Medieval History* (New York: American Book Company, 1907), pp. 345-350.

10.3

"ON THE ETERNALITY OF THE WORLD," ST. BONAVENTURA

Scholasticism was the pre-eminent medieval intellectual system, which attempted to unite faith and reason into one coherent system. It is also a manifestation of the classical legacy; scholastic theologians endeavored to use classical philosophy to prove, logically, the existence and nature of God. The reintroduction of Aristotelian texts in the twelfth century became a primary motivation of scholastic explorations. Aristotle's ideas became so popular he was referred to simply as the Philosopher in most scholastic works.

Bonaventura (c. 1217-1274) was a Franciscan theologian at the University of Paris who argues here for rational proof that God, the Eternal, created the known world.

QUESTIONS

1. How did the creation of universities, such as the previous charter, promote scholasticism?
2. How does Bonaventura use "time" as evidence of creation?
3. Why did the scholastics feel it necessary to prove God using reason and logical philosophy?

ST. BONAVENTURA

(In *II Sent.* d.1, a.1, q.2)

The question is: Has the world been produced in time or from eternity. That it has not been produced in time is shown:

1. By the arguments based on motion, the first of which is demonstrative in the following way: *Before every motion and change, there is the motion of the first moveable thing (primum mobile)*; but everything which begins to be begins by way of motion or change; therefore that motion (viz., of the first moveable thing) is before all that which begins to be. But that motion could not have preceded itself or its movable thing (*mobile*); therefore it could not possibly have a beginning. The first proposition is a basic one and its proof is as follows: It is a basic principle in philosophy that "in every kind the complete is prior to the incomplete of that kind"; but movement toward place is the more perfect among all the kinds of motion inasmuch as it is the motion of a complete being, and circular motion is both the swifter and the more perfect among all the kinds of local motion; but the motion of the heaven is of this kind, therefore most perfect, therefore the first. Therefore it is evident that, etc.

2.   This is likewise shown by an absurdity consequent upon the alternative. *Everything which comes to be comes to be through motion or change*; consequently, if motion comes to be it comes to be through motion or change, and with regard to this latter motion the question is similarly raised. Therefore, either there is to be an infinite regress or a positing of some motion lacking a beginning; if the motion, then also the moveable thing and, consequently, also the world.

3.   Similarly, a demonstrative argument based on time as follows: *Everything which begins to be either begins to be in an instant or in time*. If, therefore, the world begins to be, it does so either in an instant or in time. But before every time there is time, and time is before every instant. Consequently there is time before all those things which have begun to be. But it could not have been before the world and motion; therefore the world has not had a beginning. The first proposition is *per se* known. The second, namely that before every time there is time, is evident from the fact that if it is flowing, it was of necessity flowing beforehand. Similarly, it is evident that there is time before every instant since time is a circular measure suited to the motion and the movable thing; but every point in a circle is a beginning even as it is an end; therefore every instant of time is a beginning of the future even as it is a terminus of the past. Accordingly, before every "now" there has been a past. It is evident, therefore, etc.

4.   Again, this is shown by the absurdity consequent upon the alternative. If time is produced, it is produced either in time or in an instant; therefore in time. But in every time there is a prior and a posterior, both a past and a future. Consequently, if time has been produced in time, there has been time before every time, and this is impossible. Therefore, etc.

These are Aristotle's arguments based on the character of the world itself.

5.   Besides, these, there are other arguments based on the character of the producing cause. In general, there can be reduced to two, the first of which is demonstrative and the second based on the absurdity consequent upon the alternative. The first is as follows: *Given an adequate and actual cause, the effect is given*; but God from eternity has been the adequate and actual cause of this world; therefore, etc. The major premise is *per se* known. The minor, namely that God is the adequate cause, is evident. Since He needs nothing extrinsic for the creating of the world, but only the power, wisdom and goodness which have been most perfect in God from eternity, evidently He has, from eternity, been the adequate cause. That He has also been the actual cause is evident as follows: God is pure act and is His own act of willing, as Aristotle says; and our philosophers (*Sancti*) say that He is His own acting. It follows, therefore, etc.

6.   Also, by the absurdity of the alternative. *Everything which begins to act or produce, when it was not producing beforehand, passes from rest into act*. If, therefore, God begins to produce the world, He passes from rest into act; but all such things are subject to rest and change or mutability. Therefore God is subject to rest and mutability. This, however, contradicts His absolute goodness and absolute simplicity, and, consequently, is impossible. It is to blaspheme God; and to say that the world has had a beginning amounts to the same thing.

These are the arguments which the commentators and more recent men (*moderniores*) have added over and beyond the arguments of Aristotle; or, at least, they are reducible to these.

But there are arguments to the contrary, based on *per se* known propositions of reason and philosophy.

1.   The first of these is: It is impossible to add to the infinite. This is *per se* evident because everything which receives an addition becomes more; "but nothing is more infinite." If the world lacks a beginning, however, it has had an infinite duration, and consequently there can be no addition to its duration. But this is certainly false because every day a revolution is added to a revolution; therefore, etc. If you were to say that it is infinite in past time and yet is actually finite with respect to the present, which now is, and, accordingly, that it is in this respect, in which it is finite, that the "more" is to be found, it is pointed out to you that, to the contrary, it is in the past that the "more" is to be found. This is an infallible truth: If the world is eternal, then the revolutions of the sun in its orbit are infinite in number. Again, there have necessarily been twelve revolutions of the moon for every one of the sun. Therefore the moon has revolved more times than the sun, and the sun an infinite number of times. Accordingly, that which exceeds the infinite as infinite is discovered. But this is impossible; therefore, etc.

2.   The second proposition is: *It is impossible for the infinite in number to be ordered.* For every order flows from a principle toward a mean. Therefore, if there is no first, there is no order; but if the duration of the world or the revolutions of the heaven are infinite, they do not have a first; therefore they do not have an order, and one is not before another. But since this is false, it follows that they have a first. If you say that it is necessary to posit a limit (*statum*) to an ordered series only in the case of things ordered in a causal relation, because among causes there is necessarily a limit, I ask why not in other cases. Moreover, you do not escape in this way. For there has never been a revolution of the heaven without there being a generation of animal from animal. But an animal is certainly related causally to the animal from which it is generated. If, therefore, according to Aristotle and reason it is necessary to posit a limit among those things ordered in a causal relation, then in the generation of animals it is necessary to posit a first animal. And the world has not existed without animals; therefore, etc.

3.   The third proposition is: *It is impossible to traverse what is infinite.* But if the world had no beginning, there has been an infinite number of revolutions; therefore it was impossible fore it to have traversed them; therefore impossible for it to have come down to the present. If you say that they (i.e., numerically infinite revolutions) have not been traversed because there has been no first one, or that they well could be traversed in an infinite time, you do not escape in this way. For I shall ask you if any revolution has infinitely preceded today's revolution or none. If none, then all are finitely distant from this present one. Consequently, they are all together finite in number and so have a beginning. If some one is infinitely distant, then I ask whether the revolution immediately following it is infinitely distant. If not, then neither is the former (infinitely) distant since there is a finite distance between the two of them. But if it (i.e. the one immediately following) is infinitely distant, then I ask in a similar way about the third, the fourth, and so on to infinity. Therefore, one is not more distant than another from this present one, one is not before anothers, and so they are all simultaneous.

4.   The fourth proposition is: *It is impossible fore the infinite to be grasped by a finite power.* But if the world had no beginning, then the infinite is grasped by a finite power; therefore, etc. The proof

of the major is *per se* evident. The minor is shown as follows. I suppose that God alone is with a power actually infinite and that all other things have limitation. Also I suppose that there has never been a motion of the heaven without there being a created spiritual substance who would either cause or, at least, know it. Further, I also suppose that a spiritual substance forgets nothing. If, therefore, there has been no revolution of the heaven which he would not know and which would have been forgotten. Therefore, he is actually knowing all of them and they have been infinite in number. Accordingly, a spiritual substance with finite power is grasping simultaneously an infinite number of things. If you assert that this is not unsuitable because all the revolutions, being of the same species and in every way alike, are known by a single likeness, there is the objection that not only would he have known the rotations, but also their effects as well, and these various and diverse effects are infinite in number. It is clear, therefore, etc.

5. The fifth proposition is: *It is impossible that there be simultaneously an infinite number of things*. But if the world is eternal and without a beginning, then there has been an infinite number of men, since it would not be without there being men — for all things are in a certain way for the sake of man and a man lasts only for a limited length of time. But there have been as many rational souls as there have been men, and so an infinite number of souls. But, since they are incorruptible forms, there are as many souls as there have been; therefore an infinite number of souls exist. If this leads you to say that there has been a transmigration of souls or that there is but the one soul for all men, the first is an error in philosophy, because, as Aristotle holds, "appropriate act is in its own matter." Therefore, the soul, having been the perfection of one, cannot be the perfection of another, even according to Aristotle. The second position is even more erroneous, since much less is it true that there is but the one soul for all.

6. The last argument to this effect is: *It is impossible for that which has being after non-being to have eternal being*, because this implies a contradiction. But the world has being after nonbeing. Therefore it is impossible that it be eternal. That it has being after non-being is proven as follows: everything whose having of being is totally from another is produced by the latter out of nothing; but the world has its being totally from God; therefore the world is out of nothing. But not out of nothing as a matter (*materialiter*); therefore out of nothing as an origin (*originaliter*). It is evident that everything which is totally produced by something differing in essence has being out of nothing. For what is totally produced is produced in its matter and form. But matter does not have that out of which it would be produced because it is not out of God (*ex Deo*). Clearly, then, it is out of nothing. The minor, viz., that the world is totally produced by God, is evident from the discussion of another question.

Conclusion

Whether positing that all things have been produced out of nothing would imply saying that the world is eternal or has been produced eternally.

I answer: It has to be said that to maintain that the world is eternal or eternally produced by claiming that all things have been produced by claiming that all things have been produced out of nothing is entirely against truth and reason, as the last of the above arguments proves; and it is so against reason that I do not believe that any philosopher, however slight his understanding, has maintained this.

For such a position involves an evident contradiction. But, with the eternity of matter presupposed, to maintain an eternal world seems reasonable and understandable, and this by way of two analogies which can be drawn. For the procession of earthly things from God is after the fashion of an imprint (*vestigium*). Accordingly, if a foot and the dust in which its print were formed were eternal, nothing would prevent our understanding that the footprint is co-eternal with the foot and, nevertheless, it still would be an imprint from the foot. If matter, or the potential principle, were in this fashion coeternal with the maker, what would keep that imprint from being eternal? Rather, on the contrary, it would seem quite fitting that it should be.

Again, another reasonable analogy offers itself. For, from God the creature proceeds as a shadow, the Son as brightness. But as soon as there is light, there is immediately brightness, and immediately shadow if there should be an opaque object in its way. If, therefore, matter, as opaque, is coeternal with the maker, just as it is reasonable to posit the Son, the brightness of the Father, to be coeternal, so it seems reasonable that creatures or the world, shadow in relation to the Highest Light, is eternal. Moreover, this view is more reasonable than its contrary, viz., that matter has been eternally incomplete, without form or the divine influence, as certain philosophers have maintained. In fact, it is more reasonable to such an extent that even that outstanding philosopher, Aristotle, has fallen into this error, according to the charges of our philosophers (*Sancti*), the exposition of the commentators, and the apparent meaning of his text.

On the other hand, modern scholars say that the Philosopher has never thought this nor did he intend to prove that the world had no beginning *in any way at all*, but rather that it did not begin *by way of natural motion*.

Which of these interpretations is the truer one I do not know. This one thing I do know, that if he held that the world has not begun *according to nature*, he maintained what is true, and his arguments based on motion and time are conclusive. But if he thought that it has *in no way begun*, he has clearly erred, as has been shown above by many arguments. Moreover, in order to avoid self-contradiction, he had to maintain either that the world has not been made, or that it has not been made out of nothing. In order to avoid an actual infinity, however, he had to hold for either the corruption of the rational soul, or its unicity, or its transmigration; thus, in any case, had had to destroy its beatitude. So it is that this error has both a bad beginning and the worst of endings.

Reprinted from *Readings in Medieval History, third edition*, edited by Patrick J. Geary, Ontario: Broadview Press, 2003, pp. 493-497. Reprinted by permission of Broadview Press.

10.4

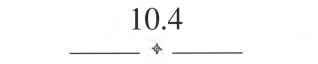

"ON GOD'S KNOWLEDGE," AVERROËS

Not all of the scholastic philosophers of the High Middle Ages were Christian. In fact, Aristotelian philosophy had been lost to the Christian West from the sixth century onward, as the ability to read Greek was lost. Aristotle and other Greek texts had been preserved, largely through Arabic and Syrian translations, by Muslim scholars throughout the Islamic world. Ibn Rushd (1126-1198) was one of the most exceptional minds of the High Middle Ages. He excelled at medicine, pure philosophy, law, and of course theology, which in both Muslim and Christian worlds was considered to be the highest field of study. In the end, Muslim intellectual conservatism turned against philosophy and Ibn Rushd's works were lost, but they were translated into Latin and studied for centuries, in the West. Particularly important were his commentaries on Aristotle. The Latinized version of his name is Averroës.

QUESTIONS

1. Compare the Averroës selection with the previous one by Bonaventura. Do their definitions of God differ substantially?
2. How is human knowledge different from God's knowledge?
3. Because of its association with the universities, Christian scholasticism was very much an urban philosophy; can we say the same of Averroës?

The difficulty is compelling, as follows. If all these things were in the Knowledge of God the Glorious before they existed, are they in their state of existence [the same] in His Knowledge as they were before their existence, or are they in their state of existence other in His Knowledge than they were before they existed? If we say that in their state of existence they are other in God's knowledge than they were before they existed, it follows that the eternal Knowledge is subject to change, and that when they pass from nonexistence to existence, there comes into existence additional Knowledge: but that is impossible for the eternal Knowledge. If on the other hand we say that the Knowledge of them in both states is one and the same it will be asked, 'Are they in themselves', i.e. the beings which come into existence, 'the same before they exist as when they exist?' The answer will have to be 'No, in themselves they are not the same before they exist as when they exist'; otherwise the existent and the non-existent would be one and the same. If the adversary admits this, he can be asked, 'Is not true Knowledge acquaintance with existence as it really is?' If he says 'Yes', it will be said, 'Consequently if the object varies in itself, the knowledge of it must vary; otherwise it will not be known as it really is'. Thus one of two alternatives is necessary: either the eternal Knowledge varies in Itself, or the things that come into existence are not know to It. But both alternatives are impossible for God the Glorius.

This difficulty is confirmed by what appears in the case of man: His knowledge of non-existent things depends on the supposition of existence, while his knowledge of them when they exist depends [on existence itself]. For it is self-evident that the two states of knowledge are different; otherwise he would be ignorant of things' existence at the time when they exist....

It is impossible to escape from this [difficulty] by the usual answer of the theologians about it, that God the Exalted knows things before their existence as they will be at the time of their existence, in respect of time, place and other attributes proper to each being. For it can be said to them: 'Then when they come to exist, does there occur any change or not?' — with reference to the passage of the thing from non-existence to existence. If they say "No change occurs', they are merely being supercilious. But if they say 'There does occur a change', it can be said to them: 'Then is the occurrence of this change known to the eternal Knowledge or not?' Thus the difficulty is compelling. In sum, it can hardly be conceived that the knowledge of a thing before it exists can be identical with the knowledge of it after it exists. Such, then, is the formulation of this problem in its strongest possible form, as we have explained it to you in conversation....

The way to resolve this difficulty, in our opinion, is to recognize that the position of the eternal Knowledge with respect to beings is different from the position of originated knowledge with respect to beings, in that the existence of beings is a cause and reason for our knowledge, while the eternal Knowledge is a cause and reason for beings. If, when beings come to exist after not having existed, there occurred an addition in the eternal Knowledge such as occurs in originated knowledge, it would follow that the eternal Knowledge would be an effect of beings, not their cause. Therefore there must not occur any change such as occurs in originated knowledge. The mistake in this matter has arisen simply from making an analogy between the eternal Knowledge and originated knowledge, i.e. between the suprasensible and the sensible; and the falsity of this analogy is well known. Just as no change occurs in an agent when his act comes into being, i.e. no change which has not already occurred, so no change occurs in the eternal Glorious Knowledge edge when the object of Its Knowledge results from It.

Thus the difficulty is resolved, and we do not have to admit that if there occurs no change, i.e. in the eternal Knowledge, He does not know beings at the time of their coming into existence just as they are; we only have to admit that He does not know them with originated knowledge but with eternal Knowledge. For the occurrence of change in knowledge when beings change is a condition only of knowledge which is caused by beings, i.e. originated knowledge....

Therefore eternal Knowledge is only connected with beings in a manner other than that in which originated knowledge is connected with them. This does not mean that It is not connected at all, as the philosophers have been accused of saying, in the context of this difficulty, that the Glorious One does not know particulars. Their position is not what has been imputed to them; rather they hold that He does not know particulars with originated knowledge, the occurrence of which is conditioned by their occurrence, since He is a cause of them, not caused by them as originated knowledge is. This is the furthest extent to which purification [of concepts] ought to be admitted.

For demonstration compels the conclusion that He knows things, because their issuing from Him is solely due to His knowing; it is not due to His being merely Existent or Existent with a certain attribute, but to His knowing, as the Exalted has said: 'Does He not know, He who created? He is the Penetrating, the Omniscient!' But demonstration also compels the conclusion that He does not know things with a knowledge of the same character as originated knowledge. Therefore there must be another knowledge of beings which is unqualified, the eternal Glorious Knowledge. And how is it conceivable that the Peripatetic philosophers could have held that the eternal Knowledge does not comprehend particulars, when they held that It is the cause of warning in dreams, of revelation, and of other kinds of inspiration?

[Conclusion]

This is the way to resolve this difficulty, as it appears to us; and what has been said is incontestable and indubitable. It is God who helps us to follow the right course and directs us to the truth. Peace on you, with the mercy and blessing of God.

SELECTION II

[Aristotle] means: Because of its not intellecting anything outside its own essence (since it is simple), its intellection of its own essence is something which can be subject to no mutation through all eternity; nor can there by any doubt regarding the fact that it is not subject therein to any weariness such as is the case in our intellection. The situation must be the same in the case of the rest of the separated intellects, save that the First is the simplest of them and for this reason is the One absolutely, since there is no multiplicity whatsoever in it, either through the intellect's being other than the intelligible or through the multiplicity of the intelligibles. For the multiplicity of intelligibles in one and the same intellect (as is the situation with our intellection) is something that is consequent on the otherness which exists in it, *acil.*, between the act of intellection and the intelligible. For when the intellect and the intelligible are united in a perfect union it follows that the many intelligibles which belong to that intellect and that intellect [itself] are united so as to become on thing, simple in all respects; but when the intelligibles that are actual in the single intellect remain many they are not united with its essence and its essence, then, is other than them.

This is what escaped Themistius where he holds that it is possible for the intellect to understand many intelligibles simultaneously. This contradicts our statement that it understands its own essence and understands nothing extrinsic to it and that the intellect and what it understands are one in all respects. He says that it understands all things by virtue of its understanding that it is a principle of theirs. All of this exemplifies the speech of one who does not grasp Aristotle's proofs here. Indeed, a disgraceful conclusion may follow, viz., that God is ignorant of what is here. Because of this, some people have said that he knows what is here through a universal knowledge, not through a particular knowledge. The truth is that since he knows his own essence alone he knows existent beings in that existence which is the cause of their [individual] existences. For example, one does not say of him who knows the heat of fire alone that he has no knowledge of the heat that is present in hot things but on the contrary it is he who knows the nature of heat *qua* heat. Thus it is the First (Be He Praised) who knows the nature of the existent *qua* existent absolutely which [existent] is his essence.

QUESTIONS FOR PART 10

1. Why did universities not appear before this part of the Middle Ages?
2. Scholastic Christians were reading writers such as Averroës at the same time as the crusades; how do we reconcile the contradiction two cultures sharing central theological ideas while they are also at war with one another?
3. Compare the *Rule* of St. Francis with the texts of Bonaventura and Averroës; is the Franciscan order anti-intellectual?

PART 11

❧

EUROPEAN KINGDOMS OF THE MIDDLE AGES

The previous chapter explored the intellectual and spiritual developments of the High Middle Ages; this chapter explores the economic and political developments of the same period. One of the defining trends in these two fields was that of centralization; kings and popes alike were both seeking to consolidate their authority over land and subjects. Yet at the same time the newly emerging cities were also trying to protect their independence from the control of the new states. Individual elements within medieval society were more aware than ever of their personal liberties, and of the potential for states to infringe upon them. Furthermore, as kings and popes grew more powerful individually, they inevitably came into conflict with one another. Each after all was trying to rule over the same populaces. The documents of this section include regulations from the merchants of Southampton who wanted to protect their freedom of trade, two documents reflecting royal subjects trying to protect their rights against those of their kings, and finally, a series of documents illustrating the complex relationship between church and state.

11.1

✦

MERCHANT'S GUILD REGULATIONS

Southampton was a town on the southeast coast of England, with heavy trade in raw wool for finished textiles and wine from the continent. Wool was the single most common trade good for England throughout most of the Middle Ages; controlling trade in that commodity was therefore of tremendous importance to the kings of England. Until 1199, Southampton was a royal demesne land, meaning it was directly under the control of the king. In that year, however, the merchants of Southampton formed an association known as a guild (or gild) and negotiated with King John for some autonomy. Over the next few centuries, the guild and various royal governments would add to the liberties of the guild. In turn, the guild effectively became the rulers of the town. In other cities, individual crafts would form their own guilds to negotiate with town and noble rulers, and to set standards for their own work and prices. The craft guilds were somewhat similar to the modern day labor unions, but played a much more central role in the day-to-day life of cities and citizens.

✦

Questions

1. Why do the merchants of Southampton ensure that guild members will be self-policing?
2. How does Regulation 20 ensure that the merchants' guild will be the most powerful organization in the town?
3. What advantage was there to the kings of England in agreeing to these concessions of power?

THE MERCHANTS OF SOUTHAMPTON

ORDANCES OF THE GILD MERCHANT OF SOUTHAMPTON

1 In the first place, there shall be elected from the gild merchant, and established, an alderman, a steward, a chaplain, four skevins, and an usher. And it is to be known that whosoever shall be alderman shall receive from each one entering into the gild fourpence, the steward, twopence; the chaplain, twopence; and the usher, one penny. And the gild shall meet twice a year: that is to say, on the Sunday next after St. John the Baptist's day, and on the Sunday next after St. Mary's day.

2. And when the gild shall be sitting, no one of the gild is to bring in any stranger, except when required by the alderman or steward. And the alderman shall have a sergeant to serve before him, the steward another sergeant, and the two skevins a sergeant, and the other two skevins a sergeant, and the chaplain shall have his clerk.

3. And when the gild shall sit, the alderman is to have, each night, so long as the gild sits, two gallons of wine and two candles, and the steward the same; and the four skevins and the chaplain, each of them one gallon of wine and one candle, and the usher one gallon of wine.

4. And when the gild shall sit, the lepers of La Madeleine shall have of the alms of the gild, two sesters of ale, and the sick of God's House and of St. Julian shall have two sesters of ale. And the Friars Minor shall have two sesters of ale and one sester of wine. And four sesters of ale shall be given to the poor whenever the gild shall meet.

5. And when the gild is sitting, no one who is of the gild shall go outside of the town for any business, without the permission of the steward. And if anyone does so, let him be fined two shillings, and pay them.

6. And when the gild sits, and any gildsman is outside of the city so that he does not know when it will happen, he shall have a gallon of wine, if his servants come to get it. And if a gildsman is ill and is in the city, wine shall be sent to him, two loaves of bread and a gallon of wine and a dish from the kitchen; and two approved men of the gild shall go to visit him and look after his condition.

7. And when a gildsman dies, all those who are of the gild and are in the city shall attend the service of the dead, and gildsmen shall bear the body and bring it to the place of burial. And whoever will not do this shall pay according to his oath, two pence, to be given to the poor. And those of the ward where the dead man shall be ought to find a man to watch over the body the night that the deal shall lie in his house. And so long as the service of the dead shall last, that is to say the vigil and the mass, there ought to burn four candles of the gild, each candle of two pounds weight or more, until the body is buried. And these four candles shall remain in the keeping of the steward of the gild.

8. The steward ought to keep the rolls and the treasure of the gild under the seal of the alderman of the gild.

9. And when a gildsman dies, his eldest son or his next heir shall have the seat of his father, or of his uncle, if his father was not a gildsman, and of no other one; and he shall give nothing for his seat. No husband can have a seat in the gild by right of his wife, nor demand a seat by right of his wife's ancestors.

10. And no one has the right or power to sell or give his seat in the gild to any man; and the son of a gildsman, other than his eldest son, shall enter into the gild on payment of ten shillings, and he shall take the oath of the gild.

11. And if a gildsman shall be imprisoned in England in time of peace, the alderman with the steward and with one of the skevins shall go, at the cost of the gild, to procure the deliverance of the one who is in prison.

12. And if any gildsman strikes another with his fist and is convicted thereof, he shall lost the gild until he shall have bought it back for ten shillings, and taken the oath of the gild again like a new member. And if a gildsman strikes another with a stick, or a knife, or any other weapon, whatever it may be, he shall lost the gild and the franchise, and shall be held as a stranger until he shall have been reconciled to the good men of the gild and has made recompense a fine to the gild of twenty shillings; and this shall not be remitted.

13. If any one does an injury, who is not of the gild, and is of the franchise or strikes a gildsman and is reasonably convicted, he shall lose his franchise and go to prison for a day and a night.

14. And if any stranger or any other who is not of the gild nor of the franchise strikes a gildsman, and is reasonable convicted thereof, let him be in prison two days and two nights, unless the injury is such that he should be more severely punished.

15. And if a gildsman reviles or slanders another gildsman, and a complaint of it comes to the alderman, and if he is reasonably convicted thereof, he shall pay two shillings fine to the gild, and if he is not able to pay he shall lose the gild.

16. And if anyone who is of the franchise speaks evil of a gildsman, and is convicted of this before the alderman, he shall pay five shillings for a fine or lose the franchise.

17. And no one shall come to the council of the gild if he is not a gildsman.

18. And if anyone of the gild forfeits the gild by any act or injury, and is excluded by the alderman and the steward and the skevins and the twelve sworn men of the city, and he wishes to have the gild again, he shall do all things anew just as one who has never been of the gild, and shall make amends for his injury according to the discretion of the alderman and the aforesaid approved men. And if anyone of the gild or of the franchise brings a suit against another outside of the city, by a writ or without a writ, he shall lose the gild and the franchise if he is convicted of it.

19. And no one of the city of Southampton shall buy anything to sell again in the same city, unless he is of the gild merchant or of the franchise. And if anyone shall do so and is convicted of it, all which he has so bought shall be forfeited to the king; and no one shall be quit of custom unless he proves that he is in the gild or in the franchise, and this from year to year.

20. And no one shall buy honey, fat, salf herrings, or any kind of oil, or millstones, or fresh hides, or any kind of fresh skins, unless he is a gildsman: nor keep a tavern for wine, nor sell cloth at retail, except in market or fair days, nor keep grain in his granary beyond five quarters, to sell at retail, if he is not a gildsman; and whoever shall do this and be convicted shall forfeit all to the king.

21. No one of the gild ought to be partner or joing dealer in any of the kinds of merchandise before mentioned with anyone who is not of the gild, by any manner of coverture, or art, or contrivance, or

collusion, or in any other manner. And whosoever shall do this and be convicted, the goods in such manner bought shall be forfeited to the king, and the gildsman shall lose the gild.

22. If any gildsman falls into poverty and has not the wherewithal to live, and is not able to work or to provide for himself, he shall have one mark from the gild to relieve his condition when the gild shall sit. No one of the gild nor of the franchise shall avow anothers goods for his by which the custom of the city shall be injured. And if any one does so and is convicted, he shall lose the gild and the franchise; and the merchandise so avowed shall be forfeited to the king.

23. And no private man nor stranger shall bargain for or buy any kind of merchandise coming into the city before a burgess of the gild merchant, so long as the gildsman is present and wishes to bargain for and buy this merchandise; and if anyone does so and is convicted, that which he buys shall be forfeited to the king.

24. And anyone who is of the gild merchant shall share in all merchandise which another gildsman shall buy or any other person, whosoever he is, if he comes and demands part and is there where the merchandise is bought, and also if he gives satisfaction to the seller and gives security for his part. But no one who is not a gildsman is able or ought to share with a gildsman, without the will of the gildsman.

25. And if any guildsman or other of the city refuse a part to the gildsman in the manner above said, he shall not buy or sell in that year in the town, except his victuals.

26. And if any merchant of the town buys wine or grain so that all the risk shall be on the buyer, he shall not pay custom for this merchandise. And if any risk is upon the seller, he shall pay.

27. It is provided that the chief alderman of the town, or the bailiffs and the twelve sworn men, shall give attention to the merchants as well strangers as private men, as often as it shall be required, to see that they have sufficient security for their debts, and recognizance from their debtors; and the day of this shall be enrolled before them, so that if the day is not kept, on proof by the creditor, the debtor should be then distrained according to the recognizance which he has made, in lands and chattels, to give satisfaction according to the usage of the town, without any manner of pleading, so that the men of the town should not have damage by the default of payment of the debtors aforesaid.

28. And if any guildsman for any debt which he may owe will not suffer himself to be distrained, or when he has been distrained, shall break through, or make removal or break the king's lock, and be convicted thereof, he shall lose his gildship until he has bought it again for twenty shillings, and this each time that he offends in such manner. And he shall be none the less distrained until he has made satisfaction for the debt he owes; and if he will not submit to justice as aforesaid and be thereof convicted, he shall go to prison for a day and a night like one who is against the peace; and if he will not submit to justice let the matter be laid before the king and his council in manner aforesaid....

32. Every year, on the morrow of St. Michael, shall be elected by the whole community of the town, assembled in a place provided, to consider the estate and treat of the common business of the town — then shall be elected by the whole community, twelve discreet men to execute the king's commands, together with the bailiffs, and to keep the peace and protect the franchise, and to do and keep justice to all persons, as well poor as rich, natives or strangers, all that year; and to this they shall be sworn in the form provided. And these twelve discreet men shall choose the same day two discreet men from among themselves and the other profitable and wise men to be bailiffs for the ensuing year, who shall take care that the customs shall be well paid; and they shall receive their jurisdiction the day after Michaelmas, as has been customary. And this shall be renewed every year, and the twelve aforesaid, if there is occasion. The same shall be done as to clear and sergeants of the city, in making and removing....

35. The common chest shall be in the house of the chief alderman or of the steward, and the three keys of it shall be lodged with three discreet men of the aforesaid twelve sworn men, or with three of the

skevins, who shall loyally take care of the common seal, and the charters and the treasure of the town, and the standards, and other muniments of the town, and no letter shall be sealed with the common seal, nor any charter taken out of the common-chest but in the presence of sex or twelve sworn men, and of the alderman or steward; and nobody shall sell by any kind of measure or weight that it is not sealed, under forfeiture of two shillings.....

63. No one shall go out to meet a ship bringing wine or other merchandise coming to the town, in order to buy anything, before the ship be arrived and come to anchor for unlading; and if any one does so and is convicted, the merchandise which he shall have bought shall be forfeited to the king.

Source: Andrea, Alfred, ed. *The Medieval Record: Sources of Medieval History*. Boston: Houghton Mifflin Company, 1997), pp. 249-252.

11.2

COMPLAINTS TO LOUIS IX FROM NORMAN SUBJECTS

Louis IX, the king of France from 1226 to 1270, is remembered for reforming the civil administration and for twice leading Crusades. Before setting out for the Holy Land on his first crusade, Louis sent out royal judges known as enquêteurs *to collect any grievances against royal administrators. He collected the grievances from Normandy, a dukedom that had been brought under French royal control in 1204 by King Philip II Augustus. The following excerpts from those complaints illustrate the centrality of revenue collection from royal lands.*

QUESTIONS

1. According to *Enquêt 423*, who is responsible for supplying the parish churches with money for the host?
2. Why are so many of the *Enquêts* petitions by women for restoration of land or revenue? What does this say about the power women had over their own lands?
3. What ultimately do the *Enquêts* say about the king's power over his subjects?

355. R...de Clerdoit, Richard Flori,...Herberti, Hugues Herberti, Buillaume, son of Hugh de Clerdoit, of Saint Jaques de...t, complain that both they and all others from the said parish for whom they similarly complain, were forced by the *baillis* and revenue farmers of the Lord King to pay a customs duty on all things they sell and purchase, wherever they sell or purchase them, just as they had been accustomed to do when there was a market at Montpinçon...on the Tuesday of each week, at the time when Raoul de Grandvilliers, knight and baron, held peaceful possession of his land before he want to England with King John; at which time he forfeited the land. And they say that they paid the said customs duty unjustly because, from the time when the land of the said baron came to the hand of King

Philip, there has been no market in the village of Montpinçon, as there had been at the aforesaid time; and nevertheless, they have paid the said customs duty from that time till the present and are still compelled to pay it....

359. Mabel, widow of Richard, son of Fulk, the knight, of Vieuxpont-en-Auge, complains that Girard de La Boiste acquired for the Lord King land lying in the parish of Castillon, of the diocese of Lisieux, and worth approximately 100s. annually, because the brother of the said woman, a lay person, after the death of his brother the priest, also died in England. It is the priest who had given the said land to Mabel, on the condition that he peacefully and with no interference hold the aforesaid land at farm from Mabel and her heirs throughout his lifetime for one pair of gloves worth 6d. The land was acquired by the Lord King last year on the previous Nativity of the Lord....

366. Emeline, daughter of Alain of Bretteville-sur-Dive complains that the revenue farmers of the Lord King acquired for the King 1-1/2 acres of land, which lie in the aforesaid parish. She was not able to recover them after the death of her father, who used to hold them from the said Lord King in fief for 3 capons, 3 hens, and 3 loaves to be paid annually; and the land was taken into the King's hand approximately 12 years ago. Nor in this matter was the Lord King injured....

374. Robert, called "the Blockhead" of Eraines, complains on behalf of his wife, since she is ill, saying that 20 years ago the Lord King retained in his possession the 3 quarts of barley that his wife used to collect in a certain land lying in the parish of Aubigny; for the *baillis* of the King did not wish to return the land to his wife's mother nor to her after the year and a day that it had been held in the hand of the King. [It was held] because of the outlawry of one of her men, who had been holding that land from [his wife's] mother; although it ought to have been returned after a year and a day....

385. Leceline, widow of G. Ferant, and Guillaume, her son, of the parish of Saint-Loup-Canivet, complain that they are not able to recover 4 acres of land, lying next to a certain field, which they hold from the Lord King, and which the Lord King gave 8 years ago to aforesaid Leceline to hold for herself and her heirs in return for 20s. to be paid annually for the said acres and the said field. And Girard de La Boiste was commanded to transfer the property to her, but he refused even though Jean de Vignes had commanded him to do it....

388. Giroth *de Treperel*, of the parish of Martigny, complains that Girard de La Boiste acquired for the Lord King 1 acre of land that Morel [de Falaise] the Jew had purchased in his fief during the life of his father [but] without the assent and permission of the said father. Giroth is not able to recover [the land] for the price that the Jew had given for the land....

395. Nicholas, rector of the church of Ussy, and Jean de Soulangy, priest, and Hugues, called "the Englishman," a clerk of the Lord King, complain for themselves and for all persons and vicars of the churches of the deanery of Aubigny, saying that the *prévôts* of Falaise exact a duty from them on those things, pertaining to [their] livelihood, which they buy for their own use — if they exceed the price of 5 pennies; briefly, on all the things that they purchase for their use and the use of their churches, just as from lay dues payers, so they say. The dean of Falaise and Thomas of Morteaux-Couliboeuf, a priest, make a similar complaint for all the priests of the aforesaid deanery....

411. Agnes *de Veilleio*, of Falaise, complains that King Philip, of illustrious memory, 2 years after the conquest of Normandy acquired possession of 2 plots, worth 48s. annually, and there fortified the castle of Falaise with moat-battlements and other structures; nor did he exchange [anything for them] with her although the said plots had been given to her as a marriage portion....

415. Acelin le Telier, of the parish of Aubigny, complains that 28 years ago, Pierre du Thillai took his son, W. Acelini into the King's hand, on account of land lying in the aforesaid parish and worth to the Lord King 5 bushels of barley at the Falaise measure to the Lord King. Pierre claimed that a certain

cousin of [Acelin's], whose land it had been, had gone into Poitou against the King, but [in fact] before he had left his province to set out for Poitou, the said cousin had sold the land to Acelin, so he says.

416. Raoul *de Cantepie* and Pierre, his brother, of Beaumais, complain that 40 years ago, Jean le Guerrier acquired for the King 20 acres of land and 1 fishpond, lying in the aforesaid parish and worth 40s. per year to the King, by asserting that their father owed one-third of 18l. to Morel [de Falaise] the Jew. However, King Philip, of illustrious memory, had quit him of that third part and had returned him that land which he had handed over to Morellus in pledge, so they say....

421. Robert Caffrei, of Olendon, complains that 6 years ago, Girard de La Boiste took in the Lord King's hand a certain *vavassoria* lying in the aforesaid parish and worth 10s. annually to [Robert], after the death of a certain man who was holding the said *vavassoriai* from him [Robert] — because the son of that man had acknowledged the lordship of the King after the death of [his] father; however, through an investigation [by jury] made about this it was discovered that the said *vavassoria* should have been held from the said Robert. And the said Girard had [collected] for the relief, 32s, for the aid of the host, 13s, and 10s from [Robert] for bailing himself out of jail — in which [Girard] had put him for claiming the said *vavassoria*....

423. Guillaume Martin, cleric, Buillaume de Villeray, Geoffroy *de Hamello*, Nicolas Chaperon, Roger Tustain, and Elnaud *de Fonte*, of Beaumais, complain that the revenue farmers of the Lord King refuse to help them pay the 36s. of aid for the host, which they were accustomed to pay for the demesne of the King. And they make the complaint for themselves and for their fellows. For the revenue farmers have not paid the said money for 3 years, although they [Guillaume Martin and company] have paid the aid for the host each year....

425. Nicolas *de Hamello*, of Cordey, Guillaume Fuchier, [and] Guillaume Eemelench complain on behalf of the entire parish, saying that they were accustomed to have a certain quittance, such that they did not pay the duty in Falaise on either wood or fields, for 1 penny, which each bordar of those [aforesaid] men used to pay to the *prévôt* of Falaise annually at the Circumcision of the Lord. Nevertheless, for the past 9 years the duty on forests and fields is demanded from them, although they are quit from the said rent.

Reprinted from *Readings in Medieval History, third edition*, edited by Patrick J. Geary, Ontario: Broadview Press, 2003, pp. 705-711. Reprinted by permission of Broadview Press.

11.3

MAGNA CARTA

In 1215 King John of England was confronted by his nobles, presented with a document called the Great Charter (Magna Carta), and told to sign it or risk being deposed. The Charter is famous for promoting individual freedoms, and protecting the common folk from royal abuses of power. In reality, the Charter only protects the noble class, and it includes few new protections that the nobles did not already have. The most important is the assurance by the king that he will respect the right of the nobles to approve taxes before he demanded them. It does, however, present a clear example of the feudal balance of power between kings and nobles.

The circumstances that precipitated the confrontation between John and his barons (as English nobles were collectively known) were a series of military and political failures by John. He had lost Normandy to the French in 1204 and another war to them in 1214. In both instances he turned to the barons and demanded extra taxes. He had lost a confrontation with Pope Innocent III over the archbishop of Canterbury. In 1213, Innocent legally deposed John, who had to sign a feudal oath of loyalty to the pope in order to get his title back. Collectively the barons felt manipulated, ignored, and bitter at John's repeated lack of success.

---- ⚜ ----

QUESTIONS

1. Is there anything innovative in the *Great Charter*?
2. Under what circumstances are women mentioned in the *Charter*?
3. At the end of the *Charter* John promises that the Church of England shall be free; from whom is he promising it freedom?

MAGNA CARTA

...1. In the first place we have granted to God, and by this our present charter confirmed, for us and our hears forever, that the English church shall be free, and shall hold its rights entire and its liberties uninjured; and we will that it thus be observed; which is shown by this, that the freedom of elections, which is considered to be most important and especially necessary to the English church, we, of our pure and spontaneous will, granted, and by our charter confirmed, before the contest between us and our barons had arisen; and obtained a confirmation of it by the lord pope Innocent III; which we will observe and which we will shall be observed in good faith by our heirs forever.

We have granted moreover to all free men of our kingdom for us and our heirs forever all the liberties written below, to be had and held by themselves and their heirs from us and our heirs.

2. If any of our earls or barons, or others holding from us in chief by military service shall have died, and when he has died his heir shall be of full age and owe relief, he shall have his inheritance by the ancient relief; that is to say, the heir or heirs of an earl for the whole barony of an earl and hundred pounds; the heir or heirs of a baron for a whole barony a hundred pounds; the heir or heirs of a knight, for a whole knight's fee, a hundred shillings at most; and who owes less let him give less according to the ancient custom of fiefs.

3. If moreover the heir of any one of such shall be under age, and shall be in wardship, when he comes of age he shall have his inheritance without relief [that is, inheritance tax] and without a fine.

4. The custodian of the land of such a minor heir shall not take from the land of the heir any except reasonable products, reasonable customary payments, and reasonable services, and this without destruction or waste of men or of property; and if we shall have committed the custody of the land of any such a one to the sheriff or to any other who is to be responsible to us for its proceeds, and that man shall have caused destruction or waste from his custody we will recover damages from him, and the land shall be committed to two legal and discreet men of that fief, who shall be responsible for its proceeds to us or to him to whom we have assigned them; and if we shall have given or sold to anyone the custody, an it shall be handed over to two legal and discreet men of that fief who shall be in like manner responsible to us as is said above.

5. The custodian moreover, so long as he shall have the custody of the land, must keep up the houses, parks, warrens, fish ponds, mills, and other things pertaining to the land, from the proceeds of the land itself; and he must return to the heir, when he has come to full age, all his land, furnished with plows and implements of husbandry according as the time of cultivation requires and as the proceeds of the land are able reasonably to sustain.

6. Heirs shall be married without disparity, but so that before the marriage is contracted, it shall be announced to the heir's blood relatives.

7. A widow, after the death of her husband, shall have her marriage portion and her inheritance immediately and without obstruction, nor shall she give anything for her dowry or for her marriage portion, or for her inheritance which inheritance her husband and she held on the day of the death of her husband; and she may remain in the house of her husband for forty days after his death, within which time her dowry shall be assigned to her.

8. No widow shall be compelled to marry so long as she prefers to live without a husband, provided she gives security that she will not marry without our consent, if she holds from us, or without the consent of her lord from whom she holds, if she holds from another.

9. Neither we nor our bailiffs will seize any land or rent, for any debt, so long as the chattels of the debtor are sufficient for the payment of the debt; nor shall the pledges of a debtor be distrained so long as the principal debtor himself has enough for the payment of the debt; and if the principal debtor fails in the payment of the debt, not having the wherewithal to pay it, the pledges shall be responsible for the debt and if they wish, they shall have the lands and the rents of the debtor until they shall have been satisfied for the debt which they have before paid for him, unless the principal debtor shall have shown himself to be quit in that respect towards those pledges.

10. If anyone has taken anything from the Jews, by way of a loan, more or less, and ideas before that debt is paid, the debt shall not draw interest so long as the heir is under age, from whomsoever he holds; and if that debt falls into our hands, we will take nothing except the chattel contained in the agreement.

11. And if anyone dies leaving a debt owing to the Jews, his wife shall have her dower, and shall pay nothing of that debt; and if there remain minor children of the dead man, necessaries shall be provided for them corresponding to the holding of the dead man; and from the remainder shall be paid the debt, the service of the lords being retrained. In the same way debts are to be treated which are owed to others than the Jews.

12. No scutage or aid shall be imposed in our kingdom except by the common council of our kingdom, except for the ransoming of our body, for the making of our oldest son a knight, and for once marrying our oldest daughter, and for these purposes it shall be only a reasonable aid; in the same way it shall be done concerning the aids of the city of London.

13. And the city of London shall have all its ancient liberties and free customs, as well by land as by water. Moreover, we will and grant that all other cities and boroughs and villages and ports shall have all their liberties and free customs.

14. And for holding a common council of the kingdom concerning the assessment of an aid otherwise than in the three cases mentioned above, or concerning the assessment of a scutage [that is, payment by a vassal in lieu of military service], we shall cause to be summoned the archbishops, bishops, abbots, earls, and grater barons by our letters under seal; and besides we shall cause to be summoned generally, by our sheriffs and bailiffs, all those who hold from us in chief, for a certain day, that is at the end of forty days at least, and for a certain place; and in all the letters of that summons, we will express the cause of the summons, and when the summons has thus been given the business shall proceed on the

appointed day, on the advice of those who shall be present, even if not all of those who were summoned have come.

15. We will not grant to anyone, moreover, that he shall take an aid from his free men, except for ransoming his body, for making his oldest son a knight, and for once marrying his oldest daughter; and for these purposes only a reasonable aid shall be taken.

16. No one shall be compelled to perform any greater service for a knight's fee, or for any other free tenement, than is owed from it.

17. The common pleas shall not follow our court, but shall be held in some certain place.

18. The recognitions of *novel disseisin*, *mort d'ancestor*, and *darrein presentment* [that is, the common law procedures determining temporary possession of disputed land] shall be held only in their own counties and in this manner: we, or, if we are outside of the kingdom, our principal justiciar, will send two justiciars through each county four times a year, who with four knights of each county, elected by the county, shall hold in the county and one the day and in the place of the county court, the aforesaid assizes of the county.

19. And if the aforesaid assizes cannot be held within the day of the county court, a sufficient number of knights and free-holders shall remain from those who were present at the county court on that day to give the judgments, according as the business is more or less.

20. A free man shall not be fined for a small offense, except in proportion to the measure of the offense; and for a great offense he shall be fined in proportion to the magnitude of the offense, saving this freehold; and a merchant in the same way, saving his merchandise; and the villain shall be fined in the same way, saving his tools of civilization, if he shall be at our mercy; and none of the above fines shall be imposed except by the oaths of honest men of the neighborhood.

21. Earls and barons shall only be fined by their peers, and only in proportion to their offense.

22. A clergyman shall be fined, like those before mentioned, only in proportion to his lay holding, and not according to the extent of his ecclesiastical benefice.

23. No manor or man shall be compelled to make bridges over the rivers except those which ought to do it of old and rightfully.

24. No sheriff, constable, coroners, or other bailiffs of ours shall hold pleas of our crown.

25. All counties, hundreds, wapentakes, and tithings [that is, small traditional units of land] shall be at the ancient rents and without any increase, excepting our demesne manors.

26. If any person holding a lay fief from us shall die, and our sheriff or bailiff shall show our letters-patent of our summons concerning a debt which the deceased owed to us, it shall be lawful for our sheriff or bailiff to attach and levy on the chattels of the deceased found on his lay fief, to the value of that debt, in the view of legal men, but in such a way that nothing be removed thence until the clear debt to us shall be paid; and the remainder shall be left to the executors for the fulfillment of the will of the deceased, saving to his wife and children their reasonable shares.

27. If any free man dies intestate, his chattels shall be distributed by the hands of his near relatives and friends, under the oversight of the church, saving to each one the debts which the deceased owed to him.

28. No constable or other bailiff of ours shall take anyone's grain or other chattels, without immediately paying for them in money, unless he is able to obtain a postponement at the good-will of the seller.

29. No constable shall require any knight to give money in place of his ward of a castle if he is willing to furnish that ward in his own person or through another honest man, if he himself is not able to

do it for a reasonable cause; and if we shall lead or send him into the army he shall be free from ward in proportion to the amount of time by which he has been in the army for us.

30. No sheriff or bailiff of ours or anyone else shall take horses or wagons of any free man for carrying purposes except on the permission of that free man.

31. Neither we nor our bailiffs will take the wood of another man for castles, or for anything else which we are doing, except by the permission of him to whom the wood belongs.

32. We will not hold the lands of those convicted of a felony for more than a year and a day, after which the lands shall be returned to the lords of the fiefs.

33. All the fish-weirs in the Thames and the Medway, and throughout all England, shall be done away with, except those on the coast.

34. The writ which is called *praecipe* shall not be given for the future to anyone concerning any tenement by which a free man can lose his court.

35. There shall be one measure of wine our whole kingdom, and one measure of ale, and one measure of grain, that is the London quarter, and one width of died cloth and of russets and of halbergets, that is two ells within the selvages; of weights, moreover, it shall be as of measures.

36. Nothing shall henceforth be given or taken for a writ of inquisition concerning life or limbs, but it shall be given freely and not denied.

37. If anyone holds from us by fee farm or by non-military tenure or by urban tenure, and from another he holds land by military service, we will not have the guardianship of the heir of his land by military service, we will not have the guardianship of the heir of his land which is of the fief of another, on account of that fee farm, or soccage, or burgage; nor will we have the custody of that fee farm, or soccage, or burgage, unless that fee farm itself owes military service. We will not have the guardianship of the heir or of the land of anyone, which he holds from another by military service of paying to us knives or arrows, or things of that kind.

38. No bailiff for the future shall place anyone to his law on his simple affirmation, without credible witnesses brought for this purpose.

39. No free man shall be taken or imprisoned or dispossessed, or outlawed, or banished, or in any way destroyed, nor will we go upon him, nor send upon him, except by the legal judgment of his peers or by the law of the land.

40. To no one will we sell, to no one will we deny or delay, right or justice.

41. All merchants shall be safe and secure in going out from England and coming into England and in remaining and going through England, as well by land as by water, for buying and selling, free from all evil tolls, by the ancient and rightful customs, except in time of war; and if they are of a land at war with us, and if such are found in our land at the beginning of war, they shall be attached without injury to their bodies or goods, until it shall be known from us or from our principal justiciar in what way the merchants of our land are treated who shall be then found in the country which is at war with us; and if ours are safe there, the others shall be safe in our land.

42. It is allowed henceforth to anyone to go out from our kingdom, and to return, safely and securely, by land and by water, saving their fidelity to us, except in time or war for some short time, for the common good of the kingdom; excepting persons imprisoned and outlawed according to the law of the realm, and people of a land at war with us, and merchants, or whom it shall be done as is before said.

43. If anyone holds from any escheat [that is, a fief reverting to the lord in the absence of an heir], as from the honor of Wallingford, or Nottingham, or Boulogne, or Lancaster, or from other escheats which are in our hands and are baronies, and he dies, his heir shall not give any other relief, nor do to us

any other service than he would do to the baron, if that barony was in the hands of the baron; and we will hold it in the same way as the baron held it.

44. Men who dwell outside the forest shall not henceforth come before our justiciars of the forest, on common summons, unless they are in a plea of the forest, or are pledges for any person or persons who are arrested on account of the forest.

45. We will not make justiciars, constables, sheriffs or bailiffs except of such as know the law of the realm and are well inclined to observe it.

46. All barons who have founded abbeys for which they have charters of kings of England, or ancient tenure, shall have their custody when they have become vacant, as they ought to have.

47. All forests which have been afforested in our time shall be disafforested immediately; and so it shall be concerning river banks which in our time have been fenced in.

48. All the bad customs concerning forests and warrens and concerning foresters and warreners, sheriffs and their servants, river banks and their guardians shall be inquired into immediately in each county by twelve sworn knights of the same county, who shall be elected by the honest men of the same county, and within forty days after the inquisition has been made, they shall be entirely destroyed by them, never to be restored, provided that we be first informed of it, or our justiciar, if we are not in England.

49. We will give back immediately all hostages and charters which have been delivered to us by Englishmen as security for peace or for faithful service.

50. We will remove absolutely from their bailiwicks the relatives of Gerard de Athyes, so that for the future they shall have no bailiwick in England; Engelard de Cygony, Andrew, Peter and Gyon de Chancelles, Gyon de Cygony, Geoffrey de Martin and his brothers, Philip Mark and his brothers, and Geoffrey his nephew and their whole retinue.

51. And immediately after the re-establishment of peace we will remove from the kingdom all foreign-born soldiers, cross-bow men, servants, and mercenaries who have come with horses and arms for the injury of the realm.

52. If anyone shall have been dispossessed or removed by us without legal judgment of his peers, from his lands, castles, franchises, or his right we will restore them to him immediately; and if contention arises about this, then it shall be done according to the judgment of the twenty-five barons, of whom mention is made below concerning the security of the peace. Concerning all those things, however, from which anyone has been removed or of which he has been deprived without legal judgment of his peers by King Henry our father, or by King Richard our brother, which we have in our hand, or which others hold, and which is our duty to guarantee, we shall have respite till the usual term of crusaders; excepting those things about which the suit has been begun or the inquisition made by our writ before our assumption of the cross; when, however, we shall return from our journey, or if by chance we desist from the journey, we will immediately show full justice in regard to them.

53. We shall, moreover, have the same respite, in the same manner, about doing justice in regard to the forests which are to be disafforested or to remain forests, which Henry our father or Richard our brother made into forests; and concerning the custody of lands which are in the fief of another, custody of which we have until now had on account of a fief which anyone has held from us by military service; and concerning the abbeys which have been founded in fiefs of others than ourselves, in which the lord of the fee has asserted for himself a right; and when we return or if we should desist from our journey we will immediately show full justice to those complaining in regard to them.

54. No one shall be seized nor imprisoned on the appeal of a woman concerning the death of anyone except her husband.

55. All fines which have been imposed unjustly and against the law of the land, and all penalties imposed unjustly and against the law of the land are altogether excused, or will be on the judgment of the twenty-five barons of whom mention is made below in connection with the security of the peace, or on the judgment of the majority of them, along with the aforesaid Stephen, archbishop of Canterbury, if he is able to be present, and others whom he may wish to call for this purpose along with him. And if he should not be able to be present, nevertheless the business shall go on without him, provided that if any one or more of the aforesaid twenty-five barons are in a similar suit they should be removed as far as this particular judgment goes, and others who shall be chosen and put upon oath by the remainder of the twenty-five shall be substituted for them for this purpose along with him. And if he should not be able to be present, nevertheless the business shall go on without him, provided that if any one or more of the aforesaid twenty-five barons are in a similar suit they should be removed as far as this particular judgment goes, and others who shall be chosen and put upon oath by the remainder of the twenty-five shall be substituted for them for this purpose.

56. If we have dispossessed or removed any Welshmen from their lands, or franchises, or other things, without legal judgment of their peers, in England, or in Wales, they shall be immediately returned to them; and if a dispute shall have arisen over this, then it shall be settled in the borderland by judgment of their peers, concerning holdings of England according to the law of England, concerning holdings of Wales according to the law of Wales, and concerning holdings of the borderland according to the law of the borderland. The Welsh shall do the same to us and ours.

57. Concerning all those things, however, from which any one of the Welsh shall have been removed or dispossessed without legal judgment of his peers by King Henry our father, or King Richard our brother, which we hold in our hands, or which others hold, and we are bound to warrant to them, we shall have respite till the usual period of crusaders, except those about which suit was begun or inquisition made by our command before our assumption of the cross. When, however, we shall return or if by chance we shall desist from our journey, we will show full justice to them immediately, according to the laws of the Welsh and the aforesaid parts.

58. We will give back the son of Llewellyn immediately, and all the hostages from Wales and the charters which had been delivered to us as a security for peace.

59. We will act toward Alexander, king of the Scots, concerning the return of his sisters and his hostages, and concerning his franchises and his right, according to the manner in which we shall act toward our other barons of England, unless it ought to be otherwise by the charters which we hold from William his father, formerly king of the Scots, and this shall be by the judgment of his peers in our court.

60. Moreover, all those customs and franchises mentioned above which we have conceded in our kingdom, and which are to be fulfilled, as far as pertains to us, in respect to our men, all men of our kingdom shall observe as far as pertains to them, clergy as well as laymen, in respect to their men.

61. Since, moreover, for the sake of God, and for the improvement of our kingdom, and for the better quieting of the hostility sprung up lately between us and our barons, we have made all these concessions; wishing them to enjoy these in a complete and firm stability forever, we make and concede to them the security described below; that is to say, that they shall elect twenty-five barons of the kingdom, whom they will, who ought with all their power to observe, hold, and cause to be observed, the peace and liberties which we have conceded to them, and by this our present charter confirmed to them; in this manner, that if we or our justiciar, or our bailiffs, or any one of our servants shall have done wrong in any way toward anyone, or shall have transgressed any of the articles of peace or security; and the wrong shall have been shown to four barons of the aforesaid twenty-five barons, let those four barons come to us or to our justiciar, if we are out of the kingdom, laying before us the transgression, and let

them ask that we cause that transgression to be corrected without delay. And if we shall not have corrected the transgression, or if we shall be out of the kingdom, if our justiciar shall not have corrected it within a period of forty days, counting from the time in which it has been shown to us or to our justiciar, if we are out of the kingdom; the aforesaid four barons shall refer the matter to the remainder of the twenty-five barons, and let those twenty-five barons with the whole community of the country distress and injure us in every way they can; that is to say by the seizure of our castles, lands, possessions, and in such other ways as they can until it shall have been corrected according to their judgment, saving our person and that of our queen, and those of our children; and when the correction has been made, let them devote themselves to us as they did before. And let whoever in the country wishes take an oath that in all the above-mentioned measures he will obey the orders of the aforesaid twenty-five barons, and that he will injure us as far as he is able with them, and we give permission to swear publicly and freely to each one who wishes to swear, and no one will we ever forbid to swear. All those, moreover, in the country who of themselves and their own will are unwilling to take an oath to the twenty-five barons as to distressing and injuring us along with them, we will compel to take the oath by our mandate, as before said. And if any one of the twenty-five barons shall have died or departed from the land or shall in any other way be prevented from taking the above-mentioned action, let the remainder of the aforesaid twenty-five barons choose another in his place, according to their judgment, who shall take an oath in the same way as the others. In all those things, moreover, which are committed to those five and twenty barons to carry out, if perhaps the twenty-five are present, and some disagreement arises among them about something, or if any of them when they have been summoned are not willing or are not able to be present, let that be considered valid and firm which the greater part of those who are present arrange or command, just as if the whole twenty-five had agreed in this; and let the aforesaid twenty-five swear that they will observe faithfully all the things which are said above, and with all their ability cause them to be observed. And we will obtain nothing from anyone, either by ourselves or by another by which any of these concessions and liberties shall be revoked or diminished; and if any such thing shall have been obtained, let it be invalid and void, and we will never use it by ourselves or by another.

62. And all ill-will, grudges, and anger sprung up between us and our men, clergy and laymen, from the time of the dispute, we have fully renounced and pardoned all. Moreover, all transgressions committed on account of this dispute, from Easter in the sixteenth year of our reign till the restoration of peace, we have fully remitted to all, clergy and laymen, and as far as pertains to us, fully pardoned. And moreover we have caused to be made for them testimonial letters-patent of lord Stephen, archbishop of Canterbury, lord Henry, archbishop of Dublin, and of the aforesaid bishops and of master Pandulf, in respect to that security and the concession named above.

63. Wherefore we will and firmly command that the church of England shall be free, and that the men of our kingdom shall have and hold all the aforesaid liberties, rights and concessions, well and peacefully, freely and quietly, fully and completely, for themselves and their heirs, from us and our heirs, in all things and places, forever, as before said. It has been sworn, moreover, as well on our part as on the part of the barons, that all these things spoken of above shall be observed in good faith and without any evil intent. Witness the above names and many others. Given by our hand in the meadow which is called Runnymede, between Windsor and Staines, on the fifteenth day of June, in the seventeenth year of our reign.

Reprinted from *Medieval England, 1000-1500: A Reader*, edited by Emilie Amt, Ontario: Broadview Press, 2001, pp. 241-223. Reprinted by permission of Broadview Press.

11.4

--- ✤ ---

INVESTITURE CONTROVERSY DOCUMENTS

The Magna Carta came about, in part, because of a struggle for power between a king and a pope. Such struggles were common throughout the High and Late Middle Ages. No such struggle had as substantial an effect as the Investiture Controversy between the Holy Roman Emperor Henry IV and Pope Gregory VII. The controversy began in 1075, when the pope issued a list of papal claims to authority and power, Dictatus Papae ("Proclamations of the Pope"). In 1076 Henry IV responded by calling for a synod, or council, to reform abuses within the church, clearly ignoring the pope's authority to call such councils; in fact, the "abuses" Henry intended to clear up included Gregory's claims to power. In Henry IV then decided to test papal claims to jurisdiction over internal church appointments in the Holy Roman Empire by appointing, or investing, his own choices for bishops, without the pope's approval, leading to his deposition and excommunication by Gregory. Henry would get his title back, and his excommunication lifted, but only after public penance. Gregory would re-depose and re-excommunicate Henry again in 1080; finally Henry would have Gregory himself deposed and exiled in 1084. The feud does not officially end until the Concordat of Worms in 1122, between Calixtus II (pope from 1119-1124) and Emperor Henry V (r. 1106-1125).

It must be noted that there are antecedents to this struggle which go back to centuries of conflicting theories about imperial and papal power, and that even the oath taken by Henry V at Worms in 1122 did not really resolve this underlying power struggle. It merely settled the specific fight over investiture.

--- ✤ ---

QUESTIONS

1. Who ultimately do you think wins the Investiture Controversy, the pope or the king?
2. What authorities does Gregory VII base the claims of *Dictatus Papae* on?
3. What do these documents tell us about how emperors viewed the function of the earthly church?

DICTATUS PAPAE

1. That the Roman church was established by God alone.
2. That the Roman pontiff alone is rightly called universal.
3. That he alone has the power to depose and reinstate bishops.
4. That his legate, even if he be of lower ecclesiastical rank, presides over bishops in council, and has the power to give sentence of deposition against them.
5. That the pope has the power to depose those who are absent.
6. That, among other things, we ought not to remain in the same house with those whom he has excommunicated.

7. That he alone has the right, according to the necessity of the occasion, to make new laws, to create new bishoprics....
8. That he alone may use the imperial insignia.
9. That all princes shall kiss the foot of the pope alone.
10. That his name alone is to be recited in the churches.
11. That the name applied to him belongs to him alone.
12. That he has the power to depose emperors.
13. That he has the right to transfer bishops from one see to another when it becomes necessary.
14. That he has the right to ordain as a cleric anyone from any part of the church whatsoever.
15. That anyone ordained by him may rule [as bishop] over another church....
16. That no general synod may be called without his order.
17. That no action of a synod and no book shall be regarded as canonical without his authority.
18. That his decree can be annulled by no one, and that he can annul the decrees of anyone.
19. That he can be judged by no one.
20. That no one shall dare to condemn a person who has appealed to the Apostolic See.
21. That the important cases of any church whatsoever shall be referred to the Roman Church.
22. That the Roman Church has never erred and will never err to all eternity, according to the testimony of the holy scriptures.
23. That the Roman pontiff who has been canonically ordained is made holy by the merits of St. Peter....
24. That by his command or permission subjects may accuse their rulers.
25. That he can depose and reinstate bishops without the calling of a synod.
26. That no one can be regarded as catholic who does not agree with the Roman Church.
27. That he has the power to absolve subjects from their oath of fidelity to wicked rulers.

⚜ ⚜ ⚜

THE LETTER OF HENRY IV TO GREGORY VII, JANUARY 24, 1076

Henry, king not by usurpation, but by the holy ordination of God, to Hildebrand, not pope, but false monk.

This is the salutation which you deserve, for you have never held any office in the Church without making it a source of confusion and a curse to Christian men instead of an honor and a blessing. To mention only the most obvious cases out of many, you have not only dared to touch the Lord's anointed, the archbishops, bishops, and priests, but you have scorned them and abused them, as if they were ignorant servants not fit to know what their master was doing. This you have done to gain favor with the vulgar crowd. You have declared that the bishops know nothing and that you know everything; but if you have such great wisdom you have used it not to build but to destroy. Therefore we believe that St. Gregory, whose name you have presumed to take, had you in mind when he said: "The heart of the prelate is puffed up by the abundance of subjects, and he thinks himself more powerful than all others." All this we have endured because of our respect for the papal office, but you have mistaken our humility for fear, and have dared to make an attack upon the royal and imperial authority which we received from God. You have even threatened to take it away, as if we had received it from you, and as if the empire and kingdom were in your disposal and not in the disposal of God. Our Lord Jesus Christ has called us to the government of the empire, but he never called you to the rule of the Church. This is the way you have gained advancement in the Church: through craft you have obtained wealth; through wealth you have obtained favor; through favor, the power of the sword; and through the power of the sword, the papal seat, which is the seat of peace; and then from the seat of peace you have expelled peace. For you have incited subjects to rebel against their prelates by teaching them to despise the bishops, their rightful rulers. You have given to laymen the authority over priests, whereby they condemn and depose those whom the bishops have put over them to teach them. You have attacked me, who, unworthy as I am, have yet been anointed to rule among the anointed of God, and who, according to the teaching of the fathers, can be judged by no one save God alone, and can be deposed for no crime except infidelity. For the holy fathers in the time of the apostate Julian did not presume to pronounce sentence of deposition against him, but left him to be judged and condemned by God. St. Peter himself said: "Fear God, honor the king" [1 Pet. 2:17]. But you, who fear not God, have dishonored me, whom He has established. St. Paul, who said that even an angel from heaven should be accursed who taught any other than the true doctrine, did not make an exception in your favor, to permit you to teach false doctrines. For he says: "But though we, or an angel from heaven, preach any other gospel unto you than that which we have preached unto you, let him be accursed" [Gal. 1:8]. Come down, then, from that apostolic seat which you have obtained by violence; for you have been declared accursed by St. Paul for your false doctrines and have been condemned by us and our bishops for your evil rule. Let another ascend the throne of St. Peter, one who will not use religion as a cloak of violence, but will teach the life-giving doctrine of that prince of the apostles. I, Henry, king by the grace of God, with all my bishops, say unto you: "Come down, come down, and be accursed through all the ages."

❖ ❖ ❖

GREGORY VII'S FIRST EXCOMMUNICATION AND DEPOSITION OF HENRY IV

St Peter, prince of the apostles, incline your ear to me, I beseech you, and hear me, your servant, whom you have nourished from my infancy and have delivered from my enemies who hate me for my fidelity to you. You are my witness, as are also my mistress, the mother of God, and St. Paul your brother, and all the other saints, that your holy Roman church called me to its government against my own will, and that I did not gain your throne by violence; that I would rather have ended my days in exile than have obtained your place by fraud or for worldly ambition. It is not by my efforts, but by your grace, that I am set to rule over the Christian world which was specially entrusted to you by Christ. It is by your grace and as your representative that God has given to me the power to bind and to loose in heaven and in earth. Confident of my integrity and authority, I now declare in the name of omnipotent God, the Father, Son, and Holy Spirit, that Henry, son of the emperor Henry, is deprived of his kingdom of Germany and Italy; I do this by your authority and in defense of the honor of your church, because he has rebelled against it. He who attempts to destroy the honor of the Church should be deprived of such honor as he may have held. He has refused to obey as a Christian should, he has not returned to God from whom he had wandered, he has had dealings with excommunicated persons, he has done many iniquities, he has despised the warnings which, as you are witness, I sent to him for his salvation, he has cut himself off from your Church, and has attempted to rend it asunder; therefore, by your authority, I place him under a curse. It is in your name that I curse him, that all people may know that you are Peter, and upon your rock the Son of the living God has built his Church, and the gates of hell shall not prevail against it.

✢ ✢ ✢

THE CONCORDAT OF WORMS

The Oath of Calixtus II

Calixtus, bishop, servant of the servants of God, to his beloved son, Henry, by the grace of God emperor of the Romans, Augustus.

We hereby grant that in Germany the elections of the bishops and abbots who hold directly from the crown shall be held in you presence, such elections to be conducted canonically and without simony or other illegality. In the case of disputed elections you shall have the right to decide between the parties, after consulting with the archbishop of the province and his fellow-bishops. You shall confer the regalia of the office upon the bishop or abbot elect by the scepter, and this shall be done freely without exacting any payment from him; the bishop or abbot elect on his part shall perform all the duties that go with the holding of the regalia.

In other parts of the empire the bishops shall receive the regalia from you in the same manner within six months of their consecration, and shall in like manner perform all the duties that go with them. The undoubted rights of the Roman Church, however, are not to be regarded as prejudiced by this concession. If at any time you shall have occasion to complain of the carrying out of these provisions, I will undertake to satisfy your grievances as far as shall be consistent with my office. Finally, I hereby make a true and lasting peace with you and with all of your followers, including those who supported you in the recent controversy.

The Oath of Henry V

In the name of the holy and undivided Trinity.

For the love of God and his holy church and of Pope Calixtus, and for the salvation of my soul, I, Henry, by the grace of God, emperor of the Romans, Augustus, hereby surrender to God and his apostles, Sts. Peter and Paul, and to the holy Catholic Church, all investiture by ring and staff. I agree that elections and consecrations shall be conducted canonically and shall be free from all interference. I surrender also the possessions and regalia of St. Pater which have been seized by me during this quarrel, or by my father in his lifetime, and which are now in my possession, and I promise to aid the Church to recover such as are held by any other persons. I restore also the possessions of all other churches and princes, clerical or secular, which have been taken away during the course of this quarrel, which I have, and promise to aid them to recover such as are held by any other persons.

Finally, I make true the lasting peace with Pope Calixtus and with the holy Roman Church and with all who are or have ever been of his party. I will aid the Roman Church whenever my help is asked, and will do justice in all matters in regard to which the Church may have occasion to make compliant.

Source: Andrea, Alfred, ed. *The Medieval Record: Sources of Medieval History*. Boston: Houghton Mifflin Company, 1997), pp. 314-317.

—————— ✥ ——————

Questions for Part 11

1. By the end of the High Middle Ages, which has more power over individual Europeans, the church or the state?
2. What options did royal subjects have to express their dissatisfaction with their kings? Were those options class based?
3. Compare these documents with those of the previous section; what common themes can you identify from this three hundred year period of Western history?

PART 12

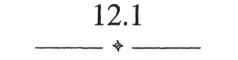

INTERSECTION OF MEDIEVAL CULTURES: THE CRUSADES

From Spain to Jerusalem, the most common interaction between western Europeans and other cultures in the High and Late Middle Ages was one of warfare. In addition to warfare, there were other modes of contact between Europe and other cultures, primarily trade and missionary activity, although it usually overlapped with military activity. In Spain, Christian kingdoms had been fighting to regain control of the peninsula since the Muslim invasion of the eighth century. The *Reconquista* would finally end in 1492, when Ferdinand of Aragon defeated the last Muslim stronghold of Granada and the last Spanish Jews were either exiled or converted to Christianity. Other Jewish communities in Europe were also targets of Christian violence. From 1096 onward Jews were massacred, marginalized by the Catholic Church at the Fourth Lateran Council of 1215, and exiled by England and France.

In 1095, Western Christians turned their military attention outside the continent, launching a series of Crusades that would last until the thirteenth century. The First Crusade turned out to be only one of many, and the end result was not just warfare between Christian and Muslim, but ultimately between Christian and Christian. In 1204 Venice led a Crusade against the city of Constantinople itself, and in 1226 a Crusade was called against Christian heretics in France, known as the Albigensian Crusade.

12.1

URBAN II'S CALL FOR THE FIRST CRUSADE

The First Crusade began in 1095 when Pope Urban II sent out a call for all "servants of God" to take up arms and rescue the Byzantine Empire from Muslim expansion. Urban also wanted to recapture the Holy Land, restoring Christian control to Jerusalem. The Call came in response to a plea from Byzantine Emperor Alexius II Comnenus, who had written a letter to Urban requesting soldiers to augment his forces. Instead, Christians of all social classes answered the Call; the first Crusader "army" to reach Constantinople was made up of ordinary pilgrims, men and women, most of who lacked any military training. Successive waves of actual soldiers, divided by feudal allegiance and nationality into fiercely competitive armies, succeeded in capturing the Holy Land in 1099, and established several Christian kingdoms.

✤

QUESTIONS

1. How does Urban use the Call for a Crusade to bolster his own power as pope?
2. What benefit does Urban promise those who die in battle or on the way to the Crusade? What else might motivate someone to go on Crusade?
3. Of the four accounts, Guibert of Nogent was probably not present when Urban gave the actual speech. How does his account differ from the other three?

Fulcher of Chartres

Most beloved brethren: Urged by necessity, I Urban, by the permission of God chief bishop and prelate over the whole world, have come into these parts as an ambassador with a divine admonition to you, the servants of God....

"Although, O sons of God, you have promised more firmly than ever to keep the peace among yourselves and to preserve the rights of the church, there remains still an important work for you to do. Freshly quickened by the divine correction, you must apply the strength of your righteousness to another matter which concerns you as well as God. For your brethren who live in the east are in urgent need of your help, and you must hasten to give them the aid which has often been promised them. For, as most of you have heard, the Turks and Arabs have attacked them and have conquered the territory of Romania [that is, the Greek empire] as far west as the shore of the Mediterranean and the Hellespont, which is called the Arm of St. George. They have occupied more and more of the lands of those Christians, and have overcome them in seven battles. They have killed and captured many, and have destroyed the churches and devastated the empire. If you permit them to continue thus for a while with impunity, the faithful of God will be much more widely attacked by them. On this account I, or rather the Lord, beseech you as Christ's heralds to publish this everywhere and to persuade all people of whatever rank, footsoldiers and knights, poor and rich, to carry aid promptly to those Christians and to destroy that vile race from the lands of our friends. I say this to those who are present, but it is meant also for those who are absent. Moreover, Christ commands it.

"All who die by the way, whether by land or by sea, or in battle against the pagans, shall have immediate remission of sins. This I grant them through the power of God with which I am invested. O what a disgrace, if such a despised and base race, which worships demons, should conquer a people which has the faith of omnipotent God and is made glorious with the name of Christ! With what reproaches will the Lord overwhelm us if you do not aid those who, with us, profess the Christian religion! Let those who have been accustomed to wage unjust private warfare against the faithful now go against the infidels and end with victory this war which should have been begun long ago. Let those who for a long time have been robbers now become knights. Let those who have been fighting against their brothers and relatives now fight in a proper way against the barbarians. Let those who have been serving as mercenaries for small pay now obtain the eternal reward. Let those who have been wearing themselves out in both body and should now work for a double honor. Behold! on this side will be the sorrowful and poor, on that, the rich; on this side, the enemies of the Lord, on that, his friends. Let those who go not put off the journey, but rent their lands and collect money for their expenses; and as soon as winter is over and spring comes, let them eagerly set out on the way with God as their guide."

Robert the Monk

In 1095 a great council was held at Auvergne, in the city of Clermont. Pope Urban II, accompanied by cardinals and bishops, presided over it. It was made famous by the presence of many bishops and princes from France and Germany. After the council had attended to ecclesiastical matters, the pope went out into a public square, because no house was able to hold the people, and addressed them in a very persuasive speech, as follows:

"O race of Franks, O people who live beyond the mountains [that is, from Rome], O people loved and chosen by God, as is clear from your many deeds, distinguished over all other nations by the situation of your land, your catholic faith, and your regard for the holy church, we have a special message and exhortation for you. For we wish you to know what a grave matter has brought us to your country. The sad news has come from Jerusalem and Constantinople that the people of Persia, an accursed and foreign race, enemies of God, 'a generation that set not their heart aright, and whose spirit was not steadfast with God' [Ps. 78-8], have invaded the lands of those Christians and devastated them with the sword, rapine, and fire. Some of the Christians they have carried away as slaves; others they have put to death. The churches they have either destroyed or turned into mosques. They desecrate and overthrow the altars. They circumcise the Christians and pour the blood from the circumcision on the altars or in the baptismal fonts. Some they kill in a horrible way by cutting open the abdomen, taking out a part of the entrails and tying them to a stake; they then beat them and compel them to walk until all their entrails are drawn out and they fall to the ground. Some they use as targets for their arrows. They compel some to stretch out their necks, and then they try to see whether they can cut off their heads with one stroke of the sword. It is better to say nothing of their horrible treatment of the women. They have taken from the Greek empire a tract of land so large that it takes more than two months to walk through it. Whose duty is it to avenge this and recover that land, if not yours? For to you more than to other nations the Lord has given military spirit, courage, agile bodies, and the bravery to strike down those who resist you. Let your minds be stirred to bravery by the deeds of your forefathers, and by the efficiency and greatness of Charles the Great, and of Louis his son, and of the other kings who have destroyed Turkish kingdoms and established Christianity in their lands. You should be moved especially by the holy grave of our Lord and Savior which is now held by unclean peoples, and by the holy places which are treated with dishonor and irreverently befouled with their uncleanness.

"O bravest knights, descendants of unconquered ancestors, do not be weaker than they, but remember their courage. If you are kept back by your love for your children, relatives, and wives, remember what the Lord says in the Gospel: 'He that loveth father or mother more than me is not worthy of me' [Matt. 10:37]; 'and everyone that hath forsaken houses, or brothers, or sisters, or father, or mother, or wife, or children, or land for my name's sake shall receive a hundredfold and shall inherit everlasting life' [Matt. 19:29]. Let no possessions keep you back, no solicitude for your property. Your land is shut in on all sides by the sea and mountains and is too thickly populated. There is not much wealth here and the soil scarcely yields enough to support you. On this account you kill and devour each other, and carry on war and mutually destroy each other. Let your hatred and quarrels cease, your civil wars come to an end and all your dissensions stop. Set out on the road to the holy sepulcher, take the land from that wicked people and make it your own. That land which, as the scriptures says, if lowing with milk and honey, God gave to the children of Israel. Jerusalem is the best of all lands, more fruitful than all others, as it were a second paradise of delights. This land our Savior made illustrious by his birth, beautiful with his life, and sacred with his suffering; he redeemed it with his death and glorified it with his tomb. This royal city is now held captive by her enemies, made pagan by those who know not God.

She asks and longs to liberated and does not cease to beg you to come to her aid. She asks aid especially from you because, as I have said, God has given more of the military spirit to you than to other nations. Set out on this journey and you will obtain the remission of your sins and be sure of the incorruptible glory of the kingdom of heaven."

When Pope Urban had said this and much more of the same sort, all who were present were moved to cry out with one accord, "It is the will of God, it is the will of God." When the pope heard this he raised his eyes to heaven and gave thanks to God, and commanding silence with a gesture of his hand, he said: "My dear brethren, today there is fulfilled in you that which the Load says in the Gospel, 'Where two or three are gathered together in my name, there I am in the midst' [Matt. 18:20]. For unless the Lord God had been in your minds you would not all have said the same thing. For although you spoke with many voices, nevertheless, it was one and the same thing that made you speak. So I say unto you, God, who put those words into your hearts, has caused you to utter them. Therefore let these words be your battle cry because God caused you to speak them. Whenever you meet the enemy in battle, you shall all cry out, 'It is the will of God, it is the will of God.' And we do not command the old or weak to go, or those who cannot bear arms. No women shall go without their husbands, or brothers, or proper companions, for such would be a hindrance rather than a help, a burden rather than an advantage. Let the rich aid the poor and equip them for fighting and take them with them. Clergymen shall not go without the consent of their bishop, for otherwise the journey would be of no value to them. Nor will this pilgrimage be of any benefit to a layman if he goes without the blessing of his priest. Whoever therefore shall determine to make this journey and shall make a vow to God and shall offer himself as a living sacrifice, holy, acceptable to God [Rom. 12:1], shall wear a cross on his brow or on his breast. And when he returns after having fulfilled his vow he shall wear the cross on his back. I this way he will obey the command of the Lord, 'Whosoever doth not bear this cross and come after me is not worthy of me'" [Luke 1:27].

When these things had been done, while all prostrated themselves on the earth and beat their breasts, one of the cardinals, named Gregory, made confession for them, and they were given absolution for all their sins. After the absolution, they received the benediction and permission to go home.

Baldric of Dol

"We have heard, most beloved brethren, and you have heard what we cannot recount without deep sorrow — how, with great hurt and dire sufferings, our Christian brothers, members in Christ, are scourged, oppressed, and injured in Jerusalem, in Antioch, and the other cities of the East. Your own blood-brothers, your companions, your associates (for you are sons of the same Christ and the same church) are either subjected in their inherited homes to other masters, or are driven from them, or they come as beggars among us; or, which is far worse, they are flogged and exiled as slaves for sale in their own land. Christian blood, redeemed by the blood of Christ, has been shed, and Christian flesh, akin to the flesh of Christ, has been subjected to unspeakable degradation and servitude. Everywhere in those cities there is sorrow, everywhere misery, everywhere groaning (I say it with a sigh). The churches in which divine mysteries were celebrated in olden times are now, to our sorrow, used as stables for the animals of these people! Holy men do not possess those cities; nay, base and bastard Turks hold sway over our brothers. The blessed Peter first presided as bishop at Antioch; behold, in his own church the gentiles [that is, the non-Christians] have established their superstitions, and the Christian religion, which they ought rather to cherish, they have basely shut out from the hall dedicated to God! The estates given for the support of the saints and the patrimony of nobles set aside for the sustenance of the poor are subject to pagan tyranny, while cruel masters abuse for their own purposes the returns from these lands. The priesthood of God has been ground down into the dust. The sanctuary of God (unspeakable shame!) is everywhere profaned. Whatever Christians still remain in hiding there are sought out with unheard of tortures.

"Of holy Jerusalem, brethren, we dare not speak, for we are exceedingly afraid and ashamed to speak of it. This very city, in which, as you all know; Christ himself suffered for us, because our sins demanded it, has been reduced to the pollution of paganism and, I say it to our disgrace, withdrawn from the service of God. Such is the heap of reproach upon us who have so much deserved it! Who now serves the church of the blessed Mary in the valley of Josaphat, in which church she herself was buried in body? But why do we pass over the Temple of Solomon, nay of the Lord, in which the barbarous nations placed their idols contrary to law, human and divine? Of the Lord's Sepulcher we have refrained from speaking, since some of you with your own eyes have seen to what abominations it has been given over. The Turks violently took from it the offerings which you brought there for alms in such vast amounts, and in addition, they scoffed much and often at your religion. And yet in that place (I say only what you already know) rested the Lord; there he died for us; there he was buried. How precious would be the longed-for, incomparable place of the Lord's burial, even if God failed there to perform the yearly miracle! For in the days of his passion all the lights in the Sepulcher and round about in the church, which have been extinguished, are re-lighted by divine command. Whose heart is so stony, brethren, that it is not touched by so great a miracle? Believe me, that man is bestial and senseless whose heart such divinely manifest grace does not move to faith! And yet the gentiles see this in common with the Christians and are not turned from their ways! They are, indeed, afraid, but they are not converted to the faith; nor is it to be wondered at, for a blindness of mind rules over them. With what afflictions they wronged you who have returned and are now present, you yourselves know too well, you who there sacrificed your substance and your blood for God....

"What are we saying? Listen and learn! You, girt about with the badge of knighthood, are arrogant with great pride; you rage against your brothers and cut each other in pieces. This is not the [true] soldiery of Christ which rends asunder the sheep-fold of the Redeemer. The holy church has reserved a soldiery for herself to help her people, but you debase her wickedly to her hurt. Let us confess the truth, whose heralds we ought to be; truly, you are not holding to the way which leads to life. You, the oppressors of children, plunderers of widows; you, guilty of homicide, of sacrilege, robbers of another's rights, you who await the pay of thieves for the shedding of Christian blood — as vultures smell fetid corpses, so do you sense battles from afar and rush to them eagerly. Verily, this is the worst way, for it is utterly removed from God! If, forsooth, you wish to be mindful of your souls, either lay down the girdle of such knighthood, or advance boldly, as knights of Christ, and rush as quickly as you can to the defense of the eastern church. For she it is from whom the joys of your whole salvation have come forth, who poured into your mouths the milk of divine wisdom, who set before you the holy teachings of the Gospels. We say this, brethren, that you may restrain your murderous hands from the destruction of your brothers, and in behalf of your relatives in the faith oppose yourselves to the gentiles. Under Jesus Christ, our leader, may you struggle for your Jerusalem, in Christian battle-line, most invincible line, even more successfully than did the sons of Jacob of old — struggle, that you may assail and drive out the Turks, more execrable than the Jebusites, who are in this land, and may you deem it a beautiful thing to die for Christ in that city in which he died for us. But if it befall you to die this side of it, be sure that to have died on the way is of equal value, if Christ shall find you in his army. God pays with the same shilling, whether at the first or eleventh hour. You should shudder, brethren, you should shudder at raising a violent hand against Christians; it is less wicked to brandish your sword against Saracens. It is the only warfare that is righteous, for it is charity to risk your life for your brothers. That you may not be troubled about the concerns of tomorrow, know that those who fear God want nothing, nor those who cherish him in truth. The possessions of the enemy, too, will be yours, since you will make spoil of their treasures and return victorious to your own; or empurpled with our own blood, you will have gained everlasting glory. For such a commander you ought to fight, for one who lacks neither might nor wealth with which to reward you. Short is the way, little the labor, which, nevertheless, will repay you with the crown that fades not away. Accordingly, we speak with the authority of the prophet: 'Gird they sword upon thy thigh, O mighty one.' Gird yourselves, everyone of you, I say, and be valiant sons; for it is better for you to die in battle than to behold the sorrows of your race and of your holy places. Let neither property nor the alluring charms of your wives entice you from going; nor let the trials that are to be borned so deter you that you remain here."

And turning to the bishops, he said, "You brothers and fellow bishops; you, fellow priests and sharers with us in Christ, make this same announcement through the churches committed to you, and with your whole soul vigorously preach the journey to Jerusalem. When they have confessed the disgrace of their sins, do you, secure in Christ, make this same announcement through the churches committed to you, and with your whole soul vigorously preach the journey to Jerusalem. When they have confessed the disgrace of their sins, do you, secure in Christ, grant them speedy pardon. Moreover, you who are to go shall have us praying for you; we shall have you fighting for God's people. It is our duty to pray, yours to fight against the Amalekites [that is, biblical enemies of the Hebrews]. With Moses, we shall extend unwearied hands in prayer to heaven, while you go forth and brandish the sword, like dauntless warriors, against Amalek."

As those present were thus clearly informed by these and other words of this kind from the apostolic lord, the eyes of some were bathed in tears; some trembled, and yet others discussed the matter. However, in the presence of all at that same council, and as we looked on, the bishop of Puy, a man of great renown and of highest ability, went to the pope with joyful countenance and on bended knee sought and entreated blessing and permission to go. Over and above this, he won from the pope the command that all should obey him, and that he should hold sway over al the army in behalf of the pope, since all knew him to be a prelate of unusual energy and industry.

From *The Crusades: A Reader*, edited by S. J. Allen and Emilie Amt, Ontario: Broadview Press, 2003, pp. 39-45. Reprinted by permission of Broadview Press.

12.2

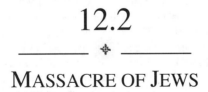

MASSACRE OF JEWS

On their way to Constantinople to join with other Crusading armies, the first pilgrims who responded to Urban's Call (source 12.1) for the First Crusade launched a series of attacks on Jewish communities in Germany. These Crusaders decided that Jewish "infidels" were just as worthy a target as Muslims. This source is a Jewish description of the massacre of Jews in Mayence (Mainz) in 1096.

———— ✦ ————

QUESTIONS

1. Why do the Jews view their own destruction as a sentence from God?
2. Why do some of the Jews choose suicide, or to kill their own families, when threatened by the Christians?
3. Besides the religious differences between Christians and Jews, what other motivation might the Crusaders have had for killing Jews?

. . . The hand of the Lord was heavy against His people. All the Gentiles were gathered together against the Jews in the courtyard to blot out their name, and the strength of our people weakened when they saw the wicked Edomites overpowering them. [The Edomites were the traditional foes of the Jews; here, Christians are meant.] The bishop's men, who had promised to help them, were the very first to flee, thus delivering the Jews into the hands of the enemy. They were indeed a poor support; even the bishop himself fled from his church for it was thought to kill him also because he had spoken good things of the Jews….[Archbishop Ruthard had been paid to remain and defend the Jews. He was later accused of having received some of the plunder taken from them.]

When the children of the holy covenant saw that the heavenly decree of death had been issued and that the enemy had conquered them and had entered the courtyard, then all of them — old men and young, virgins and children, servants and maids — cried out together to their Father in heaven and, weeping for themselves and for their lives, accepted as just the sentence of God. One to another they said: "Let us be strong and let us bear the yoke of the holy religion, for only in this world can the enemy kill us — and the easiest of the four deaths is by the sword. But we, our souls in paradise, shall continue to live eternally, in the great shining reflection [of divine glory]." [In Jewish law the four death penalties were: stoning, burning, beheading, strangulation.]

With a whole heart and with a willing soul they then spoke: "After all it is not right to criticize the acts of God — blessed by He and blessed by His name — who has given to us His Torah and a command to put ourselves to death, to kill ourselves for the unity of His holy name. Happy are we if we do His will. Happy is anyone who is killed or slaughtered, who dies for the unity of His name, so that he is ready to enter the World to Come, to dwell in the heavenly camp with the righteous — with Rabbi Akiba and his companions, the pillars of the universe, who were killed for His name's sake. [The Romans martyred Akiba during the Bar Kikba revolt, about 135 C.E.] Not only this; but he exchanges the world of darkness for the world of light, the world of trouble for the world of joy, and the world that passes away for the world that lasts for all eternity." Then all of them, to a man, cried out with a loud voice: "Now we must delay no longer for the enemy are already upon us. Let us hasten and offer ourselves as a sacrifice to the Lord. Let him who has a knife examine it that it not be nicked, and let him come and slaughter us for the sanctification of the Only One, the Everlasting, and then let him cut his own throat or plunge the knife into his own body." [A nick in the slaughterer's knife would make it ritually unfit.]

As soon as the enemy came into the courtyard they found some of the very pious there with our brilliant master, Isaac ben Moses. He stretched out his neck, and his head they cut off first. The others, wrapped in their fringed praying-shawls, sat by themselves in the courtyard, eager to do the will of their Creator. They did not care to flee into the chamber to save themselves for this temporal life, but out of love they received upon themselves the sentence of God. The enemy showered stones and arrows upon them, but they did not care to flee; and [Esther 9:5] "with the stroke of the sword, and with slaughter, and destruction" the foe killed all of those whom they found there. When those in the chambers saw the deed of these righteous ones, how the enemy and already come upon them, they then cried out, all of them: "There is nothing better than for us to offer our lives as a sacrifice." [The outnumbered Jews had no chance to win: Emico is reported to have had about 12,000 men.]

The women there girded their loins with strength and slew their sons and their daughters and then themselves. Many men, too, plucked up courage and killed their wives, their sones, their infants. The tender and delicate mother slaughtered the babe she had played with; all of them, men and women arose and slaughtered one another. The maidens and the young brides and grooms looked out of the windows and in a loud voice cried: "Look and see, O our God, what we do for the sanctification of Thy great name in order not to exchange you for a hanged and crucified one...."

Thus were the precious children of Zion, the Jews of Mayence, tried with ten trials like Abraham, our father, and like Hananiah, Mishael, and Azariah [who were thrown into a fiery furnace, Daniel 3:21]. They tied their sons as Abraham tied Isaac his son, they received upon themselves with a willing soul the yoke of the fear of god, the King of the Kings of Kings, the Holy One, blessed be He, rather than deny and exchange the religion of our King for [Isaiah 14:19] "an abhorred offshoot [Jesus]...." [Christians and Jews of those days often spoke contemptuously of each other's religion.] They stretched out their necks to the slaughter and they delivered their pure souls to their Father in heaven. Righteous and pious women bared their throats to each other, offering to be sacrificed for the unity of the Name. A father turning to his son or brother, a brother to his sister, a woman to her son or daughter, a neighbor to a neighbor or a friend, a groom to a bride, a fiancée to a fiancée, would kill and would be killed, and blood touched blood. The blood of the men mingled with their wives', the blood of the fathers with their children's, the blood of the brothers with their sisters', the blood of the teachers with their disciples', the blood of the grooms with their brides', the blood of the leaders with their cantors', the blood of the judges with their scribes', and the blood of infants and sucklings with their mothers'. For the unity of the honored and awe-inspiring Name were they killed and slaughtered.

The ears of him who hears these things will tingle, for who has ever heard anything like this? Inquire now and look about, was there ever such an abundant sacrifice as this since the days of the primeval Adam? Were there ever eleven hundred offerings on one day, each one of them like the sacrifice of Isaac, the son of Abraham?

For the sake of Isaac who was ready to be sacrificed on Mount Moriah, the world shook, as it is said [Isaiah 33:7]: "Behold their valiant ones cry without; [the angels of peace weep bitterly]" and [Jeremiah 4:28] "the heavens grow dark." Yet see what these martyrs did! Why did the heavens not grow dark and the stars not withdraw their brightness? Why did not the moon and the sun grow dark in their heavens when on one day, on the third of Siwan, on a Tuesday, eleven hundred souls were killed and slaughtered, among them so many infants and sucklings who had not transgressed nor sinned, so many poor, innocent souls?

Wilt Thou, despite this, still restrain Thyself, O Lord? For Thy sake it was that these numberless souls were killed. Avenge quickly the blood of Thy servants which was spilt in our days and in our sight. Amen.

II. Rachel and Her Children

Now I shall recount an tell of the most unusual deeds that were done on that day [May 27, 1096] by these righteous ones....Who has ever seen anything like this? Who has ever heard of a deed like that which was performed by this righteous and pious woman, the young Rachel, the daughter of Rabbi Isaac ben Asher, the wife of Rabbi Judah? For she said to her friends: "I have four children. Do not spare even them, lest the Christians come, take them alive, and bring them up in their false religion. Through them, too, sanctify the name of the Holy God."

So one of her companions came and picked up a knife to slaughter her son. But when the mother of the children saw the knife, she let out a loud and bitter lament and she beat her face and breast, crying: "Where are Thy mercies, O God?" In the bitterness of her soul she said to her friend: "Do not slay Isaac in the presence of his brother Aaron lest Aaron see his brother's death and run away." The woman then took the lad Isaac, who was small and very pretty, and she slaughtered him while the mother spread out her sleeves to receive the blood, catching it in her garment instead of a basin. When the child Aaron saw that his brother Isaac was slain, he screamed again and again: "Mother, mother, do not butcher me," and ran and hid under a chest.

She had two daughters also who still lived at home, Bella and Matrona, beautiful young girls, the children of her husband Rabbi Judah. The girls took the knife and sharpened it themselves that it should not be nicked. Then the woman bared their necks and sacrificed them to the Lord God of Hosts who has commanded us not to change His pure religion but to be perfect with Him, as it is written [Deuteronomy 18:13]: "Perfect shall you be with the Lord your God."

When this righteous woman had made an end of sacrificing her three children to their Creator, she then raised her voice and called out to her son Aaron: "Aaron, where are you? You also I will not spare nor will I have any mercy." Then she dragged him out by his foot from under the chest where he had hidden himself, and she sacrificed him before God, the high and exalted. She put her children next to her body, two on each side, covering them with her two sleeves, and there they lay struggling in the agony of death. When the enemy seized the room they found her witting and wailing over them. "Show us the money that is under your sleeves," they said to her. But when it was the slaughtered children they saw, they struck her and killed her, upon her children, and her spirit flew away and her soul found peace at last. To her applied the Biblical verse [Hosea 10:14]: "The mother was dashed in pieces with her children.". . .

When the father saw the death of his four beautiful, lovely children, he cried aloud, weeping and wailing, and threw himself upon the sword in his hand so that his bowels came out, and he wallowed in blood on the road together with the dying who were convulsed, rolling in their life's blood. The enemy killed all those who were left in the room and then stripped them naked; [Lamentations 1:11] "See, O Lord, and behold, how abject I am become." Then the crusaders began to give thanks in the name of "the hanged one" because they had done what they wanted with all those in the room of the bishop so that not a soul escaped. [The crusaders now held a thanksgiving service in the archbishop's palace where the massacre took place.]

From *The Jew in the Medieval World: A Sourcebook: 315-1791*, by Jacob R. Marcus, pp. 116-120. Copyright © 1938 Jewish Publication Society of America. Reprinted with permission.

12.3

RICHARD I AND SALADIN: THE THIRD CRUSADE

After nine decades of Christian control, Muslims re-conquered Jerusalem in 1187. Inevitably this led to a renewed call for crusading. Unlike previous crusades, this time the Europeans faced well-organized Muslim forces, which were unified under a Sunni Kurd named Saladin. Saladin proved a formidable enemy but also earned the respect of the Crusaders. Three European kings set sail for the Third Crusade: Richard I (d. 1199) of England, Philip II (d. 1223) of France, and Holy Roman Emperor Frederick Barbarossa (d. 1190). Only Richard I, the Lionhearted, would achieve any success, although he would fail to take Jerusalem.

Richard had to settle for capturing Acre in 1187. It is one of the most controversial moments in the history of the Crusades. In the capture of Jerusalem Saladin had promised not to harm Christian civilians; Richard made no such promises and slaughtered thousands of Muslim prisoners at Acre. Saladin responded by ending his ban on killing Christian prisoners. In the end, however, Richard and Saladin negotiated access for Christian pilgrims to Jerusalem.

The following descriptions provide a chance to compare Saladin and Richard. The first is from Baha ad-Din, an Arab biographer of Saladin, and the second is from the Deeds of Richard.

QUESTIONS

1. Baha ad-Din states that Saladin showed respect for infidels by suggesting they convert to Islam. How is this respectful?
2. What are the political and military advantages for Saladin in not slaughtering Christian prisoners?
3. What are the political and military advantages for Richard in slaughtering the Muslim prisoners?

1. What I have observed of Saladin's attachment to the principles of religion, and his respect for every part of the holy law

In our collection of authentic traditions stands the following saying of the holy Prophet [that is, Mohammed]: "Islam is built upon five columns: confession of the unity of God, the regular performance of prayer, payment of the tenth in charity, the fast of the month Ramadon, and pilgrimage to the holy house of God [in Mecca]. Saladin — may God be merciful to him! — truly believed in the doctrines of the faith, and often recited prayers in praise of God. He had accepted the dogmas of religion upon demonstrable proofs, the result of his conversations with the most learned doctors and the most eminent jurisconsults. In these arguments he acquired knowledge that enabled him to speak to the purpose when a discussion took place in his presence, although he did not employ the technical language of the lawyers. These conversations confirmed him in a true faith, which remained undisturbed by any doubt, and, in his case, prevented the arrow of speculation from overshooting the mark, and striking at last on doubt and infidelity.

The learned doctor Kotb ed-Uin en-Nisaburi had composed an exposition of Islam for the benefit of this prince, containing all that was necessary for him to know. As [Saladin] was much pleased with this treatise, he made his younger sons learn it by heart, so that good doctrine might be established in their souls from their tenderest years. I have myself seen him take this book and read it aloud to his children, after they had committed its contents to memory.

As to prayer, he was always regular in his attendance at the public service [on Fridays], and he said one day that for several years he had never failed in this duty. When he was ill, he used to send for the imam [that is, teacher] alone, and forcing himself to keep on his feet, would recite the Friday prayers. He recited the usual prayers regularly, and, if he woke during the night, said a prayer. If he did not wake, he used to pray before the morning prayer. As long as consciousness lasted, he never failed to say his prayers. I saw him perform this duty regularly during his last illness, and he discontinued it only during the three days in which his mind was wandering. When he was traveling, he used to get down from his horse at the appointed hours to pray.

Let us speak of his tenth in charity. The sum of money he left at his death was not large enough to be submitted to this tax; his private charities had absorbed everything. He who had possessed such abundant wealth left in his treasury, when he died, only forty-seven Nasri dirhems [equivalent to Greek drachmas], and a single Tyrian gold piece [that is, a gold coin minted at Tyre]. He left neither goods, nor house, nor real estate, neither garden, nor village, nor cultivated land, nor any other species of property....

5. *Of his zeal in fighting in God's cause*

God almighty said (Quran 29:69): "Those who fight strenuously for us we will surely guide in our way, for, verily, God is with those who do well." There are numerous texts in the Quran exhorting us to fight for the faith. And, of a truth, the sultan entertained an ardent passion for the holy war; his mind was always filled with it. Therefore one might swear, in absolute security and without risk of perjury, that from the time when he first issued forth to fight the infidel, he spent not a single piece of gold or silver except for the carrying on of the holy war or for distribution among his troops. With him to wage war in God's name was a veritable passion; his whole heart was filled with it, and he gave body and soul to the cause. He spoke of nothing else; all his thoughts were of instruments of war; his soldiers monopolized every idea. He showed all deference to those who talked of the holy war and who encouraged the people to take part in it. His desire to fight in God's cause forced him to leave his family, his children, his native land, the place of his abode, and all else in his land. Leaving all these earthly enjoyments, he contented himself with dwelling beneath the shadow of a tent, shaken to the right hand and to the left by the breath of every wind....

8. *His care to be polite:*

The holy Prophet said: "I have been sent to make manifest in all their beauty the noble qualities of the soul." When any man gave his hand to the Prophet he clasped it until the other withdrew it. And so, too, our sultan was very noble of heart; his face expressed kindliness, his modesty was great, and his politeness perfect. No visitor ever came to him without being given to eat, and receiving what he desired. He greeted everyone, even infidels, politely. For instance, after the conclusion of peace in the month of

Shawâl, in the year 588 [that is, Oct. to Nov. 1192], he left Jerusalem to journey to Damascus, and whilst he was on his way he saw the [Frankish] prince of Antioch, who had come up unexpectedly, and was standing at the entrance of his tent. This prince had come to ask something from him, and the sultan gave him back el 'Amk, which territory he had acquired in the year 584 [that is, 1188-1189), at the time of the conquest of the coastal lands. So, too, I was present at Nazareth when the sultan received the visit of the [Frankish] lord of Sidon; he showed him every mark of respect, treated him with honor, and admitted him to his own table. He even proposed to him that he should embrace Islam, set before him some of the beauties of our religion, and urged him to adopt it....

I was present one day when a Frankish prisoner was brought before him. This man was in such a state of excitement that his terror was visible in every feature. The interpreter asked him the cause of his fear, and God put the following answer in the mouth of the unfortunate fellow: "Before I saw his face I was greatly afraid, but now that I am in the presence [of Saladin] and can see him, I am certain that he will do me no harm." The sultan, moved by these words, gave him his life, and sent him away free.

I was attending the prince on one of the expeditions he used to make on the flanks of the enemy, when one of the scouts brought up a woman, rending her garments, weeping and beating her breast without ceasing. "This woman," the soldier said, "came out from among the Franks, and asked to be taken to the sultan; so I brought her here." The sultan asked her, through his interpreter, what was the matter, and she replied: "Some Muslim thieves got into my tent last night and carried off my child, a little girl. All night long I have never ceased begging for help, and our princes advised me to appeal to the king of the Muslims. 'He is very merciful,' they said. 'We will allow you to go out to seek him and ask for your daughter.' Therefore they permitted me to pass through the lines, and in you lies my only hope of finding my child." The sultan was moved by her distress; tears came into his eyes, and, acting from the generosity of his heart, he sent a messenger to the market-place of the camp, to seek her little one and bring her away, after repaying her purchaser the price he had given. It was early morning when her case was heard, and in less than an hour the horseman returned, bearing the little girl on his shoulder. As soon as the mother caught sight of her, she threw herself on the ground, rolling her face in the dust, and weeping so violently that it drew tears from all who saw her. She raised her eyes to heaven, and uttered words which we did not understand. We gave her back her daughter, and she was mounted to return to the enemy's army.

The sultan was very averse to the infliction of corporal punishment on his servants, even when they cheated him beyond endurance. On one occasion two purses filled with Egyptian gold pieces had been lodged in the treasury; these were stolen, and two purses full of copper coins left in their place. All he did was to dismiss the people employed in that department of his service.

In the year 583 [that is, 1187], at the battle of Hattin — a famous day's fight of which, please God, we shall speak in its proper place — Prince Arnat [that is, Reynald of Châtillon], lord of el-Kerak, and the king of the Franks of the seacoast [that is, Guy of Lusignan], were both taken prisoner, and the sultan commanded them to be brought before him. This accursed Arnat was a great infidel, and a very strong man. On one occasion, when there was a truce between the Muslims and the Franks, he had treacherously attacked and carried off a caravan that passed through his territory, coming from Egypt. He seized these people, put them to torture, and put some of them in grain-pits, and imprisoned some in narrow cells. When they objected that there was a truce between the two peoples, he replied: "Ask your Mohammed to deliver you." The sultan, to whom these words were reported, took an oath to slay the infidel with his own hand, if God should ever place him in his power. The day of the battle of Hattin God delivered this man into the hands of the sultan, and he resolved at once to slay him, that he might fulfill his oath. He commanded him to be brought before him, together with the king. The latter complained of thirst, and the sultan ordered a cup of sherbet to be given him. The king, having drunk some of if, handed the cup to Arnat, whereupon the sultan said to the interpreter: "Say to the king, 'It is you who give him drink, but I give him neither to drink nor to eat.'" By these words he wished it to be understood that honor forbade him to harm any man who had tasted his hospitality. He then struck him on the neck with his own hand, to fulfill the vow he had made. After this, when he had taken Acre, he delivered all the prisoners, to the number of about four thousand, from their wretched durance, and sent them back to their own country and their homes, giving each of them a sum of money for the expenses of his journey. This is what I have been told by many persons, for I was not present myself when it took place....

King Richard...turned his attention to packing up the petraries and mangonels for transportation. For when the time had expired which had been fixed by the Turks for the restoration of the cross and the ransom of the hostages, after waiting three weeks, according to the conditions, to see if Saladin would keep his word and covenant, the king regarded him as a transgressor, as Saladin appeared not to care about it at all; and perhaps this happened by the dispensation of God, so that something more advantageous might be obtained. But the Saracens asked further time to fulfill their promise and make search for the cross....

When it became clearly evident to King Richard that a longer period had elapsed than had been agreed, and that Saladin was obdurate and would not bother to ransom the hostages, he called together a council of the chiefs of the people, by whom it was resolved that the hostages should all be hanged, except a few nobles of the higher class, who might ransom themselves or be exchanged for some Christian captives. King Richard, aspiring to destroy the Turks root and branch, and to punish their wanton arrogance, as well as to abolish the law of Mohammed, and to vindicate the Christian religion, on the Friday before the Assumption of the blessed virgin Mary, ordered 2,700 of the Turkish hostages to be led forth from the city and hanged; his soldiers marched forward with delight to fulfill his commands and to retaliate, with the assent of divine grace, by taking revenge upon those who had destroyed so many of the Christians with missiles from bows and crossbows.... [The crusaders then moved toward Jerusalem, arriving in it vicinity in mid-1192, after much fighting and many delays.]

✤ ✤ ✤

Itinerary of the Pilgrims and Deeds of Richard

The [German] army now entered the Armenian territories: all rejoiced at having left a hostile kingdom, and at their arrival in the country of the faithful. But, alas! a more fatal land awaited them, which was to extinguish the light and joy of all.... On the boarders of Armenia there was a place, surrounded on one side by steep mountains, on the other side by the river Selesius. While the packhorses and baggage were passing this river, the victorious emperor [Frederick Barbarossa] halted... [and] in consequence of the packhorses crossing the river, became at last impatient of the delay; and wishing to accelerate the march, he prepared to cross the nearest part of the stream, so as to get front of the packhorses and be at liberty to proceed. O sea! O earth! O heaven! the ruler of the [Holy] Roman Empire, ever august, in whom the glory of ancient Rome again flourished,...was overwhelmed in the waters and perished! And though those who were near him hastened to his assistance, yet his aged spark of life was extinguished by a sudden through not premature death....

When his funeral rites had been performed, they left the fatal spot as soon as possible, bearing with them the body of the emperor adorned with royal magnificence, that it might be carried to Antioch. There the flesh, being boiled from the bones, reposes in the church of the apostolic see, and the bones were conveyed by sea to Tyre, to be transported from there to Jerusalem…. The [emperor's army], arriving at Antioch after many and long fastings, gave way too plentifully to their appetites, and [many] died of sudden repletion, and so…the greater part of the great army perished, and most of the survivors returned to their own countries. A small body of them, ashamed to return, served under the emperor's son….

After Easter [1191] there arrived [at Acre] Philip, king of France, and not long after him, Richard, king of England…. Around [Acre] the besiegers lay in countless multitudes, chosen from every nation throughout Christendom and under the face of heaven, and well fitted for the labors and fatigues of war; for the city had now been besieged a long time, and had been afflicted by constant toil and tribulation, but the pressure of famine, and every kind of adversity, as we have before described. Moreover, beyond the besiegers was seen the Turkish army, not in a compact body, but covering the mountains and valleys, hills and plains, with tents, the colors of whose various forms were reflected by the sun…. King Richard beheld and counted all their army, and when he arrived in port, the king of France and a whole army of natives, and the princes, chiefs, an nobles, came forth to meet him and welcome him, with joy and exultation, for they had eagerly long for his arrival….

The city of Acre, from its strong position, and its being defended by the choicest men of the Turks, appeared difficult to take by assault. The French had hitherto spent their labor in vain in constructing machines and engines for breaking down the walls, with the greatest care; for whatever they erected, at a great expense, the Turks destroyed with Greek fire or some devouring conflagration….

From *The Crusades: A Reader*, edited by S. J. Allen and Emilie Amt, Ontario: Broadview Press, 2003, pp. 148-153, 170-172. Reprinted by permission of Broadview Press.

12.4

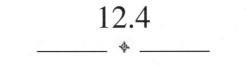

TEUTONIC KNIGHTS IN POLAND

Crusading orders — knights who took religious vows yet remained primarily soldiers — became popular after the success of the First Crusade. The Knights Templar, the Knights of St. John (the Hospitallers) and the Teutonic Knights are just three of these warrior monastic orders. Even when there were no more crusades to the Holy Land these orders remained active; the Templars became bankers until their dissolution in 1312, the Knights of St. John controlled Rhodes and established hospitals, and the Teutonic Knights turned their attention to eastern Europe and the conquest of the Prussians of Poland, and the conversion of the Slavs.

QUESTIONS

1. Do these German chronicles present anything to admire about the Prussians?
2. Compare these documents to the following source on the Mongols (Source 12.5); do the European observers view each of these groups the same?
3. Which temporal lord had final authority over the Teutonic Knights?

Concerning Brother Herman von Salza, fourth master of the German house

This powerful hero received God's blessing in many manifestations of grace. In all his actions he was eloquent, wise, far-seeing, just, honorable, and kind. When he saw the order, as master of which the brothers had elected him, in such a miserable condition, he said with a sigh: "Oh, heavenly God, I would gladly lose an eye if only the order, in my time, would increase enough so that it could equip ten knightly brothers." Thus he prayed fervently. And you, most gentle Christ, who are always willing to fulfill the wishes of the just who beseech you, what did you do? Did you let his prayer go unheard? No, your sweet kindness gave him all he prayed for: while he was master, the order increased in wealth and power so greatly that after his death it numbered two thousand brothers of German origin and of excellent manly strength....

Master Hermann also acquired for his order the most useful and best papal and imperial privileges. Also the order was given many a territory in Apulia, Greece, Cilicia, and Germany, Transylvania, Livonia, and Prussia....

God loved Master Hermann because he obeyed his orders, and he therefore helped him to rise high. All people loved him; pope and emperor, kings, dukes, famous princes, and other courageous lords were drawn to Master Hermann to such an extent that all his wishes were fulfilled to the benefit, honor, and advantage of the order.

How the Prussians devastated the land of Duke Conrad of Masovia and Kujavia

The Prussians often did much harm to these lands. They burned, destroyed, murdered men and drove women and children into eternal slavery. And if a pregnant woman could not keep up with their army, they killed her, together with the unborn child. They tore children from their mothers' arms and impaled them on fence poles where the little ones died in great misery, kicking and screaming. They devastated the duke's lands to such an extent that, of all the weaker and stronger fortresses of his territory, only Plock on the Vistula was left to him.

The heathen also destroyed about two hundred and fifty parish houses and many beautiful monasteries in which monks, nuns, and the secular clergy had served God. The heathen stormed about everywhere like madmen. They killed the priests before their altars while the body and blood of our Lord Jesus Christ were devoutly being consecrated. The heathen threw God upon the ground to the outrage and infamy of the sacred object, and stamped upon the sacred body of Christ and his blood in their fury. One could further see the unclean heathen stealing in their hate chalices, lamps, and all sorts of sacred vessels. It was pitiful to see how they treated not only the worldly virgins but also those devoted to God. The devilish crowd dragged them out of the cloisters by force and, to their great distress of heart, used them for their disgusting lust.

The Brothers of the Sword

When Duke Conrad saw his land so miserable destroyed, and he was not able to protect it, he conferred with Bishop Christian of Prussia and the great nobles of his court about what would help him and them most. He thus created for the protection of his country the Brotherhood of the Knights of Christ. They wore white tunics with red swords and stars on them. (The duke gave the order the castle of Dobrin on the Vistula.)

How the lands of Prussia and Kulm were given to the brothers of the order of the German house

The fame of the heroic deeds of the Teutonic order spread so far that Conrad of Masovia heard of it. Then the idea came to him — and the spirit of God moved him so that he did not relinquish it again — to invite these brothers for the protection of his country; to ask them whether they could not, with their force, free the Christians from their heathen oppressors since the Brothers of the Sword were unable to do so.

Imperial confirmation of the gift of land of Kulm to the Teutonic order (1226)

In the name of the holy and undivided Trinity, Amen. Frederick II, by the grace of God, emperor of the Romans, Augustus, king of Jerusalem and Sicily. God has raised our emperorship over all kings of the earth, and expanded the sphere of our power over different zones that his name may be magnified in this world and the faith be spread among the heathen peoples. Just as he created the Holy Roman Empire for the preaching of the Gospel, so likewise we must turn our care and attention to the conquest and conversion of the heathen....

For this reason we make known to and inform with this proclamation all living and future members of our empire: Brother Hermann, the worthy master of the Holy German Hospital of St. Mary at Jerusalem and our trustworthy servant, has informed us in all submissiveness that our dear Conrad, duke of Masovia and Kujavia, intends to make provision for him and his brothers in the land of Kuhn and the land between his march and the territories of the Prussians. Therefore the brothers shall take upon themselves the trouble and, on a suitable occasion, to the honor and glory of the true God, enter into the Prussian land and occupy it. Hermann postponed the acceptance of this offer and approached our majesty first with his submissive application; if we should deign to agree, he would begin the great task, trusting in our authorization. Our majesty should then confirm to him and his house all the land which the duke gave him, as well as all the land they would gain in Prussia through their efforts; also we should grant his house through a charter all rights and liberties for this area. Then he would accept the gift of said duke and use the goods and men of his house for the invasion and conquest of the county in tireless, unremitting effort.

Considering the attitude of active Christianity of this master, and how he eagerly desires to acquire these lands for his house in the name of God, and since this land belongs to our empire; trusting also in the wisdom of this master, a man mighty in word and deed, who will take up the matter forcefully with his brothers and carry through the conquest manfully, not abandoning it as many did before him, who wasted so much energy in this undertaking for nothing, we give this master the authority to invade the land of Prussia with the forces of his house, and with all means at his disposal.

We also permit and confirm to this master, his successors and his house for all time that they shall hold the said land which they will get from Duke Conrad according to his promise, any other lands which he may give them in the future, finally, all they conquer in Prussia with the grace of God, with rights to the mountains, the flat country, rivers, forests, and lakes as if it were an ancient imperial right, freely and unencumbered by any services or taxes, without any ordinary burdens, and no one shall have to give account for this, their land. They also shall be allowed in the land they conquer now or in the future, for the benefit of their house to erect road and other toll stations, hold fairs and markets, coin money, collect taxes and other tributes, set up traffic laws for their rivers and the sea as it seems good to them; they also shall always have the right of mining gold, silver, and other metals, and salt if such are at present found in their territories, or should be found there in the future. We also give them the right to set up judges and administrators, thus to govern and lead justly the people subject to them, both those who have been converted to the true faith as well as those who live in their delusion; to punish crimes of evil-doers wisely, to examine civil and criminal matters and to make decisions according to the dictates of reason. To this we add, out of our especial grace, that this master and his successors shall have and exercise sovereign rights in all their lands in the same manner as they are enjoyed by princes of the empire exercising the fullest rights in their lands, so that they may introduce good customs and promulgate regulations through which the faith of the Christians may be strengthened and their subjects enjoy peace and quiet.

Through this charter we prohibit any prince, duke, margrave, count, court official, magistrate, bailiff, every person of high or low estate, whether temporal or spiritual, to infringe on these privileges and authorizations. Should anyone dare to do so, let him know that he will have to pay a fine of one thousand pounds of gold, one half to our treasury, the other to the ones that were injured....

Of the images, disbeliefs, and customs of the Prussians

[The Prussians knew neither writing nor books.] and they were very much surprised at first when they saw the letters of the knights. And thus God was unknown to them; and thence came their error that they, in their foolishness, worshipped any creature as god: thunder, sun, moon, stars, birds, animals, and even toads. They also had fields, woods, and waters which were holy to them, so that they neither plowed nor fished nor cut wood in them....

The Prussians also believed in a resurrection, but not correctly. They believed that as he is on earth, noble or common, poor or rich, powerful or not, just so would he be after the resurrection. Therefore it was customary after the death of a noble to burn with him his weapons and horse, servants and maids, beautiful clothes, hunting dogs, falcons, and whatever else belongs to the equipment of a noble. Also with the common people everything they owned was burned, because they believed it all would rise with them and continue to serve them.

Also there was a devilish fraud connected with such a death, for the relatives of the dead came to the priest and asked if he had seen somebody go or drive by his house at such and such a time of the day or night. The priest then generally described to them exactly the figure of the dead man, his gestures, his weapons and dress, servants and horses. And to make them believe him more readily, he often showed them some mark which the dead man cut or scratched into his door while driving by.

After a victory, the heathen, for their salvation, usually sacrificed to their idols one-third of their booty which they gave to the priest, who burned it for the gods. [They also sacrificed horses and cast lots.]...

Wealth and good-looking clothes they value very slightly; as they take off their furs today, they put them on tomorrow. They are ignorant of soft beds and fine food. They drink, since ancient times, only three things: water, mead, and mares' milk....

[Their greatest virtue is hospitality.] They freely and willingly share food and drink. They think they have not treated their guests politely and well if they are not so full of drink that they vomit. Usually they urge each other mutually to take an innumerable number of drinks of equal measure. When they sit down to drink, every member of the household brings a measure to his host, drinks to him out of it, and the host then gladly finishes the drink. Thus they drink to each other, and let the cup go round without rest, and it runs to and fro, now full, now empty. They do this until man and woman, host and friends, big and small, all are drunk; that is pastime to them and a great honor — to me that does not seem honorable at all.

According to an old custom, they buy their women with money. The husband keeps his wife like a maid; she is not allowed to eat at his table, and daily has to wash the feet of the members of the household and the guests.

Nobody has to beg, because the poor man can go from house to house and eat wherever he likes.

If there is a murder, there is no reconciliation until the friends of the dead have killed the guilty person or one of his close relatives. If a Prussian is met suddenly by a great calamity, he usually kills himself in his distress....

Some Prussians, in honor of their gods, bathe daily; others never. Man and woman spin thread; some wool, the others linen, whichever they think the gods like most. Some never mount a black horse; some never a white one, or one of some other color.

As found in *The Crusades: A Reader*, ed. by S. J. Allen and Emilie Amt, pp. 280-284. Copyright © 2003 Broadview Press. Reprinted with permission of Suhrkamp Verlag.

12.5

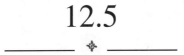

ENCOUNTERING THE MONGOLS, WILLIAM OF RUBRUCK

The Mongols were a nomadic, tribal people from the Asiatic steppes who were virtually unknown to the West until c. 1167. In that year, a warrior named Temuchin unified the tribes under his control and conquered the Far East, Central Asia, and the Russian kingdoms, reaching as far west as Poland and Hungary. Temuchin was granted the title of Genghis Khan, or "universal ruler." When he died in 1227, his vast empire was divided amongst his four grandsons. The European part of his empire, known as the Golden Horde, lasted only a few more decades before being gradually pushed back into the east or converted to Christianity and absorbed into the emerging Russian state.

In 1253 a Franciscan monk named William of Rubruck was sent by Louis IX of France into the Golden Horde to convert the Mongols (or Tartars) to Christianity. He wrote the following account of the Mongol culture for the king.

QUESTIONS

1. What does William hope the Crusaders of Europe will learn from his description of the Mongols?
2. How do the Mongols treat their dead?
3. Do you feel that William's mission to the Mongols was successful?

WILLIAM OF RUBRUCK ON THE MONGOLS

William of Rubruck, and Franciscan friar, traveled into Mongol territories in 1253 as part of the ongoing Christian missionary effort to convert the Mongols to Christianity. He was probably in the service of the French king Louis IX, to whom his account of his journey, excerpted below, is addressed. William's writings are important for their detailed (albeit western) view of Mongol life.

Source: trans. W.W. Rockhill, *The Journey of William Rubruck to the Eastern Parts of the World, 1253-55...* (London: The Hakluyt Society, 1900), second series, vol. 4, pp. 52-55, 75-84, 95-96, 1-3-105, 107, 116, 281-82; revised.

After having left Sodaia we came on the third day across the Tartars, and when I found myself among them it truly seemed to me that I had been transported into another century. I will describe to you as well as I can their mode of living and manners.

Nowhere do they have fixed dwelling-places, nor do they know where their next will be. They have divided Scythia among themselves, which extends from the Danube to the rising of the sun; and every captain, depending on the number of men under him, knows the limits of his pasture lands and where to graze in winter and in summer, spring and autumn. For in winter they go down to warmer regions in the south: in summer they go up to cooler regions towards the north. The pasture lands without water they graze over in winter when there is snow there, for the snow serves them as water.

They set up the dwelling in which they sleep on a circular frame of interlaced sticks converging into a little round hoop on the top, from which projects above a collar as a chimney, and this framework they cover over with white felt.... and they make these houses so large that they are sometimes 30 feet in width. I myself once measured the width between the wheel-tracks of a cart 20 feet, and when the house was on the cart it projected beyond the wheels on either side five feet at least....

It is the duty of the women to drive the carts, get the dwellings on and off them, milk the cows, make butter and sour curds, and dress and sew skins, which they do with a thread made of tendons. They divide the tendons into fine shreds, and then twist them into one long thread. They also sew boots, the socks and the clothing. They never wash clothes, for they say that God would be angered at this, and that it would thunder if they hung them up to dry. They will even beat those they find washing them.... Furthermore, they never wash their bowls, but when the meat is cooked they rinse out the dish in which they are about to put it with some of the boiling broth from the kettle, which they pour back into it. The women also make the felt and cover the houses.

The men make bows and arrows, manufacture stirrups and bits, make saddles, do the carpentering on [the framework] of their dwellings and the carts; they take care of the horses, milk the mares, churn the *cosmos* or mare's milk, make the skins in which it is put; they also look after the camels and load them. Both sexes look after the sheep and goats, sometimes the men, other times the women milking them....

As to their marriages, you must know that no one among them has a wife unless he buys her; so it sometimes happens that girls are well past marriageable age before they marry, for their parents always keep them until they sell them. They observe the first and second degrees of consanguinity, but no degree of affinity; thus one [man] will have at the same time or successively two sisters [as his wives]. Among them no widow marries, for the following reason: they believe that all who serve them in this life shall serve them in the next, so they believe that a widow will always return to her first husband after death. Hence this shameful custom prevails among them: that sometimes a son marries all his father's wives, except his own mother; for the dwellings of the father and mother always belong to the youngest son, so it is he who must provide for all his father's wives who come to him with the paternal household, and if he wishes it he uses them as wives, for he does not think himself injured if they return to his father after death. So when anyone has made a bargain with a man to marry his daughter, the father of the girl gives a feast, and the girl flees to her relatives and hides there. Then the father says: "Here, my daughter is yours: take her wherever you find her." Then [the bridegroom] searches for her with his friends till he finds her, and must take her by force and carry her off with a semblance of violence to his house....

When anyone dies, they lament with loud wailing, and then they are free, for they pay no taxes for the year. And if anyone is present at the death of an adult, he may not enter the dwelling even of Mangu Khan [the emperor] for the year. If it is a child who dies, the person who was present may not enter it for a month. Beside the tomb of the dead they always leave a tent if he is one of the nobles, that is, of the family of Genghis Khan, who was their first father and lord. Of him who is dead, the burying place is not known. And around these palaces where they bury their nobles there is always a camp with men watching the tombs. I did not understand that they bury treasures with their dead....

When therefore we found ourselves among these barbarians, it seemed to me, as I said before, that I had been transported into another world. They surrounded us on their horses, after having made us wait for a long while seated in the shade under our carts. The first question [they asked] was whether we had ever been among them before.... Then they asked where we came from and where we wanted to go. I told them...that we had heard that Sartach was a Christian, and that I wanted to go to him, for I had your letters to deliver to him....

There were five of us [Europeans], and the three [Mongols] who were conducting us, two driving the carts and one going with us to Sartach. The meat they had given us was insufficient, and we could find nothing to buy with money. To add to this, when we were seated in the shade under our carts, [the people of the neighborhood] pushed in most importunately among us, to the point of crushing us, in their eagerness to see all our things.... Above all this, however, I was distressed because I could do no preaching to them; the interpreter would say to me, "You cannot make me preach, I do not know the proper words to use." And he spoke the truth; for after a while, when I had learned something of the language, I saw that when I said one thing, he said a totally different one, according to what came uppermost in his mind. So, seeing the danger of speaking through him, I made up my mind to keep silence....

And so we came to Sartach's dwelling, and they raised the felt which hung before the entry, so that he could see us. Then they made the clerk and the interpreter bow [to him]; of us they did not demand it. Then they enjoined us earnestly to be most careful in going in and coming out not to touch the threshold of the dwelling, and also to chant some blessing for him. So we went in chanting, "*Salve, regina!*"...Then Coiac [A Nestorian priest who served Sartach] handed [Sartach] the censer with the incense, and he examined it, holding it in his hand most carefully. After that he handed the psalter [we had brought], at which he took a good look, as did the wife who was seated beside him. Then he handed him the Bible, and he asked if the Gospels were in it. I said that it contained all the sacred writings. He also took in his hand the cross, and asked if the image on it were that of Christ. I replied that it was. Those Nestorians and Hermenian [Christians] never make the figure of Christ on their crosses; they would thus appear to entertain some doubt of the Passion, or to be ashamed of it. Then I presented to him your letter, with translations in Arabic and Syiac, for I had had them both translated and written in these languages at Acon....

Before we left Sartach, the above-mentioned Coiac and a number of scribes of the court said to us, "You must not say that our lord is a Christian. He is not a Christian, but a Moal" [or Mongol]. For the name of Christian seems to them that of a nation. They have risen so much in their pride, that though they may believe somewhat in Christ, yet they do not wish to be called Christians, wishing to exalt their own name of Moal above all others, nor do they wish to be called Tartars. The Tartars were another people....

Of Sartach I know not whether he believes in Christ or not. This I do know, that he will not be called a Christian, and it even seemed to me that he mocked the Christians. For he is on the road of the [local] Christians,…all of whom pass by him when going to his father's household carrying presents to him, so he shows himself most attentive to them. Should, however, Saracens come along carrying more presents than they, they are sent along more expeditiously. He has Nestorian priests around him who [conduct their worship services]….

…[I]f the army of the church were to come to the Holy Land, it would be very easy to conquer or to pass through [the lands on the way]. The king of Hungary has at most 30,000 soldiers. From Cologne to Constantinople it is not more than forty days in a cart. From Constantinople it is not so far as that to the country of the king of Hermenia. In times past valiant men passed through these countries, and succeeded, though they had most powerful adversaries, whom God has since removed from the earth. Nor should we [if we followed the road] be exposed to the dangers of the sea or to the mercies of the sailor men, and the price which would have to be given for a fleet would be enough for the expenses of the land journey. I state it with confidence, that if you peasants—to say nothing of the princes and noblemen—would only travel like the Tartar princes, and be content with similar provisions, they would conquer the world.

It seems to me inexpedient to send another friar to the Tartars as I went, or as the preaching friars go; but if the lord pope, who is head of all Christians, wishes to send with proper state a bishop, and reply to the foolishness [the Mongols] have already written three times to the Franks (once to Innocent IV of blessed memory [from Guyuk Khan], and twice to you…), he would be able to tell them whatever he pleased, and also make them reply in writing. They listen to whatever an ambassador [as opposed to a lower-level envoy like a friar] has to say, and always ask if he has more to say; but he must have a good interpreter—nay, several interpreters—abundant travelling funds, and so on.

From *The Crusades: A Reader*, edited by S. J. Allen and Emilie Amt, Ontario, Broadview Press, 2003, pp. 393-396. Reprinted by permission of Broadview Press.

--- ✛ ---

QUESTIONS FOR PART 12

1. In what ways did all the warfare of the High Middle Ages benefit Europe economically and culturally?
2. Were the Crusades an indication of how powerful the Christian faith had become in Europe, or a sign of weakness within the faith?
3. What role did monarchs play in crusading? How did the Crusades help them politically?

PART 13

❧

CRISES OF THE LATER MIDDLE AGES

The fourteenth and fifteenth centuries were two of the most catastrophic throughout the Middle Ages. Western Europe faced a series of disasters in this period: the first appearance of the Black Death in 1347, dramatic social upheavals exemplified by peasant rebellions and renewed persecutions of Jews, disintegration of the Catholic Church through the Avignon exile and the Great Schism, over a century of warfare between England and France, and finally the eruption of civil war in England. The results of these calamities were diverse, although in general the mood of Europe was one of doom and gloom for most of the period.

In spite of the dark mood, it was also a period of tremendous advancement and development. New technologies were discovered, admittedly most of them military. The decrease in population from the plague eased the burden on Europe's over-extended food supplies. Overall, cities grew more prosperous in spite of populations fleeing disease and warfare for the countryside. Although people's faith was weakened by the crises of Avignon and Schism, the Church emerged stronger. External and internal warfare only revealed the resilience of England and France. Finally, during (and often in direct response to) all of this, Europe rediscovered its classical past and the artistic and cultural movement known as the Renaissance began.

13.1

✦

BONIFACE VIII'S BULL "UNAM SANCTUM"

Boniface VIII was only pope for nine years, between 1294 and 1303, yet his impact on the Catholic Church was felt for the next century and a half. In 1296, Philip IV, the Fair, levied a tax on French clergy. Boniface saw this as an infringement of ecclesiastical privilege and ordered the clergy to ignore the tax. The feud between king and pope escalated, resulting in the bull "Unam Sanctum" in 1302, the broadest claim of papal power yet issued. In retaliation, royal troops seized Boniface, who was freed by Italians but quickly died (perhaps of shock from the attack). Upon the death of Boniface, Philip forced the College of Cardinals to elect a French pope, Clement V, who was encouraged to move the papal court from Rome to Avignon, where Philip promised the protection of French troops. This began the Babylonian Captivity of the Papacy, which lasted from 1305-1377.

————— ✣ —————

QUESTIONS

1. According to Boniface, who has the authority to judge the pope?
2. What is the two-sword theory of power?
3. Do you feel that Boniface has any justification for his claims of authority?

(From the latest revision of the text in "Revue des Questions historiques," July, 1889, p. 255.)

We are compelled, our faith urging us, to believe and to hold — and we do firmly believe and simply confess — that there is one holy catholic and apostolic church, outside of which there is neither salvation nor remission of sins; her Spouse proclaiming it in the canticles: "My dove, my undefiled is but one, she is the choice one of her that bare her;" which represents one mystic body, of which body the head is Christ; but of Christ, God. In this church there is one Lord, one faith and one baptism. There was one ark of Noah, indeed, at the time of the flood, symbolizing one church; and this being finished in one cubit had, namely, one Noah as helmsman and commander. And, with the exception of this ark, all things existing upon the earth were, as we read, destroyed. This church, moreover, we venerate as the only one, the Lord saying through His prophet: "Deliver my soul from the sword, my darling from the power of the dog." He prayed at the same time for His soul — that is, for Himself the Head — and for His body, — which body, namely, he called the one and only church on account of the unity of the faith promised, of the sacraments, and of the love of the church. She is that seamless garment of the Lord which was not cut but which fell by lot. Therefore of this one and only church there is one body and one head — not two heads as if it were a monster: — Christ, namely, and the vicar of Christ, St. Peter, and the successor of Peter. For the Lord Himself said to Peter, Feed my sheep. My sheep, He said, using a general term, and not designating these or those particular sheep; from which it is plain that He committed to Him *all* His sheep. If, then, the Greeks or others say that they were not committed to the care of Peter and his successors, they necessarily confess that they are not of the sheep of Christ; for the Lord says, in John, that there is one fold, one shepherd and one only. We are told by the word of the gospel that in this His fold there are two swords, — a spiritual, namely, and a temporal. For when the apostles said "Behold here are two swords" — when, namely, the apostles were speaking in the church — the Lord did not reply that this was too much, but enough. Surely he who denies that the temporal sword is in the power of Peter wrongly interprets the world of the Lord when He says: "Put up thy sword in its scabbard." Both swords, the spiritual and the material, therefore, are in the power of the church; the one, indeed, to be wielded for the church, the other by the church; the one by the knights, but at the will and sufferance of a priest. One word, moreover, ought to be under the other, and the temporal authority to be subjected to the spiritual. For when the apostle says "there is no power but of God, and the powers that are of God are ordained," they would not be ordained unless sword were under sword and the lesser one, as it were, were led by the other to great deeds. For according to St. Dionysius the law of divinity is to lead the lowest through the intermediate to the highest things. Not therefore, according to the law of the universe, are all things reduced to order equally and immediately; but the lowest through the intermediate to the highest things. Not therefore, according to the law of the universe, are all things reduced to order equally and immediately; but the lowest through the intermediate, the intermediate through the higher. But that the spiritual exceeds any earthly power in dignity and nobility we ought the more openly to confess the more spiritual things excel temporal ones. This also is made plain to our eyes from the giving of tithes, and the benediction and the sanctification; from the acceptation of this same power, from the control over those same things. For, the truth bearing witness, the spiritual power has to establish the earthly power, and to judge it if it be not good. Thus concerning the church and the ecclesiastical power is verified the prophecy of Jeremiah: "See, I have this day set thee over the nations and over the kingdoms," and the other things which follow. Therefore if the earthly power err it shall be judged by the spiritual power; but if the lesser spiritual power err, by the greater. But if the greatest, it can be judged by God alone, not by man, the apostle bearing witness. A spiritual man judges all things, but he himself is judged by no one. This authority, moreover, even though it is given to man and exercised through man, is not human but rather divine, being given by divine lips to Peter and founded on a rock for him and his successors through Christ himself whom he has confessed; the Lord himself saying to Peter: "Whatsoever thou shalt bind," etc. Whoever, therefore, resists this power thus ordained by God, resists the ordination of God, unless he makes believe, like the Manichean, that there are two beginnings. This we consider false and heretical, since by the testimony of Moses, not "in the beginnings," but "in the beginning" God created the Heavens and the earth. Indeed we declare, announce and define, that it is altogether necessary to salvation for every human creature to be subject to the Roman pontiff.

The Lateran, Nov. 14, in our 8th year. As a perpetual memorial of this matter.

Source: Ernest Henderson, ed. *Select Historical Documents of the Middle Ages* (New York: AMS Press, 1968), pp. 435-37.

13.2

PEASANT REBELLION OF 1381

There were several peasant rebellions in the fourteenth century. In 1320, French peasants rebelled, and again in the 1358 Jacquerie ("Jack Goodman," which was a colloquial term for peasant). In 1381 English peasants revolted against Richard II, and there were also rebellions that year in Flanders and in the Italian city-states. There were many reasons why individual rebellions occurred, but one common theme was the frustration by the peasants with taxes and feudal dues.

Jean Froissart's Chronicle *recorded many significant events of the century, including the English Peasant Rebellion, as excerpted here.*

QUESTIONS

1.   What role does the Catholic Church play in causing this rebellion?
2.   As they marched toward London, why do the rebels claim that they stand "for the King"?
3.   If this is a rebellion about feudal dues and taxes, why to the rebels attack Lombards (i.e., foreigners) in London?

I n these machinations they had been greatly encouraged originally by a crack-brained priest of Kent called John Ball, who had been imprisoned several times for his reckless words by the Archbishop of Canterbury. This John Ball had the habit on Sundays after mass, when everyone was coming out of church, of going to the cloisters or the graveyard, assembling the people round him and preaching thus:

'Good people, things cannot go right in England and never will, until goods are held in common and there are no more villains and gentlefolk, but we are all one and the same. In what way are those whom we call lords greater masters than ourselves? How have they deserved it? Why do they hold us in bondage? If we all spring from a single father and mother, Adam and Eve, how can they claim or prove that they are lords more than us, except by making us produce and grow the wealth which they spend? They are clad in velvet and camlet lined with squirrel and ermine, while we go dressed in coarse cloth. They have the wines, the spices and the good bread; we have the rye, the husks and the straw, and we drink water. They have shelter and ease in their fine manors, and we have hardship and toil, the wind and the rain in the fields. And from us must come, from our labour, the things which keep them in luxury. We are called serfs and beaten if we are slow in our service to them, yet we have no sovereign lord we can complain to, none to hear us and do us justice. Let us go to the King — he is young — and show him how we are oppressed, and tell him that we want things to be changed, or else we will change them ourselves. If we go in good earnest and all together, very many people who are called serfs and are held in subjection will follow us to get their freedom. And when the King sees and hears us, he will remedy the evil, either willingly or otherwise.'

These were the kind of things which John Ball usually preached in the villages on Sundays when the congregations came out from mass, and many of the common people agreed with him. Some, who were up to no good, said: 'He's right!' and out in the fields, or walking together from one village to another, or in their homes, they whispered and repeated among themselves: 'That's what John Ball says, and he's right.'...

These promises incited the people of Kent, Essex, Sussex, Bedford and the neighbouring districts and they set off and went towards London. They were a full sixty thousand and their chief captain was one Wat Tyler. With him as his companions were Jack Straw and John Ball. These three were the leaders and Wat Tyler was the greatest of them. He was a tiler of roofs, and a wicked and nasty fellow he was....

When those people saw that they would obtain nothing more, they were aflame with fury. They went back to the hill where the main body was and reported what had been said to them and that the King had gone back to the Tower. The whole mass of them began shouting together: 'To London! Straight to London!' They started off and swept down towards the city, ransacking and destroying the houses of abbots, lawyers and court officials, and came to the immediate outskirts, which are fine and extensive. They levelled several fine buildings and, in particular, the King's prisons, which are called Marshalseas, setting free all the prisoners inside. They committed many outrages in the suburbs and, when they reached the bridge, they began to threaten the Londoners because they had closed its gates. They said they would set fire to all the suburbs and then take London by storm, burning and destroying it. The common people of London, many of whom were on their side, assembled together and said: 'Why not let these good people come into the town? They are our own people and they are doing all this to help us.' So the gates had to be opened and all those famished men entered the town and rushed into the houses which had stocks of provisions. Nothing was refused them and everyone made haste to welcome them in and set out food and drink to appease them. After that, their leaders John Ball, Jack Straw and Wat Tyler, with more than thirty thousand men, went straight through London to the Palace of the Savoy, a very fine building on the Thames as you go towards the King's Palace of Westminster, and belonging to the Duke of Lancaster. They quickly got inside and killed the guards, and then sent it up in flames. Having committed this outrage they went on to the palace of the Hospitallers of Rhodes, known as St. John of Clerkenwell, and burnt it down, house, church, hospital and everything. Besides this, they went from street to street, killing all the Flemings they found in churches, chapels, and houses. None was spared. They broke into many houses belonging to Lombards and robbed them openly, no one daring to resist them. In the town they killed a wealthy man called Richard Lyon, whose servant Wat Tyler had once been during the wars in France. On one occasion Richard Lyon had beaten his servant and Wat Tyler remembered it. He led his men to him, had his head cut off in front of him, and then had it stuck on a lance and carried through the streets. So those wicked men went raging about in wild frenzy, committing many excesses on that Thursday throughout London....

They were all agreeing to this plan when suddenly the King appeared, accompanied by perhaps sixty horsemen. He had not been thinking about them, but had been intending to go on and leave London behind. When he reached the Abbey of St. Bartholomew which stands there, he stopped and looked at the great crowd and said that he would not go on without hearing what they wanted. If they were discontented, he would placate them. The nobles who were with him stopped when he did, as they must. When Wat Tyler saw this, he said to his men: 'Here's the King, I'm going to talk to him. Don't budge from here unless I give you the signal, but if I make this sign (he showed them one), move forward and kill the lot. Except the King, don't touch the King. He's young, we will make him do as we want, we can take him with us anywhere in England and we shall be the lords of the realm. No doubt of that.' There was a tailor there called John Tickle, who had delivered sixty doublets for some of those scoundrels to wear and Tyler was wearing one himself. Tickle said to him: 'Hi, sir, who's going to pay for my doublets? I want at least thirty marks.' 'Be easy now,' said Tyler. 'You'll be paid in full by tomorrow. Trust me, I'm a good enough guarantee.'

With that, he stuck his spurs into a horse he had mounted, left his companions and went straight up to the King, going so near that his horse's tail was brushing the head of the King's horse. The first words he said to the King were: 'Well, King, you see all those men over there?' 'Yes,' said the King. 'Why do you ask?' 'Because they are all under my command. They've sworn their sacred oath to do anything I tell them.' 'Good,' said the King, 'I see nothing wrong in that.' 'So,' said Tyler, who only wanted a quarrel, 'do you think, King, that these men here, and as many again in London, all under my command, are going to leave you without getting their letters? No, we're going to take them with us.'...

Just then the Lord Mayor of London arrived on horseback with a dozen others, all fully armed beneath their robes, and broke through the crowd. He saw how Tyler was behaving and said to him in the sort of language he understood: 'Fellow, how dare you say such things in the King's presence? You're getting above yourself.' The King lost his temper and said to the Mayor: 'Lay hands on him, Mayor.' Meanwhile Tyler was answering: "I can say and do what I like. What's it to do with you?' 'So, you stinking boor,' said the Mayor, who had once been a King's Advocate, 'you talk like that in the presence of the King, my natural lord? I'll be hanged if you don't pay for it.'

With that he drew a great sword he was wearing and struck. He gave Tyler such a blow on the head that he laid him flat under his horse's feet. No sooner was he down than he was entirely surrounded, so as to hide him from the crowds who were there, who called themselves his men. One of the King's squires called John Standish dismounted and thrust his sword into Tyler's belly so that he died.

Those crowds of evil men soon realized that their leader was dead. They began to mutter: 'They've killed our captain. Come on, we'll slay the lot!" They drew themselves up in the square in a kind of battle-order, each holding before him the bow which he carried. Then the King did an extraordinarily rash thing, but it ended well. As soon as Tyler was dispatched, he left his men, saying: 'Stay here, no one is to follow me,' and went alone towards those half-crazed people, to whom he said: 'Sirs, what more do you want? You have no other captain but me, I am your king, behave peaceably.' On hearing this, the majority of them were ashamed and began to break up. They were the peace-loving ones. But the bad ones did not disband; instead they formed up for battle and showed that they meant business. The King rode back to his men and asked what should be done next. He was advised to go on towards the country, since it was no use trying to run away. The Mayor said: 'That is the best thing for us to do, for I imagine the loyal men on our side who are waiting armed in their houses with their friends.'…

So those crazy men departed and split up, some going one way, some another. The King, with the nobles and their companies, went back in good order into London, to be received with joy. The first thing the King did was to visit his lady mother the Princess, who was still in the Tower Royal. When she saw her son, she was overjoyed and said: 'Ah, my son, how anxious I have been today on your account!' 'Yes, my lady,' the King answered, 'I know you have. But now take comfort and praise God, for it is a time to praise him. Today I have recovered my inheritance, the realm of England which I had lost.'

The King remained with his mother for the whole day and the lords and nobles went back peaceably to their houses. A royal proclamation was drawn up and cried from street to street, ordering all persons who were not natives of London or had lived there for less than a year to leave at once. If they were still found three at sunrise on the Sunday, they would be counted as traitors to the King and would lose their heads. When this order became known, none dared to disobey it. Everyone left in haste on that same Saturday and started back for their own districts. John Ball and Jack Straw were found hiding in an old ruined building, where they had hoped to escape the search. But they did not; their own people gave them away. The King and the nobles were delighted by their capture, for then their heads were cut off, and Tyler's too, although he was dead already, and posted up on London Bridge in place of those of the worthy men whom they had beheaded on the Thursday. News of this quickly spread around London. All the people from the distant counties who had flocked there at the summons of those wicked men set off hurriedly for their own places, and never dared to come back again.

From Jean Froissart, *Chronicles*, trans. Geoffrey Brereton, pp. 212-213, 217-218, 225-229. Copyright © 1968, 1978 Penguin Books, Ltd. Reproduced by permission of Penguin Books Limited.

13.3

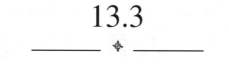

THE TWELVE CONCLUSIONS OF THE LOLLARDS

In late fourteenth-century England the first heresy native to England appeared. John Wyclif (c. 1328-1384) was an Oxford theologian who questioned and ultimately rejected papal claims of authority as well as many traditional Catholic beliefs and practices. His objections were based on his close reading of scripture, which he claimed did not support the traditional power of the papacy. Wyclif's ideas were officially declared heretical by the Church, but continued to find support across England and on the continent. His English followers were known as Lollards. In 1394 they offered the following list of twelve "conclusions" on the corruption of the Church.

✤

QUESTIONS

1. How do the Conclusions of the Lollards represent a type of crisis for the later Middle Ages?
2. Who do the Lollards blame most for what they see as the corruption of the fourteenth-century Church: the papacy, the priests, or the laity? Why?
3. Are the Lollards hopeful about humanity's potential to be saved?

1 That when the Church of England began to go mad after temporalities, like its great step-mother the Roman Church, and churches were authorized by appropriation in divers places, faith, hope, and charity began to flee from our Church, because pride, with its doleful progeny of moral sins, claimed this under title of truth. This conclusion is general, and proved by experience, custom, and manner or fashion, as you shall afterwards hear.

2. That our usual priesthood which began in Rome, pretended to be of power more lofty than the angels, is not that priesthood which Christ ordained for His apostles. This conclusion is proved because the Roman priesthood is bestowed with signs, rites, and pontifical blessing, of small virtue, nowhere exemplified in Holy Scripture, because the bishop's ordinal and the New Testament scarcely agree, and we cannot see that the Holy Spirit, by reason of any such signs, confers the gift, for He and all His excellent gifts cannot consist in any one with mortal sin. A corollary to this is that it is a grievous play for wise men to see bishops trifle with the Holy Spirit in the bestowal for orders, because they give the tonsure in outward appearance in the place of white hearts; and this is the unrestrained introduction of antichrist into the Church to give colour to idleness.

3. That the law of continence enjoined on priests, which was first ordained to the prejudice of women, brings sodomy into all the Holy Church, but we excuse ourselves by the Bible because the decree says that we should not mention it, though suspected. Reason and experience prove this conclusion: reason, because the good living of ecclesiastics must have a natural outlet or worse; experience, because the secret proof of such men is that they find delight in women, and when thou hast proved such a man mark him well, because he is one of them. A corollary to this is that private religions and the originators or beginning of this sin would be specially worthy of being checked, but God of His power with regard to secret sin sends open vengeance in His Church.

4. That the pretended miracle of the sacrament of bread drives all men, but a few, to idolatry, because they think that the Body of Christ which is never away from heaven could by power of the priest's word be enclosed essentially in a little bread which they show the people; but God grant that they might be willing to believe what the evangelical doctor says in his Trialogus (iv 7), that the bread of the altar is habitually the Body of Christ, for we take it that in this way any faithful man and woman can by God's law perform the sacrament of that bread without any such miracle. A final corollary is that although the Body of Christ, for we take it that in this way any faithful man and woman can by God's law perform the sacrament of that bread without any such miracle. A final corollary is that although the Body of Christ has been granted eternal joy, the service of Corpus Christi, instituted by Brother Thomas [Aquinas], is not true but is fictitious and full of false miracles. It is no wonder; because Brother Thomas, at that time holding with the pope, would have been willing to perform a miracle with a hen's egg; and we know well that any falsehood openly preached turns to the disgrace of Him who is always true and without any defect.

5.　That exorcisms and blessings performed over wine, bread, water and oil, salt, wax, and incense, the stones of the altar, and church walls, over clothing, mitre, cross, and pilgrims' staves, are the genuine performance of necromancy rather than of sacred theology. This conclusion is proved as follows, because by such exorcisms creatures are honoured as being of higher virtue than they are in their own nature, and we do not see any change in any creature which is so exorcized, save by false faith which is the principal characteristic of the Devil's art. A corollary: that if the book of exorcizing holy water, read in church, were entirely trustworthy we think truly that the holy water used in church would be the best medicine for all kinds of illnesses—sores, for instance; whereas we experience the contrary day by day.

6.　That king and bishop in one person, prelate and judge in temporal causes, curate and officer in secular office, puts any kingdom beyond good rule. This conclusion is clearly proved because the temporal and spiritual are two halves of the entire Holy Church. And so he who has applied himself to one should not meddle with the other, for no one can serve two masters. It seems that hermaphrodite or ambidexter would be good names for such men of double estate. A corollary is that we, the procurators of God in this behalf, do petition before Parliament that all curates, as well superior as inferior, be fully excused and should occupy themselves with their own charge and no other.

7.　That special prayers for the souls of the dead offered in our Church, preferring one before another in name, are a false foundation of alms, and for that reason all houses of alms in England have been wrongly founded. This conclusion is proved by two reasons: the one is that meritorious prayer, and of any effect, ought to be a work proceeding from deep charity, and perfect charity leaves out no one, for 'Thou shalt love thy neighbour as thyself.' And so it is clear to us that the gift of temporal good bestowed on the priesthood and houses of alms is a special incentive to private prayer which is not far from simony. For another reason is that special prayer made for men condemned is very displeasing to God. And although it be doubtful, it is probable to faithful Christian people that founders of a house of alms have for their poisonous endowment passed over for the most part to the broad road. The corollary is: effectual prayer springing from perfect love would in general embrace all whom God would have saved, and would do away with that well-worn way or merchandise in special prayers made for the possessionary mendicants and other hired priests, who are a people of great burden to the whole realm, kept in idleness: for it has been proved in one book, which the king had, that a hundred houses of alms would suffice in all the realm, and from this would rather accrue possible profit to the temporal estate.

8.　That pilgrimages, prayers, and offerings made to blind crosses or roods, and to deaf images of wood or stone, are pretty well akin to idolatry and far from alms, and although these be forbidden and imaginary, a book of error to the lay folk, still the customary image of the Trinity is specially abominable. This conclusion God clearly proves, bidding alms to be done to the needy man because they are the image of God, and more like than wood or stone; or God did not say, 'let us make wood or stone in our likeness and image,' but man; because the supreme honour which clerks call *latria* appertains to the Godhead only; and the lower honour which clerks call *dulia* appertains to man and angel and to no inferior creature. A corollary is that the service of the cross, performed twice in any year in our church, is full of idolatry, for if that should, so might the nails and lance be so highly honoured; then would the lips of Judas be relics indeed if any were able to possess them. But we ask you, pilgrim, to tell us when you offer to the bones of saints placed in a shrine in any spot, whether you relieve the saint who is in joy, or that almshouse which is so well endowed and for when men have been canonized. God knows how. And to speak more plainly, a faithful Christian supposes that the wounds of that noble man, whom men call St. Thomas, were not a case of martyrdom.

9.   That auricular confession which is said to be so necessary to the salvation of a man, with its pretended power of absolution, exalts the arrogance of priests and gives them opportunity of other secret colloquies which we will not speak of; for both lords and ladies attest that, for fear of their confessors, they dare not speak the truth. And at the time of confession there is a ready occasion for assignation, that is for 'wooing,' and other secret understandings leading to mortal sins. They themselves say that they are God's representatives to judge of every sin, to pardon and cleanse whomsoever they please. They say that they have the keys of heaven and of hell, and can excommunicate and bless, bind and loose, at their will, so much so that for a drink, or twelve pence, they will sell the blessing of heaven with charter and close warrant sealed with the common seal. This conclusion is so notorious that it needs not any proof. It is a corollary that the pope of Rome, who has given himself out as treasurer of the whole Church, having in charge that worthy jewel of Christ's passion together with the merits of all saints in heaven, whereby he grants pretended indulgence from penalty and guilt, is a treasurer almost devoid of charity, in that he can set free all that are prisoners in hell at his will, and cause that they should never come to that place. But in this any Christian can well see there is much secret falsehood hidden away in our Church.

10.   That manslaughter in war, or by pretended law of justice for a temporal cause, without spiritual revelation, is expressly contrary to the New Testament, which indeed is the law of grace and full of mercies. This conclusion is openly proved by the examples of Christ's preaching here on earth, for he specially taught a man to love his enemies, and to show them pity, and not to slay them. The reason is this, that for the most part, when men fight, after the first blow, charity is broken. And whoever dies without charity goes the straight road to hell. And beyond this we know well that no clergyman can by Scripture or lawful reason remit the punishment of death for one mortal sin and not for another; but the law of mercy, which is the New Testament, prohibits all manner of manslaughter, for in the Gospel: 'It was said unto them of old time, Thou shalt not kill.' The corollary is that it is indeed robbery of poor folk when lords get indulgences from punishment and guilt for those who aid their army to kill a Christian people in distant lands for temporal gain, just as we too have seen soldiers who run into heathendom to get them a name for the slaughter of men; much more do they deserve ill thanks from the King of Peace, for by our humility and patience was the faith multiplied, and Christ Jesus hates and threatens men who fight and kill, when He says: 'He who smites with the sword shall perish by the sword.'

11.   That the vow of continence made in our Church by women who are frail and imperfect in nature, is the cause of bringing in the gravest horrible sins possible to human nature, because, although the killing of abortive children before they are baptized and the destruction of nature by drugs are vile sins, yet connexion with themselves or brute beasts of any creature not having life surpasses them in foulness to such an extent as that they should be punished with the pains of hell. The corollary is that, widows and such as take the veil and the ring, being delicately fed, we could wish that they were given in marriage, because we cannot excuse them from secret sins.

12.   That the abundance of unnecessary arts practised in our realm nourishes much sin in waste, profusion, and disguise. This, experience and reason prove in some measure, because nature is sufficient for a man's necessity with few arts. The corollary is that since St. Paul says: 'having food and raiment, et us be therewith content,' it seems to us that goldsmiths and armourers and all kinds of arts not necessary for a man, according to the apostle, should be destroyed for the increase of virtue; because although these two said arts were exceedingly necessary in the old law, the New Testament abolishes them and many others.

This is our embassy, which Christ has bidden us fulfil, very necessary for this time for several reasons. And although these matters are briefly noted here they are however set forth at large in another book, and many others besides, at length in our own language, and we wish that these were accessible to all Christian people. We ask God then of His supreme goodness to reform our Church, as being entirely out of joint, to the perfectness of its first beginning.

Source: Henry Bettenson, ed., *Documents of the Christian Church*, (New York: Oxford University Press, 1963), pp. 175-179.

13.4

❖

TALE OF JOAN OF ARC, CHRISTINE DE PIZAN

Few medieval figures still attract as much debate as Joan of Arc. An illiterate peasant born in 1412, she claimed to have visions that led her to fight against the English on behalf of the Dauphin Charles, heir to the French throne. After Joan defeated the English at Orleans in 1429, the Dauphin was crowned Charles VII and the tide of the Hundred Years' War turned in favor of the French. In 1430 Joan was captured by the Burgundians, who although French were allies of the English. Joan was tried by French clergy, under English control, and executed for witchcraft and heresy in 1431. She was nineteen years old. Rallying around the memory of Joan, Charles and his French forces gradually reconquered his kingdom and by 1453 English territory in France was reduced to one town, Calais. In 1920 the Catholic Church declared Joan a saint.

The controversies surrounding Joan then and now center on the questions of whether her visions were "true," and what role she actually played in the battle. In 1429, immediately after the capture of Orleans, a French writer named Christine de Pizan wrote a poem (or ditiè, *a song) applauding Joan's success and her holiness. It is the first poem dedicated to Joan.*

❖

QUESTIONS

1. What significance is there in the fact that the author of the poem is a woman?
2. How does Christine use Biblical examples to explain the success of Joan?
3. Why does Christine think God has chosen to use a young girl for this "miraculous" victory over the English?

1. I, Christine, who have wept for eleven years in a closed abbey, where I have lived ever since Charles (what a strange thing!), the king's son, fled, if I dare say it, in haste from Paris, enclosed here because of this treachery, I begin now for the first time to laugh....

3. In 1429 the sun began to shine again. It brings back the good new season which we had not really seen for a long time, which made many people live in sorrow. But I no longer grieve over anything, for now I see what I desire....

5.   All this because the cast-out child of the legitimate king of France, who has suffered for a long time great troubles and who now approaches, rose up like one who goes to prime, coming as a crowned king, in wonderful and great power, wearing spurs of gold.

6.   Now let us celebrate our king! May he be welcomed on his return! Rejoice at his noble appearance, let us all go, great and small—may no one hold back—and joyfully greet him, praising God who has protected him and loudly shout "Noel…."

10.   Who, then, has seen something so extraordinary occur—which should be noted and remembered in all regions—that France, who in everyone's opinion was defeated, has, by divine command, changed from evil to such great good,

11.   and truly through such a miracle that, if the matter were not so well-known and obvious in every way, no one would believe it? This is well worth remembering: that God has wished to bestow His grace on France—and this is true—through a tender virgin.

12.   Oh, what an honor given to the French crown by this divine proof! For by the grace He gives it is obvious that he supports it and that more than anywhere else He finds faith in the royal estate of which I read—and there is nothing new in this—that the Lilies of France never erred in the faith.

13.   And you Charles, French king, seventh of that noble name, who waged a great war before things changed for the better for you: But now, by God's grace, see how your renown is exalted by the Maid, who has subjugated your enemies under your flag—and this is something new—

14.   In a short time; people thought that it was impossible that you would ever get back your country which you were losing. Now it is clearly yours, for against all those who harmed you, you have recovered it! And through the clever Maid, who thank God has done her share!

15.   I firmly believe that God would not bestow on you this grace if it were not ordained by Him that you should, in the course of time, bring to fruition and a good end a great and solemn task, and if it were not destined for you to be the leader of the greatest events….

[Christine pursues the idea that there was a prophecy predicting the current events and appeals to the king to be worthy of his great mission. She thanks God for His mercy and then turns to the maid, Joan of Arc.]

21.   And you blessed Maid, should you be forgotten in all this? For God has honored you so much that you undid the rope that held France tightly bound. Could one praise you enough when you have given peace to this country humiliated by war?

22.   You, Joan, were born at a propitious hour, blessed be He who created you! Maid, ordained by God, in whom the Holy Spirit (in whom there was and is the greatest generosity with noble

gifts) poured His great grace and never refused any of your requests, how can we ever reward you?

23. How could one say more of anyone else or of the great deeds of the past? Moses, on whom God in His generosity bestowed many blessings and virtues, by a miracle led his people out of Egypt, without tiring of it. In the same way you have led us from evil, elected Maid!

24. When we reflect on your person, you who are a young maid, to whom God has given the strength and power to be a champion who gives to France her breast of peace and sweet nourishment and cast down the rebels. See how this goes beyond nature!

25. For if God performed so many miracles through Joshua who conquered so many places and routed so many enemies—he was a strong and powerful man! But after all, a woman, a simple shepherdess, braver that any man ever was in Rome! For God, this was an easy thing to do.

26. But for us, we never heard tell of such a great marvel, for all the brave men from the past cannot measure up in prowess against this woman who strives to cast out our enemies. But this is God's doing who counseled her, who from Him received more courage than any man.

27. We make much of Gideon who was a simple laborer, so the story goes, God made him fight, none could hold out against him, he conquered everything. But whatever orders He gave him, He never did such a clear miracle as He did in our case.

28. I have learned about Esther, Judith, and Deborah, worthy ladies, through whom God restored His people which was so oppressed, and I also learned about many others who were brave, but there was none through whom He has performed a greater miracle than through the Maid.

29. She was sent by divine command, guided by God's angel to the king, in his support. Her deeds are not an illusion, for she was well tested in a council (we conclude that a thing is proved by its effect),

30. and before one wanted to believe her, and before it became known that God sent her to the king she was led before clerks and wise men and was well examined to see whether she spoke the truth. But one found in history books that she was destined for these deeds....

33. Oh, how clear was this at the siege of Orleans where her power first appeared! No miracle, I believe, was ever clearer, for God helped His people so much that the enemies were as helpless as dead dogs. There they were captured and put to death.

34. Oh, what an honor to the female sex! That God loves it is clear with all these wretched people and traitors who laid waste the whole kingdom cast out and the realm elevated and restored by a woman—something a hundred thousand men could not have done! Before, one would not have believed it possible.

35. A young girl of sixteen years (is this not something beyond nature?), to whom arms seem

weightless, she seems to have been brought up for this, she is so strong and hardy. And the enemies flee before her, not one can last in front of her. She does this, with many eyes looking on,

36.   and rids France of her enemies, recapturing castles and towns. Never was there such great strength, not in a hundred or a thousand men. And she is the supreme leader of our brave and skilled people. Neither Hector nor Achilles had such strength! But all this God does who guides her.

37.   And you, trusty men-at-arms who do the deeds and prove yourselves good and loyal, one should certainly mention you (you will be praised for it in all countries!) and speak of you above all else, and of your courage,

38.   you who in such harsh pain risk blood, body, and life for justice and dare to go forward in such great peril. Be constant, for I promise you, for this you will receive glory and praise in heaven. For I dare say, whoever fights for justice will win Paradise....

40.   You thought you had already conquered France, and that she would be yours forever. Things have turned out differently, you false people! You'll have to beat your drums elsewhere if you do not want to taste death like your companions whom the wolves may well devour, for they lie dead in the fields.

41.   And may it be known that she will cast down the English, there will be no getting up, for this is the will of God who hears the voices of the good people whom they wanted to harm! The blood of those forever dead cries out against them. God will no longer stand for this, but condemn them as evil—this is decided.

42.   In Christendom and the Church harmony will reign through her. She will destroy the unbelievers one talks about and the heretics with their vile ways, for thus it is prophesied; she will have no pity for any place where one speaks ill of God.

43.   She will destroy the Saracens, by conquering the Holy Land. There she will lead Charles, whom God may protect! Before he dies he will make this trip, he is the one who will conquer it. There she will end her life, and both will gain glory. There things will be fulfilled.

44.   Therefore, above all the brave men of the past she must wear the crown, for her deeds show dearly that God has given her more courage than all those men one talks about. And she has not finished yet! I believe that she is God's gift to those of us on earth, so that through her deeds peace may be made.

45.   And destroying the English is the least of her worries, for her desires lie rather elsewhere: to guard against the destruction of the Faith. As for the English, whether one laughs or cries about it, they are done for. One will mock them in times to come. They have been vanquished!

46.   And all you lowly rebels who make common cause with them, now you can see that you should

have gone forward rather than backward and become the serfs of the English. Watch out that nothing else will happen to you (for you have been tolerated long enough), and think well about the end result!

47.   Don't you realize, you blind people, that God has a hand in this? Those who don't see this are truly stupid, for how could this Maid have been sent to us in this way, she who strikes all of you down dead? You do not have sufficient strength! Do you want to go into combat against God?…

From *The Selected Writings of Christine de Pizan, A Norton Classical Edition* by Christine de Pizan, Renate Blumenfeld-Kosinski, ed., translated by Renate Blumenfeld-Kosinski. Copyright © 1997 by W. W. Norton & Company, Inc. Used by permission of W. W. Norton & Company, Inc.

❖

Questions for Part 13

1.   In what ways do all four of these documents reflect a new awareness of the individual?
2.   Although the crises of the fourteenth and fifteenth centuries were traumatic, how do these documents also present positive opportunities?
3.   Had the status of women changed since the Early Middle Ages?

PART 14

ITALIAN RENAISSANCE

Between 1350-1550, a new artistic, cultural, and political movement began in Italy and moved gradually northward across the continent. The movement was later called the "Renaissance," a French word meaning "rebirth." Most prominent was the rediscovery of classical ideas, techniques, and philosophy. The very languages of the classical world were revived; throughout the Middle Ages, Latin was the language of the Church and Greek was virtually unknown in western Europe. In the fourteenth and fifteenth centuries, classical Latin was studied again, and Greek was re-introduced into Europe by Byzantine scholars fleeing the conquest of Constantinople in 1453 by Ottoman Turks.

It was also a period of rebirth of trade and cities, particularly after the 1450's, when the Hundred Years' War had ended and more wealth increased the interest in luxury goods. Warfare was certainly not over; if anything it increased between the Italian city-states, and between the Italians and the French. But new theories about states and war changed how both were organized and conducted. Faith also underwent a revolution; the Protestant Reformation was a manifestation of the Renaissance, although in a more subtle way.

The single most important Renaissance philosophy was humanism, which was a part of every endeavor of European culture during this period. Humanist ideals emphasized the potential of humanity and praised human endeavors and led to the celebration of humanity in a characteristically classical manner. Humanism also sought to counter the rigidity to which scholasticism had been reduced by the thirteenth century. The sources in this chapter show the poetic, artistic, and political sides of the Renaissance.

14.1

SONNETS, DANTE ALIGHIERI

Dante Alighieri (1265-1321) was both a Medieval and a Renaissance writer, thus perfectly indicative of the gradual shift in literary styles and tastes that took place in the fourteenth century. Although his masterpiece epic, The Divine Comedy, is a classic example of medieval piety and world-view, his sonnets (three of which are included here) show the humanist influences of the early Renaissance. The sonnets are dedicated to Beatrice, with whom Dante first fell in love when they were both children and continued to love and idealize long after her death.

It is worth noting that Dante was from Florence, as with many of the most influential Renaissance artists (in many media) and thinkers. The Florence of Dante's day was wracked with internal strife and blood feuds (Dante was himself exiled from Florence because of one such feud), and torn between imperial and papal politics. None of this would change over the course of the Renaissance, but within a century of Dante's death Florence would also be the most powerful and wealthy city in Italy.

---- ✢ ----

QUESTIONS

1. Can you pick out examples of classical influence from these sonnets?
2. Is Beatrice a real woman for Dante?
3. Are these Christian poems?

To every captive soul and gentle lover
  Into whose sight this present rhyme may chance,
  That, writing back, each may expound its sense,
  Greetings in Love, who is their Lord, I offer.
  Already of those hours a third was over
  Wherein all stars display their radiance,
  When lo! Love stood before me in my trance:
  Recalling what he was fills me with horror.
Joyful Love seemed to me and in his keeping
  He held my heart; and in his arms there lay
  My lady in a mantle wrapped, and sleeping.
  Then he awoke her and, her fear not heeding,
  My burning heart fed to her reverently.
  Then he departed from my vision, weeping

✢ ✢ ✢

These eyes of mine beheld the tenderness
  Which marked your features when you turned your gaze
  Upon my doleful bearing and the ways
  I many times assume in my distress.
  I understood then that you fain would guess
  The nature of the dolour of my days;
  And so straightway I grew afraid to raise
  My eyes lest they reveal my abjectness.
And as I from your vision then withdrew
  The tears within my heart began to well,
  Where all was stirred to tumult by your sight;
  And to my soul I murmured in my plight:
  'With her indeed that self-same Love must dwell
  Who makes you go thus weeping as you do.'...

❖ ❖ ❖

N̲o woman's countenance has ever worn
In such miraculous degree the hue
Of love and pity's look, from yielding to
The sight of gentle eyes or folk who mourn,
As does your own when I approach forlorn
And with my grieving face for mercy sue.
Such thoughts then come to mind because of you
My heart with fear and suffering is torn.
My wasted eyes I find I cannot keep
From gazing at you ever and again,
For by a tearful longing they are led.
Beholding you then so augments their pain
They are consumed by their desire to weep,
Yet in your presence tears they cannot shed.

From Dante Alighieri, *La Vita Nuova (Poems of Youth)*, trans. Barbara Reynolds, pp. 33, 90-91.
Copyright © 1969 Penguin Books, Ltd. Reproduced by permission of Penguin Books Limited.

14.2

THE LIFE OF LEONARDO DA VINCI

The term "renaissance man" might have been invented just to describe Leonardo da Vinci (1452-1519). Da Vinci was a painter, sculptor, and poet; his notebooks are filled with writings and drawings in mathematics, optics, anatomy, mechanics, chemistry, and philosophical speculation. Although not the most successful artist in his day (that title belongs to Michelangelo), to many people da Vinci was the epitome of everything that made up the Renaissance fusion of classical and Christian humanism. Two of the most famous pieces of art ever created by Western civilization are paintings by him: Mona Lisa *and* The Last Supper.

The following passages are from a biography of da Vinci by a contemporary painter, Vasari, who wrote biographies of several of his fellow artists.

❖

QUESTIONS

1. How is the very idea of writing a biography of an artist a "Renaissance" concept?
2. Why, according to Vasari, does da Vinci leave so many of his works unfinished?
3. What is humanist about da Vinci's approach to art?

Leonardo's disposition was so lovable that he commanded everyone's affection. He owned, one might say, nothing and he worked very little, yet he always kept servants as well as horses. These gave him great pleasure as indeed did all the animal creation which he treated with wonderful love and patience. For example, often when he was walking past the places where birds were sold he would pay the price asked, take them from their cages, and let them fly off into the air, giving them back their lost freedom. In return he was so favoured by nature that to whatever he turned his mind or thoughts the results were always inspired and perfect; and his lively and delightful works were incomparably graceful and realistic.

Clearly, it was because of his profound knowledge of painting that Leonardo started so many things without finishing them; for he was convinced that his hands, for all their skill, could never perfectly express the subtle and wonderful ideas of his imagination. Among his many interests was included the study of nature; he investigated the properties of plants and then observed the motion of the heavens, the path of the moon, and the course of the sun.

I mentioned earlier that when he was still young Leonardo entered the workshop of Andrea del Verrocchio. Now at that time Verrocchio was working on a panel picture showing the baptism of Christ by St. John, for which Leonardo painted an angel who was holding some garments; and despite his youth, he executed it is such a manner that his angel was far better than the figures painted by Andrea. This was the reason why Andrea would never touch colours again, he was so ashamed that a boy understood their use better than he did. Leonardo was then commissioned to make a cartoon (for a tapestry to be woven of gold and silk in Flanders an sent to the king of Portugal) showing the sin of Adam and Eve in the Garden of Paradise. For this he drew with the brush in chiaroscuro, with the lights in lead-white, a luxuriant meadow full of different kinds of animals; and it can truthfully be said that for diligence and faithfulness to nature nothing could be more inspired or perfect. There is a fig tree, for example, with its leaves foreshortened and its branches drawn from various aspects, depicted with such loving care that the brain reels at the thought that a man could have such patience. And there is a palm tree, the radiating crown of which is drawn with such marvellous skill that no one without Leonardo's understanding and patience could have done it. The work was not carried any farther and so today the cartoon is still in Florence, in the blessed house of the Magnificent Ottaviano de' Medici to whom it was presented not long ago by Leonardo's uncle....

Leonardo also executed in Milan, for the Dominicans of Santa Maria delle Grazie, a marvellous and beautiful painting of the Last Supper. Having depicted the heads of the apostles full of splendour and majesty, he deliberately left the head of Christ unfinished, convinced he would fail to give it the divine spirituality it demands. This all but finished work has ever since been held in the greatest veneration by the Milanese and others. In it Leonardo brilliantly succeeded in envisaging and reproducing the tormented anxiety of the apostles to know who had betrayed their master; so in their faces one can read the emotions of love, dismay, and anger, or rather sorrow, at their failure to grasp the meaning of Christ. And this excites no less admiration than the contrasted spectacle of the obstinacy, hatred, and treachery in the face of Judas or, indeed, than the incredible diligence with which every detail of the work was executed. The texture of the very cloth on the table is counterfeited so cunningly that the linen itself could not look more realistic.

It is said that the prior used to keep pressing Leonardo, in the most importunate way, to hurry up and finish his work, because he was puzzled by Leonardo's habit of sometimes spending half a day at a time contemplating what he had done so far; if the prior had had his way, Leonardo would have toiled like one of the labourers hoeing in the garden and never put his brush down for a moment. Not satisfied with this, the prior then complained to the duke, making such a fuss that the duke was constrained to send for

Leonardo and, very tactfully, question him about the painting, although he showed perfectly well that he was only doing so because of the prior's insistence. Leonardo, knowing he was dealing with a prince of acute and discerning intelligence, was willing (as he never had been with the prior) to explain his mind at length; and so he talked to the duke for a long time about the art of painting. He explained that men of genius sometimes accomplish most when they work the least; for, he added, they are thinking out inventions and forming in their minds the perfect ideas which they subsequently express and reproduce with their hands. Leonardo then said that he still had two heads to paint: the head of Christ was one, and for this he was unwilling to look for any human model, nor did he dare suppose that his imagination could conceive the beauty and divine grace that properly belonged to the incarnate Deity. Then, he said, he had yet to do the head of Judas, and this troubled him since he did not think he could imagine the features that would form the countenance of a man who, despite all the blessing he had been given, could so cruelly steel his will to betray his own master and the creator of the world. However, added Leonardo, he would try to find a model for Judas, and if he did not succeed in doing so, why then he was not without the head of that tactless and importunate prior. The duke roared with laughter at this and said that Leonardo had every reason in the world for saying so. The unfortunate prior retired in confusion to worry the labourers working in his garden, and he left off worrying Leonardo, who skilfully finished the head of Judas and made it seem the very embodiment of treachery and inhumanity. The head of Christ remained, as was said, unfinished.

This noble painting was so finely composed and executed that the King of France subsequently wanted to remove it to his kingdom. He tried all he could to find architects to make cross-stays of wood and iron with which the painting could be protected and brought safely to France, without any regard for expense, so great was his desire to have it. But as the painting was done on a wall his majesty failed to have his way and it remained in the possession of the Milanese. While he was working on the Last Supper, in the same refectory where there is a painting of the Passion done in the old manner, on the end wall, Leonardo portrayed Ludovico himself with his eldest son, Massimiliano; and on the other side, with the Duchess Beatrice, his other son Francesco, both of whom later became dukes of Milan; and all these figures are beautifully painted....

For Francesco del Giocondo Leonardo undertook to execute the portrait of his wife, Mona Lisa. He worked on this painting for four years, and then left it still unfinished; and today it is in the possession of King Francis of France, at Fontainebleau. If one wanted to see how faithfully art can imitate nature, one could readily perceive it from this head; for here Leonardo subtly reproduced every living detail. The eyes had their natural lustre and moistness, and around them were the lashes and all those rosy and pearly tints that demand the greatest delicacy of execution. The eyebrows were completely natural, growing thickly in one place and lightly in another and following the pores of the skin. The nose was finely painted, with rosy and delicate nostrils as in life. The mouth, joined to the flesh-tints of the face by the red of the lips, appeared to be living flesh rather than paint. On looking closely at the pit of her throat one could swear that the pulses were beating. Altogether this picture was painted in a manner to make the most confident artist — no matter who — despair and lose heart. Leonardo also made use of this device: while he was painting Mona Lisa, who was a very beautiful woman, he employed singers and musicians or jesters to keep her full of merriment and so chase away the melancholy that painters usually give to portraits. As a result, in this painting of Leonardo's there was a smile so pleasing that it seemed divine rather than human; and those who saw it were amazed to find that it was as alive as the original....

Leonardo went to Rome with Duke Giuliano de' Medici on the election of Pope Leo who was a great student of natural philosophy, and especially of alchemy. And in Rome he experimented with a paste made out of a certain kind of wax and made some light and billowy figures in the form of animals which he inflated with his mouth as he walked along and which flew above the ground until all the air escaped. To the back of a very odd-looking lizard that was found by the gardener of the Belvedere he attached with a mixture of quicksilver some wings, made from the scales stripped from other lizards, which quivered as it walked along. Then, after he had given it eyes, horns, and a beard he tamed the creature, and keeping it in a box he used to show it to this friends and frighten the life out of them. Again, Leonardo used to get the intestines of a bullock scraped completely free of their fat, cleaned and made so fine that they could be compressed into the palm of one hand; then he would fix one end of them to a pair of bellows lying in another room, and when they were inflated they filled the room in which they were and forced anyone standing there into a corner. Thus he could expand this translucent and airy stuff to fill a large space after occupying only a little, and he compared it to genius. He perpetrated hundreds of follies of this kind, and he also experimented with mirrors and made the most outlandish experiments to discover oils for painting and varnish for preserving the finished works....

From Georgio Vasari, *The Lives of the Artists*, trans. George Bull, pp. 257-258, 262-263, 266-269. Copyright © 1965 Penguin Books, Ltd. Reproduced by permission of Penguin Books Limited.

14.3

✤

THE PRINCE, MACHIAVELLI

The Renaissance was much more than an artistic change. It also included new approaches to politics and new definitions of power. Nothing epitomizes this new idea of power better than Niccolo Machiavelli's political treatise The Prince. *Written in 1513,* The Prince *was a radically different approach to statecraft; according to Machiavelli (d. 1527), rulers were justified in taking whatever actions that are necessary to protect their own power, whether that action is morally acceptable or not, or if it benefits the ruler's subjects or not. He used as his model contemporary rulers from Italy (Machiavelli was himself from Florence) as well as his knowledge of Roman political history. Perhaps the most important innovation of Machiavelli's political theory was his secularism.*

✤

QUESTIONS

1. *The Prince* has been described as either a cynical or realistic view of politics. Which do you think it is?
2. According to Machiavelli, why should a ruler avoid a reputation for generosity?
3. Is there a place for faith in Machiavelli's theory of statehood?

CHAPTER XVII — CONCERNING CRUELTY: WHETHER IT IS BETTER TO BE LOVED THAT TO BE FEARED, OR THE REVERSE

Turning to some other of the afrementioned qualities, I say that ever prince ought to wish to be considered kind rather than cruel. Nevertheless, he must take care to avoid misusing his kindness. Cesare Brogia was considered cruel; yet his cruelty restored Romagna, uniting it in peace and loyalty. If this result is considered good, then he must be judged much kinder than the florentines who, to avoid being called cruel, allowed Pistoia to be destroyed. A prince, therefore, must be indifferent to the charge of cruelty if he is to keep his subjects loyal and united. Having set an example once or twice, he may thereafter act far more mercifully than the princes who, through excessive kindness, allow disorders to arise from which murder and rapine ensue. Disorders harm the entire citizenry, while the executions ordered by a prince harm only a few individuals. Indeed, of all princes, the newly-established one can least of all escape the charge of cruelty, for new states are encumbered with dangers. As Virgil has Dido say,

> *Res dura, et regni novitas me talia cogunt*
> *Moliri, et late fines custode tueri.*

Nevertheless, he ought to be slow to believe what he hears and slow to act. Nor should he fear imaginary dangers, but proceed with moderation, prudence, and humanity, avoiding carelessness born of overconfidence and unbearable harshness born of excessive distrust.

Here a question arises: whether it is better to be loved than feared, or the reverse. The answer is, of course, that it would be best to both loved and feared. But since the two rarely come together, anyone compelled to choose will find greater security in being feared than in being loved. For this can be said about the generality of men: that they are ungrateful, fickle, dissembling, anxious to flee danger, and covetous of gain. So long as you promote their advantage, they are all yours, as I said before, and will offer you their blood, their goods, their lives, and their children when the need for these is remote. When the need arises, however, they will turn against you. The prince who bases his security upon their word, lacking other provision, is doomed; for friendships that are gained by money, not by greatness and nobility of spirit, may well be earned, but cannot be kept; and in time of need, they will have fled your purse. Men are less concerned about offending someone they have cause to love than someone they have cause to fear. Love endures by a bond which men, being scoundrels, may break whenever it serves their advantage to do so; but fear is supported by the dread of pain, which is ever present.

Still a prince should make himself feared in such a way that, though he does not gain love, he escapes hatred; for being feared but not hated go readily together. Such a condition he may always attain if he will not touch the property of his citizens and subjects, nor their women. And if he finds it necessary to take someone's life, he should do so when there is suitable justification and manifest cause; but above all, he should refrain from the property of others, for men are quicker to forget the death of a father than the loss of a patrimony. Furthermore, excuses for seizing property are never lacking and, indeed, anyone who begins to live by plunder will always find pretexts for taking over what belongs to someone else. On the other hand, pretexts for taking someone's life arise more rarely and last a shorter time.

But when a prince is at the head of his armies and must command multitudes of soldiers, then more than ever must he be indifferent to a reputation for cruelty, for without such a reputation no army was ever held together, nor was it every fit for combat. Among the marvelous deeds of Hannibal is numbered this one: that though he had an enormous army composed of a great variety of races fighting in a foreign land, no dissension ever arose among the troops or between the troops and their leader, either in good times or in bad. This could have had no other source but his inhuman cruelty which, together with his extraordinary qualities of leadership, made him an object of constant reverence and terror to his soldiers. To produce such an effect without this cruelty, his other qualities would have been insufficient. Writers of scant judgment in this matter have, on the one hand, admired his accomplishments and, on the other, condemned their chief source.

The proof that his other qualities would have been insufficient may be seen in the case of Scipio — a most exceptional man not only in his own times but in all remembered history — whose soldiers mutinied in Spain for no reason other than his excessive leniency, which allowed them more freedom than was consonant with military discipline. Fabius Maximus reproved him for it in the Senate and called him the corrupter of Roman arms. When one of his lieutenants ravaged the Locrians, Scipio neither avenged them nor took action to correct his lieutenant's insolence. This too grew out of his mild nature, so much so, in fact, that someone seeking to excuse Scipio's conduct before the Senate observed that many men have more skill in avoiding errors than in correcting them. This propensity would in time have damaged Scipio's fame and glory if he had persevered in it, but since he was ruled by the Senate, its potential harmfulness remained hidden, and it redounded to his glory.

Returning to the question, then, of being loved or feared, I conclude that since men love as they themselves determine but fear as their ruler determines, a wise prince must rely upon what he and not others can control. He need only strive to avoid being hated, as I said....

CHAPTER XXIII — HOW TO AVOID FLATTERERS

One important point I do not want to overlook concerns a failing against which princes cannot easily protect themselves unless they are especially prudent or have good advisers. I refer to the flatterers with whom the courts of princes are crowded. Because men are so easily pleased with their own qualities and are so readily deceived in them, they have difficulty in guarding against these pests, and in attempting to guard against them, they run the risk of being scorned. For there is no way of avoiding flattery except by letting men know that they will not offend by telling the truth; yet if every man is free to tell you the truth, you will not receive due respect.

Therefore, a prudent prince will pursue a third course, choosing the wise men of his state and granting only to them the freedom to tell him the truth, but only concerning those matters about which he asks, and no others. Yet he should question them about all maters, listen to their opinions, and then decide for himself as he wishes. He should treat these councils and the individual advisers in such a way as to make it clear that their words will be the more welcome the more freely they are spoken. Except for these men, he should listen to no one, but rather pursue the course agreed upon and do so resolutely. Anyone who does otherwise will fall victim to flatterers or, as a result of the various opinions he hears, will often change his mind and thereby lose reputation.

Regarding this, I should like to cite a recent example. Pre' Luca, the ambassador of Maximilian, the present emperor, used to say that His Majesty never sought counsel from anyone, yet never did anything as he wished to do it. This grows out of his acting contrary to what has just been suggested. Being a very secretive man, the Emperor never consults anyone and never reveals his intentions. But as soon as he begins to put them into effect, they are discovered. Then they are opposed by the men he has about him, and, lacking resolution, he is easily dissuaded from them. The result in that what he does on one day he destroys on the next, and it is never possible to know what he is seeking or planning, or to have any confidence in his decisions.

A prince, therefore, should always seek advice, but only when he, not someone else, chooses. Indeed, he should discourage everyone from giving advice unless he has asked for it. In fact, if he should observe that someone is withholding the truth for some reason, he should show annoyance. Since many people believe that some princes are reputed wise, thanks rather to their wise counselors than to their own natural gifts, they ought to be told that they deceive themselves. For this is a general rule that never fails: a prince who is not wise himself cannot be wisely counseled, unless by chance he should have a sole counselor by whom he is ruled in all matters. There could be such a situation, but it would not last long, for the counselor would soon deprive the prince of his state. An unwise prince, having to consider the advice of several counselors, would never receive concordant opinions, and he would not be able to reconcile them on his own. His counselors would pursue their own interests and he would know neither how to rule them nor how to understand them. They could not do otherwise, for men will always prove bad unless necessity compels them to be good. Therefore I conclude that good advice, no matter where it comes from, ultimately derives from the prudence of the prince, and the prudence of the prince does not derive from good advice.

From *The Prince and Selected Discourses by Niccolo Machiavelli*, translated by Daniel Donno, copyright © 1966 by Bantam, a division of Random House, Inc. Used by permission of Bantam Books, a division of Random House, Inc.

14.4

BOOK OF THE COURTIER, CASTIGLIONE

Machiavelli was not the only political theorist of the Renaissance. Indeed, the field of political philosophy seemed to explode in the fifteenth and sixteenth centuries, and would forever remain one of the most popular fields of Western intellectual endeavor. Baldesar Castiglione (1478–1529) wrote the definitive handbook for the aristocratic class of Italy. Unlike Machiavelli, who focused on the skills necessary to be a good ruler, Castiglione's Book of the Courtier *was aimed at all aristocrats and thus presented a broader picture of what education, skills, morals, and even fashion sense an ambitious nobleman needed to have. It drew very heavily on classical learning as well as current Italian history.*

QUESTIONS

1. Compare Castiglione's discussion of flattery with Machiavelli's in the previous source.
2. What kind of education should a courtier have? Why?
3. In what way does Castiglione use classical references? Which ones does he choose, and why?

' I should like our courtier to be a more than average scholar, at least in those studies which we call the humanities; and he should have a knowledge of Greek as well as Latin, because of the many different things that are so beautifully written in that language. He should be very well acquainted with the poets, and no less with the orators and historians, and also skilled at writing both verse and prose, especially in our own language; for in addition to the satisfaction this will give him personally, it will enable him to provide constant entertainment for the ladies, who are usually very fond of such things. But if because of his other activities or through lack of study he fails to achieve a commendable standard in his writing, then he should take pains to suppress his work, to avoid ridicule, and he should show it only to a friend he can trust. And the exercise of writing will be profitable for him at least to the extent that it will teach him how to judge the work of others. For it is very unusual for someone who is not a practised writer, however erudite he may be, to understand completely the demanding work done by writers, or appreciate their stylistic accomplishments and triumphs and those subtle details characteristic of the writers of the ancient world. Moreover, these studies will make our courtier well informed and eloquent and (as Aristippus said to the tyrant) self-confident and assured no matter whom he is talking to. However, I should like our courtier to keep one precept firmly in mind: namely, that in what I have just discussed and in everything else he should always be diffident and reserved rather than forward, and he should be on his guard against assuming that he knows what he does not know. For we are instinctively all too greedy for praise, and there is no sound or song that comes sweeter to our ears; praise, like Sirens' voices, is the king of music that causes shipwreck to the man who does not stop his ears to its deceptive harmony. Recognizing this danger, some of the philosophers of the ancient world wrote books giving advice on how a man can tell the difference between a true friend and a flatterer. Even so, we may well ask what use is this, seeing that there are so many who realize perfectly well that they are listening to flattery, and yet love the flatterer and detest the one who tells them the truth. Indeed, very often, deciding that the one who praises them is not being fulsome enough, they lend him a hand themselves and say such things that even the most outrageous flatterer feels ashamed. Let us leave these blind fools to their errors and decide that our courtier should possess such good judgement that he will not be told that black is white or presume anything of himself unless he is certain that it is true, and especially in regard to those flaws which, if you remember, when he was suggesting his game for the evening Cesare recalled we had often used to demonstrate the particular folly of this person or another. To make no mistake at all, the courtier should, on the contrary, when he knows the praises he receives are deserved, not assent to them too openly nor let them pass without some protest. Rather he should tend to disclaim them modestly, always giving the impression that arms are, as indeed they should be, his chief profession, and that all his other fine accomplishments serve merely as adornments; and this should especially be his attitude when he is in the company of soldiers, lest he behave like those who in the world of scholarship want to be taken for warriors and among warriors want to seem men of letters. In this way, as we have said, he will avoid affectation, and even his modest achievements will appear great.'

At this point, Pietro Bembo interrupted: 'I cannot see, my dear Count, why you wish this courtier, who is so literate and so well endowed with other worthy qualities, to regard everything as serving to adorn the profession of arms, and not arms and the rest as serving to adorn the profession of letter, which, taken by themselves, are as superior in dignity to arms as is the soul to the body, since letters are a function of the soul, just as arms are of the body.'

Then the Count answered: 'On the contrary, the profession of arms pertains both to the soul and to the body. But I should not want you to be the judge of this, Pietro, because by one of the parties concerned it would be assumed that you were prejudiced. And as this is a controversy that the wisest men have already thrashed out, there is no call to re-open it. As it is, I consider that it has been settled in favour of arms; and since I may form our courtier as I wish, I want him to be of the same opinion. If you think the contrary, wait until you hear of a contest in which the man who defends the cause of arms is allowed to use the, just as those who defend the cause of letters make use of letters in their defence; for if each one uses his own weapons, you will see that the men of letters will lose.'

'Ah,' said Pietro Bembo, 'you were only too ready earlier on to damn the French for their scant appreciation of letters, and you mentioned the glory that they bring to men and the way they make a man immortal. And now you seem to have changed your mind. Do you not remember that:

> Giunto Alessandro alla famosa tomba
> del fero Achille, sospirando disse:
> O fortunato, che si chiara tromba
> trovasti, e chi di te sì alto scrisse!

And if Alexander was envious of Achilles not because of what he had done himself but because of the way he was blessed by fortune in having his deeds celebrated by Homer, we must conclude that he put a higher value on the writings of Homer than on the arms of Achilles. What other judge do you want, or what other verdict on the relative worth of arms and letters than the one delivered by one of the greatest commanders that has ever lived?

The Count replied: 'I blame the French for believing that letters are harmful to the profession of arms, and I maintain myself that it is more fitting, joined together in our courtier. I do not think that this means I have changed my opinion. But, as I said, I do not wish to argue which of them is more praiseworthy. Let it be enough that men of letters hardly ever choose to praise other than great men and glorious deeds, which deserve praise both on their own account and because, in addition, they provide writers with a truly noble theme. And this subject-matter embellishes what is written and, no doubt, is the reason why such writings endure, for otherwise, if they dealt not with noble deeds but with vain and trivial subjects, they would surely be read and appreciated less. And if Alexander was envious of Achilles because he was praised by Homer, it still does not necessarily follow that he thought more of letters than of arms; and if he had thought that he was as inferior to Achilles as a soldier as he believed that all those who would write about him were inferior to Homer as writers, he would, I am sure, have far preferred brave exploits on his own part to brave talk from others. Therefore I believe that when he said what he did, Alexander was tacitly praising himself, and expressing a desire for what he thought he lacked, namely supreme ability as a writer, rather than for what he took for granted he already had, namely prowess as a warrior, in which he was far from acknowledging Achilles as his superior. So when he called Achilles fortunate he meant that if so far his own fame did not rival that of Achilles (which had been made bright and illustrious through so inspired a poem) this was not because his valour and merits were less notable or less deserving of the highest praise but because of the way fortune had granted Achilles a born genius to be his herald and to trumpet his deeds to the world. Moreover, perhaps Alexander wanted to encourage some gifted person to write about him, showing that his pleasure in this would be as great as his love and respect for the sacred monuments of literature. And now we have said enough about this subject.'...

...the Count continued as follows:

'Gentlemen, I must tell you that I am not satisfied with our courtier unless he is also a musician and unless as well as understanding and being able to read music he can play several instruments. For, when we think of it, during our leisure time we can find nothing more worthy or commendable to help our bodies relax and our spirits recuperate, especially at Court where, besides the way in which music helps everyone to forget his troubles, many things are done to please the ladies, whose tender and gentle souls are very susceptible to harmony and sweetness. So it is no wonder that both in ancient times and today they have always been extremely fond of musicians and have welcomed music as true refreshment for the spirit.'

From Baldesar Castiglione, *The Book of Courtier*, trans. George Bull, pp. 90-94. Copyright © 1967, 1986 Penguin Books, Ltd. Reproduced by permission of Penguin Books Limited.

Questions for Part 14

1. The term "renaissance" literally means rebirth. What was reborn and how?
2. How was the Renaissance also a time of continuity of medieval culture?
3. Why did the Renaissance begin first in the Italian city-states?

PART 15

❧

REFORMATION AND THE WARS OF RELIGION

There were many Reformations in the sixteenth century. Some of the movement's leaders began as reformers and became protesters, while others remained reformers. Furthermore, these Reformations did not appear without precedent or cause; humanism and renaissance ideas also contributed to the Reformations. Martin Luther's objections to particular Catholic practices in 1517 was certainly one starting point of one Reformation, but it had inherited fifteenth-century humanism and movements that emphasized personal piety. John Calvin and Ulrich Zwingli introduced their own Reformations in the decade after Luther's, and while they both agreed with Luther (and each other) on some doctrines and beliefs, they disagreed with Luther (and each other) on many more. All three, as well as other reformers were influenced by emerging national awareness. It seemed as if every European country had its own version of a Reformation. The Catholic Church had its own as well, although it did so without changing any doctrine; instead it underwent an internal renewal and rid itself of abuses.

All Reformations, whether Protestant or Catholic, ended up the period embroiled in violence. Religious wars swept across Europe in the mid-sixteenth century and would continue into the seventeenth. One particularly horrific manifestation of the religious violence was the witch hunts, which admittedly began in the Late Middle Ages, but which increased in both scope and degree of violence as the Reformation progressed. Reformation and religious violence were both aided by the new technology of printing, which made ideas more readily available to a wider audience than ever before.

15.1

✤

NINETY-FIVE THESES, MARTIN LUTHER

The most important document of the Protestant Reformation was the Ninety-Five Theses *of Martin Luther. Luther (1483-1546) was an intensely devout monk with legal training and humanist interests who was obsessed with salvation. In 1517 Luther was teaching at the university in Wittenberg when the Dominican Tetzel arrived to preach a special indulgence. Indulgences were papal dispensations (releases) from either penance or time in purgatory in exchange for an act of faith. The Crusades are an example of how indulgences had been used by the Church; Crusaders had been promised full remission of their sins in exchange for fighting. Tetzel promised salvation if people donated money for the construction of St. Peter's in Rome. Luther was confused by the theology of the indulgence and offended by the apparent "sale" of salvation preached by Tetzel. Luther posited ninety-five points on penance, indulgences, and salvation; he proposed this topic for discussion in the traditional university manner by posting his theses on the church door.*

QUESTIONS

1. How does Luther's legal background reveal itself in how he thinks about indulgences?
2. Find an example of how Luther uses scripture to argue against the theory of indulgence.
3. How is Luther using this opportunity to criticize papal abuses?

NINETY-FIVE THESES *or* DISPUTATION ON THE POWER AND EFFICACY OF INDULGENCES

1. When our Lord and Mater Jesus Christ said, "Repent" [Matt. 4:17], he willed the entire life of believers to be one of repentance.
2. This word cannot be understood as referring to the sacrament of penance, that is, confession and satisfaction, as administered by the clergy.
3. Yet it does not mean solely inner repentance; such inner repentance is worthless unless it produces various outward mortifications of the flesh.
4. The penalty of sin remains as long as the hatred of self, that is, true inner repentance, until our entrance into the kingdom of heaven.
5. The pope neither desires nor is able to remit any penalties except those imposed by his own authority or that of the canons.
6. The pope cannot remit any guilt, except by declaring and showing that it has been remitted by God; or, to be sure, by remitting guilt in cases reserved to his judgment. If his right to grant remission in these cases were disregarded, the guilt would certainly remain unforgiven.
7. God remits guilt to no one unless at the same time he humbles him in all things and makes him submissive to his vicar the priest.
8. The penitential canons are imposed only on the living, and, according to the canons themselves, nothing should be imposed on the dying.
9. Therefore the Holy Spirit through the pope is kind to us insofar as the pope in his decrees always makes exception of the article of death and of necessity.
10. Those priests act ignorantly and wickedly who, in the case of the dying, reserve canonical penalties for purgatory.
11. Those tares of changing the canonical penalty to the penalty of purgatory were evidently sown while the bishops slept [Matt. 13:25].
12. In former times canonical penalties were imposed, not after, but before absolution, as tests of true contrition.
13. The dying are freed by death from all penalties, are already dead as far as the canon laws are concerned, and have a right to be released from them.

14. Imperfect piety or love on the part of the dying person necessarily brings with it great fear; and the smaller the love, the greater the fear.
15. This fear or horror is sufficient in itself, to say nothing of other things, to constitute the penalty of purgatory, since it is very near the horror of despair.
16. Hell, purgatory, and heaven seem to differ the same as despair, fear, and assurance of salvation.
17. It seems as though for the souls in purgatory fear should necessarily decrease and love increase.
18. Furthermore, it does not seem proved, either by reason or Scripture, that souls in purgatory are outside the state of merit, that is, unable to grow in love.
19. Nor does it seem proved that should in purgatory, at least not all f them, are certain an assured of their own salvation, even if we ourselves may be entirely certain of it.
20. Therefore the pope, when he uses the words "plenary remission of all penalties," does not actually mean "all penalties," but only those imposed by himself.
21. Thus those indulgence preachers are in error who say that a man is absolved from every penalty and saved by papal indulgences.
22. As a matter of fact, the pope remits to souls in purgatory no penalty which, according to canon law, they should have paid in this life.
23. If remission of all penalties whatsoever could be granted to anyone at all, certainly it would be granted only to the most perfect, that is, to very few.
24. For this reason most people are necessarily deceived by that indiscriminate and high-sounding promise of release from penalty.
25. That power which the pope has in general over purgatory corresponds to the power which any bishop or curate has in a particular way in his own diocese and parish.
26. The pope does very well when he grants remission to souls in purgatory, not by the power of the keys, which he does not have, but by way of intercession for them.
27. They preach only human doctrines who say that as soon as the money clinks into the money chest, the soul flies out of purgatory.
28. It is certain that when money clinks in the money chest, greed and avarice can be increased; but when the church intercedes, the result is in the hands of God alone.
29. Who knows whether all souls in purgatory wish to be redeemed, since we have exceptions in St. Severinus and St. Paschal, as related in a legend.
30. No one is sure of the integrity of his own contrition, much less of having received plenary remission.
31. The man who actually buys indulgences is as rare as he who is really penitent; indeed, he is exceedingly rare.
32. Those who believe that they can be certain of their salvation because they have indulgence letters will be eternally damned, together with their teachers.
33. Men must especially be on guard against those who say that the pope's pardons are that inestimable gift of God by which man is reconciled to him.
34. For the graces of indulgences are concerned only with the penalties of sacramental satisfaction established by man.
35. They who teach that contrition is not necessary on the part of those who intend to buy souls out of purgatory or to buy confessional privileges preach unchristian doctrine.
36. Any truly repentant Christian has a right to full remission of penalty and guilt, even without indulgence letters.
37. Any true Christian, whether living or dead, participates in all the blessings of Christ and the church; and this is granted him by God, even without indulgence letters.

38. Nevertheless, papal remission and blessing are by no means to be disregarded, for they are, as I have said (Thesis 6), the proclamation of the divine remission.

39. It is very difficult, even for the most learned theologians, at one and the same time to commend to the people the bounty of indulgences and the need of true contrition.

40. A Christian who is truly contrite seeks and loves to pay penalties for his sins; the bounty of indulgences, however, relaxes penalties and causes men to hate them -- at least it furnishes occasion for hating them.

41. Papal indulgences must be preached with caution, lest people erroneously think that they are preferable to other good works of love.

42. Christians are to be taught that the pope does not intend that the buying of indulgences should in any way be compared with works of mercy.

43. Christians are to be taught that he who gives to the poor or lends to the needy does a better deed than he who buys indulgences.

44. Because love grows by works of love, man thereby becomes better. Man does not, however, become better by means of indulgences but is merely freed from penalties.

45. Christians are to be taught that he who sees a needy man and passes him by, yet gives his money for indulgences, does not buy papal indulgences but God's wrath.

46. Christians are to be taught that, unless they have more than they need, they must reserve enough for their family needs and by no means squander it on indulgences.

47. Christians are to be taught that they buying of indulgences is a matter of free choice, not commanded.

48 Christians are to be taught that the pope, in granting indulgences, needs and thus desires their devout prayer more than their money.

49. Christians are to be taught that papal indulgences are useful only if they do not put their trust in them, but very harmful if they lose their fear of God because of them.

50. Christians are to be taught that if the pope knew the exactions of the indulgence preachers, he would rather that the basilica of St. Peter were burned to ashes than built up with the skin, flesh, and bones of his sheep.

51. Christians are to be taught that the pope would and should wish to give of his own money, even though he had to sell the basilica of St. Peter, to many of those from whom certain hawkers of indulgences cajole money.

52. It is vain to trust in salvation by indulgence letters, even though the indulgence commissary, or even the pope, were to offer his soul as security.

53. They are the enemies of Christ and the pope who forbid altogether the preaching of the Word of God in some churches in order that indulgences may be preached in others.

54. Injury is done to the Word of God when, in the same sermon, an equal or larger amount of time is devoted to indulgences than to the Word.

55. It is certainly the pope's sentiment that if indulgences, which are a very insignificant thing, are celebrated with one bell, one procession, and one ceremony, then the gospel, which is the very greatest thing, should be preached with a hundred bells, a hundred processions, a hundred ceremonies.

56. The true treasures of the church, out of which the pope distributes indulgences, are not sufficiently discussed or known among the people of Christ.

57. That indulgences are not temporal treasures is certainly clear, for many indulgence sellers do not distribute them freely but only gather them.

58. Nor are they the merits of Christ and the saints, for, even without the pope, the latter always work grace for the inner man, and the cross, death, and hell for the outer man.
59. St. Lawrence said that the poor of the church were the treasures of the church, but he spoke according to the usage of the word in his own time.
60. Without want of consideration we say that the keys of the church, given by the merits of Christ, are that treasure.
61. For it is clear that the pope's power is of itself sufficient for the remission of penalties and cases reserved by himself.
62. The true treasure of the church is the most holy gospel of the glory and grace of God.
63. But this treasure is naturally most odious, for it makes the first to be last (Mt. 20:16).
64. On the other hand, the treasure of indulgences is naturally most acceptable, for it makes the last to be first.
65. Therefore the treasures of the gospel are nets with which one formerly fished for men of wealth.
66. The treasures of indulgences are nets with which one now fishes for the wealth of men.
67. The indulgences which the demagogues acclaim as the greatest graces are actually understood to be such only insofar as they promote gain.
68. They are nevertheless in truth the most insignificant graces when compared with the grace of God and the piety of the cross.
69. Bishops and curates are bound to admit the commissaries of papal indulgences with all reverence.
70. But they are much more bound to strain their eyes and ears lest these men preach their own dreams instead of what the pope has commissioned.
71. Let him who speaks against the truth concerning papal indulgences be anathema and accursed.
72. But let him who guards against the lust and license of the indulgence preachers be blessed.
73. Just as the pope justly thunders against those who by any means whatever contrive harm to the sale of indulgences.
74. Much more does he intend to thunder against those who use indulgences as a pretext to contrive harm to holy love and truth.
75. To consider papal indulgences so great that they could absolve a man even if he had done the impossible and had violated the mother of God is madness.
76. We say on the contrary that papal indulgences cannot remove the very least of venial sins as far as guilt is concerned.
77. To say that even St. Peter if he were now pope, could not grant greater graces is blasphemy against St. Peter and the pope.
78. We say on the contrary that even the present pope, or any pope whatsoever, has greater graces at his disposal, that is, the gospel, spiritual powers, gifts of healing, etc., as it is written, 1 Co 12[:28].
79. To say that the cross emblazoned with the papal coat of arms, and set up by the indulgence preachers is equal in worth to the cross of Christ is blasphemy.
80. The bishops, curates, and theologians who permit such talk to be spread among the people will have to answer for this.
81. This unbridled preaching of indulgences makes it difficult even for learned men to rescue the reverence which is due the pope from slander or from the shrewd questions of the laity.
82. Such as: "Why does not the pope empty purgatory for the sake of holy love and the dire need of the souls that are there if he redeems an infinite number of souls for the sake of miserable money with which to build a church?" The former reason would be most just; the latter is most trivial.

83. Again, "Why are funeral and anniversary masses for the dead continued and why does he not return or permit the withdrawal of the endowments founded for them, since it is wrong to pray for the redeemed?"

84. Again, "What is this new piety of God and the pope that for a consideration of money they permit a man who is impious and their enemy to buy out of purgatory the pious soul of a friend of God and do not rather, because of the need of that pious and beloved soul, free it for pure love's sake?"

85. Again, "Why are the penitential canons, long since abrogated and dead in actual fact and through disuse, now satisfied by the granting of indulgences as though they were still alive and in force?"

86. Again, "Why does not the pope, whose wealth is today greater than the wealth of the richest Crassus, build this one basilica of St. Peter with his own money rather than with the money of poor believers?"

87. Again, "What does the pope remit or grant to those who by perfect contrition already have a right to full remission and blessings?"

88. Again, "What greater blessing could come to the church than if the pope were to bestow these remissions and blessings on every believer a hundred times a day, as he now does but once?"

89. "Since the pope seeks the salvation of souls rather than money by his indulgences, why does he suspend the indulgences and pardons previously granted when they have equal efficacy?"

90. To repress these very sharp arguments of the laity by force alone, and not to resolve them by giving reasons, is to expose the church and the pope to the ridicule of their enemies and to make Christians unhappy.

91. If, therefore, indulgences were preached according to the spirit and intention of the pope, all these doubts would be readily resolved. Indeed, they would not exist.

92. Away, then, with all those prophets who say to the people of Christ, "Peace, peace," and there is no peace! (Jer 6:14)

93. Blessed be all those prophets who say to the people of Christ, "Cross, cross," and there is no cross!

94. Christians should be exhorted to be diligent in following Christ, their Head, through penalties, death and hell.

95. And thus be confident of entering into heaven through many tribulations rather than through the false security of peace (Acts 14:22).

Source: *Luther's Works, Volume 31, Career of the Reformer: I*, ed. Harold J. Grimm (Philadelphia: Muhlenberg Press, 1957), pp. 25-33.

15.2

✛

SIXTY-SEVEN ARTICLES, ULRICH ZWINGLI

With the Ninety-Five Theses of Luther, the Protestant Reformation had begun. Luther had probably not intended to break away from the church when he first questioned the practice of indulgences, but that was the end result. Particularly appealing to many Christians across Europe was Luther's insistence that scripture alone should be the source of Christian doctrine. Ulrich Zwingli (1484-1531) began preaching on the centrality of scripture in 1523 and was immediately controversial; a town council was called after much debate proclaimed Zwingli to be the spiritual leader of the city and encouraged him to continue his preaching. The Reformation begun by Luther in Germany had spread to Switzerland.

Although he was influenced by Luther, Zwingli was no Lutheran. The two theologians differed greatly on certain doctrines, particularly their interpretation of the nature of the sacraments and the relationship between church and state. Zwingli envisioned Zurich as a "Christian" city, and theorized that the civil authority came from God.

The following source lists Zwingli's plan for Zurich.

---- ✢ ----

QUESTIONS

1. What is Zwingli's view of the papacy?
2. According to Zwingli, what is the relationship between the individual and God?
3. How does Zwingli define the priesthood?

The articles and opinions below, I, Ulrich Zwingli, confess to have preached in the worthy city of Zurich as based upon the Scriptures which are called inspired by God, and I offer to protect and conquer with the said articles, and where I have not now correctly understood said Scriptures I shall allow myself to be taught better, but only from said Scriptures.

I. All who say that the Gospel is invalid without the confirmation of the Church err and slander God.

II. The sum and substance of the Gospel is that our Lord Jesus Christ, the true Son of God, has made known to us the will of his heavenly Father, and has with his innocence released us from death and reconciled God.

III. Hence Christ is the only way to salvation for all who ever were, are and shall be.

IV. Who seeks or points out another door errs, yea, he is a murderer of souls and a thief.

V. Hence all who consider other teachings equal to or higher than the Gospel err, and do not know what the Gospel is.

VI. For Jesus Christ is the guide and leader, promised by God to all human beings, which promise was fulfilled.

VII. That he is an eternal salvation and head of all believers, who are his body, but which is dead and can do nothing without him.

VIII. From this follows first that all who dwell in the head are members and children of God, and that is the church or communion of the saints, the bride of Christ, *Ecclesia catholica*.

IX. Furthermore, that as the members of the body can do nothing without the control of the head, so no one in the body of Christ can do the least without his head, Christ.

X. As that man is mad whose limbs (try to) do something without his head, tearing, wounding, injuring himself; thus when the members of Christ undertake something without their head,

Christ, they are mad, and injure and burden themselves with unwise ordinances.

XI. Hence we see in the clerical (so-called) ordinances, concerning their splendor, riches, classes, titles, laws, a cause of all foolishness, for they do not also agree with the head.

XII. Thus they still rage, not on account of the head (for that one is eager to bring forth in these times from the grace of God,) but because one will not let them rage, but tries to compel them to listen to the head.

XIII. Where this (the head) is hearkened to one learns clearly and plainly the will of God, and man is attracted by his spirit to him and changed into him.

XIV. Therefore all Christian people shall use their best diligence that the Gospel of Christ be preached alike everywhere.

XV. For in the faith rests our salvation, and in unbelief our damnation; for all truth is clear in him.

XVI. In the Gospel one learns that human doctrines and decrees do not aid in salvation.

ABOUT THE POPE

XVII. That Christ is the only eternal high priest, wherefrom it follows that those who have called themselves high priests have opposed the honor and power of Christ, yea, cast it out.

ABOUT THE MASS

XVIII. That Christ, having sacrificed himself once, is to eternity a certain and valid sacrifice for the sins of all faithful, wherefrom it follows that the mass is not a sacrifice, but is a remembrance of the sacrifice and assurance of the salvation which Christ has given us.

XIX. That Christ is the only mediator between God and us.

XX. That God desires to give us all things in his name, whence it follows that outside of this life we need no mediator except himself.

XXI. That when we pray for each other on earth, we do so in such fashion that we believe that all things are given to us through Christ alone.

ABOUT GOOD WORKS

XXII. That Christ is our justice, from which follows that our works in so far as they are good, so far they are of Christ, but in so far as they are ours, they are neither right nor good.

CONCERNING CLERICAL PROPERTY

XXIII. That Christ scorns the property and pomp of this world, whence from it follows that those who attract wealth to themselves in his name slander him terribly when they make him a pretext for their avarice and wilfullness.

CONCERNING THE FORBIDDING OF FOOD

XXIV. That no Christian is bound to do those things which God has not decreed, therefore one may eat at all times all food, wherefrom one learns that the decree about cheese and butter is a Roman swindle.

ABOUT HOLIDAY AND PILGRIMAGE

XXV. That time and place is under the jurisdiction of Christian people, and man with them, wherefrom is learnt that those who fix time and place deprive the Christians of their liberty.

ABOUT HOODS, DRESS, INSIGNIA

XXVI. That God is displeased with nothing so much as with hypocrisy; whence is learnt that all is gross hypocrisy and profligacy which is mere show before men. Under this condemnation fall hoods, insignia, plates, etc.

ABOUT ORDER AND SECTS

XXVII. That all Christian men are brethren of Christ and brethren of one another, and shall create no father (for themselves) on earth. Under this condemnation fall orders, sects, brotherhoods, etc.

ABOUT THE MARRIAGE OF ECCLESIASTS

XXVIII. That all which God has allowed or not forbidden is righteous, hence marriage is permitted to all human beings.

XXIX. That all who are called clericals sin when they do not protect themselves by marriage after they have become conscious that God has not enabled them to remain chaste.

ABOUT THE VOW OF CHASTITY

XXX. That those who promise chastity [outside of matrimony] take foolishly or childishly too much upon themselves, whence is learnt that those who make such vows do wrong to the pious being.

ABOUT THE BAN

XXXI. That no special person can impose the ban upon any one, but the Church, that is the congregation of those among whom the one to be banned dwells, together with their watch man, *i.e.,* the pastor.

XXXII. That one may ban only him who gives public offence.

ABOUT ILLEGAL PROPERTY

XXXIII. That property unrighteously acquired shall not be given to temples, monasteries, cathedrals, clergy or nuns, but to the needy, if it cannot be returned to the legal owner.

ABOUT MAGISTRY

XXXIV. The spiritual (so-called) power has no justification for its pomp in the teaching of Christ.

XXXV. But the lay has power and confirmation from the deed and doctrine of Christ.

XXXVI. All that the spiritual so-called state claims to have of power and protection belongs to the lay, if they wish to be Christians.

XXXVII. To them, furthermore, all Christians owe obedience without exception.

XXXVIII. In so far as they do not command that which is contrary to God.

XXXIX. Therefore all their laws shall be in harmony with the divine will, so that they protect the oppressed, even if he does not complain.

XL. They alone may put to death justly, also, only those who give public offence (if God is not offended let another thing be commanded).

XLI. If they give good advice and help to those for whom they must account to God, then these owe to them bodily assistance.

XLII. But if they are unfaithful and transgress the laws of Christ they may be deposed in the name of God.

XLIII. In short, the realm of him is best and most stable who rules in the name of God alone, and his is worst and most unstable who rules in accordance with his own will.

ABOUT PRAYER

XLIV. Real petitioners call to God in spirit and truly, without great ado before men.

XLV. Hypocrites do their work so that they may be seen by men, also receive their reward in this life.

XLVI. Hence it must always follow that church-song and outcry without devoutness, and only for reward, is seeking either fame before the men or gain.

ABOUT OFFENCE

XLVII. Bodily death a man should suffer before he offend or scandalize a Christian.

XLVIII. Who through stupidness or ignorance is offended without cause, he should not be left sick or weak, but he should be made strong, that he may not consider as a sin which is not a sin.

XLIX. Greater offence I know not than that one does not allow priests to have wives, but permits them to hire prostitutes. Out upon the shame!

ABOUT REMITTANCE OF SIN

L. God alone remits sin through Jesus Christ, his Son, and alone our Lord.

LI. Who assigns this to creatures detracts from the honor of God and gives it to him who is not God; this is real idolatry.

LII. Hence the confession which is made to the priest or neighbor shall not be declared to be a remittance of sin, but only a seeking for advice.

LIII. Works of penance coming from the counsel of human beings (except the ban) do not cancel sin; they are imposed as a menace to others.

LIV. Christ has borne all our pains and labor. Hence whoever assigns to works of penance what belongs to Christ errs and slanders God.

LV. Whoever pretends to remit to a penitent being any sin would not be a vicar of God or St. Peter, but of the devil.

LVI. Whoever remits any sin only for the sake of money is the companion of Simon and Balaam, and the real messenger of the devil personified.

ABOUT PURGATORY

LVII. The true divine Scriptures know naught about purgatory after this life.

LVIII. The sentence of the dead is known to God only.

LVIX. And the less God has let us know concerning it, the less we should undertake to know about it.

LX. That man earnestly calls to God to show mercy to the dead I do not condemn, but to determine a period of time therefor (seven years for a mortal sin), and to lie for the sake of gain, is not human, but devilish.

ABOUT THE PRIESTHOOD.

LXI. About the consecration which the priests have received in late times the Scriptures know nothing.

LXII. Furthermore, they know no priests except those who proclaim the word of God.

LXIII. They command honor should be shown, i.e., to furnish them with food for the body.

ABOUT THE CESSATION OF MISUSAGES

LXIV. All those who recognize their errors shall not be allowed to suffer, but to die in peace, and thereafter arrange in a Christian manner their bequests to the Church.

LXV. Those who do not wish to confess, God will probably take care of. Hence no force shall be used against their body, unless it be that they behave so criminally that one cannot do without that.

LXVI. All the clerical superiors shall at once settle down, and with unanimity set up the cross of Christ, not the money-chests, or they will perish, for I tell thee the ax is raised against the tree.

LXVII. If any one wishes conversation with me concerning interest, tithes, unbaptized children or confirmation, I am willing to answer.

Let no one undertake here to argue with sophistry or human foolishness, but come to the

Scriptures to accept them as the judge (foras cares! the Scriptures breathe the Spirit of God), so that the truth either may be found, or if found, as I hope, retained.

Amen.

Thus may God rule.

The basis and commentary of these articles will soon appear in print.

Sources: *Ulrich Zwingli (1484-1531): Selected Works*, ed. Samuel Macauley Jackson (Philadelphia: University of Philadelphia Press, 1901, 1972), pp. 111-117.

15.3

"RAPTURE OF THE SOUL," TERESA OF AVILA

The Catholic Church was not unresponsive to the charges of reformers such as Luther and Zwingli. There were two stages to the Counter-Reformation that took place within the Catholic Church. One was the official response by both pope and emperor, which were to condemn Luther and the Protestants, and to summon a church council at Trent in 1545-1563, which confirmed all Catholic doctrines and practices. The second response was a movement of spiritual renewal, which promoted a more personal relationship between humanity and God. New religious orders such as the Society of Jesus (the Jesuits) and the Capuchins (a reformed Franciscan order) emerged. Missionary activity also increased, helped by the discovery of the Americas and new access to Asia. Mysticism had a resurgence in popularity, which incorporated personal piety and traditional Catholic faith. Teresa of Avila (1515-1582) was a Carmelite nun who had intense visions of God. In the following excerpt from her mystical text, the Interior Castle, she discusses the soul's rapturous union with God.

QUESTIONS

1. How is Teresa's understanding of rapture related to her gender?
2. Compare this with Luther's Ninety-Five Theses. How do the two differ in their description of how the soul knows God?
3. Who do you think was the intended audience of this mystical text?

... I want to put down here some kinds of rapture that I've come to understand because I've discussed them with so many spiritual persons. But I don't know whether I shall succeed as I did when I wrote elsewhere about them and other things that occur in this dwelling place. On account of certain reasons it seems worthwhile to speak of these kinds of rapture again — if for no other reason, so that everything related to these dwelling places will be put down here together.

3. One kind of rapture is that in which the soul even though not in prayer is touched by some word it remembers or hears about God. It seems that His Majesty from the interior of the soul makes the spark we mentioned increase, for He is moved with compassion in seeing the soul suffer so long a time from its desire. All burnt up, the soul is renewed like the phoenix, and one can devoutly believe that its faults are pardoned. Now that it is so pure, the Lord joins it with Himself, without anyone understanding what is happening except these two; nor does the soul itself understand in a way that can afterward be explained. Yet, it does have interior understanding, for this experience is not like that of fainting or convulsion; in these latter nothing is understood inwardly or outwardly.

4. What I know in this case is that the soul was never so awake to the things of God nor did it have such deep enlightenment and knowledge of His Majesty. This will seem impossible, for if the faculties are so absorbed that we can say they are dead, and likewise the senses, how can a soul know that it

understands this secret? I don't know, nor perhaps does any creature but only the Creator. And this goes for many other things that take place in this state — I mean in these two dwelling places, for there is no closed door between the one and the other. Because there are things in the last that are not revealed to those who have not yet reached it, I thought I should divide them.

5. When the soul is in this suspension, the Lord likes to show it some secrets, things about heaven, and imaginative visions. It is able to tell of them afterward, for these remain so impressed on the memory that they are never forgotten. But when the visions are intellectual, the soul doesn't know how to speak of them. For there must be some visions during these moments that are so sublime that it's not fitting for those who live on this earth to have the further understanding necessary to explain them. However, since the soul is in possession of its senses, it can say many things about these intellectual visions.

It could be that some of you do not know what a vision is, especially an intellectual one. I shall explain at the proper time, for one who has the authority ordered me to do so. And although the explanation may not seem pertinent, it will perhaps benefit some souls.

6. Well now you will ask me: If afterward there is to be no remembrance of these sublime favors granted by the Lord to the soul in this state, what benefit do they have? O daughters, they are so great one cannot exaggerate! For even though they are unexplainable, they are well inscribed in the very interior part of the soul and are never forgotten.

But, you will insist, if there is no image and the faculties do not understand, how can the visions be remembered? I don't understand this either; but I do understand that some truths about the grandeur of God remain so fixed in this soul that even if faith were not to tell it who God is and of its obligation to believe that He is God, from that very moment it would adore Him as God, as did Jacob when he saw the ladder. By means of the ladder Jacob must have understood other secrets that he didn't know how to explain, for by seeing just a ladder on which angels descended and ascended he would not have understood such great mysteries if there had not been deeper interior enlightenment. I don't know if I'm guessing right in what I say, for although I have heard this story about Jacob, I don't know if I'm remembering it correctly.

7. Nor did Moses know how to describe all that he saw in the bush, but only what God wished Him to describe. But if God had not shown secrets to his soul along with a certitude that made him recognize and believe that they were from God, Moses could not have entered into so many severe trials. But he must have understood such deep things among the thorns of that bush that the vision gave him the courage to do what he did for the people of Israel. So, sisters, we don't have to look for reasons to understand the hidden things of God. Since we believe He is powerful, clearly we must believe that a worm with as limited a power as ours will not understand His grandeurs. Let us praise Him, for He is pleased that we come to know some of them.

8. I have been wanting to find some comparison by which to explain what I'm speaking about, and I don't think there is any that fits. But let's use this one: You enter into the room of a king or great lord, or I believe they call it the treasure chamber, where there are countless kinds of glass and earthen vessels and other things so arranged that almost all of these objects are seen upon entering. Once I was brought to a room like this in the house of the Duchess of Alba where, while I was on a journey, obedience ordered me to stay because of this lady's insistence with my superiors. I was amazed on entering and wondered what gain could be gotten from that conglomeration of things, and I saw that one could praise the Lord at seeing so many different kinds of objects, and now I laugh to myself on realizing how the experience has helped me here in my explanation. Although I was in that room for a while, there was so much there to see that I soon forgot it all; none of those pieces has remained in my memory any more than if I had never seen them, nor would I know how to explain the workmanship of any of them. I can

only say in general that I remember seeing everything. Likewise with this favor, the soul, while it is made one with God, is placed in this empyreal room that we must have interiorly. For, clearly, the soul has some of these dwelling places since God abides within it. And although the Lord must not want the soul to see these secrets every time it is in this ecstasy, for it can be so absorbed in enjoying Him that a sublime good like that is sufficient for it, sometimes He is pleased that the absorption decrease and the soul see at once what is in that room. After it returns to itself, the soul is left with that representation of the grandeurs it saw; but it cannot describe any of them, nor do its natural powers grasp any more than what God wished that it see supernaturally.

9. You, therefore, might object that I admit that the soul sees and that the vision is an imaginative one. But I'm not saying that, for I'm not dealing with an imaginative vision but with an intellectual one. Since I have no learning, I don't know how in my dullness to explain anything. If what I have said up to now about this prayer is worthwhile, I know clearly that I'm not the one who has said it.

I hold that if at times in its raptures the soul doesn't understand these secrets, its raptures are not given by God but are caused by some natural weakness. It can happen to persons with a weak constitution, as is so with women, that any spiritual force will overcome the natural powers, and the soul will be absorbed as I believe I mentioned in reference to the prayer of quiet. These experiences have nothing to do with rapture. In a rapture, believe me, God carries off for Himself the entire soul, and, as to someone who is His own and His spouse, He begins showing it some little part of the kingdom that it has gained by being espoused to Him. However small that part of His kingdom may be, everything that there is in this great God is magnificent. And He doesn't want any hindrance from anyone, neither from the faculties nor from the senses, but He immediately commands the doors of all these dwelling places to be closed; and only that door to His room remains open so that we can enter. Blessed be so much mercy; they will be rightly cursed who have not wanted to benefit by it and who have lost this Lord.

10. O my sisters, what nothingness it is, that which we leave! Nor is what we do anything, nor all that we could do for a God who thus wishes to communicate Himself to a worm! And if we hope to enjoy this blessing even in this present life, what are we doing? What is causing us to delay? What is enough to make us, even momentarily, stop looking for this Lord as did the bride in the streets and in the squares? Oh, what a mockery everything in the world is if it doesn't lead us and help us toward this blessing even if its delights and riches and joys, as much of them as imaginable, were to last forever! It is all loathsome dung compared to these treasures that will be enjoyed without end. Nor are these anything in comparison with having as our own the Lord of all the treasures of heaven and earth.

11. O human blindness! How long, how long before this dust will be removed from our eyes! Even though among ourselves the dust doesn't seem to be capable of blinding us completely, I see some specks, some tiny pebbles that if we allow them to increase will be enough to do us great harm. On the contrary, for the love of God, Sisters, let us benefit by these faults so as to know our misery, and they will give us clearer vision as did the mud to the blind man cured by our Spouse. Thus, seeing ourselves so imperfect, let us increase our supplications that His Majesty may draw good out of our miseries so that we might be pleasing to Him.

12. I have digressed a great deal without realizing it. Pardon me, Sisters, and believe me that having reached these grandeurs of God (I mean, reached the place where I must speak of them), I cannot help but feel very sorry to see what we lose through our own fault. Even though it is true that these are blessing the Lord gives to whomever He wills, His Majesty would give them all to us if we loved Him as He loves us. He doesn't desire anything else than to have those to whom to give. His riches do not lessen because He gives them away.

13. Well now, to get back to what I was saying, the Spouse commands that the doors of the dwelling places be closed and even those of the castle and the outer wall. For in desiring to carry off this soul, He takes away the breath so that, even though the other senses sometimes last a little longer, a person cannot speak at all; although at other times everything is taken away at once, and the hands and the body grow cold so that the person doesn't seem to have any life; nor sometimes is it known whether he is breathing. This situation lasts but a short while, I mean in its intensity; for when this extreme suspension lets up a little, it seems that the body returns to itself somewhat and is nourished so as to die again and give more life to the soul. Nevertheless, so extreme an ecstasy doesn't last long.

Excerpt from Teresa of Avila, Interior Castle, from *Classics of Western Spirituality*, translated by Kieran Kavanaugh, OCD, and Otillo Rodriquez, OCD, copyright © 1979 by the Washington Province of Discalced Carmelites, Inc., Paulist Press, Inc., New York/Mahwah, N.J. Used with permission. www.paulistpress.com

15.4

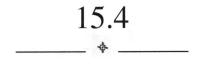

THE EDICT OF NANTES

The Wars of Religion began in 1524 with a peasant rebellion in Germany. In France, the religious divisions turned into a civil war between noble families. John Calvin (1509–1564) began preaching in Paris in 1533, although he fled in 1536 to avoid persecution. Many people (including nobles) were still drawn to Calvinism (known in France as Huguenots) for spiritual reasons; others saw this as a chance to demand social and political reforms. In 1559 the monarchy faced another crisis: a series of weak kings, whose state was run by their mother Catherine de' Medici and the fanatically anti-Protestant Guise family. By 1562 the powerful Bourbons, relatives of the king and rivals of the Guise, were Huguenots. War broke out in 1562 when the Duc of Guise massacred Huguenots. In 1572 a larger massacre of Huguenots occurred on St. Bartholomew's Day, ordered by the king, Catherine, and Guise family. Huguenots had been invited to Paris to celebrate the marriage of Henry of Navarre (a Huguenot himself) to the king's sister.

But Henry did marry Margaret, the king's sister. When her two remaining brothers died, Henry became the next king of France (1594). He agreed to convert to Catholicism, but remained sympathetic to the Huguenots. In 1598 he issued this Edict.

QUESTIONS

1. Does the Edict offer full toleration to the Huguenots? Explain why or why not.
2. How does Henry think the state should best deal with the recent violence?
3. How much freedom is actually promised to the Huguenots?

Henry, by the grace of God king of France and of Navarre, to all to whom these presents come, greeting:

Among the infinite benefits which it has pleased God to heap upon us, the most signal and precious is his granting us the strength and ability to withstand the fearful disorders and troubles which prevailed on our advent in this kingdom. The realm was so torn by innumerable factions and sects that the most legitimate of all the parties was fewest in numbers. God has given us strength to stand out against this storm; we have finally surmounted the waves and made our port of safety, — peace for our state. For which his be the glory all in all, and ours a free recognition of his grace in making use of our instrumentality in the good work.... We implore and await from the Divine Goodness the same protection and favor which he has ever granted to this kingdom from the beginning....

We have, by this perpetual and irrevocable edict established and proclaimed and do establish and proclaim:

I. First, that the recollection of everything done be one party or the other between March, 1585, and our accession to the crown, and during all the preceding period of troubles, remain obliterated and forgotten, as if no such things had ever happened.

III. We ordain that the Catholic Apostolic and Roman religion shall be restored and reestablished in all places and localities of this our kingdom and countries subject to our sway, where the exercise of the same has been interrupted, in order that it may be peaceably and freely exercised, without any trouble or hindrance: forbidding very expressly all persons, of whatsoever estate, quality, or condition, from troubling, molesting, or disturbing ecclesiastics in the celebration of divine service, in the enjoyment or collection of tithes, fruits, or revenues of their benefices, and all other rights and dues belonging to them: and that all those who during the troubles have taken possession of churches. Houses, goods or revenues, belonging to the said ecclesiastics, shall surrender to them entire possession and peaceable enjoyment of such rights, liberties, and sureties as they had before they were deprived of them.

VI. And in order to leave no occasion for troubles or differences between our subjects, we have permitted, and herewith permit, those of the said religion called Reformed to live and abide in all the cities and places of this our kingdom and countries of our sway, without being annoyed, molested, or compelled to do anything in the matter of religion contrary to their consciences, . . . upon condition that they comport themselves in other respects according to that which is contained in this our present edict.

VII. It is permitted to all lords, gentlemen, and other persons making profession of the said religion called Reformed, holding the right of high justice [or a certain feudal tenure], to exercise the said religion in their houses.

IX. We also permit those of the said religion to make and continue the exercise of the same in all villages and places of our dominion where it was established by them and publicly enjoyed several and divers times in the year 1597, up to the end of the month of August, notwithstanding all decrees and judgments to the contrary.

XIII. We very expressly forbid to all those of the said religion its exercise, either in respect to ministry, regulation, discipline, or the public instruction of children, or otherwise, in this our kingdom and lands of our dominion, otherwise than in the places permitted and granted by the present edict.

XIV. It is forbidden as well to perform any function of the said religion in our court or retinue, or in our lands and territories beyond the mountains, or in our city of Paris. or within five leagues of the said city.

XVIII. We also forbid all our subjects, of whatever quality and condition, from carrying off be force or persuasion, against the will of their parents, the children of the said religion, in order to cause them to be baptized or confirmed in the Catholic Apostolic and Roman Church; and the same is forbidden to those of the said religion called Reformed, upon penalty of being punished with especial severity.

XXI. Books concerning the said religion called Reformed may not be printed and publicly sold, except in cities and places where the public exercise of the said religion is permitted.

XXII. We ordain that there shall be no difference or distinction made in respect to the said religion, in receiving pupils to be instructed in universities, colleges, and schools; nor in receiving the sick and poor into hospitals, retreats and public charities.

XXIII. Those of the said religion called Reformed shall be obliged to respect the laws of the Catholic Apostolic and Roman Church, recognized in this our kingdom, for the consummation of marriages contracted, or to be contracted, as regards the degrees of consanguinity and kinship.

Source: James Harvey Robinson, ed., *Readings in European History*, Vol. II, (Boston: Ginn and Company, 1904, 1934), pp. 183-85.

15.5

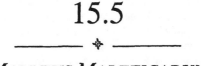

MALLEUS MALEFICARUM

Another manifestation of the Wars of Religion was the witch hunts. There had been restrictions against witchcraft within the medieval Catholic Church, but active persecution of people suspected of witchcraft began in 1484 with a papal bull, which specifically allowed the inquisition to use torture on suspected witches. The witch trials begin in earnest in the mid-sixteenth century, and continue until about mid-seventeenth century. "Witches" were yet another target of religious violence: both Catholics and Protestants persecuted men and women suspected of witchcraft.

The following source is from 1486. It is an excerpt from the Malleus Maleficarum, *the "Hammer of Witches" written by two Dominican friars. It was intended to be handbook for the identification, capture, torturing, and execution of suspected witches. The* Malleus *was popular with both Catholics and Protestants. The following excerpt identifies a group that was deemed particularly susceptible to interest in witchcraft: women.*

QUESTIONS

1. How exactly is "witch craft" being defined in this period?
2. Why were women supposed to be so susceptible?
3. This text was written by a Catholic, yet the basic principles of it were also used by Protestant witch hunters. What "authority" does this text have for Protestants?

Why Superstition is chiefly found in Women.

As for the first question, why a greater number of witches is found in the fragile feminine sex than among men; it is indeed a fact that it were idle to contradict, since it is accredited by actual experience, apart from the verbal testimony of credibly witnesses. And without in any way detracting from a sex in which God has always taken great glory that His might should be spread abroad, let us say that various men have assigned various reasons for this fact, which nevertheless agree in principle. Wherefore it is good, for the admonition of women, to speak of this matter; and it has often been proved by experience that they are eager to hear of it, so long as it is set forth with discretion.

For some learned men propound this reason; that there are three things in nature, the Tongue, an Ecclesiastic, and a Woman, which know no moderation in goodness or vice; and when they exceed the bounds of their condition they reach the greatest heights and the lowest depths of goodness and vice. When they are governed by a good spirit, they are most excellent in virtue; but when they are governed by an evil spirit, they indulge the worst possible vices....

Now the wickedness of women is spoken of in *Ecclesiasticus* xxv: There is no head above the head of a serpent: and there is no wrath above the wrath of a woman. I had rather dwell with a lion and a dragon than to keep house with a wicked woman. And among much which in that place precedes and follows about a wicked woman, he concludes: All wickedness is but little to the wickedness of a woman. Wherefore S. John Chrysostom says on the text, It is not good to marry (*S. Matthew* xix): What else is woman but a foe to friendship, an unescapable punishment, a necessary evil, a natural temptation, a desirable calamity, a domestic danger, a delectable detriment, an evil of nature, painted with fair colours! Therefore if it be a sin to divorce her when she ought to be kept, it is indeed a necessary torture; for either we commit adultery by divorcing her, or we must endure daily strife. Cicero in his second book of *The Rhetorics* says: The many lusts of men lead them into one sin, but the lust of women leads them into all sins; for the root of all women's vices is avarice. And Seneca says in his *Tragedies:* A woman either loves or hates; there is no third grade. And the tears of woman are a deception, for they may spring from true grief, or they may be a snare. When a woman thinks alone, she thinks evil....

And all this is made clear also in the New Testament concerning women and virgins and other holy women who have by faith led nations and kingdoms away from the worship of idols to the Christian religion. Anyone who looks at Vincent of Beauvais (*in Spe. Histo.*, XXVI. 9) will find marvellous things of the conversion of Hungary by the most Christian Gilia, and of the Franks by Clotilda, the wife of Clovis. Wherefore in many vituperations that we read against women, the word woman is used to mean the lust of the flesh. As it is said: I have found a woman more bitter than death, and good woman subject to carnal lust.

Other again have propounded other reasons why there are more superstitious women found than men. And the first is, that they are more credulous; and since the chief aim of the devil is to corrupt faith, therefore he rather attacks them. See *Ecclesiasticus* xix: He that is quick to believe is light-minded, and shall be diminished. The second reason is, that women are naturally more impressionable, and more ready to receive the influence of a disembodied spirit; and that when they use this quality well they are very good, but when they use it ill they are very evil.

The third reason is that they have slippery tongues, and are unable to conceal from the fellow-women those things which by evil arts they know; and, since they are weak, they find an easy and secret manner of vindicating themselves by witchcraft. See *Ecclesiasticus* as quoted above: I had rather dwell with a lion and a dragon than to keep house with a wicked woman. All wickedness is but little to the wickedness of a woman. And to this may be added that, as they are very impressionable, they act accordingly.

There are also others who bring forward yet other reasons, of which preachers should be very careful how they make use. For it is true that in the Old Testament the Scriptures have much that is evil to say about women, and this because of the first temptress, Eve, and her imitators; yet afterwards in the New Testament we find a change of name, as from Eva to Ave (as S. Jerome says), and the whole sin of Eve taken away by the benediction of Mary. Therefore preachers should always say as much praise of them as possible.

But because in these times this perfidy is more often found in women than in men, as we learn by actual experience, if anyone is curious as to the reason, we may add to what has already been said the following: that since they are feebler both in mind and body, it is not surprising that they should come more under the spell of witchcraft.

For as regards intellect, or the understanding of spiritual things, they seem to be of a different nature from men; a fact which is vouched for by the logic of the authorities, backed by various examples from the Scriptures. Terence says: Women are intellectually like children. And Lactantius (*Institutiones*, III): No woman understood philosophy except Temeste. And *Proverbs* xi, as it were describing a woman, says: As a jewel of gold in a swine's snout, so is a fair woman which is without discretion.

But the natural reason is that she is more carnal than a man, as is clear from her many carnal abominations. And it should be noted that there was a defect in the formation of the first woman, since she was formed from a bent rib, that is, a rib of the breast, which is bent as it were in a contrary direction to a man. And since through this defect she is an imperfect animal, she always deceives. For Cato says: When a woman weeps she weaves snares. And again: When a woman weeps, she labours to deceive a man. And this is shown by Samson's wife, who coaxed him to tell her the riddle he had propounded to the Philistines, and told them the answer, and so deceived him. And it is clear in the case of the first woman that she had little faith; for when the serpent asked why they did not eat of every tree in Paradise, she answered: Of every tree, etc. - lest perchance we die. Thereby she showed that she doubted, and had little in the word of God. And all this is indicated by the etymology of the word; for *Femina* comes from *Fe* and *Minus*, since she is ever weaker to hold and preserve the faith. And this as regards faith is of her very nature; although both by grace and nature faith never failed in the Blessed Virgin, even at the time of Christ's Passion, when it failed in all men.

Therefore a wicked woman is by her nature quicker to waver in her faith, and consequently quicker to abjure the faith, which is the root of witchcraft.

And as to her other mental quality, that is, her natural will; when she hates someone whom she formerly loved, then she seethes with anger and impatience in her whole soul, just as the tides of the sea are always heaving and boiling. Many authorities allude to this cause. *Ecclesiasticus* xxv: There is no wrath above the wrath of a woman. And Seneca (*Tragedies*, VIII): No might of the flames or the swollen winds, no deadly weapon, is so much to be feared as the lust and hatred of a woman who has been divorced from the marriage bed....

And indeed, just as through the first defect in their intelligence they are more prone to abjure the faith; so through their second defect of inordinate affections and passions they search for, brood over, and inflict various vengeances, either by witchcraft, or by some other means. Wherefore it is no wonder that so great a number of witches exist in this sex.

Women also have weak memories; and it is a natural vice in them not to be disciplined, but to follow their own impulses without any sense of what is due; this is her whole study, and all that she keeps in her memory. So Theophrastus says: If you hand over the whole management of the house to her, but reserve some minute detail to your own judgement, she will think that you are displaying a great want of faith in her, and will stir up strife; and unless you quickly take counsel, she will prepare poison for you, and consult seers and soothsayers; and will become a witch....

If we inquire, we find that nearly all the kingdoms of the world have been overthrown by women. Troy, which was a prosperous kingdom, was, for the rape of one woman, Helen, destroyed, and many thousands of Greeks slain. The kingdom of the Jews suffered much misfortune and destruction through the accursed Jezebel, and her daughter Athaliah, queen of Judah, who caused her son's sons to be killed, that on their death she might reign herself; yet each of them was slain. The kingdom of the Romans endured much evil through Cleopatra, Queen of Egypt, that worst of women. And so with others. Therefore it is no wonder if the world now suffers through the malice of women.

And now let us examine the carnal desires of the body itself, whence has arisen unconscionable harm to human life. Justly may we say with Cato of Utica: If the world could be rid of women, we should not be without God in our intercourse. For truly, without the wickedness of women, to say nothing of witchcraft, the world would still remain proof against innumerable dangers. Hear what Valerius said to Rufinus: You do not know that women is the Chimaera, but it is good that you should know it; for that monster was of three forms; its face was that of a radiant and noble lion, it had the filthy belly of a goat, and it was armed with the virulent tail of a viper. And he means that a woman is beautiful to look upon, contaminating to the touch, and deadly to keep.

Let us consider another property of hers, the voice. For as she is a liar by nature, so in her speech she stings while she delights us. Wherefore her voice is like the song of the Sirens, who with their sweet melody entice the passers-by and kill them. For they kill them by emptying their purses, consuming their strength, and causing them to forsake God. Again Valerius says to Rufinus: When she speaks it is a delight which flavours the sin; the flower of love is a rose, because under its blossom there are hidden many thorns. See *Proverbs* v, 3-4: Her mouth is smoother than oil; that is, her speech is afterwards as bitter as absinthium. [Her throat is smoother than oil. But her end is as bitter as wormwood.]

Let us consider also her gait, posture, and habit, in which is vanity of vanities. There is no man in the world who studies so hard to please the good God as even an ordinary woman studies by her vanities to please men. An example of this is to be found in the life of Pelagia, a worldly woman who was wont to go about Antioch, tired and adorned most extravagantly. A holy father, name Nonnus, saw her and began to weep, saying to his companions, that never in all his life had he used such diligence to please God; and much more he added to this effect, which is preserved in his orations.

It is this which is lamented in *Ecclesiastes* vii, and which the Church even now laments on account of the great magnitude of witches. And I have found a woman more bitter than death, who is the hunter's snare, and her heart is a net, and her hands are bands. He that pleaseth God shall escape from her; but he that is a sinner shall be caught by her. More bitter than death, that is, than the devil: *Apocalypse* vi, 8, His name was Death. For though the devil tempted Eve to sin, yet Eve seduced Adam. And as the sin of Eve would not have brought death to our soul and body unless the sin had afterwards passed on to Adam, to which he was tempted by Eve, not by the devil, therefore she is more bitter than death....

To conclude. All witchcraft comes from carnal lust, which is in women insatiable. See *Proverbs* xxx: There are three things that are never satisfied, yea, a forth thing which says not, It is enough; that is, the mouth of the womb. Wherefore for the sake of fulfilling their lusts they consort even with devils.

Source: Heinrich Kramer and James Sprenger, *The Malleus Maleficarum,* trans. Montague Summers (New York: Dover Publications, Inc., 1971), pp. 41-47. Reprinted with permission.

❖

QUESTIONS FOR PART 15

1. Did Luther and Zwingli see their Reformation as making Christianity easier for believers?
2. Was the Reformation (Protestant or Catholic) good for women?
3. How did the Reformation exacerbate the witch-hunts?

PART 16

NEW WORLD ENCOUNTERS

The late fifteenth and sixteenth centuries are often called the Age of Exploration or the Age of Discovery. Both were certainly two of the major themes of the period. This was also the time of the Reformation, itself an exploration of sorts, one that examined the spiritual discoveries of the period. This chapter will examine the geographic explorations. In 1492, in a story well known to most students of Western history, Christopher Columbus made the second (to the Vikings) European discovery of the American continents. In the decades prior to this, Portuguese and Spanish navigators had begun to explore the western coast of North Africa. In the century following Columbus, Portuguese, Spanish, English, French, and Dutch sailors continued these earlier explorations of Africa and the Americas, and eventually moved into Asia as well. The drive to explore was fueled by many factors: a desire to find new routes to the riches (spices, gold, goods) of the East without having to go through the usual Muslim merchants, religious fervor (increased by the keen interests in all things religious thanks to the Reformation), a strong sense of competition against those same Muslim merchants who had for so many centuries dominated trade, and a very simple craving for adventure. Exploration was also inspired by a long tradition of tales that emphasized the mysteriousness of the East and a growing sense of curiosity about these relatively unknown lands.

Europe went into the Age of Exploration confident in itself religiously, politically, and culturally. The encounters with non-European cultures that resulted from the "new world" discoveries only increased that confidence. All too quickly the interest in exploration, discovery, and adventure became the need to conquer. Exploration for Europe meant expansion; colonies were quickly founded and empires created. Western history was effectively transformed into world history at this moment.

16.1

"COURT OF THE GREAT KHAN," MARCO POLO

Discovery of the newly Americas was not the beginning of European explorations. An earlier exploration of Asia occurred in 1271 when a Venetian merchant family followed the Silk Road, a major trade route, from Italy to China. The Polos were looking for financial gain and trading opportunities; however, the youngest member of the family, Marco took advantage of the chance to meet with various Asian cultures and peoples. When he returned to Venice in he recorded his observations in what was known alternatively as the "Wonders of the East" or the "Millions of the East" and was tremendously popular for its colorful stories and was popular with later explorers, who sometimes used Polo's text as a literal navigational guide. Columbus not only read Polo's text, he took it with him on his voyage in 1492.

The following excerpts describe the court of Kublai Khan, emperor of China in when Polo reached China.

QUESTIONS

1. Polo's text tells of the many wives and concubines of Kublai Khan; what impression about the Far East do you think this helped to create for Europe?
2. In describing the palace of Kublai, what aspects does Polo remark upon and emphasize?
3. Does Polo have an opinion about the Khan?

[Chapter 8]

Of the figure and stature of the Great Khan — of his four principal Wives — and of the annual selection of young women for him in the province of Ungut

Kublai, who is styled Great Khan, or Lord of Lords, is of the middle stature, that is, neither tall nor short. His limbs are well formed, and in his whole figure there is a just proportion. His complexion is fair, and occasionally suffused with red, like the bright tint of the rose, which adds much grace to his countenance. His eyes are black and handsome, his nose is well shaped and prominent.

He has four wives of the first rank, who are esteemed legitimate, and the eldest born son of any one of these succeeds to the empire, upon the decease of the Great Khan. They bear equally the title of empress, and have their separate courts. None of them have fewer than three hundred young female attendants of great beauty, together with a multitude of youths as pages, and other eunuchs, as well as ladies of the bedchamber; so that the number of persons belonging to each of their respective courts amounts to ten thousand.

When his majesty is desirous of the company of one of his empresses, he either sends for her, or goes himself to her palace. Besides these, he has many concubines provided for his use, from a province of Tartary named Ungut, the inhabitants of which are distinguished for beauty of features and fairness of complexion. Every second year, or oftener, as it may happen to be his pleasure, the Great Khan sends thither his officers, who collect for him, one hundred or more, of the handsomest of the young women, according to the estimation of beauty communicated to them in their instructions.

The mode of their appreciation is as follows. Upon the arrival of these commissioners, they give orders for assembling all the young women of the province, and appoint qualified persons to examine them, who, upon careful inspection of each of them separately, that is to say, of the hair, the countenance, the eyebrows, the mouth, the lips, and other features, as well as the symmetry of these with each other, estimate their value at sixteen, seventeen, eighteen, or twenty, or more carats, according to the greater or less degree of beauty. The number required by the Great Khan, at the rates, perhaps, of twenty or twenty-one carats, to which their commission was limited, is then selected from the rest, and they are conveyed to his court.

Upon their arrival in his presence, he causes a new examination to be made by a different set of inspectors, and from amongst them a further selection takes place, when thirty or forty are retained for his own chamber at a higher valuation. These are committed separately to the care of the elderly ladies of the palace, whose duty it is to observe them attentively during the course of the night, in order to ascertain that they have not any concealed imperfections, that they sleep tranquilly, do not snore, have sweet breath, and are free from unpleasant scent in any part of the body. Having undergone this rigorous scrutiny, they are divided into parties of five, one of which parties attends during three days and three nights, in his majesty's interior apartment, where they are to perform every service that is required of them, and he does with them as he likes.

When this term is completed, they are relieved by another party, and in this manner successively, until the whole number have taken their turn; when the first five recommence their attendance. But whilst the one party officiates in the inner chamber, another is stationed in the outer apartment adjoining; in order that if his majesty should have occasion for anything, such as drink or victuals, the former may signify his commands to the latter, by whom the article required is immediately procured. In this way the duty of waiting upon his majesty's person is exclusively performed by these young females. The remainder of them, whose value had been estimated at an inferior rate, are assigned to the different lords of the household; under whom they are instructed in cookery, in dressmaking, and other suitable works; and upon any person belonging to the court expressing an inclination to take a wife, the Great Khan bestows upon him one of these damsels, with a handsome portion. In this manner he provides for them all amongst his nobility.

It may be asked whether the people of the province do not feel themselves aggrieved in having their daughters thus forcibly taken from them by the sovereign? Certainly not; but, on the contrary, they regard it as a favour and an honour done to them; and those who are the fathers of handsome children feel highly gratified by his condescending to make choice of their daughters. "If," say they, "my daughter is born under an auspicious planet and to good fortune, his majesty can best fulfill her destinies, by matching her nobly; which it would not be in my power to do." If, on the other hand, the daughter misconducts herself, or any mischance befalls her, by which she becomes disqualified, the father attributes the disappointment to the malign influence of her stars....

[Chapter 10]

...In the middle of each division of these walls is a handsome and spacious building, and consequence within the enclosure there are eight such buildings, in which are deposited the royal military stores; one building being appropriated to the reception of each class of stores. Thus, for instance, the bridles, saddles, stirrups, and other furniture serving for the equipment of cavalry, occupy one storehouse; the bows, strings, quivers, arrows, and other articles belonging to archery, occupy another; cuirasses, corselets, and other armour formed of leather, a third storehouse; and so of the rest....

Within these walls, which constitute the boundary of four miles, stands the palace of the Great Khan, the most extensive that has ever yet been known. It reaches from the northern to the southern wall, leaving only a vacant space (or court), where persons of rank and the military guards pass and re-pass. It has no upper floor, but the roof is very lofty. The paved foundation or platform on which it stands is raised ten spans above the level of the ground, and a wall of marble, two paces wide, is built on all sides, to the level of this pavement, within the line of which the palace is erected; so that the wall, extending beyond the ground plan of the building, and encompassing the whole, serves as a terrace, where those who walk on it are visible from without. Along the exterior edge of the wall is a handsome balustrade, with pillars, which the people are allowed to approach. The sides of the great halls and the apartments are ornamented with dragons in carved work and gilt, figures of warriors, of birds, and of beasts, with representations of battles. The inside of the roof is contrived in such a manner that nothing besides gilding and painting presents itself to the eye.

On each of the four sides of the palace there is a grand flight of marble steps, by which you ascend from the level of the ground to the wall of marble which surrounds the building, and which constitute the approach to the palace itself.

The grand hall is extremely long and wide, and admits of dinners being there served to great multitudes of people. The palace contains a number of separate chambers, all highly beautiful, and so admirably disposed that it seems impossible to suggest any improvement to the system of their arrangement The exterior of the roof is adorned with a variety of colors, red, green, azure, and violet, and the sort of covering is so strong as to last for many years. The glazing of the windows is so well wrought and so delicate as to have the transparency of crystal.

In the rear of the body of the palace there are large buildings containing several apartments, where is deposited the private property of the monarch, or his treasure in gold and silver bullion, precious stones, and pearls, and also his vessels of gold and silver plate. Here are likewise the apartments of his wives and concubines; and in this retired situation he dispatches business with convenience, being free from every kind of interruption.

On the other side of the grand palace, and opposite to that in which the emperor resides, is another palace, in every respect similar, appropriated to the residence of Chinghis, his eldest son, at whose court are observed all the ceremonials belonging to that of his father, as the prince who is to succeed to the government of the empire. Not far from the palace, on the northern side, and about a bow-shot distance from the surrounding wall, is an artificial mount of earth, the height of which is full a hundred paces, and the circuit at the base about a mile. It is clothed with the most beautiful evergreen trees; for whenever his Majesty receives information of a handsome tree growing in any place, he causes it to be dug up, with all its roots and the earth about them, and however large and heavy it may be, he has it transported by means of elephants to this mount, and adds it to the verdant collection. Because the trees on this hill are always green it has acquired the name of the Green Mount.

16.2

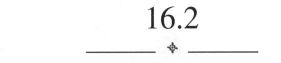

AZTEC ACCOUNT OF THE SPANISH CONQUEST

Hernán Cortés (1485–1547) arrived in Mexico in 1519 with a small (less than 600 men) force. Upon reaching Mexico he burned his ships so that his men had no option but to press on He found the area under the control of the Aztec Empire. Through alliances with smaller states that were under the domination of the Aztecs, Cortes soon controlled most of the central Mexico. He convinced the Aztecs that he had been sent by their gods and took over their state as well. In 1520 the Aztecs rebelled; the following excerpt is an Aztec description of the resulting massacre.

---- ✦ ----

Questions

1. What explanation does Motecuhzoma (Moctezuma) offer for why his people will be conquered?
2. Why do the Spanish keep Motecuhzoma a hostage and not kill him.
3. Why do the Aztecs send out magicians and wizards to negotiate with the Spanish?

The Spaniards See the Objects of Gold

Then Motecuhzoma dispatched various chiefs. Tzihuacpopocatzin was at their head, and he took with him a great many of his representatives. They went out to meet the Spaniards in the vicinity of Popocatepetl and Iztactepetl, there in the Eagle Pass.

They gave the "gods" ensigns of gold, and ensigns of quetzal feathers, and golden necklaces. And when they were given these presents, the Spaniards burst into smiles; their eyes shone with pleasure; they were delighted by them. They picked up the gold and fingered it like monkeys; they seemed to be transported by joy, as if their hearts were illuminated and made new.

The truth is that they longed and lusted for gold. Their bodies swelled with greed, and their hunger was ravenous; they hungered like pigs for that gold. They snatched at the golden ensigns, waved them from side to side and examined every inch of them. They were like one who speaks a barbarous tongue: everything they said was in a barbarous tongue....

Motecuhzoma's Despair

When the envoys arrived in the city, they told Motecuhzoma what had happened and what they had seen. Motecuhzoma listened to their report and then bowed his head without speaking a word. For a long time he remained thus, with his head bent down. And when he spoke at last, it was only to say: "What help is there now, my friends? Is there a mountain for us to climb? Should we run away? We are Mexicanos: would this bring any glory to the Mexican nation?

"Pity the old men, and the old women, and the innocent little children. How can they save themselves? But there is no help. What can we do? Is there nothing left us?

"We will be judged and punished. And however it may be, and whenever it may be, we can do nothing but wait."...

The Statue of Huitzilopochtli

On the evening before the fiesta of Toxcatl, the celebrants began to model a statue of Huitzilopochtli. They gave it such a human appearance that it seemed the body of a living man. Yet they made the statue with nothing but a paste made of the ground seeds of chicalote, which they shaped over an armature of sticks.

When the statue was finished, they dressed it in rich feathers, and they painted crossbars over and under its eyes. They also clipped on its earrings of turquoise mosaic; these were in shape of serpents, with gold rings hanging from them. Its nose plug, in the shape of an arrow, was made of gold and was inlaid with fine stones.

They placed the magic headdress of hummingbird feathers on its head. They also adorned it with an *anecuyotl*, which was a belt made of feathers, with a cone at the back. Then they hung around its neck an ornament of yellow parrot feathers, fringed like the locks of a young boy. Over this they put its nettle-leaf cape, which was painted black and decorated with five clusters of eagle feathers.

Next they wrapped it in its cloak, which was painted with skulls and bones, and over this they fastened its vest. The vest was painted with dismembered human parts: skulls, ears, hearts, intestines, torsos, breasts, hands and feet. They also put on its *maxtlatl*, or loincloth, which was decorated with images of disseevered limbs and fringed with amate paper. This *maxtlatl* was painted with vertical stripes of bright blue.

They fastened a red paper flag at its shoulder and placed on its head what looked like a sacrificial flint knife. This too was made of red paper; it seemed to have been steeped in blood.

The statue carried a *tehuehuelli*, a bamboo shield decorated with four clusters of fine eagle feathers. The pendant of this shield was blood-red, like the knife and the shoulder flag. The statue also carried four arrows.

Finally, they put the wristbands on its arms. These bands, made of coyote skin, were fringed with paper cut into little strips....

The Spaniards Attack the Celebrants

At this moment in the fiesta, when the dance was loveliest and when song was linked to song, the Spaniards were seized with an urge to kill the celebrants. They all ran forward, armed as if for battle. They closed the entrances and passageways, all the gates of the patio: the Eagle Gate in the lesser palace, the Gate of the Canestalk and the Gate of the Serpent of Mirrors. They posted guards so that no one could escape, and then rushed into the Sacred Patio to slaughter the celebrants. They came on foot, carrying their swords and their wooden or metal shields.

They ran in among the dancers, forcing their way to the place where the drums were played. They attacked the man who was drumming and cut off his arms. Then they cut off his head, and it rolled across the floor.

They attacked all the celebrants, stabbing them, spearing them, striking them with their swords. They attacked some of them from behind, and these fell instantly to the ground with their entrails hanging out. Others they beheaded: they cut off their heads, or split their heads to pieces.

They struck others in the shoulders, and their arms were torn from their bodies. They wounded some in the thigh and some in the calf. They slashed others in the abdomen, and their entrails all spilled to the ground. Some attempted to run away, but their intestines dragged as they ran; they seemed to tangle their feet in their own entrails. No matter how they tried to save themselves, they could find no escape.

Some attempted to force their way out, but the Spaniards murdered them at the gates. Others climbed the walls, but they could not save themselves. Those who ran into the communal houses were safe there for a while; so were those who lay down among the victims and pretended to be dead. But if they stood up again, the Spaniards saw them and killed them.

The blood of the warriors flowed like water and gathered into pools. The pools widened, and the stench of blood and entrails filled the air. The Spaniards ran into the communal houses to kill those who were hiding. They ran everywhere and searched everywhere; they invaded every room, hunting and killing.

The Aztecs Retaliate

When the news of this massacre was heard outside the Sacred Patio; a great cry went up: "Mexicanos, come running!" Bring your spears and shields! The strangers have murdered our warriors!"

This cry was answered with a roar of grief and anger: the people shouted and wailed and beat their palms against their mouths. The captains assembled at once, as if the hour had been determined in advance. They all carried their spears and shields.

Then the battle began. The Aztecs attacked with javelins and arrows, even with the light spears that are used for hunting birds. They hurled their javelins with all their strength, and the cloud of missiles spread out over the Spaniards like a yellow cloak.

The Spaniards immediately took refuge in the palace. They began to shoot at the Mexicans with their iron arrows and to fire their cannons and arquebuses. And they shackled Motecuhzoma in chains....

From *Broken Spears* by Miguel Leon-Portilla. Copyright © 1962, 1990 by Miguel Leon-Portilla. Expanded and Updated Edition © 1992 by Miguel Leon-Portilla. Reprinted by permission of Beacon Press, Boston.

16.3

JESUIT MISSIONARY IN CHINA, MATTEO RICCI

Explorers came in many forms. Polo was a merchant. Cortés was a conquistador (conqueror). Matteo Ricci was a Jesuit missionary, who in 1583 followed a path very similar to Polo's three hundred years' earlier. As a Jesuit, Ricci had taken vows of extreme obedience to the papacy. One of the most important functions of the Jesuit order, which was created in 1540, was missionary activity to convert people (Protestant or non-Christian) to Roman Catholicism. Ricci traveled extensively in India and China, and even reached Japan. The following excerpt is from Ricci's description of the religious practices he found in China.

QUESTIONS

1. Compare this account of the Chinese with the earlier one by Polo (Source 16.1).
2. Do you think this account of the Chinese encouraged or discouraged more Europeans from going to Asia?
3. Does Ricci view the superstitions of the Chinese as a religious belief?

9. Concerning Certain Rites, Superstitious and Otherwise

In this chapter we shall treat of the superstitious rites peculiar to certain sects, and shall touch upon such as may serve as a summary of them all....

No superstition is so common to the entire kingdom as that which pertains to the observance of certain days and hours as being good or bad, lucky or unlucky, in which to act or to refrain from acting, because the result of everything they do is supposed to depend upon a measurement of time. This imposture has assumed such a semblance of truth among them that two calendars are edited every year, written by the astrologers of the crown and published by public authority. These almanacs are sold in such great quantities that every house has a supply of them. They are produced in pamphlet form, and in them one finds directions as to what should be done and what should be left undone for each particular day, and at what precise time each and every thing should be done. In this manner the entire year is carefully mapped out in exact detail. Besides these regular calendars there are other books of this kind, more complex in their contents. Then, too, a horde of deceitful directors make a living by instructing those who consult them as to the correct day and hour for doing each particular thing in a day's routine. They charge but very little for their fraudulent advice so that no one will hesitate to have an adviser....

It is a common practice also to consult the demons, the family spirits, as the Chinese call them, and there are many of them. In this, however, they imagine that there is more of divination than anything diabolical, but in this too, they are victims of fraud and deception. In such consultations, oracles are received through the voices of little children and from the sounds of brute beasts, revealing the past and the absent, as proof of the truth of what they foretell for the future. These oracles are always produced by fraud and trickery. Of course, we read that such superstitions are common to heathens in general, but the following sample is quite peculiar to the Chinese. In choosing a place to erect a public edifice or a private house, or in selecting a plot of ground in which to bury the dead, they study the location with reference to the head and the tail and the feet of the particular dragons which are supposed to dwell beneath that spot. Upon these local dragons they believe that the good and bad fortune, not only of the family but also of the town and the province and of the entire kingdom, is wholly dependent. Many of their most distinguished men are interested in this recondite science and, when necessary, they are called in for consultation, even from a great distance. This might happen when some public building or a monument is to be erected and the machines used for that purpose are to be placed so that public misfortune might be avoided and good fortune attend the undertaking. Just as their astrologers read the stars, so their geologists reckon the fate or the fortune of a place from the relative position of mountains or rivers or fields, and their reckoning is just as deceitful as the reading of the stargazers. What could be more absurd than their imagining that the safety of a family, honors, and their entire existence must depend upon such trifles as a door being opened from one side or another, as rain falling into a courtyard from the right or from the left, a window opened here or there, or one roof being higher than another?

The streets and the taverns and all other public places abound in these astrologers and geologists, diviners and fortunetellers, or, to group them all in one class, in these imposters. Their business consists in making vain promises of prosperous fortunes at a given price. Some of them are blind men, others of low station in life, and at times, women of questionable character. According to the dictum of the Gospel, they really are, "The blind leading the blind," and their number is so great that they may be said to constitute a universal nuisance. In fact, this obnoxious class is a veritable pest in the capital cities and even in the court. Such is their means of livelihood, and not a few of them are able to support a large family in luxury and at times to accumulate considerable wealth. The high and the low, the noble and the plebeian, the educated and the illiterate are counted among their victims, as are the magistrates, the dignitaries of the realm, and even the King himself. One can readily judge from what has been said, of the auguries they read into the cackling of birds, how solicitous they are about first morning meetings and about shadows cast upon a roof by the rays of the sun. In a word, whatever misfortune befalls an individual, a city, a province, or the kingdom, they attribute it to adverse fortune, or to something wrong in the person or in the realm, as the case may be. They look upon such adversity as being a just visitation for their sins, which have called down a private or a public vindication from above.

We shall add here a few shocking practices which the Chinese look upon with indifference and which, God forbid, they even seem to consider as quite morally correct, and from these one can readily conclude to others of the same category. This people is really to be pitied rather than censured, and the deeper one finds them involved in the darkness of ignorance, the more earnest one should be in praying for their salvation.

Many of them, not being able to forgo the company of women, sell themselves to wealthy patrons, so as to find a wife among his women servants, and in so doing, subject their children to perpetual slavery. Others buy a wife when they can save money enough to do so, and when their family becomes too numerous to be supported, they sell their children into slavery for about the same price that one would pay for a pig or a cheap little donkey — about one crown or maybe one and a half. Sometimes this is done when there is really no necessity, and children are separated from their parents forever, becoming slaves to the purchaser, to be used for whatever purpose he pleases. The result of this practice is that the whole country is virtually filled with slaves; not such as are captured in war or brought in from abroad, but slaves by the Portuguese and the Spaniards. These few at least have an opportunity of becoming Christian and of thus escaping the slavery of Satan. The only ameliorating feature in this traffic of children is the fact that it lessens the great multitude of the extremely poor who have to labor incessantly in the sweat of their brow to eke out a miserable living. One might add also that slavery among the Chinese is more bearable because less exacting than among any other people in the world. A Chinese slave can purchase his freedom for the same price that was paid for him, if he can manage to acquire that amount of money.

A far more serious evil here is the practice in some provinces of disposing of female infants by drowning them. The reason assigned for this is that their parents despair of being able to support them. At times this is also done by people who are not abjectly poor, for fear the time might come when they would not be able to care for these children and they would be forced to sell them to unknown or to cruel slave masters. Thus they become cruel in an effort to be considerate. This barbarism is probably rendered less atrocious by their belief in metempsychosis, or the transmigration of souls. Believing that souls are transferred from one body that ceases to exist into another that begins to exist, they cover up their frightful cruelty with a pretext of piety, thinking that they are doing the child a benefit by murdering it. According to their way of thinking, they are releasing the child from the poverty of the family into which it was born, so that it may be reborn into a family of better means. So it happens that this slaughter of the innocents is carried on not in secret but in the open and with general public knowledge.

Another more or less common custom, and still more barbarous than that aforementioned, is the practice of committing suicide in desperation of earning a living, or in utter despair because of misfortune, or still more foolishly and more cowardly, out of spite for an enemy. They say that thousands of people, women as well as men, take their own lives in the course of a year. This is frequently done by hanging or by choking oneself to death in a public place or perhaps before the home of an enemy. Jumping into rivers and swallowing poison are other common methods and they often commit suicide for very trivial reasons. If a magistrate should pass a severe sentence upon one who is accused by the parents of a suicide of having driven their son to despair, the accused will frequently see no other way out of the difficulty than by taking his own life. Many of the magistrates show great wisdom in this respect by making it a law unto themselves never to handle a case involving a suicide and they probably save many a life by doing so.

Yet another barbarity common in the northern provinces is that of castrating a great number of male children, so they may act as servants or slaves to the King. This condition is demanded for service in the royal palace, so much so, indeed, that the King will have no others nor will he consult with or even speak to any other. Almost the whole administration of the entire kingdom is in the hands of this class of semi-men, who number nearly ten thousand in the service of the royal palace alone. They are a meager-looking class, uneducated and brought up in perpetual slavery, a dull and stolid lot, as incapable of understanding an important order as they are inefficient in carrying it out….

The Chinese look upon all foreigners as illiterate and barbarous, and refer to them in just these terms. They even disdain to learn anything from books of outsiders because they believe that all true science and knowledge belongs to them alone. If perchance they have occasion to make mention of externs in their own writings, they treat them as though there was no room for doubt that they differ but little from the beasts of the field and the forest. Even the written characters by which they express the word foreigner are those that are applied to beasts, and scarcely ever do they give them a title more honorable than they would assign to their demons. One would scarcely believe how suspicious they are of a legate or an ambassador of a neighboring country, sent in to pay respect to the King, to settle a tributary tax, or to conduct any sort of business. The fact that China may have been on friendly terms with the kingdom of the visiting legates, from time immemorial, does not exempt the visiting dignitaries from being conducted along their entire route within the realm as captives or prisoners and permitted to see nothing in the course of their journey. During their whole sojourn they are lodged in buildings, constructed like cattle barns, within the limits of the palace grounds, to which they are confined under lock and key. They are never permitted to see the King, and their diplomatic or other business is carried on with selected magistrates. No one in the whole kingdom is ever permitted to do business with foreigners, excepting at certain times and in certain places, as on the peninsula of Macao where a trading mart was established with the Portuguese in 1557. Anyone carrying on foreign trade without official sanction would be subject to the severest punishment.

From *China in Sixteenth Century* by Matthew Ricci, translated by Louis J. Gallagher, S.J., pp. 82-89. Copyright 1942, 1953 and renewed 1970 by Louis J. Gallagher, S.J. Used by permission of Random House, Inc.

16.4

❖

CAPTURE AND ENSLAVEMENT, OLAUDAH EQUIANO

There are few written accounts by Africans of their enslavement and transportation to the American colonies. That scarcity makes the autobiography of Olaudah Equiano (1745–1797), published in 1791, all the more striking. Equiano had been a member of the Ibo tribe of Benin; at age ten he was kidnapped by members of a rival tribe and sold into slavery. After passing through several African hands, he was sold to European slavers and transported to Barbados and then to Virginia. Eventually he was purchased by an English sea captain and taken to England. In 1766, with his owner's help, he was able to buy his freedom and eventually became a ship owner himself. In 1791 he published his book, The Interesting Narrative of the Life of Olaudah Equiano, *or* Gustavus Vasso, the African, *from which this selection is taken.*

⚜

QUESTIONS

1. Why is Equiano flogged for refusing to eat? Does this reveal concern on the part of the slavers?
2. How does Equiano's initial enslavement by an African family differ from his subsequent enslavement by Europeans?
3. Why does Equiano publish this narrative under both his African and European names?

Vol. I

One day, when all our people were gone out to their work as usual, and only I and my sister were left to mind the house, two men and a woman got over our walls, and in a moment seized us both; and, without giving us time to cry out, or to make resistance, they stopped our mouths, and ran off with us into the nearest wood. Here they tied our hands, and continued to carry us as far as they could, till night came on, when we reached a small house....The next morning we left the house, and continued traveling all day....

The next day proved a day of greater sorrow than I had yet experienced, for my sister and I were then separated; while we lay clasped in each other's arms. It was in vain that we besought them not to part us; she was torn from me, and immediately carried away, while I was left in a state of distraction not to be described. I cried and grieved continually; and for several days did not eat anything but what they forced into my mouth. At length, after many days' travelling, during which I had often changed masters, I got into the hands of a chieftain, in a very pleasant country. This man had two wives and some children, and they all used me extremely well....

I was there, I suppose, about a month, and they at length used to trust me some little distance from the house....I therefore determined to seize the first opportunity of making my escape, and to shape my course for that quarter; for I was quite oppressed and weighed down by grief after my mother and friends; and my love of liberty, ever great, was strengthened by the mortifying circumstance of not daring to eat with the free-born children, although I was mostly their companion....

Equiano describes the horrors of a slave ship.

The first object which saluted my eyes when I arrived on the coast was the sea, and a slave ship, which was then riding at anchor, and waiting for its cargo. These filled me with astonishment, that was soon converted into terror...when I was carried on board....

I now saw myself deprived of all chance of returning to my native country, or even the least glimpse of gaining the shore, which I now considered as friendly; and I even wished for my former slavery, in preference of my present situation, which was filled with horrors of every kind, still heightened by my ignorance of what I was to undergo. I was not long suffered to indulge my grief. I was soon put down under the decks, and there I received such a salutation in my nostrils as I had never experienced in my life: so that, with the loathsomeness of the stench, and crying together, I became so sick and low that I was not able to eat, nor had I the least desire to taste anything. I now wished for the last friend, death, to relieve me; but soon, to my grief, two of the white men offered me eatables, and, on my refusing to eat, one of them held me fast by the hands, and laid me across, I think, the windlass, and tied my feet, while the other flogged me severely. I had never experienced anything of this kind before, and although not being used to the water, I naturally feared that element the first time I saw it, yet, nevertheless, could I have got over the nettings, I would have jumped over the side, but I could not; and besides the crew used to watch us very closely who were not chained down to the decks, lest we should leap into the water; and I have seen some of these poor African prisoners most severely cut for attempting to do so, and hourly whipped for not eating. This indeed was often the case with myself.

Source: David Waldstreicher, *The Struggle Against Slavery: A History in Documents* (New York: Oxford University Press, 2001), pp. 18-20.

QUESTIONS FOR PART 16

1. Of the many reasons why Europeans explored and conquered, what do you think was the single most important?
2. What role did the Reformation and Religious Wars play in the Age of Exploration?
3. Did the Europeans treat all of the newly discovered cultures the same? Why or why not?

PART 17

&

SEVENTEENTH CENTURY STATE BUILDING

Europe faced many challenges as it entered the seventeenth century: the chaos of the Reformation, the Wars of Religion, and the rapid expansion of European states into world empires. There were several major trends in this new century: a weariness from the religions wars in many states (although they continued in the Holy Roman Empire), a growing secularization (coupled in part with the new scientific theories in the next section), increased economic activity (from those empires) and the beginning of trade wars, and above all else, the rise of new theories of royal government.

The seventeenth century was the true beginning of modern states, however much of it built upon centuries of political and legal traditions. Each European state took its own approach to state building, although the centrality of the monarchy remained constant in most of them. It was, in fact, the most powerful age of kings Europe had seen in a very long time. The pinnacle of royal power was found in the absolutist states of France under Louis XIV, Prussia under the Hohenzollern dynasty, and Russia under Peter the Great. For every monarch who successfully established absolute rule there were many more who attempted it and failed. The Habsburgs of the Holy Roman Empire saw their dominions reduced drastically by the Thirty Years' War (1618-1648), which revealed just how fractured the Empire was. Each independent state within the Empire gained recognized sovereignty, while small kingdoms such as Sweden emerged as true political contenders and the Dutch republic established one of the wealthiest international trade empires. The Stuart dynasty of England also wanted to achieve the royal dream of absolutism, yet failed. In 1648 a parliamentary republic replaced the monarchy; although the monarchy was restored in 1660, it was as a limited, constitutional monarch.

17.1

❖

CARDINAL RICHELIEU ON THE RIGHTS OF THE KING

No European monarch was ever as absolute as Louis XIV (1643-1715) of France. The concept of absolutism was tied to the belief in the divine right of kings. According to the divine right theory, a king received his power directly from God and not from the people, not from any other body of government. Because his power was divine in origin, it was thus absolute and could not be limited. At least that was the theory of absolutism. The reality was usually a bit of a compromise; James I of England had been the first monarch to articulate the concept of divine right, but was actually quite limited in power by Parliament. In France, however, Louis XIV faced no such limitation. The extent of the French king's sovereignty was established by Louis XIII's administrator Cardinal Richelieu (d. 1642). Thanks to Richelieu, Louis XIV inherited a kingdom in which private armies (the bane of medieval kings) had been abolished and the separatist Huguenots were exiled or destroyed. During his reign Louis XIV took on the French peasants and aristocracy, and attempted through a series of wars to dominate all of Europe.

The following excerpt is from a letter from Cardinal Richelieu to Louis XIII outlining his accomplishments.

---- ✤ ----

QUESTIONS

1. What was the advantage to Louis XIII in destroying all the Huguenot held castles?
2. Although the letter is written to Louis XIII, how is it also a blueprint for Louis XIV's absolutism?
3. Do you see any conflict in Richelieu's position as Cardinal to the pope and his work in centralizing the French king's power?

Richelieu's account of the condition of France when he became minister in 1624.

At the time when your Majesty resorted to admit me both to your council and to an important place in your confidence for the direction of your affairs, I may say that the Huguenots shared the state with you; that the nobles conducted themselves as if they were not your subjects, and the most powerful governors of the provinces as if they were sovereign in their offices.

I may say that the bad example of all of these was so injurious to this realm that even the best regulated *parlements* were affected by it, and endeavored, in certain cases, to diminish your royal authority as far as they were able in order to stretch their own powers beyond the limits of reason.

I may say that every one measured his own merit by his audacity; that in place of estimating the benefits which they received from your Majesty at their proper worth, all valued them only in so far as they satisfied the extravagant demands of their imagination; that the most arrogant were held to be the wisest, and found themselves the most prosperous.

I may also say that the foreign alliances were unfortunate, individual interests being preferred to those of the public; in a word, the dignity of the royal majesty was so disparaged, and so different from what it should be, owing to the malfeasance of those who conducted your affairs, that it was almost impossible to perceive its existence.

It was impossible, without losing all, to tolerate longer the conduct of those to whom your Majesty had intrusted the helm of state; and, on the other hand, everything could not be changed at once without violating the laws of prudence, which do not permit the abrupt passing from one extreme to another.

The sad state of your affairs seemed to force you to hasty decisions, without permitting a choice of time or of means; and yet it was necessary to make a choice of both, in order to profit by the change which necessity demanded from your prudence.

Thoughtful observers did not think that it would be possible to escape all the rocks in so tempestuous a period; the court was full of people who censured the temerity of those who wished to undertake a reform; all well knew that princes are quick to impute to those who are near them the bad outcome of the undertakings upon which they have been well advised; few people consequently expected good results from the change which it was announced that I wished to make, and many believed my fall assured even before your Majesty had elevated me.

Notwithstanding these difficulties which I represented to your Majesty, knowing how much kings may do when they make good use of their power, I ventured to promise you, with confidence, that you would soon get control of your state, and that in a short time your prudence, your courage, and the benediction of God would give a new aspect to the realm....

Edict of 1626 ordering the demolition of the feudal castles in France.

Whereas formerly the assemblies of the estates of this realm and those of notable persons chosen to give advice to ourselves, and to the late king, our very honorable lord and father, on important affairs of this realm, and likewise the assembly of the estates of the province of Brittany held by us in the year 1614, have repeatedly requested and very humbly supplicated our said lord and father and ourselves to cause the demolition of many strongholds in divers places of this realm, which, being neither on hostile frontiers nor in important passes or places, only serve to augment our expenses by the maintenance of useless garrisons, and also serve as retreats for divers persons who on the least provocation disturb the provinces where they are located;...

For these reasons, we announce, declare, ordain, and will that all the strongholds, either towns or castles, which are in the interior of our realm or provinces of the same, not situated in places of importance either for frontier defense or other considerations of weight, shall be razed and demolished; even ancient walls shall be destroyed so far as it shall be deemed necessary for the well-being and repose of our subjects and the security of this state, so that our said subjects henceforth need not fear that the said places will cause them any inconvenience, and so that we shall be freed from the expense of supporting garrisons in them.

Letters patent establishing the French Academy in 1635.

> *Richelieu was much interested in the encouragement of science, art, and literature. The French Academy, which he induced the king to establish by the following order, had begun with the informal conference of a few men of letters, who met at one another's houses.*

When God called us to the headship of the state we cherished the purpose not only of putting an end to the disorders caused by the civil wars which had so long distracted the realm, but we also aimed to adorn the state with all the ornaments appropriate to the oldest and most illustrious of existing monarchies. Although we have labored without intermission to realize this purpose, it has been impossible hitherto fully to accomplish it.... [But now] the confusion has at last given way to good order, which we have reestablished by the best of all means, namely, by reviving commerce, enforcing military discipline in our armies, adjusting the taxes, and checking luxury. Every one is aware of the part that our very dear and beloved cousin, the cardinal, duke of Richelieu, has had in the accomplishment of all these things.

Importance of cultivating the French language.

Consequently when we communicated our intention to him, he represented to us that one of the most glorious proofs of the happiness of a realm is that the sciences and arts flourish within it, and that letters as well as arms are held in esteem, since these constitute one of the chief ornaments of a powerful state; that, after so many memorable exploits, we had now only to add the agreeable to the essential, and to adorn the useful. He believed that we could not do better than to commence with the most noble of all arts, namely, eloquence. The French language, which has suffered much hitherto from neglect on the part of those who might have rendered it the most perfect of modern tongues, is not more capable than ever of taking its high place, owing to the great number of persons who possess a special knowledge of the advantages which it enjoys and who can augment these advantages. The cardinal informed us that, with a view of establishing fixed rules for the language, he had arranged meetings of scholars whose decisions in these matters had met with his hearty approval, and that in order to put these decisions into execution and render the French language not only elegant but capable of treating all the arts and sciences, it would only be necessary to perpetuate these gatherings. This could be done with great advantage should it please us to sanction them, to permit rules and regulations to be drawn up for the order of procedure to be observed, and to reward those who compose the association by some honorable marks of our favor.

For these reasons, and in view of the advantages which our subjects may derive from the said meetings, acceding to the desires of our said cousin:

We do permit, by our special favor, power, and royal authority, and do authorize and approve by these presents, signed by our hand, the said assemblies and conferences. We will that they continue hereafter in our good city of Paris, under the name of the *French Academy*; that our said cousin shall be designated as its head and protector; that the number of members be limited to forty persons....

Source: James Harvey Robinson, *Readings in European History,* Vol. II, (Boston: Ginn and Company, 1906, 1934), pp. 268-72.

17.2

✤

Thirty Years' War: Destruction of Magdeburg

The Thirty Years' War was the last of the Religious Wars of the Reformation, but was also very much a war of politics and national interests. It was primarily fought within the Holy Roman Empire, but not exclusively. The war went through several stages; the combatants varied from place to place and decade to decade. In Bohemia the war was fought between Catholics and Calvinists (although it was also a response to the German Habsburg dynasty's attempt to increase its power over the state). Danish Lutherans entered the war in order to protect Protestants in Germany from the attempts by the Habsburgs to re-Catholicize the German states, as they were attempting to do in Bohemia. In contrast, the war in Sweden was clearly mostly one of politics; King Gustavus Adolphus (d. 1635) used the opportunity to try and establish his kingdom's dominance over the Baltic. The settlement to the war, the Treaty of Westphalia in 1648, ensured that politics and faith would remain intertwined. The Treaty allowed for individual rulers within the Holy Roman Empire to decide what would be the official faith of his own state.

The following excerpt describes the massacre of Protestants in the German city of Magdeburg in 1631, which brought Gustavus Adolphus renewed determination to fight German Catholic princes.

QUESTIONS

1. One characteristic of the war was the improvement in guns and their efficiency; how did that affect the siege of Magdeburg?
2. Which do you think was more multinational in character, the Protestant or Catholic armies?
3. What might have been the motivation for the Imperial army sacking Magdeburg? Do you think it was about religion?

The Destruction of Magdeburg (May, 1631).

So then General Pappenheim collected a number of his people on the ramparts by the New Town, and brought them from there into the streets of the city. Von Falckenberg was shot, and fires were kindled in different quarters; then indeed it was all over with the city, and further resistance was useless. Nevertheless some of the soldiers and citizens did try to make a stand here and there, but the imperial troops kept bringing on more and more forces — cavalry, too — to help them, and finally they got the Kröckenthor open and let in the whole imperial army and the forces of the Catholic League, — Hungarians, Croats, Poles, Walloons, Italians, Spaniards, French, North and South Germans.

Thus it came about that the city and all its inhabitants fell into the hands of the enemy, whose violence and cruelty were due in part to their common hatred of the adherents of the Augsburg Confession, and in part to their being imbittered by the chain shot which had been fired at them and by the derision and insults that the Magdeburgers had heaped upon them from the ramparts.

Then was there naught but beating and burning, plundering, torture, and murder. Most especially was every one of the enemy bent on securing much booty. When a marauding party entered a house, if its master had anything to give he might thereby purchase respite and protection for himself and his family till the next man, who also wanted something, should come along. It was only when everything had been brought forth and there was nothing left to give that the real trouble commenced. Then, what with blows and threats of shooting, stabbing, and hanging, the poor people were so terrified that if they had had anything left they would have brought it forth if it had been buried in the earth or hidden away in a thousand castles. In this frenzied rage, the great and splendid city that had stood like a fair princess in the land was now, in its hour of direst need and unutterable distress and woe, given over to the flames, and thousands of innocent men, women, and children, in the midst of a horrible din of heartrending shrieks and cries, were tortured and put to death in so cruel and shameful a manner that no words would suffice to describe, nor no tears to bewail it....

Thus is a single day this noble and famous city, the pride of the whole country, went up in fire and smoke; and the remnant of its citizens, with their wives and children, were taken prisoners and driven away by the enemy with a noise of weeping and wailing that could be heard from afar, while the cinders and ashes from the town were carried by the wind to Wanzleben, Egeln, and still more distant places....

In addition to all this, quantities of sumptuous and irreplaceable house furnishings and movable property of all kinds, such as books, manuscripts, paintings, memorials of all sorts,...which money could not buy, were either burned or carried away by the soldiers as booty. The most magnificent garments, hangings, silk stuffs, gold and silver lace, linen of all sorts, and other household goods were bought by the army sutlers for a mere song and peddled about by the card load all through the archbishopric of

Magdeburg and in Anhalt and Brunswick. Gold chains and rings, jewels, and every kind of gold and silver utensils were to be bought from the common soldiers for a tenth of their real value....

Source: James Harvey Robinson, ed. *Readings in European History*, Vol. II. (Boston: Ginn and Company, 1906, 1934), pp. 211-212.

17.3

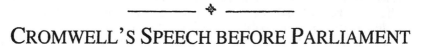

CROMWELL'S SPEECH BEFORE PARLIAMENT

As with the Thirty Years' War, the motivations of the various sides in the English Civil War (1642-1648) were diverse and complicated. The forces of Charles I, the Cavaliers, were fighting for their certainty in monarchy as the best government. Charles was himself also fighting for his conviction that he was king by divine right. The king's main adversary was Parliament, which had convened in 1640 in order to address the abuses of its sovereignty by the King. Parliament in England was already an ancient institution by 1640; its independence had been assured through such acts as the signing of Magna Carta in 1215. By 1642 Parliament's forces, the Roundheads, were led by Oliver Cromwell, a man of devoutly Puritan beliefs. One of the reasons for Parliament's hostility was its suspicion that Charles was too sympathetic to Catholicism, perhaps to the point of planning to convert to the Roman faith. After almost seventy years of uninterrupted Protestant rule, Parliament wanted to prevent the religious upheaval that having a Catholic on the throne would cause. Religion was not the only issue of disagreement between King and Parliament (taxes were, as usual, also a factor) but it was certainly one of the most pressing.

Parliament won the Civil War when it had Charles executed for tyranny. The beheading of Charles was shocking to all of Europe; in an age when kings could claim divine favor, this was tantamount to blasphemy for many Christians. Although Parliament would later depose another king (James II) for being too Catholic, it would exile rather than execute him.

In the following speech, Cromwell defends his status as the "Lord Protector" of England.

✤

QUESTIONS

1. Having won the war, why does Cromwell call himself Lord Protector and not king?
2. What are the Biblical justifications for Cromwell's actions and victories?
3. How does Cromwell defend his need to raise money from taxes?

For I look at the People of these Nations as the blessing of the Lord: and they are a People blessed by God. They have been so; and they will be so, by reason of that immortal seed which hath been, and is, among them; those Regenerated Ones in the land, of several judgments; who are all the Flock of Christ and lambs of Christ. "His," though perhaps under many unruly passions, and troubles of spirit; whereby they give disquiet to themselves and others: yet they are not so to God; since to us He is a God of other patience; and He will own the least of Truth in the hearts of His People. And the People being the blessing of God, they will not be so angry but they will prefer their safety to their passions, and their real security to forms, when Necessity calls for Supplies. Had they not well been acquainted with this principle, they had never seen this day of Gospel Liberty.

But if any man shall object, "It is an easy thing to talk of Necessities when men create Necessities: would not the Lord Protector make himself great and his family great? Doth not he make these Necessities? And then he will come upon the People with his argument of Necessity!" — This was something hard indeed. But I have *not* yet known what it is to "make Necessities," whatsoever the thoughts or judgments of men are. And I say this, not only to this Assembly, but to the world, That the man liveth not who can come to me and charge me with having, in these great Revolutions, "made Necessities." I challenge even all that fear God. And as God hath said, "My glory I will not give unto another," let men take need and be twice advised how they call His Revolutions, the things of God, and His working of things from one period to another, — how, I say, they call them Necessities of men's creation! For by so doing, they do vilify and lessen the works of God, and rob Him of His glory; which He hat said He will not give unto another, nor suffer to be taken from Him! We know what God did to Herod, when he was applauded and did not acknowledge God. And God knoweth what He will do with men, when they call His Revolutions human designs, and so detract from His glory. These issues and events have not been forecast; but were sudden Providences in things: whereby carnal and worldly men are enraged; and under and at which, many, and I fear some good men, have murmured and repined, because disappointed of their mistaken fancies. But still all these things have been the wise disposings of the Almighty; though instruments have had their passions and frailties. And I think it is an honour to God to acknowledge the Necessities to have been of God's imposing, when truly they have been so, as indeed they have. Let us take our sin in our actions to ourselves; it's much more safe than to judge things so contingent, as if there were not a God that ruled the Earth!

We know the Lord hath poured this Nation from vessel to vessel, till He poured it into your lap, when you came first together. I am confident that it came so into your hands; and was not judged by you to be from counterfeited or feigned Necessity, but by Divine Providence and Dispensation. And this I speak with more earnestness, because I speak for God and not for men. I would have any man to come and tell of the Transactions that have been, and of those periods of time wherein God hath made these Revolutions; and find where he can fix a feigned Necessity! I could recite particulars, if either my strength would serve me to speak, or yours to hear. If that you would resolve the great Hand of God in His great Dispensations, you would find that there is scarce a man who fell off, at any period of time when God had any work to do, who can give God or His work at this day a good word.

"It was," say some, "the cunning of the Lord Protector," — I take it to myself, — "it was the craft of such a man, and his plot, that hath brought it about!" And, as they say in other countries, "There are five or six cunning men in England that have skill; they do all these things." Oh, what blasphemy is this! Because men that are without God in the world, and walk not with Him, know not what it is to pray or believe, and to receive returns from God, and to be spoken unto by the Spirit of God, — who speaks without a Written Word sometimes, yet *according* to it! God hath spoken heretofore in divers manners. Let Him speak as He pleaseth. Hath He not given us liberty, nay, is it not our duty, To go to the Law and the Testimony? And there we shall find that there *have* been impressions, in extraordinary cases, as well without the Written Word as with it. And therefore there is no difference in the thing thus asserted from Truths generally received, — except we will exclude the Spirit; without whose concurrence all other teachings are ineffectual. He doth speak to the hearts and consciences of men; and leadeth them to His Law and Testimony, and there "also" He speaks to them: and so gives them double teachings. According tot hat of Job: "God speaketh once, yea twice"; and to that of David: "God hath spoken once, yea twice have I heard this." These men that live upon their *mumpsimus* and *sumpsimus*, their Masses and Service-books, their dead and carnal worship, — no marvel if they be strangers to God, and to the works of God, and to spiritual dispensations. And because *they* say and believe thus, must we do so too? We, in this land, have been otherwise instructed; even by the Word, and Works, and Spirit of God.

To say that men bring forth these things when God doth them, — judge you if God will bear this? I wish that every sober heart, though he hath had temptations upon him of deserting this Cause of God, yet may take heed how he provokes and falls into the hands of the Living god by such blasphemies as these! According to the Tenth of the *Hebrews*: "If we sin wilfully after that we have received the knowledge of the truth, there remains no more sacrifice for sin." "A terrible word." It was spoken to the Jews who, having professed Christ, apostatised from Him. What then? Nothing but a fearful "falling into the hands of the Living God!" — They that shall attribute to this or that person the contrivances and production of those mighty things God hath wrought in the midst of us; and "fancy" that they have not been the Revolutions of Christ Himself, "upon whose shoulders the government is laid," — they speak against God, and they fall under His hands without a Mediator. That is, if we deny the Spirit of Jesus Christ the glory of all His works in the world; by which He rules kingdoms, and doth administer, and is the rod of His strength, — we provoke the Mediator: and He may say: I will leave you to God, I will not intercede for you; let Him tear you to pieces! I will leave thee to fall into God's bands; thou deniest me my sovereignty and power committed to me; I will not intercede nor mediate for thee; thou fallest into the hands of the Living God! — Therefore whatsoever you may judge men for, howsoever you may say, "This is cunning and politic, and subtle," — take heed again, I say, how you judge of His Revolutions as the product of men's inventions! — I may be thought to press too much upon this theme. But I pray God it may stick upon your hearts and mine. The worldly-minded man knows nothing of this, but is a stranger to it; and thence his atheisms, and murmurings at instruments, yea, repining at God Himself. And no wonder; considering the Lord hath done such things amongst us as have not been known in the world these thousand years, and yet notwithstanding is not owned by us!

There is another Necessity, which you have put upon us, and we have not sought. I appeal to God, Angels, and Men, — if I shall "now" raise money according to the Article in the Government, whether I am not compelled to do it! Which "Government" had power to call you hither; and did: — and instead of seasonably providing for the Army, you have laboured to overthrow the Government, and the Army is now upon Free-quarter! And you would never so much as let me hear a tittle from you concerning it. Where is the fault? Has it not been as if you had a purpose to put this extremity upon us and the Nation? I hope this was not in your minds. I am not willing to judge so: — but such is the state into which we are reduced. By the designs of some in the Army who are now in custody, it was designed to get as many of them as possible, — through discontent for want of money, the Army being in a barren country, near thirty weeks behind in pay, and upon other specious pretences, — to march for England out of Scotland; and, in discontent, to seize their General there [*General Monk*], a faithful and honest man, that so another [*Colonel Overton*] might head the Army. And all this opportunity taken from your delays. Whether will this be a thing of feigned Necessity? What could it signify, but "The Army are in discontent already; and we will make them live upon stones; we will make them cast-off their governors and discipline?" What can be said to this? I list not to unsaddle myself, and put the fault upon your backs. Whether it hath been for the good of England, whilst men have been talking of this thing or the other, and pretending liberty and many good words, — whether it has been as it should have been? I am confident you cannot think it has. The Nation will not think so. And if the worst should be made of things, I know not what the Cornish men nor the Lincolnshire men may think, or other Counties; but I believe they will all think *they are not safe.* A temporary suspension of "caring for the greatest liberties and privilege" (if it were so, which is denied) would not have been of such damage as the not providing against Free-quarter hath run the Nation upon. And if it be my "liberty" to walk abroad in the fields, or to take a journey, yet it is not my wisdom to do so when my house is on fire!

Source: *British Orations from Ethelbert to Churchill* (New York: E. P. Dutton, 1960), pp. 48-52.

17.4

"A Dialogue on Sovereign Power," Thomas Hobbes

Thomas Hobbes (1588-1679) was one of the major political theorists of the seventeenth century. Hobbes lived through the English Civil War, although he did not live to see another king removed from the throne (in 1688 James II is peaceably replaced by his daughter Mary and her husband William of Orange, both devoutly Protestant). His understanding of the rights of the state is particularly affected by the events of his lifetime. In many of his writings, including his most famous political treatise, The Leviathan, he argued that the all-powerful state was the only thing that stood between humanity and its own inclination toward savage primitivism. He argued for a different type of absolutism from the Louis XIV model; Hobbes believed the state should be absolute but not necessarily the king.

This source is from a dialogue Hobbes wrote on the common law of England.

Questions

1. Does Hobbes have a theory of natural law?
2. What limits does Hobbes place on the power of kings?
3. Do you think Hobbes supported Parliament during the Civil War?

La.　I Grant you that the King is sole Legislator; but with this Restriction, that if he will not Consult with the Lords of Parliament, and hear the Complaints and Informations of the Commons, that are best acquainted with their own wants, he sinneth against God, though he cannot be Compell'd to any thing by his Subjects by Arms and Force.

Ph.　We are Agreed upon that already. Since therefore the King is sole Legislator, I think it also Reason he should be sole Supream Judge.

La.　There is no doubt of that; for otherwise there would be no Congruity of Judgments with the Laws. I Grant also that he is the Supream Judge over all Persons, and in all Causes Civil, and Ecclesiastical within his own Dominions, not only by Act of Parliament at this time, but that he has ever been so by the Common-Law: For the Judges of both the Benches have their Offices by the King's Letters Patents, and so (as to Judicature) have the Bishops. Also the Lord Chancellor hath his office by receiving from the King the Great Seal of *England*; and, to say all at once, there is no Magistrate, or Commissioner for Publick Business, neither of Judicature, nor Execution in State, or Church, in Peace, or War, but he is made so by Authority from the King.

Ph. 'Tis true; But perhaps you may think otherwise, when you Read such Acts of Parliament, as say, that the King shall have Power and Authority to do this or that by Virtue of that Act, as *Eliz. c.* I. That your Highness, your Heirs, and Successors, Kings, or Queens of this Realm, shall have full Power and Authority, by Virtue of this Act, by Letters Patents under the Great Seal of *England* to Assign, &c. Was it not this Parliament that gave this Authority to the Queen?

La. No; For the Statute in this Clause is no more than (as Sir *Edw. Coke* useth to speak) an Affirmance of the Common-Law; For she being Head of the Church of *England* might make Commissioners for the deciding of Matters Ecclesiastical, as freely as if she had been Pope, who did, you know pretend his right from the Law of God....

La. How would you have a Law defin'd?

Ph. Thus; A Law is the Command of him or them that have the Sovereign Power, given to those that be his or their Subjects, declaring Publickly and plainly what every of them may do, and what they must forbear to do....

La. By your Definition of a Law, the King's Proclamation under the Great Seal of *England* is a Law; for it is a Command, and Publick, and of the Sovereign to his Subjects.

Ph. Why not? If he think it necessary for the good of his Subjects: For this is a Maxim at the Common-Law Alleged by Sir *Edward Coke* himself. (2 *Inst.* p. 306), *Quando Lex aliquid concedit, concedere videtur et id per quod devenitur ad illud.* And you know out of the same Author, that divers Kings of *England* have often, to the Petitions in Parliament which they granted, annexed such exceptions as these, unless there be necessity, saving our Regality; which I think should be always understood, though they be not expressed; and are understood so by Common Lawyers, who agree that the King may recall any Grant wherein he was deceiv'd.

La. Again, whereas you make it of the Essence of a Law to be Publickly and plainly declar'd to the People, I see no necessity for that. Are not all Subjects Bound to take notice of all Acts of Parliament, when no Act can pass without their Consent?

Ph. If you had said that no Act could pass without their knowledge, then indeed they had been bound to take notice of them; but none can have knowledge of them but the Members of the Houses of Parliament; therefore the rest of the People are excus'd; Or else the Knights of the [Shires] should be bound to furnish People with a sufficient Number of Copies (at the People's Charge) of the Acts of Parliament at their return into the Country; that every man may resort to them, and by themselves, or friends, take notice of what they are obliged to; for otherwise it were impossible they should be obeyed: And that no Man is bound to do a thing Impossible is one of Sir *Edw. Cokes* Maxims at the Common-Law. I know that most of the Statutes are Printed, but it does not appear that every Man is bound to Buy the Book of Statutes, nor to search for them at *Westminster* or at the *Tower*, nor to understand the Language wherein they are for the most part Written....

Ph. But what are you better for your Right, if a rebellious Company at home, or an Enemy from abroad, take away the Goods, or dispossess you of the Lands you have a right to? Can you be defended, or repair'd, but by the strength and authority of the King? What reason therefore can be given by a man that endeavours to preserve his Propriety, why he should deny, or malignly contribute to the Strength that should defend him, or repair him? Let us see now what your Books say to this point, and other points of the Right of Sovereignty. *Bracton*, the most authentick author of the Common Law, *fol.* 55. saith thus: *Ipse Dominus Rex habet omnia jura in manu sua, sicut Dei Vicarius; habet etiam ea quæ sunt Pacis; habet etiam coercionem, ut Delinquentes puniat; item habet in potestate sua Leges; nihil enim prodest Jura condere, nisi sit qui Jura tueatur:* That is to say, Our Lord the King hath all Right in his own Hands; is God's Vicar; he has all that concerns the Peace; he has the power to punish Delinquents; all the Laws are in his power:; to make laws is to no purpose, unless there be some-body to make them obeyed. If *Bracton's* Law be Reason, as I, and you think it is; what temporal power is there which the King hath not? Seeing that at this day all the power spiritual which *Bracton* allows the *Pope*, is restored to the Crown; what is there that the King cannot do, excepting sin against the Law of God? The same *Bracton Lib.* ii. *c.* 8. saith thus; *Si autem a Rege petatur (cum Breve non currat contra ipsum) locus erit supplicationi, quod factum suum corrigat, et emendet; quod quidem si non fecerit, satis sufficit ei ad pœnam, quod Dominum expectet Ultorem; nemo quidem de factis ejus præsumat disputare, multo fortius contra factum suum venire:* That is to say, if any thing be demanded of the King (seeing a Writ lyeth not against him) he is put to his Petition, praying him to Correct and Amend his own Fact; which if he will not do, it is a sufficient Penalty for him, that he is to expect a punishment from the Lord: No Man may presume to dispute of what he does, much less to resist him. You see by this, that this Doctrine concerning the Rights of Sovereignty, so much Cryed down by the long Parliament, is the Ancient Common-Law, and that the only Bridle of the Kings of *England*, ought to be the fear of God. And again, *Bracton, c.* 24 of the second Book says, That the Rights of the Crown cannot be granted away; *Ea vero quæ Jurisdictionis [sunt] et Pacis, et ea quæ sunt jJustitiæ et Paci annexa, ad nullum pertinent nisi ad Coronam et Dignitatem Regiam, nec a Corona separari possunt, nec a privata persona possideri.* That is to say: those things which belong to Jurisdiction and Peace, and those things that are annexed to Justice and Peace, appertain to none, but to the Crown and Dignity of the King, nor can be separated from the Crown, nor be possest by a private Person. Again, you'l find in *Fleta* (a Law-Book written in the time of *Edw.* 2.) That Liberties though granted by the King, if they tend to the hindrance of Justice, or subversion of the Regal Power, were not to be used, nor allowed: For in that Book *c.* 20. concerning Articles of the Crown, which the jJustices Itinerant are to enquire of, the 54th Article is this, you shall inquire, *De Libertatibus concessis quæ impediunt Communem Justitiam, et Regiam Potestatem subvertunt.* Now what is a greater hindrance to Common Justice, or a greater subversion of the Regal Power, than a Liberty in Subjects to hinder the King from raising Money necessary to suppress, or prevent Rebellions, which doth destroy Justice, and subvert the power of the Sovereignty? Moreover, when a Charter is granted by the King in these words, *Dedita etc.* . . . *coram etc.* . . . *pro me et hæredibus meis*[, t]he grantor by the Common-Law (as Sir *Edw. Coke* says in his Commentaries on *Littleton*) is to warrant his Gift; and I think it Reason, especially if the Gift be upon Consideration of a price Paid. Suppose a Forraign State should lay claim to this

Kingdom ('tis no Matter as to the Question I am putting, whether the Claim be unjust), how would you have the King to warrant to every Free-holder in *England* the Lands they hold of him by such a Charter? If he cannot Levy Money, their Estates are lost, and so is the King's Estate; and if the King's Estate be gone, how can he repair the Value due upon the Warranty? I know that the King's Charters are not so meerly Grants, as that they are not also Laws; but they are such Laws as speak not to all the King's Subjects in general, but only to his Officers; implicitly forbidding them to Judge or eExecute any thing contrary to the said Grants. There be many Men that are able Judges of what is right Reason, and what not; when any of these shall know that a Man has no Superiour nor Peer in the Kingdom, he will hardly be perswaded he can be bound by any Law of the Kingdom, or that he who is Subject to none but God, can make a Law upon himself, which he cannot also as easily abrogate, as he made it. The main Argument, and that which so much taketh with the throng of People, proceedeth from a needless fear put into their minds by such Men as mean to make use of their hHands to their own ends; for if (say they) the King may (notwithstanding the Law) do what he please, and nothing to restrain him but the fear of punishment in the World to come, then (in case there come a King that fears no such punishment) he may take away from us, not only our Lands, Goods, and Liberties, but our Lives also if he will: And they say true; but they have no reason to think he will, unless it be for his own profit; which cannot be, for he loves his own Power; and what becomes of his power when his Subjects are destroyed or weakened, by whose multitude and strength he enjoys his power, and every one of his Subjects his Fortune? And lastly, whereas they sometimes say the King is bound, not only to cause his Laws to be observ'd, but also to observe them himself; I think the King causing them to be observ'd is the same thing as observing them himself: For I never heard it taken for good Law, that the King may be Indicted, or Appealed, or served with a Writ, till the long Parliament practised the contrary upon the good King *Charles*, for which divers of them were Executed, and the rest by this our present King pardoned.

Source: Thomas Hobbes, *A Dialogue Between A Philosopher and A Student of the Common Laws of England* (Chicago: University of Chicago Press, 1971), pp. 66-77.

QUESTIONS FOR PART 17

1. Compare the definitions of royal power given by Richelieu and Hobbes.
2. If most states were unsuccessful in establishing absolute monarchies, why does the idea remain popular well into the eighteenth century? Is it just royal greed?
3. Is there any move to secularize politics in the seventeenth century?

PART 18

REVOLUTIONS IN SCIENCE

As Europe transitioned out of the Middle Ages and into the Modern era, it did so with an inquisitive spirit. In matters of religion, politics, trade, and the sciences, Europeans of the sixteenth and seventeenth centuries were not satisfied with the traditional answers; the unexamined life was no longer worth living. In the end, a complete shift in worldview had occurred, although it took the West several more centuries to recognize that. Many subjects of inquiry produced dramatic change (such as the Protestant Reformation and the discovery of new worlds) while others led to more traditional results (as in the witch hunts, which represented a traditionalist response to change).

The last phase of exploration was that of the sciences. Here too a revolution in thought occurred, one that shook European culture down to its core just as Lutheranism had done in 1517. Science changed both in approach and in technique, in theory and in technology, and the changes in one realm of discourse (theory or practice) led to changes in the other, and so forth. As with the religious reformations, there was no one scientific revolution; there were many and the process continues. Perhaps the greatest single legacy of the period is the very concept that science should not stand still, that it should change and seek innovative ideas and approaches.

The scientific transformations began in astronomy, spread to physics and optics, and then to the natural sciences. The change in traditional ways of viewing, explaining, and understanding the physical world was a gradual one that encompassed many new discoveries before the old order of thought changed. It was really only with hindsight that Europe realized how volatile the new scientific discoveries were. When Columbus found the Americas, Europe had to find a new way to explain its place on the earth; similarly, when Copernicus suggested the earth was not the center of the cosmos, humanity had to rethink its place in the universe.

18.1

COPERNICAN THEORY

Nicolaus Copernicus (1473-1543) was a Polish astronomer and mathematician; his revolutionary discovery that the sun was the center of the cosmos was due more to his theoretical understanding of how the stars moved than any observations of his own. Observational proof of Copernicus' heliocentric worldview would come later. Copernicus' most important contribution was simply his willingness to question the geocentric theory that had dominated Europe since the second century AD, when a Greek astronomer named Ptolemy first described the heavens has a series of perfect spheres revolving around a still earth. The Ptolemaic theory had been challenged by some pagan astronomers, but medieval theologians built their theory of a divinely order cosmos around it. Copernicus, however, recognized that mathematically the Ptolemaic system simply did not work. He also recognized that challenging the geocentric theory was dangerous, particularly in the religious climate of the early sixteenth century and did not publish his definitive work, On the Revolution of Heavenly Spheres, *until shortly before his death. The following is an excerpt, which argues that ancient astronomers have to be challenged.*

QUESTIONS

1. How does Copernicus use comets to disprove the Ptolemaic theory of an earth-centered universe?
2. Why *must* the universe be spherical?
3. How is Copernicus' revolutionary new idea a result of Renaissance humanism?

Refutation of the arguments of the ancients that the earth remains still in the middle of the universe, as if it were its center.

From this and similar reasons it is supposed that the earth rests at the center of the universe and that there is no doubt of the fact. But if one believed that the earth revolved, he would certainly be of the opinion that this movement was natural and not arbitrary. For whatever is in accord with nature produces results which are the opposite of those produced by force. Things upon which force or an outside power has acted, must be injured and cannot long endure: what happens by nature, however, preserves itself well and exists in the best condition. So Ptolemy feared without good reason that the earth and all earthly objects subject to the revolution would be destroyed by the act of nature, since this latter is opposed to artificial acts, or to what is produced by the human spirit. But why did he not fear the same, and in a much higher degree, of the universe, whose motion must be as much more rapid as the heavens are greater than the earth? Or has the heaven become so immense because it has been driven outward from the center by the inconceivable power of the revolution; while if it stood still, on the contrary, it would collapse and fall together? But surely if this is the case the extent of the heavens would increase infinitely. For the more it is driven higher by the outward force of the movement, so much the more rapid will the movement become, because of the ever increasing circle which must be traversed in 24 hours; and conversely if the movement grows the immensity of the heavens grows, so the velocity would increase the size and the size would increase the velocity unendingly. According to the physical law that the endless cannot wear away nor in any way move, the heavens must necessarily stand still. But it is said that beyond the sky no body, no place, no vacant space, in fact nothing at all exists; then it is strange that some thing should be enclosed by nothing. But if the heaven is endless and is bounded only by the inner hollow, perhaps this establishes all the more clearly the fact that there is nothing outside the heavens, because everything is within it, but the heaven must then remain unmoved. The highest proof on which one supports the finite character of the universe is its movement. But whether the universe is endless or limited we will leave to the physiologues; this remains sure for us that the earth enclosed between the poles, is bounded by a spherical surface. Why therefore should we not take the position of ascribing to a movement conformable to its nature and corresponding to it form, rather than suppose that the whole universe whose limits are not and cannot be known moves? and why will we not recognize that the appearance of a daily revolution belongs to the heavens, but the actuality to the earth; and that the relation is similar to that of which one says: "We run out of the harbor, the lands and cities retreat from us." Because if a ship sails along quietly, everything outside of it appears to those on board as if it moved with the motion of the boat, and the boatman thinks that the boat with all on board is standing still, this same thing may hold without doubt of the motion of the earth, and it may seem as if the whole universe revolved. What shall we say, however, of the clouds and other things floating, falling or raising in the air — except that not only does the earth move with the watery elements belonging with it, but also a large part of the atmosphere, and whatever else is in any way connected with the earth; whether it is because the air immediately touching the earth has the same nature as the earth, or that the motion has become imparted to the atmosphere. A like astonishment must be felt if that highest region of the air be supposed to follow the heavenly motion, as shown by those suddenly appearing stars which the Greeks call comets or bearded stars, which belong to that region and which rise and set like other stars. We may suppose that part of the atmosphere, because of it great distance from the earth, has become free from the earthly motion. So the atmosphere which lies close to the earth and all things floating in it would appear to remain still, unless driven here and there by the wind or some other outside force, which chance may bring into play; for how is the wind in the air different from current in the sea? We must admit that the motion of things rising and falling in the air is in relation to the universe a double one, being always made up of a rectilinear and a circular movement. Since that which seeks of its own weight to fall is essentially earthy, so there is no doubt that these follow the same natural law as their whole; and it results from this same principle that those things which pertain to fire are forcibly driven on high. Earthly fire is nourished with earthly stuff, and it is said that the flame is only burning smoke. But the peculiarity of the fire consists in this that it expands whatever is seizes upon, and it carries this out so consistently that it can in no way and by no machinery be prevented from breaking its bonds and completing its work. The expanding motion, however, is directed from the center outward; therefore if any earthly material is ignited it moves upward. So to each single body belongs a single motion, and this is evinced preferably in a circular direction as long as the single body remains in its natural place and its entirety. In this position the movement is the circular movement which as far as the body itself is concerned is as if it did not occur. The rectilinear motion, however, siezes upon those bodies which have wandered or have been driven from their natural position or have been in any way disturbed. Nothing is so much opposed to the order and form of the world as the displacement of one of its parts. Rectilinear motion takes place only when objects are not properly related, and are not complete according to their nature because they have separated from their whole and have lost their unity. Moreover, objects which have been driven outward or away, leaving out of consideration the circular motion, do not obey a single, simple and regular motion, since they cannot be controlled simply by their lightness or by the force of their weight, and if in falling they have at first a slow movement the rapidity of the motion increases as they fall, while in the case of earthly fire which is forced upwards — and we have no means of knowing any other kind of fire — we will see that its motion is slow as if its earthly origin thereby showed itself. The circular motion, on the other hand, is always regular, because it is not subject to an intermittent cause. Those other objects, however, would cease to be either light or heavy in respect to their natural movement if they reached their own place, and thus they would fit into that movement. Therefore if the circular movement is to be ascribed to the universe as a whole and the rectilinear to the parts, we might say that the revolution is to the straight line as the natural state is to sickness. That Aristotle divided motion into three sorts, that from the center out, that inward toward center, and that around the center, appears to be merely a logical convenience, just as we distinguish point, line and surface, although one cannot exist without the others, and one of them are found apart from bodies. This fact is also to be considered, that the condition of immovability is held to be nobler and diviner than that of change and inconstancy, which latter therefore should be ascribed rather to the earth than to the universe, and I would add also that it seems inconsistent to attribute motion to the containing and locating element rather than to the contained and located object, which the earth is. Finally since the planets plainly are at one time nearer and at another time farther from the earth, it would follow, on the theory that the universe revolves, that the movement of the one and same body which is known to take place about a center, that is the center of the earth, must also be directed toward the center from without and from the center outward. The movement about the center must therefore be made more general, and it suffices if that single movement be about its own center. So it appears from all these considerations that the movement of the earth is more probable than its fixity, especially in regard to the daily revolution, which is most peculiar to the earth.

Source: Oliver J. Thatcher, ed., *The Ideas that have Influenced Civilization in the Original Documents, Volume V* (Boston: Roberts-Manchester Publishing Co., 1901), pp. 96-101.

18.2

❖

CONDEMNATION AND RECANTATION OF GALILEO

Copernicus was right to worry about the repercussions of publicizing his radical new understanding of the universe. If anyone had any doubts about the danger of doing so, the difficulties Galileo Galilei (1564-1642) faced in attempting to prove the Copernican theory offers proof. Between Copernicus and Galileo stand a host of observational and theoretical astronomer, such as Tycho Brahe and Johannes Kepler, who each contributed clues to the heliocentric puzzle. Using the astronomical tables assembled by these two men, Galileo was able to conclusively disprove the Ptolemaic system. Galileo had two advantages over these earlier astronomers: he was able to use their data and build upon it, and he had a telescope. Galileo was the first astronomer to use a telescope, a Flemish invention, and with his newly magnified vision he noticed one important fact about the stars. They were not perfect. The Ptolemaic system had fit so perfectly with Christian theology because both had argued that the universe was a perfect created system, reflecting a divine plan, focused on the greatest of divine creations, humanity. By placing humanity, the earth, at the center of the universe, the Ptolemaic theory supported scriptural understanding of creation. Galileo challenged this by pointing out the imperfections of the stars and planets, their movement, and his mathematical proof that the earth was just another heavenly body, no more perfect than the other created objects.

Unlike Copernicus, Galileo did not hesitate to publicize his ideas. At the University of Padua he taught the Copernican theories, and published his observations in The Starry Messenger *in 1610. The Catholic Church responded to this challenge by condemning the Copernican system and by summoning Galileo before the Inquisition for teaching heresy. Still, Galileo continued to teach Copernicanism, and in 1632 published a second book on it. This led to a second condemnation in 1633 by the Inquisition, Galileo's full recantation, and house arrest for the astronomer for the rest of his life. He was forbidden to write on or teach astronomy.*

The following source is the text of the second Condemnation of 1633 and Galileo's Recantation.

----------- ✤ -----------

QUESTIONS

1. How does the office of the Inquisition see Copernicanism as a rejection of scripture?
2. What sentence is pronounced for the second book of Galileo, the *Dialogues*?
3. Do you think Copernicus and Galileo saw their astronomical work as an attack on Christianity?

CONDEMNATION

W e...by the grace of God, cardinals of the Holy Roman Church, Inquisitors General, by the Holy Apostolic see specially deputed, against heretical depravity throughout the whole Christian Republic.

Whereas you, Galileo, son of the late Vincenzo Galilei, Florentine, aged seventy years, were in the year 1615 denounced to this Holy Office for holding as true the false doctrine taught by some that the sun is the centre of the world and immovable and that the earth moves, and also with a diurnal motion; for having disciples to whom you taught the same doctrine; for holding correspondence with certain mathematicians of Germany concerning the same; for having printed certain letters, entitled "On the Sunspots," wherein you developed the same doctrine as true; and for replying to the objections from the Holy Scriptures, which from time to time were urged against it, by glossing the said Scriptures according to your own meaning: and whereas there was thereupon produced the copy of a document in the form of a letter, purporting to be written by you to one formerly your disciple, and in this divers propositions are set forth, following the position of Copernicus, which are contrary to the true sense and authority of Holy Scripture:

This Holy Tribunal being therefore of intention to proceed against the disorder and mischief thence resulting, which went on increasing to the prejudice of the Holy Faith, by command of his Holiness and of the most eminent Lords Cardinals of this Supreme and universal Inquisition, the two propositions of the stability of the sun and the motion of the earth were by the theological "Qualifiers" qualified as follows:

The proposition that the sun is the centre of the world and does not move from its place is absurd and false philosophically and formally heretical, because it is expressly contrary to Holy Scripture.

Therefore, by our order you were cited before this Holy Office, where, being examined upon your oath, you acknowledged the book as written and published by you. You confessed that you began to write the said book about ten or twelve years ago, after the command had been imposed upon you as above; that you questioned license to print it, without however intimating to those who granted you this license that you had been commanded not to hold, defend, or teach in any way whatever the doctrine in question.

You likewise confessed that the writing of said book in its various places drawn up in such a form that the reader might fancy that arguments brought forward on the false side are rather calculated by their cogency to compel conviction than to be easy of refutation; excusing yourself for having fallen into an error, as you alleged, so foreign to your intention, by the fact that you had written in dialogue, and by the natural complacency that every man feels in regard to his own subtleties, and in showing him more clever than the generality of men, in devising, even on behalf of false propositions, ingenious and plausible arguments.

And a suitable term having been assigned to you to prepare your defence, you produced a certificate in the handwriting of his Eminence the Lord Cardinal Bellarmine, procured by you, as you asserted, in order to defend yourself against the calumnies of your enemies, who gave out that you had abjured and had been punished by the Holy Office; in which certificate it is declared that you had not abjured and had not been punished, but merely that the declaration made by his Holiness and published by the Holy Congregation of the Index, had been announced to you, wherein it is declared that the doctrine of the motion of the earth and the stability of the sun is contrary to the Holy Scriptures, and therefore cannot be defended or held. and as in this certificate there is no mention of the two articles of the injunction, namely, the order not "to teach" and "in any way," you represented that we ought to believe that in the course of fourteen or sixteen years you had lost all memory of them and that this was why you said nothing of the injunction when you requested permission to print your book. And all this you urged not by way of excuse for your error, but that it might be set down to a vainglorious ambition rather than to malice. But this certificate produced by you in your defence has only aggravated your delinquency, since although it is there stated that the said opinion is contrary to Holy Scripture, you have nevertheless dared to discuss and to defend it and to argue its probability; nor does the license artfully and cunningly extorted by you avail you anything, since you did not notify the command imposed upon you.

And whereas it appeared to us that you had not stated the full truth with regard to your intention, we thought it necessary to subject you to a rigorous examination, at which (without prejudice, however, to the matters confessed by you, and set forth as above, with regard to your said intention) you answered like a good Catholic. Therefore, having seen and maturely considered the merits of this your cause, together with your confessions and excuses above mentioned, and all that ought justly to be seen and considered, we have arrived at the underwritten final sentence against you: —

Invoking, therefore, the most holy name of our Lord Jesus Christ and of His most glorious Mother and ever Virgin Mary, by this our final sentence, which sitting in judgment, with the counsel and advice of the Reverend Masters of sacred theology and Doctors of both Laws, our assessors, we deliver in these writings, in the cause and causes presently before us between the magnificent Carlo Sinceri, Doctor of both Laws, Proctor Fiscal of this Holy Office, of the one part, and you Galileo Galilei, the defendant, here present, tried and confessed as above, have rendered yourself in the judgment of this Holy Office vehemently suspected of heresy, namely, of having believed and held the doctrine — which is false and contrary to the sacred and divine Scriptures — that the sun is the centre of the world and does not move from east to west, and that the earth moves and is not the centre of the world; and that the opinion may beheld and defended as probable after it has been declared and defined to be contrary to Holy Scriptures and that consequently you have incurred all the censures and penalties imposed and promulgated in the sacred canons and other constitutions, general and particular, against such delinquents. From which we are content that you be absolved, provided that first, with a sincere heart, and unfeigned faith, you abjure, curse, and detest the aforesaid errors and heresies, and every other error and heresy contrary to the Catholic and Apostolic Roman Church in the form to be prescribed by us.

And in order that this your grave and pernicious error and transgression may not remain altogether unpunished, and that you may be more cautious for the future, and as an example to others, that they may abstain from similar delinquencies — we ordain that the book of the *"Dialogues of Galileo Galilei"* be prohibited by public edict.

We condemn you to the formal prison of the Holy Office during our pleasure, and by way of salutary penance, we enjoin that for three years to come you repeat once a week the seven penitential Psalms.

Reserving to ourselves full liberty to moderate, commute, or take off, in whole or in part, the aforesaid penalties and penance.

And as we say, pronounce, sentence, declare, ordain, condemn and reserve, in this and any other better way and form which we can and may lawfully employ.

So we the undersigned Cardinals pronounce.

RECANTATION

❝I Galileo Galilei, son of the late Vincenzo Galilei, Florentine, aged 70 years, arraigned personally before this tribunal, and kneeling before you, most Eminent and Reverend Lord Cardinals, Inquisitor general against heretical depravity throughout the whole Christian Republic, having before my eyes and touching with my hands, the holy Gospels — swear that I have always believed, do now believe, and by God's help will for the future believe, all that is held, preached, and taught by the Holy Catholic and Apostolic Roman Church. But whereas — after an injunction had been judiciously intimated to me by this Holy Office, to the effect that I must altogether abandon the false opinion that the sun is the centre of the world and immovable, and that the earth is not the centre of the world, and moves, and that I must not hold, defend, or teach in any way whatsoever, verbally or in writing, the said doctrine, and after it had been notified to me that the said doctrine was contrary to the Holy Scripture — I wrote and printed a book in which I discuss this doctrine already condemned, and adduced arguments of great cogency in its favor, without presenting any solution of these; and for this cause I have been pronounced by the Holy Office to be vehemently suspected of heresy, that is to say, of having held and believed that the sun is the centre of the world and immovable, and that the earth is not the centre and moves: —

Therefore, desiring to remove from the minds of your Eminences, and of all faithful Christians, this strong suspicion, reasonably conceived against me, with sincere heart and unfeigned faith I abjure, curse, and detest the aforesaid errors and heresies, and generally every other error and sect whatsoever contrary to the said Holy Church; and I swear that in future I will never again say or assert, verbally or in writing, anything that might furnish occasion for a similar suspicion regarding me; but that should I know any heretic, or person suspected of heresy, I will denounce him to the Holy Office, or the Inquisitor promise to fulfil and observe in their integrity all penances that have been, or that shall be, imposed upon me by this Holy Office. And, in the event of my contravening, (which God forbid!) any of these my promises, protestations, and oaths, I submit myself to the pains and penalties imposed and promulgated in the sacred canons and other constitutions, general and particular, against such delinquents. So help me God, and His holy Gospels, which I touch with my hands.

I, the said Galileo Galilei, have abjured, sworn, promised, and bound myself as above; and in witness of the truth thereof I have with my own hand subscribed the present document of my abjuration, and recited it word for word at Rome, in the Convent of Minerva, this twenty-second day of June, 1633.

I, Galileo Galilei, have abjured as above with my own hand.❞

Source: Oliver J. Thatcher, ed., *The Ideas that have Influenced Civilization in the Original Documents*, *Volume V*, (Boston: Roberts-Manchester Publishing Co., 1901), pp. 302-307.

18.3

✤

LETTERS ON THE EXISTENCE OF GOD, ISAAC NEWTON

Isaac Newton (1642-1727) reinvented the universe. If throughout the Middle Ages the cosmos was always understood according to the Ptolemaic theory, after the publication of Newton's Principia Mathematica *in 1686, the universe would be forever understood according to a Newtonian framework. Newton's work transcends the field of astronomy. The* Principia *was not really about astronomy per se; it was about universal mechanics. With this work Newton invented the science of physics. He also theorized on optics, chemistry, economics, motion, epistemology, theology, alchemy and other magics, and of course invented a theory of universal laws (such as gravity) that explained how it all worked. Newton's influence was dramatic and widespread, then and now. As a professor at Cambridge, president of the English Royal Society of Science, and voluminous letter writer, Newton made his theories well known to a wide audience. He was also fiercely competitive and protective of his theories, and while generally promoted all scientific exploration, was known to use his influence to suppress rivals.*

Newton's purely scientific discoveries are well known, such as his laws of motion. The two letters reproduced here introduce a less familiar side of Newton, one in which he discusses the implications of his physics and the greatest enigma of his system, of whether there is a primary force or ultimate creator behind the universe as a whole. Newton wrote these letters, and two more, to Richard Bentley in 1691-92. Bentley was preparing a series of lectures at Cambridge University on proving God's existence using the new mathematical and scientific theories. Bentley to Newton and asked him to suggest what parts of the Principia might be most useful. He also asked Newton to explain to him, a non-scientist, the theory of universal forces, particularly gravity. The letters he and Newton exchanged reveal Newton thinking out his ideas further and seeking the best way to explain them to a non-specialized audience. Bentley's sermons were published as A Confutation of Atheism.

✤

QUESTIONS

1. What implications can you draw from the fact that Newton wanted to explain his ideas to an Anglican priest, and wanted to help Bentley incorporate them into sermons?
2. What do you think Newton meant by the phrase "author of the system?"
3. Why does Newton deny knowing the ultimate cause of gravity?

To the Reverend Dr. Richard Bentley, at the Bishop of Worcester's House in Parkstreet, Westminster.

S ir,

When I wrote my Treatise about our System, I had an Eye upon such Principles as might work, with considering Men, for the Belief of a Deity, and nothing can rejoice me more than to find it useful for that

Purpose. But if I have done the Public any service this way, it is due to nothing by Industry and patient Thought.

As to your first Query, it seems to me that if the Matter of our Sun and Planets, and all the Matter of the Universe, were evenly scattered throughout all the Heavens, and every Particle had an innate Gravity towards all the rest, and the whole Space, throughout which this Matter was scattered, was but finite; the Matter on the outside of this Space would by its Gravity tend towards all the Matter on the inside, and by consequence fall down into the middle of the whole Space, and there compose one great spherical Mass. But if the Matter was evenly disposed throughout an infinite Space, it could never convene into the Mass, but some of it would convene into one Mass and some into another, so as to make an infinite Number of great Masses, scattered at great Distances from one to another throughout all that infinite Space. And thus might the Sun and fixt Stars be formed, supposing the Matter were of a lucid Nature. But how the Matter should divide itself into two sorts, and that Part of it, which is fit to compose of shining Body, should fall down into one Mass and make a Sun, and the rest, which is fit to compose an opaque Body, like the shining Matter, but into many little ones; or if the Sun at first were an opaque body like the Planets, or the Planets lucid Bodies like the Sun, how he alone should be changed into a shining Body, whilst all they continue opaque, or all they be changed into opaque ones, whilst he remains unchanged, I do not think explicable by meer natural Causes, but am forced to ascribe it to the Counsel and Contrivance of a voluntary Agent.

The same Power, whether natural or supernatural, which placed the Sun in the Center of the six primary Planets, placed *Saturn* in the Center of the Orbs of his five secondary Planets, and *Jupiter* in the Center of his four secondary Planets, and the Earth in the Center of the Moon's Orb; and therefore had this Cause been a blind one, without Contrivance or Design, the Sun would have been a Body of the same kind with *Saturn, Jupiter*, and the Earth, that is, without Light and Heat. Why there is one Body in our System qualified to give Light and Heat to all the rest, I know no Reason, but because one was sufficient to warm and enlighten all the rest. For the *Cartesian* Hypothesis of Suns losing their Light, and then turning into Comets, and Comets into Planets, can have no Place in my System, and is plainly erroneous; because it is certain that as often as they appear to us, they descend into the System of our Planets, lower than the Orb of *Jupiter*, and sometimes lower than the Orbs of *Venus* and *Mercury*, and yet never stay here, but always return from the Sun with the same Degrees of Motion by which they approached him.

To your second Query, I answer, that the Motions which the Planets now have could not spring from any natural Cause alone, but were impressed by an intelligent Agent. For since Comets descend into the Region of our Plants, and here move all manner of ways, going sometimes the contrary way, and sometimes in cross ways, in Planes inclined to the Plane of the Ecliptick, and at all kinds of angles, 'tis plain that there is no natural Cause which could determine all the Planets, both primary and secondary, to move the same way and in the same Plane, without any considerable Variation: This must have been the Effect of Counsel. Nor is there any natural Cause which could give the Planets those just Degrees of Velocity, in Proportion to their distances from the Sun, and other central Bodies, which were requisite to make them move in such concentrick Orbs about those Bodies. Had the Planets been as swift as Comets, in Proportion to their Distances from the Sun (as they would have been, had their Motion been caused by their Gravity, whereby the Matter, at the first Formation of the Planets, might fall from the remotest Regions towards the Sun) they would not move in concentrick Orbs, but in such eccentrick ones as the Comets move in. Were all the Planets as swift as *Mercury*, or as slow as *Saturn* or his Satellites; or were their several Velocities otherwise much greater or less than they are, as they might have been had they arose from any other Cause than their Gravities; or had the Distances from the Centers about which they move, been greater or less than they are with the same Velocities; or had the Quantity of Matter in the Sun, or in *Saturn, Jupiter*, and the Earth, and by consequence their gravitation Power been greater or less than it is; the primary Planet could not have revolved about the Sun, nor the secondary ones about *Saturn, Jupiter*, and the Earth, in concentrick Circles as they do, but would have moved in Hyperbolas, or Parabolas, or in Ellipses very eccentrick. To make this System therefore, with all its Motions, required a Cause which understood, and compared together, the Quantities of Matter in the several Bodies of the Sun and Planets.

Source: Isaac Newton, *Isaac Newton's Papers & Letters on Natural Philosophy, Volume I*, ed. Bernard Cohen (Cambridge: Harvard University Press, 1958), pp. 279-99.

18.4

✤

OBSERVATIONS UPON EXPERIMENTAL PHILOSOPHY, MARGARET CAVENDISH

The scientific revolution was not limited to the discoveries and theories by men. Margaret Cavendish (1623-1673) is one of several prominent female scientists of the new age. Many of these women came from aristocratic backgrounds (Cavendish was the Duchess of Newcastle) and thus had the money and education that allowed them access to the new theories of men such as Galileo, Newton, and John Locke. Another example would be Madame de Châtelet, mistress of Voltaire, who first translated Newton's *Principia* from Latin into French. In eastern Europe the new scientific women will typically come from the artisan class, which provided training for the more practical (rather than theoretical) side of scientific discovery. These women were often derided by their male contemporaries as being amateurs or hobbyists; yet these same men refused to allow female scientists in the universities or membership in the scientific societies, which would have given them "professional" status.

Here Cavendish discusses empirical observations.

✤

QUESTIONS

1. According to Cavendish, how do our external sense perceptions differ from our rational perceptions?
2. How do you think Cavendish defined the concept "nature?"
3. Does Cavendish belief empirical knowledge is true knowledge?

XXVII Of Thawing or Dissolving of Frozen Bodies

As freezing or congelation is caused by contracting, condensing, and retentive motions; so thawing is nothing else but dissolving, dilating, and extending motions: for, freezing and thawing are two contrary actions; and as freezing is caused several ways, according to the various disposition of congealable bodies, and the temper of exterior cold; so thawing, or a dissolution of frozen bodies, may be occasioned either by a sympathetic agreement, (as for example, the thawing of ice in water, or other liquors) or by some exterior imitation, as by hot dilating motions. And it is to be observed, that, as the time of freezing, so the time of dissolving, is according to the several natures and tempers both of the frozen bodies, which occasion their thawing or dissolution: for, it is not only heat that doth cause ice, or snow, or other frozen bodies to melt quicker or slower; but, according as the nature of the heat is, either more or less dilative, or more or less rarefying: for surely, an exterior actual heat, is more rarefying than an interior virtual heat; as we see in strong spirituous liquors which are interiorly contracting, but being made actually hot, become exteriorly dilating: The like of many other bodies; so that actual heat is more dissolving than virtual heat. And this is the reason why ice and snow will melt sooner in some countries or places, than in others; and is much harder in some, than in others: for we see, that neither air, water, earth, minerals, nor any other sorts of creatures are just alike in all countries or climates: The same may be said of heat and cold. Besides, it is to be observed, that oftentimes a different application of one and the same object, will occasion different effects; as for example, if salt be mixed with ice, it may cause the contracted body of ice to change its present motions into its former state or figure, viz. into water; but being applied outwardly, or on the outside of the vessel wherein snow or ice is contained, it may make it freeze harder instead of dissolving it. Also, ice will oftentimes break into pieces of its own accord, and without the application of any exterior object: And the reason, in my opinion, is, that some of the interior parts of the ice endeavouring to return to their proper and natural figure by virtue of their interior dilative motions, do break and divide some of the exterior parts that are contracted by the motions of frost, especially those which have not so great a force or power as to resist them.

But concerning thawing, some by their trials have found, that if frozen eggs, apples, and the like bodies, be thawed near the fire, they will be thereby spoiled: but if they be immersed in cold water, or wrapt into ice or snow, the internal cold will be drawn out, as they suppose, but the external; and the frozen bodies will be harmlessly, though not so quickly, thawed. And truly, this experiment stands much to reason; for, in my opinion, when frozen bodies perceive heat or fire, the motions of their frozen parts, upon the perception, endeavour to imitate the motions of heat or fire; which being opposite to the motions of cold, in this sudden and hasty change, they become irregular, insomuch as to cause in most frozen parts a dissolution of their interior natural figure: Wherefore it is very probable, that frozen bodies will thaw more regularly in water, or being wrapt into ice or snow, than by heat or fire: for, thawing is a dilating action; and water, as also ice and snow, (which are nothing but congealed water) being of a dilative nature, may easily occasion a thawing of the mentioned frozen parts, by sympathy; provided the motions of the exterior cold do not overpower the motions of the interior frozen parts: for, if a frozen body should be wrapt thus into ice or snow, and continue in an open, cold, frosty air, I question whether it would cause a thaw in the same body; it would preserve the body in its frozen state, from dissolving or disuniting, rather than occasion its thawing. But that such frozen bodies, as apples, and eggs, etc. immersed in water, will produce ice on their outsides, is no wonder, by reason the motions of water imitate the motions of the frozen bodies; and those parts of water that are nearest, are the first imitators, and become of the same mode. By which we may see, that some parts will clothe themselves, others only veil themselves with artificial dresses; most of which dresses are but copies of other motions, and not original actions: It makes also evident, that those effects are not caused by an ingress of frigorific atoms in water, or other congealable bodies, but by the perceptive motions of their own parts. And what I have said of cold, the same may be spoken of heat; for it is known, that a part of a man's body being burned with fire, the burning may be cured by the heat of the fire; which, in my opinion, proceeds from a sympathetical agreement betwixt the motions of the fire, and the motions of the burned part: for every part of a man's body hath its natural heat, which is of an intermediate temper; which heat being heightened by the burning motions of ire, beyond its natural degree, causes a burning and smarting pain in the same part: And therefore, as the fire did occasion an immoderate heat, by an intermixture of its own parts with the parts of the flesh; so a moderate heat of the fire may reduce again the natural heat of the same parts, and that by a sympathetical agreement betwixt the motions of the elemental and animal heat. But it is to be observed, first, that the burning must be done by an intermixture of the fire with the parts of the body: Next, that the burning must be but skin-deep, (as we used to call it) that is, the burned part must not be totally overcome by fire, or else it will never be restored again. Neither are all burned bodies restored after this manner, but some; for one and the same thing will not in all bodies occasion the like effects; as we may see by fire, which being one and the same, will not cause all fuels to burn alike, and this makes true the old saying, "One man's meat, is another man's poison." The truth is, it cannot be otherwise: for, though nature, and natural self-moving matter is but one body, and the only cause of all natural effects; yet nature being divided into infinite, corporeal, figurative self-moving parts; these parts, as the effects of that only cause, must needs be various, and again, proceeding from one infinite cause, as one matter, they are all but one thing, because they are infinite parts of one infinite body. But some may say, If nature be but one body, and the infinite parts are all united into that same body; how comes it that there is such an opposition, strife and war, betwixt the parts of nature? I answer: Nature being material, is composable and dividable; and as composition is made by a mutual agreement of parts, so division is made by an opposition or strife betwixt parts; which opposition or division, doth not obstruct the union of nature, but, on the contrary, rather proves, that without an opposition of parts, there could not be a union or composition of so many several parts and creatures, nor no change or variety in nature; for if all the parts did unanimously conspire and agree in their motions, and move all but one way, there would be but one act or kind of motion in nature; whenas an opposition of some parts, and a mutual agreement of others, is not only the cause of the miraculous variety in nature, but it poises and balances, as it were, the corporeal figurative motions, which is the cause that nature is steady and fixt in herself, although her parts be in a perpetual motion.

Source: Margaret Cavendish, *Observations upon Experimental Philosophy,* ed. Eileen O'Neill (Cambridge: Cambridge University Press, 2001), pp. 46-48, 117-119.

QUESTIONS FOR PART 18

1. Although not everyone mentions it explicitly, how is Christian faith still inextricably linked to science even with the new discoveries?
2. Why does Newton not face the same kind of censure from the Christian churches, as does Galileo?
3. Does the heliocentric view of the universe necessarily reduce the importance of humanity?